The Joan Palevsky  Imprint in Classical Literature

In honor of beloved Virgil—

"O degli altri poeti onore e lume . . ."

—Dante, *Inferno*

The publisher gratefully acknowledges the generous support of the Classical Literature Endowment Fund of the University of California Press Foundation, which was established by a major gift from Joan Palevsky.

Lost World of the Golden King

HELLENISTIC CULTURE AND SOCIETY

General Editors: Anthony W. Bulloch, Erich S. Gruen,
A.A. Long, and Andrew F. Stewart

I.   *Alexander to Actium: The Historical Evolution of the Hellenistic Age,*
     by Peter Green

II. *Hellenism in the East: The Interaction of Greek and Non-Greek
     Civilizations from Syria to Central Asia after Alexander,* edited by
     Amélie Kuhrt and Susan Sherwin-White

III. *The Question of "Eclecticism": Studies in Later Greek Philosophy,*
     edited by J.M. Dillon and A.A. Long

IV. *Antigonos the One-Eyed and the Creation of the Hellenistic State,*
     by Richard A. Billows

V.   *A History of Macedonia, by R. Malcolm Errington,* translated
     by Catherine Errington

VI. *Attic Letter-Cutters of 229 to 86 B.C.,* by Stephen V. Tracy

VII. *The Vanished Library: A Wonder of the Ancient World,*
     by Luciano Canfora

VIII. *Hellenistic Philosophy of Mind,* by Julia E. Annas

IX. *Hellenistic History and Culture,* edited by Peter Green

X.   *The Best of the Argonauts: The Redefinition of the Epic Hero
     in Book One of Apollonius's Argonautica,* by James J. Clauss

XI. *Faces of Power: Alexander's Image and Hellenistic Politics,*
     by Andrew Stewart

XII. *Images and Ideologies: Self-definition in the Hellenistic World,*
     edited by Anthony W. Bulloch, Erich S. Gruen, A.A. Long,
     and Andrew Stewart

XIII. *From Samarkhand to Sardis: A New Approach to the Seleucid Empire*, by Susan Sherwin-White and Amélie Kuhrt

XIV. *Regionalism and Change in the Economy of Independent Delos, 314–167 B.C.*, by Gary Reger

XV. *Hegemony to Empire: The Development of the Roman Imperium in the East from 148 to 62 B.C.*, by Robert Kallet-Marx

XVI. *Moral Vision in The Histories of Polybius*, by Arthur M. Eckstein

XVII. *The Hellenistic Settlements in Europe, the Islands, and Asia Minor*, by Getzel M. Cohen

XVIII. *Interstate Arbitrations in the Greek World, 337–90 B.C.*, by Sheila L. Ager

XIX. *Theocritus's Urban Mimes: Mobility, Gender, and Patronage*, by Joan B. Burton

XX. *Athenian Democracy in Transition: Attic Letter-Cutters of 340 to 290 B.C.*, by Stephen V. Tracy

XXI. *Pseudo-Hecataeus, "On the Jews": Legitimizing the Jewish Diaspora*, by Bezalel Bar-Kochva

XXII. *Asylia: Territorial Inviolability in the Hellenistic World*, by Kent J. Rigsby

XXIII. *The Cynics: The Cynic Movement in Antiquity and Its Legacy*, edited by R. Bracht Branham and Marie-Odile Goulet-Cazé

XXIV. *The Politics of Plunder: Aitolians and Their Koinon in the Early Hellenistic Era, 279–217 B.C.*, by Joseph B. Scholten

XXV. *The Argonautika*, by Apollonios Rhodios, translated, with introduction, commentary, and glossary, by Peter Green

XXVI. *Hellenistic Constructs: Essays in Culture, History, and Historiography*, edited by Paul Cartledge, Peter Garnsey, and Erich S. Gruen

XXVII. *Josephus's Interpretation of the Bible*, by Louis H. Feldman

XXVIII. *Poetic Garlands: Hellenistic Epigrams in Context*, by Kathryn J. Gutzwiller

XXIX. *Religion in Hellenistic Athens*, by Jon D. Mikalson

XXX. *Heritage and Hellenism: The Reinvention of Jewish Tradition*, by Erich S. Gruen

XXXI. *The Beginnings of Jewishness: Boundaries, Varieties, Uncertainties,* by Shaye D. Cohen

XXXII. *Thundering Zeus: The Making of Hellenistic Bactria,* by Frank L. Holt

XXXIII. *Jews in the Mediterranean Diaspora: From Alexander to Trajan (323 B.C.E.–117 C.E.),* by John M.G. Barclay

XXXIV. *From Pergamon to Sperlonga: Sculpture and Context,* edited by Nancy T. de Grummond and Brunilde S. Ridgway

XXXV. *Polyeideia: The Iambi of Callimachus and the Archaic Iambic Tradition,* by Benjamin Acosta-Hughes

XXXVI. *Stoic Studies,* by A.A. Long

XXXVII. *Seeing Double: Intercultural Poetics in Ptolemaic Alexandria,* by Susan A. Stephens

XXXVIII. *Athens and Macedon: Attic Letter-Cutters of 300 to 229 B.C.,* by Stephen V. Tracy

XXXIX. *Encomium of Ptolemy Philadelphus,* by Theocritus, translated with an introduction and commentary by Richard Hunter

XL. *The Making of Fornication: Eros, Ethics, and Political Reform in Greek Philosophy and Early Christianity,* by Kathy L. Gaca

XLI. *Cultural Politics in Polybius's Histories,* by Craige B. Champion

XLII. *Cleomedes' Lectures on Astronomy: A Translation of The Heavens,* with an introduction and commentary by Alan C. Bowen and Robert B. Todd

XLIII. *Historical Fictions and Hellenistic Jewish Identity: Third Maccabees in Its Cultural Context,* by Sara Raup Johnson

XLIV. *Alexander the Great and the Mystery of the Elephant Medallions,* by Frank L. Holt

XLV. *The Horse and Jockey from Artemision: A Bronze Equestrian Monument of the Hellenistic Period,* by Seán Hemingway

XLVI. *The Hellenistic Settlements in Syria, the Red Sea Basin, and North Africa,* by Getzel M. Cohen

XLVII. *Into the Land of Bones: Alexander the Great in Afghanistan,* by Frank L. Holt

XLVIII. *Mediterranean Anarchy, Interstate War, and the Rise of Rome,* by Arthur M. Eckstein

XLIX. *Hellenistic Egypt: Monarchy, Society, Economy, Culture,* by Jean Bingen. Edited and introduced by Roger S. Bagnall

L. *Jewish Perspectives on Hellenistic Rulers,* edited by Tessa Rajak, Sarah Pearce, James Aitken, and Jennifer Dines

LI. *The Image of the Jews in Greek Literature: The Hellenistic Period,* by Bezalel Bar-Kochva

LII. *From Alexander to Jesus,* by Ory Amitay

LIII. *Lost World of the Golden King: In Search of Ancient Afghanistan,* by Frank L. Holt

LIV. *The Hellenistic Settlements in the East from Armenia and Mesopotamia to Bactria and India,* by Getzel M. Cohen

LV. *Creating a Common Polity: Religion, Economy, and Politics in the Making of the Greek Koinon,* by Emily Mackil

Lost World of
the Golden King

In Search of Ancient Afghanistan

Frank L. Holt

UNIVERSITY OF CALIFORNIA PRESS

Berkeley   Los Angeles   London

University of California Press, one of the most
distinguished university presses in the United
States, enriches lives around the world by
advancing scholarship in the humanities, social
sciences, and natural sciences. Its activities are
supported by the UC Press Foundation and by
philanthropic contributions from individuals
and institutions. For more information, visit
www.ucpress.edu.

University of California Press
Berkeley and Los Angeles, California

University of California Press, Ltd.
London, England

© 2012 by The Regents of the University of California

Library of Congress Cataloging-in-Publication Data
Holt, Frank Lee.
    Lost world of the golden king : in search of ancient
Afghanistan / Frank L. Holt.
        p.   cm. — (Hellenistic culture and society ; 53)
    Includes bibliographical references and index.
    ISBN 978-0-520-27342-9 (cloth, alk. paper)
    1. Bactria—Civilization.   2. Bactria—Antiquities.
3. Greeks—Afghanistan—History—To 1500.
4. Eucratides, the Great, fl. 170–145 B.C.   5. Coins,
Greek—Bactria.   6. Coins, Greek—Afghanistan.
7. Afghanistan—Civilization.   8. Afghanistan—
Antiquities.   I. Title.
DS374.B28H655   2012
939'.6—dc23   2012000828

Manufactured in the United States of America

21 20 19 18 17 16 15 14 13 12
10 9 8 7 6 5 4 3 2 1

For Alec Emery McDaniel and his parents,
Laura and Patrick,
From someone who loves them all

And so the whole great subject slept, like the enchanted princess in the fairy-tale, until the moment of awakening came.

A.H. Louis on the work of Theophilus Bayer,
April 1873

CONTENTS

List of Illustrations xv

Preface xiv

Introduction: A Lost Civilization

1

1. The Adventure Begins: Checklist Numismatics

7

2. A Dangerous Game: Framework Numismatics

27

3. The Gold Colossus: Novelty Numismatics

50

4. Telling Tales: Narrative Numismatics

67

5. Wanted—One Greek City: Archaeology

89

6. Letters Here and There: Epigraphy

113

7. A Perfect Storm: Rescue and Revisionist Numismatics

135

8. A New Beginning: Cognitive Numismatics I

160

9. Coins and the Collapse of Civilization:
Cognitive Numismatics II

184

Conclusion: The Lost World of the Golden King

211

Notes 221

Select Bibliography 297

Illustration Credits 329

Index 331

ILLUSTRATIONS

MAPS

1. Ancient Bactria 28

2. Ancient India 95

3. Ai Khanoum 98

FIGURES

1. Jacob Bruce 11

2. Bruce's tetradrachm of Eucratides 13

3. Bayer's misattributed bronze coin of Diodotus 14

4. Pellerin's tetradrachm of Eucratides 23

5. Pellerin's stater of Euthydemus 25

6. Arthur Conolly and Joseph Wolff 30

7. Alexander "Bukhara" Burnes 35

8. Heliocles and Laodice tetradrachm 41

9. Commemorative tetradrachms 45

10. The Eucratidion 51

11. Gaston L. Feuardent 56

12. Secondary symbol on some forgeries 63

13. William Woodthorpe Tarn 68

14. Edward T. Newell 79

15. Tetradrachm of Antimachus I 81

16. Inscribed potsherd from Tepe Nimlik 115

17. Example of a karshapana coin 129

18. Demetrius tetradrachm from Ai Khanoum Hoard III 140

19. Mir Zakah Hoard II 142

20. Eucratides commemorative tetradrachm 169

21. Mirror image of Amyntas double decadrachm, reverse (dot pattern emphasized) 172

22. Bronze coin of Diodotus 186

23. Imitation Eucratides tetradrachm 201

24. Tetradrachm of Diodotus 204

25. Bronze coin of Agathocles, reverse 205

26. Detail of an Afghan bank note 209

27. Drachm of Antimachus Nicephorus, obverse 213

28. Tetradrachm of Plato 216

29. Drachm of Menander I Soter 218

COLOR PLATES

Following page 88

1. Land of the Silk Road

2. The Eucratidion

3. Amyntas double decadrachms, obverse

4. Amyntas double decadrachms, reverse

5. Part of the Kuliab Hoard

6. Bactrian tetradrachm die

7. Bactrian tetradrachm die of Demetrius I

8. Bactrian tetradrachm die impression

9. Eucratides tetradrachm with parallel inscription

10. Diodotus gold stater from Mir Zakah Hoard II

PREFACE

This book originated in Paris under the most pleasant of circumstances. During a lively dinner conversation involving Professor Andrew Stewart, my wife, Linda, and our host, Professor Osmund Bopearachchi, our talk naturally turned to the archaeology and history of the Hellenistic East. Professor Stewart suggested the need for a solid introduction to this complex phase of ancient history, and it was soon proposed that I should pen such a work on the Bactrian period down to about 150 B.C.E. and that Professor Bopearachchi should produce a similar volume on the Indo-Greek period that followed. Since this project would afford me the chance to circle back to my earliest researches on Bactria, specifically my original M.A. thesis on the reign of "the Golden King," Eucratides, I readily agreed. My goal was not to write a biography of this king but to reveal how valiantly modern scholars have labored to explore and to explain his lost world. I hope that my efforts have done credit to the high aspirations of that evening in Paris. All translations in this book are my own unless indicated otherwise. For the

sake of consistency, Greek names and terms have been Latinized wherever possible (Antimachus, Nicephorus, etc.); exceptions include the Greek rendering of the Indian names Sophytos and Naratos for the sake of the acrostic verse translation
given in chapter 6.

In addition to my dinner companions in Paris, I owe much to
the assistance and encouragement of esteemed colleagues
around the world. My mentor, Stanley Burstein, offered insights
on several topics, including the epigraphy of ancient Central
Asia. Paul Bernard and Edvard Rtveladze shared their considerable firsthand archaeological knowledge. Professor Getzel
Cohen sent me a manuscript copy of his forthcoming volume
*The Hellenistic Settlements in the East from Armenia and Mesopotamia
to Bactria and India*. Elizabeth Errington provided help with
materials in the British Museum, and Charlotte Goodall did
likewise at the Bodleian Library. I have profited from conversations and correspondence with Makis Aperghis, Olivier Bordeaux, Lee Brice, Fred Hiebert, Adrian Hollis, Jens Jakobsson,
Frank Kovacs, Matthew Leeming, Charlotte Maxwell-Jones,
Mariusz Mielczarek, Valerii Nikonorov, Nataliya Smirnova,
Lloyd Taylor, Dorothy Thompson, Gail Trail, Mitch Utterback,
and L. M. Wilson. I earnestly thank my department and university for invaluable ongoing support. As always, the University of
California Press has been a delightful partner throughout this
process. I am especially grateful to classics editor Eric Schmidt
for his cheerful assistance at every turn, and to Paul Psoinos for
his careful editing.

I remain especially indebted to my friend Osmund Bopearachchi, who has never tired of helping me by supplying advice,
information, images, and so forth. I naturally owe most to my

wife, Linda, who has patiently read and improved the text and assisted with some of the research. My multitalented daughter Laura kindly produced most of the drawings and assisted with some of the modern languages, and it is to her and her family that I dedicate this book.

Houston, Texas
October 2011

Introduction

A Lost Civilization

What person doesn't dream of stumbling across the trail of some lost civilization in a little-known land like Afghanistan? Those dedicated to the study of ancient Bactria have been doing so for nearly three hundred years.[1] Along the banks of the Amu Darya and the foothills of the Hindu Kush, Bactria once thrived as an independent kingdom ruled by the descendants of Western colonists.[2] These wayward Greeks, remnants of Alexander the Great's army, waged incessant wars with their neighbors and with each other, growing richer all the while. They minted the largest gold and silver coins in the world, governed (it was said) a thousand cities, conquered deep into India (which Alexander had failed to do), and then... vanished. Their history morphed into legend, until even that was lost except for the names of a few phantom kings lingering in the quiet corners of classical and Renaissance literature.

This book is about the rediscovery of that lost civilization. Readers who wonder why we should bother owe themselves a chance to witness, in every sense, history in the making. They will see not only the process and progress of rediscovery, but also the exceptionality of Bactria as a part of world history. In fact, the collapse of Greek rule in Bactria was the first historical phenomenon ever recorded by both European and Asian sources.[3] Greek, Latin, and Chinese texts mention the occupation of Bactria by nomadic peoples, who wrested the region away from the last of the Greek rulers, including the golden king Eucratides and his family.[4] In a sense, globalism was born in Bactria, for at that same moment, the earth shrank even further when a Greek rival of Eucratides named Menander worked his solitary way into Indian literature by allegedly converting to Buddhism.[5] Menander's massive outlay of silver coins proclaimed his name and titles in both Greek and native Indian scripts, and they carried the image of Athena Alcidemus ("Defender of the People")— the patron deity of Macedonian Pella, Alexander the Great's birthplace.[6] Where else in the world could anyone find such a tangle of cultural traditions, including a Greek Buddhist raja relating to his native subjects in their own language while displaying the warlike insignia of a conqueror's hometown three thousand miles (5,555 km) away?

Although Bactria served as the easternmost edge of Greek civilization, a simple shift of the map or swing of the globe shows its centrality to half the world. At about the time that Eucratides was born somewhere in Central Asia, a massive mound of earth nearby was just settling down upon the eight thousand terracotta warriors guarding the immense tomb of Qin Shihuangdi, the unifier and first emperor of China. By the time of Eucratides' death in the middle of the second century B.C.E., Qin's Great Wall had deflected into Bactria the transformative succession of nomadic invaders that marked an epoch in world history.[7] Twenty years later, the Han emperor Wudi would dispatch his ambassador Zhang Qian to this troubled region, only to find it fragmented among numerous petty chiefs more interested in commerce than in war.[8] The only Greek kings to be found had drifted south into India, abandoning the lost world of Eucratides for that of Menander. The rich threads of the exotic Silk Road were already weaving their way across this terrain (see plate 1), which connected the far-flung peoples of India and China to those of Egypt, Greece, and Rome.[9] Traders and raiders shared these bustling paths with artists, envoys, and wandering mystics. Buddhist monks carried abroad their creed alongside lumbering caravans, and legend has it that a later king of the Bactrian realm followed a star westward along the Silk Road to deliver some luxury goods to a stable in Bethlehem.[10]

Thus faded Bactria, the hub of half the planet, into a land of legend and lost cities, mysteriously gone but for a lengthy trail of little crumbs—coins, mostly—leading us toward (though not yet to) the complete history of a lost civilization. The journey of rediscovery taken in this book begins with the antiquaries of the seventeenth and eighteenth centuries when numismatics, archaeology, art history, and epigraphy were not yet specialized disciplines (chap. 1). Using a rudimentary (but at that time quite fruitful) method best described as checklist numismatics, men like Theophilus Bayer—justly celebrated in the epigraph of this book—began to search for this enigmatic civilization in Central Asia.[11] In the dangerous lands of nascent Afghanistan, explorers found coins bearing the names of Greek kings that appeared barely—if at all—in the annals of ancient literature. Who were these monarchs, and why had they vanished? During the nineteenth century, the infamous geopolitical rivalry known as the Great Game fueled a risky competition to gather as much evidence as possible in a race to recover ancient Bactria's history (chap. 2). The pace of discovery was breathtaking, giving rise to framework numismatics as a new means of making sense of this material. In some cases, the coins coming from Central and South Asia were so remarkable that they defied conventional analysis; one gold giant among them (the coin that makes Eucratides the quintessential golden king) exemplifies the pursuit of what might be called novelty numismatics (chap. 3). The desire to reward these numismatic efforts by writing, at last, a detailed account of Bactria based largely on the coins led to narrative numismatics, an approach that still accounts for the most famous works in the field (chap. 4). Meanwhile, archaeology matured as a discipline and, in the twentieth century, slowly began to transform the quest for Bactria by including more than just coins in the search (chap. 5). Likewise, the recovery of ancient texts written in stone or on pottery, parchment, and papyrus opened new trails (chap. 6).

Unfortunately, the sad fate of Afghanistan in the late twentieth and early twenty-first centuries has forced scholars to embrace rescue and revisionist numismatics in a sometimes desperate attempt to salvage what remains of the disappearing trail (chap. 7). In spite of recent events, there exists hope that new methods may make better use of the evidence still surviving from that war-torn region. As one example, cognitive numismatics takes us in a different direction, seeking not the kings but instead the commoners whose lives and labors once made Bactria a great world civilization. The first part of this approach examines the manufacturing of the coins (chap. 8); the second follows the coins after they had left the mint (chap. 9). This allows us to consider in fresh detail the fate of the Greeks in Asia.

For the most part, readers will not find in these pages a final reconstruction of Bactrian history either for the broad sweep of antiquity from the Bronze Age to the Islamic conquest, nor even for the much shorter Hellenistic period. Instead, this book pays tribute to the extraordinary process by which scholars are finally getting close to producing such a narrative. The focus here lies on the numerous hard-won discoveries that have served so well as metaphorical breadcrumbs to the lost civilization of Bactria.

CHAPTER ONE

The Adventure Begins

Checklist Numismatics

Jean Foy Vaillant (1632–1706) could not endure another four months of slavery in the hands of Algerian pirates, so he took matters into his own mouth. The desperate Vaillant was in the midst of a dangerous numismatic journey when, about to be captured again, he swallowed his cargo of ancient gold coins.[1] This gallant French physician had developed an insatiable interest in old Greek and Roman medals soon after he was shown a hoard freshly dug from a farm near Beauvais.[2] Vaillant quickly became famous as one of the first savants to demonstrate the value of coins for the illumination of history. His erudition attracted the attention of Jean-Baptiste Colbert, Louis XIV's finance minister, who commissioned Vaillant to expand the king's collection by searching abroad for rare specimens. In 1674, while on the second of his several Mediterranean voyages, this intrepid numismatist and his fellow shipmates fell into the clutches of an Algerian corsair. The French government negotiated Vaillant's release, and the return of the twenty gold and two hundred silver coins he had painstakingly gathered for the royal collection. It was on his way back to the port of Marseilles that Vaillant, his ship laboring to outrun yet another pirate attack, gobbled down his twenty gold treasures to keep them safe.[3] The French vessel ran aground, and the numismatist escaped, though he suffered miserably from the gold still lodged in his gut. Well-meaning acquaintances suggested various *purgatifs* and *vomitifs* to speed the process of recovery. When an avid collector heard a description of what had been swallowed, he immediately purchased one of the pieces and then patiently waited with Vaillant for the hoard's final passage so that he could claim his prize. Such were the perils and payoffs of numismatics in its heroic age, at a time when—as Vaillant himself said—a collector could not always lounge comfortably in his study far from the dangers of shipwreck and slavery.[4]

Over the course of his career, Vaillant explored Italy, Greece, Sicily, Persia, and Egypt. He also traveled to nearly all the major collections of Europe, where he gathered material for his extensive and often groundbreaking publications on the coinages of ancient Rome, Seleucid Asia, Ptolemaic Egypt, and Arsacid Parthia. Vaillant's work answered the strong antiquarian impulses of his age. Men and women of means—kings, queens, nobles, ministers, merchants—collected and studied artifacts as a matter of personal pleasure, enlightenment, and profit.[5] Private cabinets of curiosities, the nuclei of future museums, could be found all over Europe. These were fed by feverish methods of acquisition, sometimes destructive, since there were as yet no professional standards of education or ethics for would-be archaeologists and numismatists; the material remains of the ancient world lay at the mercy of these well-meaning amateurs. In those times, Vaillant and his contemporaries acted the part of pioneers whose courage, energy, and genius are not to be slighted simply because their methods do not exactly square with practices not yet invented. To borrow a remark of Sir Mortimer Wheeler's: "One may as well condemn Napoleon for not using nuclear submarines at the Battle of Trafalgar."[6]

Vaillant pursued a kind of numismatics that we might now describe, but not disparage, as checklist numismatics. This approach to coins, still popular today, tends to satisfy the concerns of collectors and art connoisseurs; it treats coins as individual objects, using them to validate or illustrate some list derived from other sources.[7] In the early stages of studying any ancient topic, this straightforward methodology can be productive even if quite rudimentary. Vaillant and his patrons aimed first and foremost to match the rulers of ancient empires to the coins they minted, checking off each member of a given dynasty as his or her money came to hand. In Vaillant's last great opus, his *Arsacidarum Imperium,* which appeared posthumously in 1725, he devoted two seminal volumes to the Parthian empire.[8] He set forth a detailed chronology of the dynasty, followed by a reign-by-reign history, all supported by quotations from ancient texts. Pulling together these scattered Greek and Latin sources was itself a task of commendable erudition, marking Vaillant as an historian and philologist as well as a numismatist. For each Parthian ruler, Vaillant tried to provide drawings of a portrait coin taken either from his own collection or from that of another antiquarian such as the French king. This simple checklist approach illustrated the line of Parthian dynasts, without elaborate commentary on the coins themselves, much as some collectors still endeavor to own one coin representing each of the Twelve Caesars or to fill every slot in a notebook of U.S. state quarters. This proved to be an important beginning, even though it relegated coins to a secondary role subservient to the texts. Money did not write the story; it merely put faces to the names found in dynastic lists derived independently from ancient literature.

Among the kings discussed by Vaillant were a few from Bactria whose histories touched in some way upon his treatment of neighboring Parthia. Vaillant worked these shadowy figures into his narrative, although he naturally did not illustrate any of them since no coins from Bactria were yet known. From ancient writers, Vaillant deduced the existence of kings named Diodotus I and II, Euthydemus, Menander, Demetrius, Eucratides the Great, and Eucratides II.[9] The posthumous publication of Vaillant's book in 1725 returned these monarchs to the realm of scholarly inquiry for the first time in centuries.

Ten years later, on May 1, 1735, another numismatist posthumously gave new life to the lost world of the Bactrian kings. The deceased was Comes Iakov Vilimovich Brius (Count Jacob Daniel Bruce; see fig. 1). Born in Moscow the son of a Scottish mercenary, Bruce (1670–1735) rose to fame as a military and scientific adviser to Peter the Great.[10] An expert in all manner of practical pursuits, Bruce associated with Sir Isaac Newton and Edmund Halley; he assembled a vast personal library to support his overlapping careers as a soldier, collector, scholar, and diplomat. No foreigner anywhere in the Russian empire outranked him until he quietly retired in order to spend his remaining hours in uninterrupted study. Count Bruce died on the last day of April 1735, with one remaining good deed to perform.[11]

By prior arrangement, on the day after his death the count's considerable accumulation of antiquities passed into the collections of the Imperial Museum, in St. Petersburg. Bruce had made preparations for this bequest only a few days earlier, while meeting with a brilliant scholar named Theophilus Siegfried Bayer (1694–1738).[12] One small item in this benefaction profoundly

Figure 1. Count Jacob Daniel Bruce, collector
of the first known Bactrian coin.

impressed Bayer, and from it he derived at once the bold plan to
find what he could of the vanished Bactrians. Bayer published
the results of this research in 1738, the year of his own premature
death, in a long Latin treatise with a title to match: *Historia Regni
Graecorum Bactriani in qua simul Graecarum in India Coloniarum Vetus
Memoria* ("History of the Bactrian Kingdom of the Greeks, Together with the Ancient Tradition of Greek Colonies in India").[13]
This work was perhaps the most important of Bayer's career, and
it would not have been undertaken but for the fortuitous bequest
of Bruce.

The catalytic discovery in the dead count's collection was a unique silver coin that set Bayer on his mission (fig. 2). Bruce had acquired the tetradrachm some years earlier in either Astrakhan or Kasan, and Bayer had no doubts about its authenticity.[14] The coin showed in profile the bust of a king wearing a diadem and a plumed helmet adorned with a bull's horn and ear. The monarch also wore a Greek cavalry cloak. On the other side (the reverse), Bayer identified two cavalrymen on galloping horses, each soldier armed with a long Macedonian lance called a sarissa; Bayer failed to recognize in these figures the mythological heroes Castor and Pollux, twin sons of Zeus who were savior gods among the Greeks. What most excited Bayer were the three words stamped into the coin's design: ΒΑΣΙΛΕΩΣ ΜΕΓΑΛΟΥ ΕΥΚΡΑΤΙΔΟΥ, "[a coin] of King Eucratides the Great." This tangible evidence of a long-lost king on Vaillant's list sent Bayer rummaging for clues about the man on the coin.

Theophilus Bayer consulted the work of Vaillant to guide him toward the scattered ancient sources for the history of Bactria. Building on the basic king list and chronology compiled by Vaillant, Bayer expanded the topic into a richly documented treatise that reached back to the legendary travels of the god Dionysus and included considerable detail on geography and languages. For the period following Alexander's death, the so-called Hellenistic Age (a term not yet invented in Bayer's lifetime), Bayer found evidence of eight Greek kings who ruled in Bactria and neighboring India from about 255 to 142 B.C.E. Like Vaillant, Bayer argued that Bactria gained its independence from Alexander's successors through the agency of a rebellious regional governor named Theodotus (Diodotus) I, who was succeeded by his son, Theodotus (Diodotus) II.[15] In about 221 B.C.E., a usurper named Euthydemus ascended the Bactrian throne and later foiled an attempt by Antiochus the Great to repatriate Central Asia as part

Figure 2. Bruce's tetradrachm, showing King Eucratides (obverse) and the twin sons of Zeus (reverse).

of the Seleucid empire. During the war between Euthydemus and Antiochus, Euthydemus's son Demetrius impressed the invading king and was promised a Seleucid princess as his bride. This Demetrius, it was believed, never ruled Bactria. Instead, he governed in India for many years. Meanwhile, the Bactrian throne allegedly passed directly to Euthydemus's supposed brother Menander in 196 B.C.E. About fifteen years later, the warlike Eucratides took power in both Bactria and India, but he was eventually assassinated in 146 B.C.E. by his own son, presumably a Eucratides II—the sixth and last of these Greek kings of Bactria; two other Greeks (Demetrius and an Apollodotus) ruled only in India. Bayer put Eucratides II's death in about 142 B.C.E.[16]

Bayer's numismatic contribution lay in checking off a coin issued by one of these kings from Vaillant's list. In his zeal to mark off another, Bayer illustrated a second specimen, which he erroneously attributed to Diodotus (fig. 3).[17] This overpowering compulsion is one of the inherent dangers of checklist numismatics. The small bronze coin in question showed a bearded figure of Hercules (*Hēraklēs* in Greek) on the obverse and the hero's club

Figure 3. The bronze coin that Theophilus Bayer
erroneously attributed to Diodotus.

on the reverse. The legend read ΔΙΟ ΔΙΟΥ (*Dio Diou*) rather than
the expected ΔΙΟΔΟΤΟΥ (*Diodotou,* "of Diodotus"). As a result,
the association of this coin with King Diodotus has rarely been
accepted by other numismatists.[18] One scholar writing more than
a century after Bayer's death dared briefly to place this specimen
alongside the name of Menander on the Bactrian king list but
soon thought better of it.[19]

King Eucratides, on the other hand, at last had a portrait to
accompany his name, in spite of the many unfortunate factors
that had conspired against the survival of either. Living as we
do in a world drowning in documents and computer data, we
too often forget how easily history loses track of things. In the
premodern world, essential written sources could not be mass-
produced or instantly replicated; every copy of every volume
had to be penned by hand, often at great expense. Papyrus, the
paper of the day, was furthermore a frail custodian of the written
word, because it was constantly threatened by fire, flood, decay,
and—because of its rarity—relentless recycling. Thus, only a
sampling of ancient literature was ever handwritten in sufficient

copies to escape total eradication over time. For example, only seven of the 120 plays crafted by the wildly popular Sophocles of Athens managed to survive this winnowing effect. Weighty historical works, some of them longer than a hundred volumes (i.e., rolled papyrus scrolls), faced even greater odds. Compounding these risks was the tendency over time to abridge long works to make them cheaper and more palatable for less dedicated readers. The success of this strategy often doomed the original versions, which were essentially replaced by an abbreviated product. This practice created an inevitable historical shrinkage, with less and less useful information trickling down to later generations.

The history of a king like Eucratides had to endure these caprices of man and nature, plus another major obstacle specific to his realm: the obvious remoteness of Bactria from the main centers of classical civilization. Even the pettiest of princes living close to Greece and Rome stood a better chance of being noticed by historians working there than did a great king reigning thousands of miles away in Central Asia. Thus, even now Eucratides the Great makes no appearance in the index of one standard history of the Hellenistic Age, whereas every Ptolemy in Egypt (down to the nonentity brothers of Cleopatra VII) rates attention.[20] We might call this survival by association: persons entangled in any way with a Cleopatra or Caesar are more likely to be mentioned than the mightiest who were detached from the main dramas of the Mediterranean world. Whatever may or may not have been written about the Bactrian kings for their own sake, their continued literary existence depended largely on their connections to neighboring Parthia and India. In fact, if not for Eucratides' association with Mithridates and the Parthians, who in turn were important to Roman history, Vaillant and Bayer might never have found the name Eucratides surviving anywhere in ancient literature.[21]

In the first century B.C.E., for example, a writer named Apollodorus of Artemita composed in Greek a magisterial multivolume history called *Parthica* ("On the Parthians").[22] Sadly, this work no longer exists, but it was occasionally quoted in other ancient works for the relevance of its subject matter. The geographer Strabo (64 B.C.E.–21 C.E.) therefore cites Apollodorus's *Parthica* when describing the eastern edges of Greek civilization. Strabo complains:[23]

> Not many who have written about India in recent times, or who sail there now, report anything that is accurate. In fact, Apollodorus who wrote the *Parthica*, when referring to the Greeks who broke Bactria free from the Syrian kings descended from Seleucus Nicator, does say on the one hand that they grew in power and attacked India as well; but, on the other hand, Apollodorus discloses nothing new, and even contradicts what is known by reporting that these Greeks conquered more of India than the Macedonians [under Alexander]. He actually says that Eucratides ruled a thousand cities.

In another passage, the same geographer mentions the growth of Parthian power:[24]

> They also annexed part of Bactria, having overpowered the Scythians and, still earlier, those around Eucratides. At present, the Parthians rule so much territory and so many peoples that they have become, so to speak, rivals of the Romans.

Strabo adds that the earlier independence of Parthia coincided with the rebellion of Diodotus against the Seleucids, and that Bactria soon prospered:[25]

> Because of the excellence of the land, the Greeks who rebelled in Bactria grew so powerful that they conquered both Ariana and India

as well, according to Apollodorus of Artemita. And so they subdued more peoples than Alexander had done, especially Menander if indeed he crossed the Hypanis River toward the east and advanced as far as the Imaus; for some were subdued by Menander himself, and some by Demetrius son of Euthydemus, the king of Bactria. They took over not only Patalene but also the rest of the coast, which is called Saraostus and the kingdom of Sigerdis. In sum, Apollodorus says that Bactria is the jewel of all Ariana, and moreover its authority stretched all the way to the Seres and Phryni.

Among the "thousand cities" of this rich and powerful land, Strabo mentions:[26]

> Bactra, which they also call Zariaspa and through which flows a river of the same name that empties into the Oxus, plus the city of Darapsa, and others more. Among these was a city called Eucratidia, named after its ruler. The Greeks who took possession of the region divided it into satrapies [provinces], of which the Parthians took away from Eucratides both Turiva and Aspionus.

The linkage of Bactria with Parthia is obvious in the works of Strabo and his now-lost source Apollodorus. The same may be said of the world history published in Greek by Strabo's contemporary Pompeius Trogus, which survives only in a Latin abridgment (*epitoma*) made centuries later by Marcus Junianus Justinus (Justin). Pompeius Trogus was a Romanized Gaul who apparently relied upon the *Parthica* of Apollodorus of Artemita when, in volume 41 of his history, Trogus recounted the conjoined affairs of Parthia and Bactria.[27] For his part, Justin later condensed that narrative even further into a bare-bones recitation of selected parallel events in Parthia and Bactria, namely those that would interest a Roman audience in the third century C.E. Justin therefore summarized the origins of the Bactrian kingdom under Theodotus (Diodotus), linked to the foundation of the Parthian kingdom under Arsaces, and then the decline of the Bactrians under Eucratides, linked to the simultaneous aggrandizement of Parthia under Mithridates. About Eucratides, Justin wrote:[28]

> At about the same time that Mithridates began his reign in Parthia, Eucratides rose to power in Bactria. Both men became great, but the Parthians were more fortunate and succeeded brilliantly under their leader, whereas the Bactrians were troubled by endless wars and lost not only their lands but also their liberty. Exhausted by conflicts with the Sogdians, Arachosians, Drangians, Arians, and Indians, the Bactrians bled themselves dry and succumbed at last to the weaker Parthians. Eucratides nevertheless waged many wars with great valor. Although weakened by so much fighting and besieged by Demetrius, king of the Indians, who commanded sixty thousand troops, Eucratides with only three hundred soldiers triumphed by continual sallies. And so, after five months he freed himself from the siege and conquered India. But when Eucratides was returning to Bactria, he was killed along the way by his own son, with whom he had shared the throne. The murderer made no effort to conceal the patricide, acting instead as though he had slain an enemy rather than his father. He drove a chariot through his victim's blood and ordered the corpse to be cast aside unburied.

This summary of Eucratides' reign accounts for most of what we know about the king, depending on what we can trust in it. Is the chronology reliable, or has it been distorted to synchronize Bactrian and Parthian history? Did Eucratides usurp his position or inherit it? Can we reasonably assume that he defeated sixty thousand troops with only three hundred of his own? Was his enemy the same Demetrius who was the son of Euthydemus? Where did this extraordinary siege take place? Was Demetrius killed in the battle? Who was the son of Eucratides who so vilely desecrated his father, and why did he do it?[29] Pompeius Trogus, or his source Apollodorus, may well have answered all such questions, but in the end we are left only with the scattered details that Justin chose to preserve. We cannot know whether the Roman abridger carefully extracted the most important information or whether he just preferred sensational tidbits such as the siege and assassination. Justin may have included the story of Eucratides' horrible demise only because it would remind Roman readers of a similar legend in their own past—the death of King Servius Tullius, whose daughter, Tullia, killed him and then insolently drove her chariot through his blood.[30]

Ancient references to Bactria survived because of its close associations with Parthia, an empire that long impinged on Mediterranean history. Likewise, Bactria sometimes drifted into classical accounts by way of its eastern neighbor India, which maintained active commercial contacts by sea to Egypt and the Mediterranean. We have already seen some signs of this above, where Strabo speaks of India and the kings Eucratides, Demetrius, and Menander. In a Roman treatise titled *On the Nature of Animals,* the writer Aelian (ca. 165–230 C.E.) draws in the apparently famous Eucratides as a chronological reference:[31]

> There is a city called Perimula in India that was ruled by a man of royal blood named Soras at the time when Eucratides ruled in Bactria.

A first-century-C.E. anonymous sailing guide for merchants known as the ΠΕΡΙΠΛΟΥΣ ΤΗΣ ΕΡΥΘΡΑΣ ΘΑΛΑΣΣΗΣ ("On the Circumnavigation of the Red Sea," chap. 47) reports the spread of Bactrian coins deep into India:[32]

> Beyond Barygaza [modern Broach or Bharuch], there are many inland peoples, ... and above these to the north are the very warlike Bactrians, who have their own kingdom.... Even now in Barygaza old drachms [silver coins] stamped with inscriptions in Greek let-

tering come to hand, the coins of Apollodotus and Menander, who were kings after Alexander.

The prolific biographer and moralist Plutarch (ca. 45–125 C.E.) notes the fame in India of King Menander:[33]

> When a man named Menander died in camp after reigning well as king in Bactria, the cities [in India] observed the other usual funeral rites, but they quarreled over his actual remains and with difficulty agreed to divide up his ashes into equal shares and to set up monuments [Buddhist stupas?] in his honor.

So, from the shadow lands between Parthia and India, hints of Hellenistic Bactria survived—though just barely. Before Vaillant and Bayer, these references were too scattered and fragmented to arouse much interest. The memory of men such as Eucratides and Demetrius stirred more among the poets than the historians. In his sometimes fanciful *Chronica Polonorum* ("Polish Chronicles"), Vincenzo Kadlubeck (ca. 1150–1223) played up the pathos of Eucratides' death by adding an exotic episode involving a swallowed snake.[34] Generations later, Giovanni Boccaccio (1313–75) included Eucratides and Demetrius in his popular compendium titled *De Casibus Illustrium Virorum* ("On the Misfortunes of Famous Men," 6.6). According to Boccaccio,[35]

> Eucratides, king of the Bactrians, was besieged by Demetrius, king of the Indians; he was at last killed by his son and left to be torn asunder by wild beasts. He was lamented after the time of Mithridates.

Boccaccio's remarks in *De Casibus* were reworked by later writers such as Laurent de Premierfait (in French, ca. 1409) and John Lydgate (in English, ca. 1435).[36] In the *Canterbury Tales* of Geoffrey Chaucer (ca. 1340–1400), the poet describes an Indian king named

Emetreus, who appears to be a romanticized version of Eucratides' rival Demetrius:[37]

> Alongside Arcite, in stories as men find,
> Rode the Great Emetreus, King of India,
> Looking like the war-god Mars.
> His bay-colored steed wore trappings of steel
> Covered in gold cloth with fine trimmings.
> His tunic was made of silk cloth from Turkestan,
> Adorned with great pearls, round and white.
> His saddle gleamed with newly-wrought gold.
> A mantle draped from his shoulder
> Brimming with red rubies that sparkled like fire.
> The curly rings of his yellow hair glittered like the sun,
> And he had a high nose, bright lemony eyes,
> Round lips, ruddy complexion, and a few freckles
> Sprinkled on his face that varied from yellow to black.
> As he looked about with a lion's mien,
> I judged his age at 25 years, with a beard beginning to grow.
> His voice thundered like a trumpet.
> He wore on his head a green laurel garland
> That was delightful to see,
> And on his hand he sported a tame eagle,
> As white as a lily, for his amusement.
> With him rode a hundred lords, all fully armed
> With richly detailed splendor, except for their heads.
> For you may be sure that gathered in this company
> Were dukes, earls, and kings devoted to chivalry.
> All around this King Emetreus of India
> Many a tame lion and leopard ran.

Emetreus's obvious Greek name and European features (curly blond hair, light-colored eyes, ruddy complexion, freckled face) make him an unlikely Indian king in any context other than a fanciful evocation of ancient Bactrian history.[38]

Against this background of remembering Bactria solely as an exotic mise-en-scène, Jean Foy Vaillant and Theophilus Bayer patched the surviving sources into a narrative account for the first time in over a thousand years. This achievement in many ways overshadows their numismatic contributions. Bayer did manage to check off the silver coin of Eucratides the Great preserved in Bruce's collection, using it primarily to confirm Eucratides' existence and to give some idea of the king's personal appearance and regalia. His treatment of the coin is more descriptive than analytical, although he did hazard a date for its manufacture. Bayer noticed a Greek monogram on the tetradrachm's reverse, just ahead of the horses' legs; this he took to be the precise date of mintage.[39] Since the ancient Greek alphabet served also as a numerical system, Bayer resolved the monogram ⊬ into the letters H and P (eta and rho). Reading this as the number 108, Bayer suggested that the coin had been struck in the 108th year of some fixed era. He imagined that this Bactrian Epoch began in 255 B.C.E., when Diodotus I inaugurated the independent kingdom, thus putting the manufacture of Eucratides' coin in the year 148 B.C.E. He turned out to be fairly accurate in his guess, although for all the wrong reasons.

More than a quarter-century after Bruce's bequest, a second Eucratides coin appeared among the savants of Europe (fig. 4). In 1762, Joseph Pellerin (1684–1782) published this discovery in Paris.[40] Like Bruce, Pellerin distinguished himself as both a military expert and a scholar. A gifted linguist, Pellerin craved the classics and developed an incurable interest in ancient Greek coins. He is said to have asked the sailors of the French fleet to buy whatever such coins they could find, with assurances that their commander would in turn pay double for each one. In this way, Pellerin amassed a collection of over thirty-three thousand

Figure 4. Joseph Pellerin's tetradrachm, erroneously attributed to a second Eucratides, son of Eucratides I.

coins.[41] One of them resembled the Bruce coin published by Bayer. Comparing the two tetradrachms, Pellerin drew attention to three key observations. First, Pellerin correctly identified the twin horsemen on both specimens as the Dioscuri of Greek mythology, based on their distinctive bonnets surmounted by stars. (See below, chap. 3). Next, Pellerin noted that his coin showed a different monogram than the one discussed by Bayer. The new monogram could not be made into a number corresponding to any possible era, so Pellerin correctly dismissed Bayer's so-called year 108 of a Bactrian Epoch. The monograms on these two coins were declared to be neither numbers nor dates. Finally, Pellerin believed the portrait on the second coin to be a younger king. This allowed the antiquarian to identify the monarch on his specimen as Eucratides II and thus to check off another king-coin combination from the Vaillant-Bayer list, even though no second king of that name actually appears in the written record.[42] This attribution turned out to be an error that would burden Bactrian studies for the next century.[43]

Joseph Pellerin had actually found a second silver tetradrachm belonging to Eucratides I.[44] He then announced sixteen years later that he had in hand another Bactrian coin, this time a gold stater bearing the name of King Euthydemus (fig. 5).[45] Pellerin called this artifact one of the most precious and interesting he had ever seen, featuring it prominently below his portrait on the frontispiece of one of his books.[46] This small treasure prompted Pellerin to pen a short narrative of his own for Bactrian history.[47] He considered ancient Bactria to have been a realm distinguished above all others in the East, peopled by Greeks who were exceptionally brave and cultured.[48] Like Vaillant and Bayer, Pellerin credited Bactrian independence to the kings Diodotus I and II. Pellerin then related the few known details of the war between Bactria's third king, Euthydemus, and the Seleucid emperor Antiochus the Great. This included the remark from Polybius (11.34) regarding a promised marriage alliance uniting an unnamed daughter of Antiochus with Euthydemus' son Demetrius. To celebrate these successes, King Euthydemus allegedly minted the very gold coin owned by Pellerin. Beautifully crafted "by the hand of a Greek" (an artist perhaps lent to Euthydemus by Antiochus, according to Pellerin), this stater he considered the very first royal issue of Bactria—hence explaining the nondiscovery of any coins bearing the name of Diodotus I or II.[49] In this fashion, Pellerin considerably tightened the checklist, so that only one Bactrian combination was still missing. Bayer had found Eucratides I; Pellerin himself checked off Euthydemus and Eucratides II; the Diodotids presumably issued no coins; Demetrius and Apollodotus allegedly never ruled in Bactria—leaving only a coin of Menander yet to be discovered.

In 1825, Major James Tod informed a meeting of the Royal Asiatic Society that he had managed at last to "fill up a chasm in the Numismatic series of the Greek Kings of Bactria."[50] His suc-

Figure 5. Joseph Pellerin's gold stater, showing King Euthydemus (obverse) and Hercules (reverse).

cess capped a dozen years of concerted effort while he was residing in India. Living "amongst Mahrattas and Rajputs," Tod had hired the locals to gather all the old coins washed up by rain or unearthed by diggers.[51] From the twenty thousand thus recovered, this British officer and self-professed antiquary eventually laid hands on a coin of Menander, plus another struck in the name of Apollodotus. Both specimens had Greek letters on the obverse and "Zend" (actually Kharoshthi) characters on the reverse. They surely represented, Tod announced, the monarchs mentioned in the writings of Plutarch and Strabo, and in the anonymous tract *On the Circumnavigation of the Red Sea* that referenced coins of this very type.[52] Tod thus ticked off one king from Bayer's catalogue of princes who ruled in Bactria and one from those who governed in India. The other reported prince of India, Demetrius, had already come to light. The Russian ambassador Baron Georges de Meyendorff had acquired this remarkable discovery in Bukhara, as reported by the academician Heinrich K.E. Köhler.[53] In his publication of the coin, Köhler maintained the view of Bayer, his predecessor at the Imperial Academy in St. Petersburg, that Euthydemus's famous son founded a collateral kingdom in India—hence explaining the scalp of an Indian ele-

phant on the obverse of the coin procured by Meyendorff. Demetrius therefore reigned solely in India until (at the supposed age
of 87) he was vanquished by Eucratides the Great.

By 1825, exactly one century after the publication of Vaillant's
Arsacidarum Imperium, antiquaries had found coins associated with
the kings Euthydemus, Menander, Eucratides I and II, Demetrius, and Apollodotus; only the earliest of the recorded Bactrian
rulers, Diodotus I and II, were missing and presumed not to have
issued money. As it happened, the elusive Diodotids did indeed
strike coinage, but their mintages were not recovered and recognized until 1840.[54] It had by then taken generations of effort to
locate at least one coin each for the recorded kings of Hellenistic
Bactria and India. By the time checklist numismatics completed
its pioneering mission, expanding interests and novel circumstances had invigorated the rise of a more sophisticated approach
that we might label framework numismatics. The interests were
historical and numismatic; the circumstances, historic and nefar-
ious: The Great Game was afoot.

CHAPTER TWO

A Dangerous Game

Framework Numismatics

The trickle of Bactrian coins into the elite collections of Europe during the eighteenth century surged into a torrent early in the nineteenth. These finds accumulated rapidly as consolation prizes in the so-called Great Game of political and military intrigue in Central Asia, a high-stakes contest immortalized by Rudyard Kipling, the Nobel laureate of British imperialism.[1] Ancient Bactria, the lost world between Parthia and India, had become nascent Afghanistan, the strategic terra incognita separating czarist Russia from British India. Into that mysterious land, each side dispatched explorers, spies, soldiers, and scientists who shared the dangers with unaligned misfits of all types: charlatans, deserters, and incurable wanderers unable to resist one of the last unmarked spaces on maps of the earth.[2] Kipling's Kimball O'Hara in the novel *Kim,* and his Daniel Dravot and Peachey Carnehan in *The Man Who Would Be King,* provide archetypes of the lost souls whose very real bones still lie scattered from Bukhara and Balkh to the Khyber Pass.

One such errant soul was Captain Arthur Conolly, a British

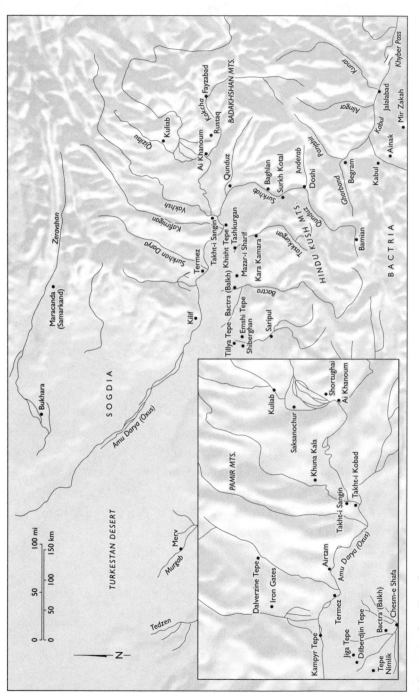

Map 1. Ancient Bactria.

intelligence officer who traveled in disguise through Central Asia under the punning name Khan Ali and wrote a book about his adventures (fig. 6).[3] He was eventually—if not inevitably—arrested, imprisoned, and beheaded as a spy, along with a fellow officer he had been sent to rescue from the notorious bug pit of Bukhara. Captain Conolly, who first coined the phrase "Great Game" long before Kipling made it famous, proved just how inappropriate the term could be.[4] In the end, his own government disavowed the mission of this heroic officer to save the imprisoned Colonel Stoddart.[5] As the suffering old Mahratta warns Kim in Kipling's novel:

> We of the Game are beyond protection. If we die, we die. Our names are blotted from the book. That is all.

Conolly and Stoddart died together, "cruelly slaughtered at Bokhara, ... masses of their flesh having been gnawn off their bones by vermin."[6] Their experiences in the Great Game should overshadow the celluloid careers of the better-known Indiana Jones and Lara Croft, but at least these officers were not blotted from history altogether.

Their story endured thanks to a daring trek to Bukhara by Reverend Joseph Wolff (1795–1862; see fig. 6), who risked his own life to learn of the officers' fate.[7] This itinerant dumpling of a man devoted his career to converting the ten lost tribes of Israel to Christianity should he ever find them somewhere in the wilds of Central Asia. Wolff did something else; like Conolly, he used his travels to search for the coins of another lost people—the Greeks of Bactria. During the lull of one April snowstorm, Wolff reported:[8]

> A Turkomaun in the tent showed to me a whole bag of Greek and Arabic coins. It is remarkable to hear these Turkomauns speak of

Figure 6. Captain Arthur Conolly, beheaded as
a spy, and his would-be rescuer, Reverend Joseph
Wolff.

the exploits of Alexander and Timur, exactly as if of a modern
occurrence.

Once he arrived at Bukhara, Wolff's numismatic interests sparked
an interrogation by the treacherous Emir Nasrullah, who had
killed Conolly and Stoddart the year before:[9]

Why do the English people like old coins? was then demanded. I explained that their value in the eyes of Englishmen arose from the circumstance that coins were looked upon as the very backbone on which the frame of history is supported. That without them we could not ascertain the duration of the world, dynasties of kings, and national events. That they were the great guides of the historian in determining his eras, and formed a metallic history of the earth.

A better explanation could not have been offered for the numismatic searches then in full force throughout Central Asia, one of the more noble by-products of the gruesome Great Game. Framework numismatics had seized the imaginations of some very daring men.

Whereas checklist numismatics aimed to find at least one coin, preferably bearing a portrait, for each king on a list derived from ancient literary texts, the appeal of framework numismatics lay in finding rulers not on that list and then working out where their unexpected reigns should fall in the succession of dynasties ruling over Hellenistic Bactria and India. Finding unexpected new coin types of already attested kings also made it necessary to tinker time and again with the basic framework of Bactrian history. The possibilities of such an approach first dawned on numismatists late in the eighteenth century, in response to a puzzling coin. In 1788, François-Paschal Gosselin and Charles Philippe Campion, the abbé de Tersan, prepared a catalogue of the impressive numismatic collection made by Michelet d'Ennery (1709–86), the former treasurer of Metz.[10] A unique silver tetradrachm of particular interest carried the name of an unknown king, Heliocles the Just.[11] The artifact appeared Syrian, which is to say Seleucid, but every numismatic expert of the time was stumped.[12] Finally, in 1799 the great French scholar Théodore Edme Mionnet (1770–1842) proposed that the Heliocles coin belonged to an unrecorded Bactrian king, based upon the overall appearance ("fabric") of the piece: "On l'a placé à la Bactriane, à cause de la fabrique."[13] Time would prove him right. The obverse portrait resembled that of Eucratides the Great, but without a helmet; the reverse featured Heliocles' name and titles, framing a figure of Zeus standing with a lightning bolt in one hand and a scepter in the other. Heliocles was placed after Eucratides in the lineage of Bactrian kings.

In 1822, Heinrich Köhler of St. Petersburg added to that of Heliocles yet another name heretofore unknown in Bactrian history: King Antimachus the God.[14] A unique tetradrachm of this king, from the collection of Prince Michael Galitzin in Moscow, featured a stunning reverse exhibiting the Greek god Poseidon. Köhler guessed that Antimachus may therefore have won a naval battle somewhere near Bactria, perhaps on the Caspian Sea or the Oxus River. This notion persists today, although it is surely a mistaken one arising from a single-minded association of Poseidon with the sea—this god also had a great deal to do with horses and cavalry, a far more important aspect of life in landlocked Central Asia than naval power.[15]

Köhler contributed new coin types as well as new kings. He announced a silver tetradrachm struck in the name of Euthydemus to match the gold stater already known, plus a "bronze" issue (actually cupronickel) that scholars would later attribute to a second Euthydemus.[16] For Eucratides I, Köhler listed the Bruce specimen and two others.[17] He discussed a second tetradrachm in the imperial collection bearing a simpler title ("King Eucratides," but not "Great"), with a different obverse and reverse design. The king wears no helmet, and Köhler thought that the monarch himself (rather than Apollo) stands on the reverse of this coin. Next, Köhler introduced to the world a smaller silver denomination, also with the simpler inscription, from the collection of Sir Gore Ouseley (1770–1844), who had served as a diplomat in both India and Persia.

Köhler still, like Pellerin, considered any Eucratides coin with a youthful portrait as a product of the son. So, alongside Pellerin's tetradrachm of "Eucratides II," Köhler recorded another type from the Galitzin collection in Moscow.[18] This specimen had all the usual features of Eucratides the Great's mintages, but with a youthful image of the king in the act of hurling a spear ("avec son bras droit il jette la lance à l'ennemi"). Köhler judged the design perfect ("parfait") in every respect, and postulated that the larger spears shown on the coins of "Eucratides II" signaled an important reform in the armament of the Bactrian cavalry.[19] Coins were thus beginning to supply a commentary on military and naval developments in Bactria, although often more imaginary than reliable.

As fresh evidence came to press, numismatists in Europe and Asia struggled to fashion it all into a reasonable framework. Monarchs like Heliocles moved up and down the evolving king list based on stylistic considerations and educated guesses about things like monograms, which some still wanted to read as dates.[20] By juggling where as well as when each king governed, it was possible to squeeze most of them together before the rise and fall of Eucratides I. Thus, a typical historical reconstruction[21] of the period 257–125 B.C.E. produced a sequence like this:

1. Diodotus I
2. Diodotus II
3. Euthydemus
4. Apollodotus the Savior
5. Menander the Savior

6. Heliocles the Just

7. Eucratides I, the Great

8. Eucratides II, the Great

This scenario still left in limbo the kings Demetrius and Antimachus the God, and already some scholars were postulating a second Demetrius, so that the son of king 3 need not be the same Demetrius who fought against king 7.[22]

The impetus for these researches came from both sides of the Great Game, and those men joining the risky hunt for personal adventure, national advantage, and valuable ancient coins occasionally crossed paths in the night. Between the travels to Bukhara by Meyendoff and Ouseley on the one hand, and poor Conolly and Stoddart on the other, Lieutenant (later Sir) Alexander "Bukhara" Burnes (fig. 7) and his companion Dr. James G. Gerard set their sights on that increasingly dangerous city.[23] Disguised as natives, the intrepid pair passed safely through Kabul and then the Hindu Kush Mountains. At Balkh, they searched for the remains of William Moorcroft, a veterinarian hired by the East India Company to improve its cavalry horses.[24] Seeking good breeding stock (and Bactrian coins), Moorcroft had traveled widely until he died mysteriously near the Amu Darya (the Oxus River of the ancients) in 1825; his body was dumped in an unmarked grave at Balkh, where Burnes and Gerard found it under the melancholy shadows of a moonlit night. Burnes's three-volume account of his travels made him a celebrity in Britain, but in 1841 he was hacked to pieces by an angry mob in Kabul at the outbreak of the First Afghan War.[25]

The Bactrian coins gathered by Burnes and Gerard vastly expanded the researches of their countrymen, most notably James Prinsep in Calcutta and Horace Hayman Wilson, who had

Figure 7. Lieutenant (later Sir) Alexander "Bukhara" Burnes, another victim of the Great Game in Central Asia.

recently departed India for a position at Oxford.[26] Under primitive conditions, and often relying on no more than "school-boy paper casts" (made by wrapping the coins in folds of paper and rubbing vigorously with a key), men like Prinsep eagerly advanced Bactrian studies.[27] The Kashmiri Mohan Lal, a talented *munshi* (secretary) who accompanied Burnes and Gerard to Bukhara, added further information on their finds of coins; he himself acquired a tetradrachm of Euthydemus "remarkable for its rich relief and exquisite workmanship."[28] Similarly, Sheikh Keramat

Ali (the sometime traveling companion of the ill-fated Conolly) collected very successfully by carrying everywhere drawings of the published coins from ancient Bactria in order to guide his efforts.[29] When he showed a new type to Dr. Gerard, the latter fire-tested the tetradrachm so violently that the coin was ruined; this turned out to be the first (but unrecognized) discovery of another new king, Euthydemus II.[30]

Meanwhile, foreigners in the employ of Maharaja Ranjit Singh (1799–1849) found time to build influential personal collections. These included the physician Martin Honigberger and the generals Jean-Francois Allard, Claude-Auguste Court, and Jean-Baptiste Ventura, alleged veterans of the Napoleonic Wars.[31] Not all their hard-won antiquities survived unscathed. Honigberger lost some of his coins to bandits when he was ambushed and held hostage near Bamian; General Court excavated so many ancient bronze coins that he melted down the rejects to make cannon for the maharaja's army.[32] Perhaps the most curious of these collectors was James Lewis (1800–1853), an English deserter from the Bengal Artillery.[33] In July 1827, Lewis walked away from his regiment at Agra and wandered about Central Asia under various guises. As the circumstance demanded, Lewis passed himself off convincingly as French or Italian; eventually, he settled upon the alias Charles Masson and the lie that he was an American explorer from Kentucky. Masson, as he is still known today, apparently learned of America through his association with a Pennsylvania Quaker named Josiah Harlan, who encountered Masson on his way to seek the maharaja's employment.[34] The unlikely pair trod and talked through a threatening landscape, both of them alert for signs of the earlier passage of Alexander the Great.[35] Harlan opined that "all the evidence to confirm the fact of Alexander's invasion is to be found in numismatology."[36] Indeed, such was the Quaker's infatuation with the ancient conqueror and his successors that he founded his own ephemeral little fiefdom, and thereby became the inspiration for Kipling's *The Man Who Would Be King*.

For his part, Charles Masson eschewed political aspirations and strove, instead, to dig as literally as possible into the region's past. He excavated nearly fifty Buddhist stupas (reliquary mounds) in search of artifacts, a pursuit popular with the maharaja's European advisors, including Honigberger, Ventura, and Court. Masson made his mark at the ruins of Begram, site of the modern airbase north of Kabul (Bagram), where he thought Alexander had built one of his many Alexandrias. The results of Masson's researches mesmerized scholars who avidly read his reports. According to Masson,[37]

> no less a number than thirty thousand coins, probably a much larger number, are found annually on the *dusht* or plain of Beghram, independently of rings, seals, and other trinkets.... The coins of Eucratides I or Great, are very numerous, and of very spirited execution.

In his second report, Masson explained his bold aspirations: "It has been my intention this year to have secured every coin of every description that should be picked up from the *dusht* of Beghram."[38] The explorer succeeded so well that in just a few years he acquired almost sixty thousand coins.[39] In 1838, the Norwegian professor of Sanskrit Christian Lassen summed up Masson's work in this way:[40]

> The interpretation of the coins, and the inferences joined to it, prove indeed, that Mr. Masson has not enjoyed a learned education; he is beside destitute in Cabul of all scientific materials; grateful there-

fore for such a laudable expenditure of time and labour, and for such a noble zeal, we shall not criticise his deficiencies, and willingly receive from him all that is capable of proof. Mr. Masson, I believe, served first in the artillery, and he knows certainly much better how to deal with numismatic inquiries, than most numismatists would know how to serve a gun.

Charles Masson's discoveries attracted the attention of another numismatist, Captain Claude Wade, who happened to be the British political officer at Ludhiana. Wade determined Masson's true identity, forcing the deserter to sign on as a British spy in exchange for a full pardon in 1835. The rebellious Masson chafed under his new responsibilities and watched bitterly as his nation careened into the First Afghan War. He has since become a more sympathetic figure, not least because of his lasting contributions to Bactrian and Buddhist studies.[41]

The numismatic data gathered by all these players of the Great Game seemed overwhelming as experts scrambled to make sense of the new evidence.[42] In France, Raoul Rochette could scarcely keep up, calling the pace of discovery unique in the annals of science.[43] He managed only by publishing supplements to his supplements, and then quickly printing addenda to those. As more and more ancient kings crowded into the historical picture, we might now liken this challenge to sorting out the casts of two plays being performed simultaneously on a single stage: Was that Prince Hamlet perhaps the son of this King Lear? In 1834, for example, a bronze specimen in the collection of Dr. Honigberger added a King Agathocles to the Bactrian playbill.[44] Where did this monarch belong in relation to the other rulers of Bactria and India? Rochette placed him first, as the founder of the Bactrian state, whereas Lassen declared his French colleague wrong: Agathocles must be a contemporary of

Demetrius and Eucratides.[45] Other numismatists decided that Agathocles might actually be the same person as Heliocles, a desperate economy that only momentarily kept the growing king list in check.[46] When the coin of a King Pantaleon appeared, it was soon wondered whether he could be dismissed as yet another emanation of Agathocles-Heliocles.[47] Meanwhile, old Euthydemus, father only of Demetrius in the ancient texts, was assigned more and more sons as numismatists strung out his family tree to accommodate Apollodotus, Menander, Antimachus, and others.[48]

To the ten or so Greek kings known prior to 1830 had been added Agathocles, Pantaleon, Philoxenus, Maues, Amyntas, Diomedes, Antialcidas, Archebius, Lysias, Hermaeus, Azes, Azilises, and others.[49] Different coin styles hinted, too, that there might be more than one Euthydemus, Demetrius, and Eucratides.[50] Notably, a few queens also surfaced among the coins. Keramat Ali found the name Queen Agathocleia the God Nourisher on a specimen "thickly coated with the rust of ages."[51] Another queen appeared on a new type of coin struck in the name of Eucratides the Great, found at Tashkurgan.[52] Prinsep, relying on a drawing by Masson and a damaged sealing-wax impression from Burnes, described this unique tetradrachm as best he could. The obverse showed Eucratides, wearing "a plain steel helmet," with the inscription "King Eucratides the Great" in the nominative rather than usual genitive (possessive) case; the reverse displayed the portrait busts of a man and woman, with the names Heliocles and Kanlodice, in the genitive. Prinsep took this to mean that Eucratides on the one side of the coin was the son of Heliocles and Kanlodice on the other. The parents bore no titles or diadems, so they were presumed to be commoners. The mother's name is not a Greek one, and its similarity to some Sanskrit words led Prinsep to decipher the name as Indian, meaning "Fairer than the Lily." He concluded: "Eucratides then was the son of a Greek officer married to a lady of the country, whom we may set down as of Hindu parentage and language."[53] Such were, and remain, the dangers of misreading any part of a coin's design, for the nature of framework numismatics (and its later derivatives) is to draw as many inferences as possible about family connections. Alexander Cunningham, a rising star among Bactrian scholars, quickly spotted Prinsep's error: the coin itself, rather than the distorted wax cast, actually read ΚΑΙΛΑΟΔΙΚΗΣ and not ΚΑΝΛΟΔΙΚΗΣ (fig. 8). The correct lettering means "and of Laodice," completing the phrase "Eucratides the Great [son] of Heliocles and of Laodice." These were indeed Eucratides' parents, but the correct name Laodice is a decidedly Greek one often favored within the Seleucid dynasty. Eucratides' Indian ancestry thus vanished almost as soon as it was imagined.[54] Naturally, some antiquaries supposed that the Heliocles shown with Laodice was the same man as King Heliocles the Just, Eucratides' son.[55] Another curious deduction drawn by Dr. Lord, who first owned the specimen, was that the reverse pictured not Heliocles and Laodice themselves, but rather another bust of Eucratides I alongside his wife. Her presence allegedly explains why the king has "a more melancholy expression" on that side of the coin.[56]

One of the greatest achievements of this period arose from the study of bilingual coinages bearing Greek texts on one side and Middle Indo-Aryan (Prakrit) inscriptions on the other. Using the mintages of Menander, Apollodotus, and others as miniature Rosetta Stones, James Prinsep endeavored to link the Greek words on the obverses directly to their Indian equivalents on the reverses:[57]

Figure 8. Heliocles and Laodice tetradrachm
of Eucratides the Great.

> It immediately struck me that if the genuine Greek names were
> faithfully expressed in the unknown character, a clue would through
> them be formed to unravel the value of a portion of the Alphabet,
> which might in its turn be applied to the translated epithets and
> titles, and thus lead to a knowledge of the language employed.
> Incompetent as I felt myself in this investigation, it was too seduc-
> tive not to lead me to an humble attempt at its solution.

The self-deprecating Prinsep managed to decipher most of the
semisyllabic Prakrit scripts now called Kharoshthi (probably
derived from Aramaic, and read from right to left) and Brahmi
(derivation contested, and read left to right).[58] Prinsep's untimely
death (April 1840) at age 40 left to others the final stages of deci-
pherment, but his legacy ought to be as celebrated today as that
of Jean-François Champollion (for hieroglyphics) and Sir Henry
Rawlinson (for cuneiform).

Lieutenant (later Major General Sir) Alexander Cunningham,
a protégé of Prinsep, took up the problem of these Prakrit legends
and other matters as well. Cunningham (1814–93), destined to
become the father of Indian archaeology (see chap. 5), juggled his
considerable military duties with a passion for coins and other
artifacts during his long posting to India. He worked amiably

with Prinsep but developed a strong antipathy for H.H. Wilson that occasionally threw off some sparks. The astute Cunningham was the first to address the inevitable appearance of forged coins among these highly prized relics. The compulsive collecting habits of the comparatively wealthy foreigners stimulated a few local craftsmen to create interesting new pieces. The irrepressible Lady Florentia Wynch Sale ("the Petticoat Grenadier"), who joined her husband Sir Robert ("Fighting Bob") at his post in Kabul, caught the collecting bug from their acquaintances Conolly, Burnes, Mohan Lal, Hay, and Cunningham.[59] She sometimes purchased from dealers in Peshawar coins of questionable authenticity. Cunningham's sharp eye caught one of them, a gold copy of a genuine bronze type minted by King Amyntas.[60] He noted another spurious coin in Conolly's collection, a cast tetradrachm of Euthydemus "forged, with many others, to satisfy the demands of our countrymen in Afghanistan, whose commendable zeal leads them to give higher prices for these coins than prudence warrants."[61] Of course, this serious problem still afflicts Bactrian studies.

Another challenge confronted by Cunningham concerned the monograms that appear on most of the coins. Cunningham at first considered it impossible that any such monograms could serve as dates, because they could be read in too many different combinations.[62] He therefore labored tirelessly, but fruitlessly, to unravel in most of them an ancient place name identifying the site of a mint in order to produce a geographic framework for Bactrian studies.[63] In doing so, he was not deterred by the fact that as names, too, the monograms could be rearranged in numerous variations. For example, he initially read the monogram ꙭ as Taukiana or Talikana, west of Balkh, but years later as Nautaka (ΝΑΥΤΑΚΑΣ), a place in Sogdiana mentioned in the Alexander sources.[64] This exercise sometimes unleashed considerable imagination, reading letters forward, backward, sideways, and up to three times each as needed to form a putative place name. In this way, Cunningham found it possible to read in the monogram ⋈ both Kapisa (ΚΑΠΙΣΣΑΣ) and Massaga (ΜΑΣΣΑΓΑΣ).[65] For the monogram 🜨, found on some coins of Eucratides, Cunningham conjured a mint city called Apolloneia or Apollonia (ΑΠΟΛΛΟΝΕΙΑΣ or ΑΠΟΛΛΩΝΙΑΣ). He admitted:[66]

> No place of this name is recorded in the lists of the geographers; but the reading is so obvious that I am tempted to suggest the probable foundation of a city of this name by Eukratides, who was a worshipper of Apollo.

Likewise, Cunningham made up the unattested Bactrian cities Diodoteia (ΔΙΟΔΟΤΕΙΑΣ) and Dionysopolis (ΔΙΟΝΥΣΟ-ΠΟΛΕΩΣ) from the monograms 🜨 and 🜨, respectively.[67] The seductive search for coded mint names inspired an obviously flawed methodology subject to nearly endless manipulation. Still, Cunningham and others could point to the use of monograms to identify mints elsewhere, such as Western Asia and Parthia. At the same time, however, other Hellenistic states clearly employed monograms to indicate the magistrates responsible for particular mintages, and some employed these letters as occasional dates.[68] Cunningham himself interpreted the same monogram ⋈ as a place name in Syria (Apameia) and a date (165 B.C.E.) in Bactria.[69] Representing places, dates, or persons, these ciphers troubled early numismatic pioneers, and still do.[70]

At about the same time that Reverend Wolff set off in vain to save Conolly and Stoddart at Bukhara, a Russian explorer named Nikolai de Khanikoff chanced upon an important find in that perilous region.[71] During a sojourn of some eight months at

Bukhara, de Khanikoff acquired a Bactrian tetradrachm with very curious features.[72] Numismatists and historians immediately quarreled over its meaning, but all agreed that this coin was the rarest, most curious, and most important artifact yet uncovered in Central Asia.[73] What distinguished this specimen from all others was the mysterious fact that it displayed the names of two kings, Diodotus and Agathocles, suggesting the existence of some significant link between them. Unraveling that connection touched off a major intellectual skirmish that quickly spread to Russia, England, France, and Germany.[74] For the next forty years, these battle lines shaped the frontiers of framework numismatics.

The coin in question, procured and published by General Jean de Bartholomaei, appeared very much like a normal issue of Diodotus, with a portrait of the king on one side and an image of Zeus hurling a thunderbolt on the other (fig. 9.1). Unlike other Diodotus issues, however, this example bore the king's name on the obverse, with a cult epithet (ΣΩΤΗΡΟΣ, "Savior") instead of the usual royal title (ΒΑΣΙΛΕΩΣ). Meanwhile, on the reverse, the complex inscription read ΒΑΣΙΛΕΥΟΝΤΟΣ ΑΓΑΘΟ-ΚΛΕΟΥΣ ΔΙΚΑΙΟΥ, a surprising grammatical construction for a coin because it includes a king's name and epithet (Agathocles the Just) plus a participle derived from the Greek verb βασιλεύω, "to rule as king." Why did this coin have the names and epithets of two different kings, and why was one described not as "king" (a noun) but rather "ruling as king" (a verb form)? For Jean de Bartholomaei, the unusual design and text suggested a special issue minted by Agathocles to honor his immediate predecessor Diodotus I, who must have recently died. Thus, the Greek inscription allegedly meant that Diodotus the Savior was being venerated by Agathocles the Just, with the latter now ruling as king.[75]

Within months, a newcomer to numismatics forcefully con-

Figure 9. Commemorative tetradrachms issued by Agathocles the Just to honor (*1*) Diodotus Soter, (*2*) Euthydemus Theos, (*3*) Antiochus Nicator.

tested the conclusions reached by Bartholomaei. Johann Gustav Droysen (1808–84), a name known to every Hellenistic scholar today, devoted several pages of his monumental *Geschichte des Hellenismus* to a description of the coin and a critique of Bartholomaei's work.[76] This precocious German historian had just recently invented the concept of a distinctive Hellenistic Age within world history. Not only was this notion quite new for contemporary scholars, but Droysen further challenged his peers to see this epoch as profoundly efficacious. Without the melding of cultures that resulted from Alexander's conquests, he argued, Christianity might never have become more than an ephemeral Jewish faction. In this grand interpretation, the hand of God deliberately planted Hellenism across the Near East so that the

Gospel could flourish in a fertile multicultural environment. How the Greeks interacted with other peoples, whether Jews, Egyptians, or Bactrians, thus became a matter of some importance to anyone interested in the rise of Christianity as a universal religion. The three centuries leading from Alexander to Jesus, once lamented for the sorry decline of classical Greek civilization under the corrupting influence of Eastern cultures, suddenly became worthy of serious study. Though Droysen adapted the term "Hellenistic" from the Greek New Testament itself, his eye wandered far afield to the coinage of Central Asia and the problems associated with studying Hellenistic kings on whom texts threw almost no light at all.[77]

Droysen's understanding of the Bactrian coinages, including the Eucratides examples bearing the names of Heliocles and Laodice, led him to believe that Agathocles ruled as a subordinate—not successor—of Diodotus I. The participle ΒΑΣΙΛΕΥΟΝΤΟΣ denoted, in his mind, not a temporal relationship (ruling after Diodotus) but an administrative relationship (ruling under Diodotus). In this way, scholars found a convenient solution to a growing problem: How to squeeze so many newly discovered Bactrian kings into the available chronology. If men like Diodotus and Agathocles reigned simultaneously within a system of kings and subkings, then all could be accommodated more easily. Many numismatists hastily lauded Droysen's interpretation, but in Russia Bartholomaei refused to relent. He responded line by line to Droysen's attack, deftly citing the example of the world-famous Rosetta Stone, which employs ΒΑΣΙΛΕΥΟΝΤΟΣ as its very first word.[78] Bartholomaei insisted that this verb form could not mean that Agathocles held an inferior position to Diodotus.

Further discoveries, at least for a time, seemed to support the position of Droysen over that of Bartholomaei. Major Hay

announced the existence of a similar coin associating Diodotus
Soter and Antimachus the God, with the inscription ΒΑΣΙΛΕ-
ΥΟΝΤΟΣ ΑΝΤΙΜΑΧΟΥ ΘΕΟΥ.[79] Now it appeared that two
kings, Agathocles and Antimachus, were somehow underlings
of Diodotus. Then, in 1858, James Gibbs of the Bombay civil service discovered a tetradrachm showing Agathocles to be linked
similarly with Euthydemus (fig. 9.2).[80] Scholars surmised that
Agathocles and Antimachus ruled different territories under the
supreme power of Diodotus, and that Agathocles continued to
do so under Euthydemus.[81] A decade later, the indefatigable collector Alexander Cunningham obtained a coin (fig. 9.3) connecting Agathocles with Antiochus the Conqueror (ΑΝΤΙΟΧΟΥ
ΝΙΚΑΤΟΡΟΣ).[82] Armed with this new evidence, Cunningham
fully supported the views of Droysen, Edward Thomas, Rochette,
Lassen, and others, that this entire series of coins attested the
junior rank of Agathocles not only to Diodotus but to Antiochus
and Euthydemus as well:[83]

> The subsequent discoveries of other coins, which show that Agath-
> okles held exactly the same relation to Euthydemus Theos and to
> Antiochus Nikator [as to Diodotus Soter], prove that this is the only
> true deduction which the coins afford.

This "only true deduction" meant that all these kings ruled more
or less together: "We know from their coins that Antimachus was
a contemporary of Diodotus, and that Agathokles was a contemporary of Diodotus, Euthydemus, and Antiochus Nikator."[84] Furthermore, since the coinage of Pantaleon so closely resembled that
of Agathocles, Cunningham placed him among this group, too, as
the older brother of Agathocles.[85] In this scenario, Diodotus I had
two daughters and, of course, a son (Diodotus II). One daughter
married the lieutenant king Agathocles, and the other wed the lieu-

tenant king Antimachus. Then, using the coins bearing the names of Eucratides, Heliocles, and Laodice, Cunningham attached these persons to the royal family tree as well. First, he imagined that Laodice, the supposed mother of Eucratides, was the daughter of Agathocles. He then abandoned that notion because her portrait lacks the "very peculiarly-shaped noses" of Agathocles and his brother Pantaleon. Undaunted, Cunningham made her the child of either Antimachus or Diodotus II.[86] Thus did Eucratides become, for a time, the great-grandson of Diodotus I.

In Berlin, the numismatist Alfred von Sallet (1842–97) waged a lonely battle against this march of scholarly opinion. He reasoned that Agathocles, Pantaleon, and Antimachus could not have reigned alongside the first rulers of Bactria; the designs of their coinage as a whole should place them later in the king list, after Demetrius and Eucratides.[87] Von Sallet called these binominal specimens "ancestor coins" ("Ahnmünzen") issued by Agathocles and Antimachus to commemorate the reigns of earlier kings. Soon, a stunning surprise vindicated this dissenting view. In 1880, Percy Gardner of the British Museum published a tetradrachm pairing Agathocles with yet another king: ΑΛΕΞΑΝΔΡΟΥ ΤΟΥ ΦΙΛΙΠΠΟΥ ("Alexander son of Philip").[88] Since Agathocles could not possibly have been a subking under Alexander the Great in the fourth century B.C.E., then it made no sense to render him a subking under Diodotus, Euthydemus, and Antiochus in the third and second centuries B.C.E. These must therefore be "medals struck in commemoration of departed worthies."[89] The inscription ΒΑΣΙΛΕΥΟΝΤΟΣ was temporal after all, rather than administrative, showing that Agathocles and Antimachus indeed reigned at a later time. "And this new light," wrote Gardner, "shows that the trained numismatic sagacity of Von Sallet saw the truth of the matter."[90]

More unexpected varieties of these ancestor coins would be found later, but the debates aired in the period 1843–80 demonstrate an important point within framework numismatics: the order in which discoveries are made often matters as much as the discoveries themselves. Had the Agathocles-Alexander coin been the first of this series found, then the entire debate going back to Bartholomaei and Droysen might have been avoided. This must be borne in mind, for it explains a great deal about the development of any scientific field, especially the intellectual dead ends that later seem so preposterous. Once this Agathocles-Alexander coin finally appeared, scholars could immediately remedy the disorder in the Bactrian king list.

Having so brilliantly superseded checklist numismatics, framework numismatics laid the foundations for all subsequent research on ancient Bactria. Through the prodigious energies of pioneering numismatists, many of whom personally endured the dangers of the Great Game, most of the kings and queens of Bactria and India were discovered by the end of the nineteenth century.[91] They established a basic "frame of history" (to quote Wolff again) that went far beyond the original list of kings compiled by Vaillant and Bayer, and that still is recognizable in all reconstructions today. At least one unusual piece among these finds exemplifies an occasional fixation with the rare for the sake of its rarity. More than any other single specimen in framework numismatics, a gigantic gold coin minted by Eucratides captured the imaginations of experts and enthusiasts alike, warranting its place in what might be called novelty numismatics.

CHAPTER THREE

The Gold Colossus

Novelty Numismatics

On July 18, 1867, a golden "monster" migrated from its home under the armpit of a murderer into a royal new residence in Paris.[1] That change of address is one of the most sensational stories in the annals of numismatics. Taking its place among the rarest treasures of the Bibliothèque Impériale (now the Bibliothèque Nationale), this huge coin became known as the Eucratidion in honor of the ancient king displayed on one side, with his name and titles wrapped around an image of the galloping Greek-hero twins, the Dioscuri, on the other (fig. 10). Weighing 169.2 grams and spanning the palm of a man's hand, it is the largest gold coin ever minted in the ancient world. Nothing more novel can be found in any numismatic collection on Earth, and the study of this piece has taken on a life of its own.

The new custodian of this gold colossus, Pierre-Marie Anatole Chabouillet (1814–99), displayed it prominently in the Cabinet des Médailles of his sovereign, Louis Napoleon III. The purchase of the Eucratidion for the incredible sum of thirty thousand francs had been specially (and, it seems, speedily) authorized by

Figure 10. The Eucratidion, largest of all gold
coins from the ancient world, minted by Eucratides
the Great.

the minister of public instruction, the historian Victor Duruy. In fact, the smitten Duruy later featured the coin in his multivolume *History of Rome.* (See plate 2.) Officially, Anatole Chabouillet claimed to have no precise knowledge of where or how this trophy had been found. He marveled that so grand a medallion managed through some unbelievable series of fortuitous circumstances ("par un concours inouï de circumstances favorables") to survive at all.[2] He could only wonder whether it had been found in Merv, around some small village in Turkestan, somewhere near Persia, or even in Persia itself.[3] Chabouillet's musings may appear to be the first and final word on the matter, but a dramatic account of the coin's discovery eventually appeared a dozen years later in the pages of the *New York Times.* That story connected the Eucratidion to the travels of a cold-blooded killer.

The 1879 *Times* article was filed under the unassuming title "A Coin of Eucratides."[4] There the anonymous reporter tells "the true story of the rarest of all coins," based on the personal recollections of an informant identified cryptically as "a French gentleman, an expert of the British Museum." In July 1867, that gentleman reportedly dined in London with General Charles Richard Fox (1796–1873), a wealthy collector and prominent member of the Royal Numismatic Society. During the dinner at Fox's Kensington mansion, the French expert learned of a "queer kind of fellow" from Bukhara who was wandering about the antiquities shops of London trying to sell a huge gold coin. The incredible size of the coin so amazed some of the London dealers that they had instinctively dismissed it as a forgery. "Just think of it," the French expert was told, "the shabby-looking fellow who was hawking the coin around had the impertinence to ask £5,000 for it!"

The dinner guest resolved at once to see this "numismatical monstrosity" for himself. General Fox, sympathizing with the expert's "fit of numismatic fever," allowed the man to quit his table and thus begin the quest of a lifetime. The excited French expert raced by cab from Kensington to Islington, where itinerant foreigners were known to congregate. A trail of inquiries soon led him to the miserable lodgings of the traveler he sought, a man said to have "black, snaky eyes" and hands like talons. Using the lodger's landlord as an interpreter, the expert asked to see the Bukharan's big gold coin. The odd little man obliged with an unusual striptease, removing in turn "his queerly-cut coat, next his embroidered waistcoat, then his waist-band, next his shirt," until, half-naked, he pulled from under his armpit "a dirty, sweat-begrimed leather case." This pouch the traveler dramatically opened to reveal the treasure inside:

> In an instant the eyes of the expert were dazzled with that peculiar soft yellow sheen which only antique gold gives forth. It was indeed a prize. One glance alone was sufficient to show that it was a grand medallion, a unique coin, the chiefest, the rarest in the world.

As the expert labored to conceal his emotions from the "wily Oriental," the latter recounted through the interpreter a remarkable story of gold, greed, and gore. He explained that he and six compatriots had discovered the coin:

> We quarreled over it. That was natural. It was worth a fight. We fell on one another with knives and daggers. After a while, for it was hot work, five of the men rolled dead in the dust.

The two survivors of this killing spree made a pact that one of them would smuggle the prize, safely lodged under his armpit, to find a rich buyer in Europe.

Feigning indifference, the French expert lit a cigarette and examined the coin dismissively. Although secretly "wild with joy," the prospective buyer casually brushed aside the seller's demand for five thousand pounds and made a cool counteroffer:

> I tell you what I will do. I will give you, right now, my check for £1,000 for the piece. If the coin is not mine in twenty minutes I shall offer you £800 for it, and so on until I get to £500. If you don't close with me tonight, tomorrow I will not take it at any price.

The buyer smoked, and the seller sulked, for the full twenty minutes, when suddenly the man from Bukhara snatched the check and handed over the Eucratidion. That night the expert never closed his eyes, so excited was he to possess safely under his pillow the most expensive coin in the world. Even at the cost of five lives and a small fortune, he firmly believed that the coin was a bargain "even had fifty or one hundred lives been sacrificed" for it. As quickly as possible, the patriotic French buyer carried his treasure to Paris. Emperor Louis Napoleon III took an interest in it, as did the minister of public instruction. Through the agency of a dealer named Feuardent, French officials purchased the Eucratidion for thirty thousand francs (20% more than the expert had paid for it in London). The coin thus took residence in the Cabinet des Médailles of the Bibliothèque Impériale in Paris, where it remains today, having first traveled across two continents under the armpit of a self-professed murderer.

That, at least, is the famous story long entrenched in numismatic lore.[5] Can a single word of it be true? Some scholars have naturally condemned this melodramatic account as an outright fabrication.[6] Only recently has anyone sought to investigate the claims made by the anonymous source behind it.[7] That attempt focused on General Fox, an avid collector with deep pockets who was a Francophile with residences in both London (site of the infamous dinner) and Paris (where the coin was hastened). The theory is that Fox actually bought the Eucratidion. He allegedly steered the French expert to the seller with instructions to verify the coin's authenticity. That being done, it was Fox's own cash that finalized the deal. Afterward, Fox and his expert friend took the gold prize to Paris and sold it. This interesting reconstruction, however, does not take into account a number of relevant newspaper reports and other publications that fill out the story of a coin still appreciated primarily for its novelty.[8]

General Fox played only a minor role in the affair and most certainly was not the source for the original newspaper account, which appeared six years after his death. We can now state that the man at the center of events was in fact the French expert, Gaston L. Feuardent (1843–93; fig. 11), son of the Feuardent mentioned in the newspaper account.[9] The elder Feuardent (1819–1907), named Félix, was a successful antiquities dealer and partner in the firm of Rollin et Feuardent in Paris, which sold the Eucratidion to the Bibliothèque Impériale. The firm had opened a London branch in 1867, represented by the son, Gaston.[10] This younger Feuardent became quite active in London numismatic circles and procured many items for the collections of the British Museum, hence his description as "an expert of the British Museum." He was a member of the London Numismatic Society and knew well its other members, including General Fox. His place at Fox's table, his reaction to the news of the great gold coin, his ability to purchase it, and his immediate conveyance of the prize to the firm's Paris offices all make perfect sense of the newspaper story.

Gaston Feuardent's decision to relate his adventure to the *New York Times* can also be easily explained. In 1876, Gaston moved to New York City, where he formed a very active relationship with the staff of the *Times*. He was frequently consulted by the newspaper on all manner of antiquarian subjects, from rare coins to a

Figure 11. Gaston L. Feuardent, the French numismatist who procured the Eucratidion and sold it
to Louis Napoleon.

huge sword alleged to have fallen in a fireball from the heavens.[11]
He acted soberly as the paper's debunker in chief, discrediting
hoaxes and forgeries of various kinds. In fact, his rigid no-nonsense
nature embroiled him in one of the most famous dustups of
the day—the astonishing Cesnola affair.[12] This very public case
shows just how much Gaston Feuardent jealously guarded his

widespread reputation as a disciplined expert. In 1880, Gaston created a stir by vigorously challenging the authenticity of a collection of Cypriot antiquities sold by General Luigi Palma di Cesnola to the Metropolitan Museum of Art.[13] Tempers flared and great egos clashed on the battlefields of the press and the courts. The ensuing vitriol seriously strained relations between, on the one hand, the Metropolitan Museum and its first director (none other than Cesnola himself) and, on the other, the American Numismatic and Archaeological Society (ANAS) and one of its most prominent members, Gaston Feuardent. With its own reputation on the line against that of the Metropolitan, the ANAS prudently investigated Gaston's reliability, focusing on his record of professionalism and even his "moral fiber."[14] The result was a resounding vote of confidence, publicly expressed in a resolution appearing in the *New York Times* that lauded Feuardent's "unselfish devotion to the truth."[15] Whether or not such circumstances so confirm the habitual trustworthiness of the man that we may believe everything he reported about the Eucratidion, at least we now know that it was he who bought the coin and conveyed it to France in July 1867.

Gaston Feuardent actually reinforced his account a few years later in his "Peculiar History of the Most Valuable Coin Known to Numismatists," a newspaper story that has heretofore escaped scholarly attention.[16] Interviewed by the New York correspondent of the *Chicago Daily* in December 1882, Gaston is described as "the Nemesis of Di Cesnola." He is credited as the only real "numismatician" in America, a man "so skilled in knowledge of coins, in classical archaeology, and in antiquarian lore of all sorts that others are scarcely to be mentioned in comparison." In the course of answering the reporter's questions about coins in general, Gaston Feuardent made the following statement:

I, myself, sold to Louis Napoleon the most valuable coin in the world. When I first heard of this I was at dinner with some gentlemen in London. One of them told about a ragged stroller who had that day offered to sell to him a splendid gold coin from Central Asia nearly as large as the palm of his hand. He sent him off as a mountebank and swindler. The description of the coin fired my imagination in a way that all collectors will understand. I hastily excused myself, called a cab, and went out to the suburbs, to a wretched quarter where I knew these Indian traders were wont to congregate. I searched some hours before I found the man from Bokhara, and got him out of his squalid bed. We went into a room alone, and there, removing his outer clothing, the tawny man drew from his arm-pit a sweaty bag, and from the bag he brought forth the most magnificent coin I had ever seen. It was obviously A GENUINE ANTIQUE stamped by King Eucratides of India, one of the successors of Alexander the Great. I was much excited, but strove to appear cool. On the obverse was an engraved head of the King, on the reverse a fine relief of Castor and Pollux [the Dioscuri]. It bore date about 185 B.C. [*sic*] He said the coin had at first been found by seven men, but they got into a deadly feud over it, and five were slain. He and a friend were the only survivors. He put an extravagant price on it, but I refused to pay it. At last I offered him £1,000—about $5,000—and gave him only ten minutes to consider the proposition. After that I told him I should take off $100 each minute from my offer. Before the ten minutes were up the coin was mine. I carried it to the Emperor, Napoleon. He offered me $6,000 for it, and I accepted it as a command that so rare a treasure should never leave France. It may now be seen in Paris among the antique trophies, honored by being placed in a case all by itself beneath the eye of the sentinel. It is the finest coin in the world.

In almost every respect, this version tallies with Gaston's earlier account in the *New York Times*. The only notable differences are the absence of the interpreter and the time allotted the Bukharan seller to accept the offer of £1,000. Again, Feuardent credits Fox with no active role in the proceedings, and none need be imagined. The French expert seems certain of these events, and he clearly enjoyed recounting to all and sundry this greatest adventure of his life. His associations with the press of nineteenth-century America made the Eucratidion the most famous novelty in ancient numismatics.

We may go further than Feuardent's recollections in U.S. newspapers. The earliest known report of the huge gold Eucratides coin actually appears in the published diary of Sir Mountstuart Elphinstone Grant Duff (1829–1906). Sir Mountstuart recorded on July 1, 1867, that he "saw the great gold coin of Eucratides" at a meeting of the Council of the Asiatic Society.[17] This viewing of the Eucratidion must have taken place just days before the July dinner at which Gaston Feuardent learned of the piece, for the coin was settled into Paris's Bibliothèque Impériale by July 18. The diarist, who was indeed a council member of the Asiatic Society, correctly describes the coin as "weighing about twenty of our sovereigns." He adds:

> This very remarkable piece was brought from Bokhara by a Jew, who, on his first arrival in Paris, knowing that the West was rich and fond of curious objects, modestly demanded a million of francs for it. No one being willing to go into the transaction at that figure, he came to London, and entered into negotiations with the British Museum. Of course people there were charmed with it, and they soon began to discuss the question of price. "What," said the Jew, "is its intrinsic value?" So much, they replied. "When was it struck?" he then asked. About such and such a year, was the answer. "Well," rejoined the Jew, "I will be satisfied with interest at 5 percent from that date."

These scribblings unfortunately intensify the jingoistic tone detectable in Gaston Feuardent's reminisces: the wily, sinister, shabby Oriental with talon hands and snaky eyes who is bested by the cool French expert; the greedy Bukharan Jew totaling up two thousand years' interest on an ancient coin.[18] Sir Mountstuart's final remarks complete the story:

> After a good deal of bargaining, it was ultimately bought by Feuardent for, I have heard, £1,100, and it passed to the Imperial Library for, I believe, £1,300.

The diarist is here correct in identifying Feuardent (and not Fox) as the owner of the coin, although off a bit on the sums paid and received (£100 in each case). Nothing in his last sentence could Sir Mountstuart have known on July 1, so this must be a later elaboration for the published version of the diary.

The next known mention of the coin can be found in a letter of Major General Alexander Cunningham written to Colonel Charles Seton Guthrie. These men, members of the Royal Engineers, shared a keen interest in ancient coins, a passion that both officers nurtured during their years of service in India. An extract from Cunningham's letter, printed in the *Journal of the Asiatic Society of Bengal*, reads:[19]

> But what is a double gold-mohur compared to the great gold Eucratides which has just been brought from Bokhara by Aga Zebalun Bokhari? It is $2\frac{1}{2}$ inches in diameter, and weighs ten staters, or eleven guineas? It has the usual helmeted head on one side, with the horsemen and inscription on the reverse. The owner has refused 700£ for it. It is genuine—and beats all the Greek coins hitherto discovered.

Since this letter reached Colonel Guthrie in India and was then passed along to Arthur Grote of the Asiatic Society of Bengal in time for publication in the November 1 issue of its journal, it must have been composed much earlier.[20] Several points in the letter are noteworthy. Cunningham names the foreigner from Bukhara, insists that the coin is authentic, and knows of at least one unsuccessful bid for the piece. These details square nicely with Gaston Feuardent's account published twelve years later, and with Mountstuart Duff's reference to a Bukharan seller.[21] Yet, Cunningham describes the coin in terms that do not match the Eucratidion seen by Mountstuart and sold to the Cabinet des Médailles; Cunningham reports a coin that is half the weight but a quarter-inch larger. Are these careless errors, or the dimensions of a different specimen altogether?

Hyde Clarke, a numismatist who traveled in the same circles as Gaston Feuardent, wondered the same thing about Cunningham's report.[22] When a copy of Cunningham's letter appeared in the London *Athenaeum* on March 21, 1868, Clarke responded for the very next issue (March 28). The journal reported:

> Last week we spoke of a very remarkable gold coin, a great gold Eucratides. "The first gold Eucratides," writes Mr. Hyde Clarke, "came into the possession of M. Svoboda, of Bagdad, and after being offered to the British Museum, was sold to the Imperial Museum at Paris for 30,000 francs, or 1,200£. Is this the same as that described by General A. Cunningham? M. Svoboda has now on hand a silver Eucratides of the same size."

Had two large gold Eucratides coins, one a twenty-stater and the other a ten-stater, crossed paths on the London market in 1867? The existence of two genuine variants of the Eucratidion seems very unlikely, and Cunningham's own numismatic research makes the existence of two a remote possibility at best. In an article published about Eucratides' coins in 1869, Cunningham lists all known specimens in gold, silver, and bronze; he references the twenty-stater piece and makes no mention of any other variety in gold.[23] By this time, then, the famed numismatist had corrected his earlier confusion about the size of the coin he labels "Unique, from Bokhara." Indeed, Cunningham's original uncertainty about the coin's weight can be seen in the question mark he placed in the letter: "It… weighs ten staters, or eleven guineas?" In all quotations of that sentence in later journals and newspapers, editors have replaced the original question mark with an exclamation point, as if Cunningham were emphatic rather than unsure about the coin's size.[24] We may assume that General Cunningham had seen (or heard of) the same coin mentioned in Mountstuart Duff's diary, namely the unique twenty-stater Eucratidion.

Hyde Clarke's remarks to the *Athenaeum* do include two odd new bits of information. First, he avers that the Eucratidion was at some time owned by a Mr. Svoboda of Baghdad. Up to this point, all references to the seller identify him as a man from Bukhara, perhaps named Aga Zebalun Bokhari; the buyer, Gaston Feuardent, later confirmed this provenance. The latter's version of events has no place for Svoboda anywhere in the coin's history from its first discovery to its final disposition in the Bibliothèque Impériale. Is Hyde Clarke therefore wrong on this point? The answer to this question may rest upon his other curious revelation: the existence of a large silver Eucratides coin, also in the possession of Mr. Svoboda. This detail raises the very real possibility that Svoboda was trafficking in gold and silver imitations of the original Eucratidion. This practice often follows the sale of a sensational coin.[25] In fact, by the early twentieth century there were at least a half-dozen gold and silver imitations of the genuine Eucratidion, and twice that number are known today. Svoboda's "silver Eucratides of the same size" may have been one of the two examples known from casts that are kept in the cabinets of the British Museum.[26] In 1901, one of these silver imita-

Figure 12. The elaborate secondary symbol, representing one of the caps of the Dioscuri, found on some forgeries of the Eucratidion.

tions was owned by Professor Torrey, surely Charles Cutler Torrey (1863–1956), who later wrote a book about coins from Bukhara.[27] This specimen was said to weigh 1,014 grains (about 66 grams, the size of four large silver tetradrachms); it has a secondary symbol on the reverse that resembles an elaborate conical headdress (fig. 12). This symbol is actually a copy of one of the caps worn by the Dioscuri, which are displayed separately on Eucratides' obols and small square bronzes.[28] The other huge silver imitation, attributed to "Baldwin 1954" according to the museum identification ticket, carries a rudimentary form of this ancillary symbol. This suggests that the Baldwin specimen is a secondary derivative of the Torrey imitation.

Copies in gold range in weight from three to nineteen staters. Solid-gold varieties include two auctioned from the collection of Joseph Avent in November 1897 (sold as fakes for about £20 each).[29] Another at the time was owned by Dr. Guerson da Cunha, purchased as genuine for over £600 but later condemned as a forgery.[30] Two imitations are associated with the famous American financier John Pierpont Morgan. One was auctioned from his collection in 1953; the other now lies in the forgery trays of the American Numismatic Society.[31] A gold imitation owned by Syed Ali Bilgrame passed through the British Museum in 1902 and again in 1923.[32] A fifteen-stater copy appeared in an exhibition at the Smithsonian Institution in 1985–86.[33] This last example shows the same elaborate ancillary symbol of the Dioscuri cap as seen on the silver coin owned by Professor Torrey. It does not seem, however, that the forgers quite understood the headdress they were copying, since the horsemen themselves do not wear them. Instead, the engraved Dioscuri have rays prominently radiating from their heads. A gold-plated specimen in the British Museum that belonged to a Mrs. Thornton in 1909 captures this same effect; the note with the coin in the forgery trays actually describes the Dioscuri as wearing "Indian feather headdress."[34] This gilded piece, like the silver Baldwin example, bears the rudimentary version of the ancillary symbol (and a simplified monogram), so that it too is clearly a later derivative—a copy of a copy. All these take us back to the comment by Hyde Clarke, and the strong possibility that imitations in gold and silver were circulating soon after the sale of the original coin to Gaston Feuardent.

The early proliferation of Eucratidion knockoffs prompted one numismatist to ask: "Are they concoctions altogether, the work of some skilful Persian goldsmith? Or does there exist more than one genuine piece, from which the da Cunha and Avent examples have been imitated?"[35] The existence of a second genuine twenty-stater Eucratides has long been rumored but never confirmed.[36] As for the existence of "some skilful Persian goldsmith," we should probably look farther east for the manufacturer of most of these fakes, since so many have derived from collections formed in India.[37] Meanwhile, the fame of the specimen in Paris, which had inspired the forgeries, continued to grow year by year. The Eucratidion, after all, had become the most notable numismatic celebrity in the world thanks to its extraordinary size and price.[38] In nearly every reference to it, this "monster" was regarded for its novelty rather than for anything it might contribute to framework numismatics.

Similar stories swirl around Eucratides' other gold issues. The first appearance of a normal-sized Eucratides gold coin, a battered stater, happened to be on the finger of an Afghan army officer, where it apparently caught the attention of an avid British collector named Charles Strutt.[39] The latter purchased the artifact and chiseled it free of the ring to which it had been attached. Though badly scarred, the coin became a great prize for successive owners.[40] Weighing 8.53 grams, this piece preserves the same basic features as its gigantic cousin, though with a different monogram (ᗖ). The obverse portrait of Eucratides has been mashed, perhaps during its long service as a signet ring, and the Dioscuri reverse suffers a deep cut from end to end. (See chap. 9, below.) The edges of the coin are misshapen, marked here and there by the bite of pliers used in removing the ring. More than once, this marred novelty made its way through Sotheby's as the stater meandered through some of the finest collections in Europe and America.[41]

By the end of the nineteenth century, Bactrian studies finally had the benefit of an impressive corpus of ancient coins. Some finds had fulfilled the first ambitions of checklist numismatics; a few extraordinary pieces mesmerized the aficionados of novelty numismatics, and most of the coins served the broader interests of framework numismatics. By 1888, the sesquicentennial of Bayer's *Historia Regni Graecorum Bactriani,* what might be called the heroic age of numismatic exploration in Central Asia had filled public and private coin cabinets on several continents. The single specimen of Eucratides known to Bayer could be compared to a growing array of this king's mintages in gold, silver, and bronze. The largest accumulation of Eucratides' coins resided at that time in the British Museum, which had managed to absorb much of the material from the pioneering collectors Prinsep, Masson, Court, and especially Sir Alexander Cunningham. Thus, to the sixty-five Eucratides specimens published by the British Museum in 1886 (32 silver, 33 bronze), Cunningham's coins eventually brought that number to well above a hundred.[42] Dozens more specimens could be studied elsewhere in France, Britain, Russia, and India, although there existed as yet no major Bactrian collections in the United States.[43]

Cataloguing major collections like that in the British Museum laid the foundations for a new phase of numismatic studies. Scholars now had a burgeoning framework that invited them to build more complex historical narratives. The use of photography, beginning in 1874, replaced less reliable line drawings, so that even non-numismatists closeted in their libraries might consult these catalogues and dare to write histories based upon them. In their hands, the money of ancient Bactria was made to talk under sometimes torturous interrogation.

CHAPTER FOUR

Telling Tales

Narrative Numismatics

At the very outset of the twentieth century, a young British barrister on the eve of a serious breakdown indulged his passion for a subject far outside his profession. William Woodthorpe Tarn (1869–1957; see fig. 13) loved Hellenistic history. He had studied classics at Cambridge and traveled throughout mainland Greece and the islands before settling, at his father's request, upon a career at law.[1] His practice proved a great success, but it could never displace his enthusiasm for ancient history. Tarn's avocation blossomed into an article on the Oxus trade route published in 1901, and another treatise the following year on Hellenism in Bactria and India.[2] These contributions to a prestigious academic journal set the stage for a new career when, in 1905, Tarn's ill health forced him to relinquish his law practice and retire from London. He lived thenceforth as an aristocratic country gentleman, researching and writing history at a prodigious pace.[3] Tarn never held a university post, yet he became a dominant figure in classical scholarship and, in addition to his world-famous work on Alexander the Great, rose to the highest ranks

Figure 13. Sir William Woodthorpe Tarn, a towering figure in Bactrian studies.

of Bactrian studies. Naturally, his views on these subjects have been closely scrutinized and inevitably criticized over the years, but they will always stand as milestones.[4]

When Tarn first delved into the subject of Bactria, he essentially accepted at face value the fruits of framework numismatics. Thus, he wrote confidently in 1902 that Heliocles was the son and murderer of Eucratides, for this was the view of most coin experts at the time.[5] By 1938, however, Tarn the historian had lost confidence in the numismatists on this point: "There is no chance whatever of it being true as it stands."[6] Such boldness on his part reflected his growing sense that Bactrian studies needed a new approach. Tarn suggested:[7]

The coins of course are all-important, and one cannot overpraise the work done on them by generations of numismatists; it seems to me one of the wonders of scholarship. But the numismatist as such has sometimes been unable to place or explain the facts which he has elicited; naturally so, for he is not expected to be a Hellenistic historian.

Tarn wished to expand the work of countless numismatic specialists into something more than a mere framework; he insisted upon a deep, complex narrative full of details about personalities and family relationships.[8] The task of the Hellenistic historian was to find in the coin evidence those thousands of subtle connections to other sources and events that the numismatists had missed. Thus, Tarn saw his mission as one to mend the gap between the increasingly independent disciplines of history and numismatics. After all, a similar parting of the ways had already begun to isolate numismatists from archaeologists in a way that has been unfortunate for both camps.[9] In 1907, for example, what had been the American Numismatic and Archaeological Society since 1865 voted to excise "and Archaeological" from its name.[10] In his presidential address leading up to this decision, Archer Huntington insisted:[11]

The character of the Society, and of its collection, has increasingly rendered this title inappropriate. We are not, except in a vague sense, an Archaeological Society.

He added that the society's main brief was to appreciate the art of the medalist and to promote the aesthetics of U.S. coins. His successful proposal was consummated by disbanding the society's standing committee on archaeology once and for all.

Tarn the historian not only wanted numismatics to be made more narrative; he also had strong ideas about where that narrative should belong. In his own work, Tarn emphasized Hellenistic history in reaction to the tendency of Bactrian studies to be treated as an adjunct of orientalists. In the decades between his first attempt, in 1902, to investigate the Hellenism per se of Bactria and, in 1938, his full treatment of the subject in *The Greeks in Bactria and India,* other scholars had continued to associate Bactria primarily with Indian history and culture. In 1909, Hugh George Rawlinson's dissertation on Bactria won the Hare Prize in classics at Cambridge, but the book was then published in Probstbain's Oriental Series alongside volumes on Chinese philosophy, and its author went on to a brilliant career as a scholar of Indian history.[12] In 1922, two important chapters on Bactria appeared in *The Cambridge History of India,* one written by the noted numismatist (Sir) George Macdonald and the other by Edward James Rapson, professor of Sanskrit at Cambridge.[13] Such works probably account for Tarn's famous complaint:[14]

> It is unfortunate that in Britain, and I think everywhere, the story of the Greeks in India has been treated as part of the history of India alone. For in the history of India the episode of Greek rule has no meaning; it is really part of the history of Hellenism, and that is where its meaning resides.

Tarn's Hellenocentric viewpoint would later inspire a rousing rebuttal from Indian scholars, but in 1938 the reaction was largely positive and, at times, even adulatory. Professor Charles Alexander Robinson, Jr., raved that Tarn's book "may well represent the greatest triumph of historical scholarship in our day."[15]

Unlike the short, tentative steps taken in the first two centuries of Bactrian studies, Tarn marked its bicentennial by daring to make some amazing leaps. The first edition of *The Greeks in Bactria and India* sucked up evidence from every quarter, and

Tarn fitted each available piece—no matter how obscure—into a long, seamless narrative that exceeded anything ever ventured before.[16] What Rawlinson, Macdonald, and Rapson had covered in just a few pages, Tarn needed nine densely packed chapters and twenty-one appendixes to argue. In so doing, Tarn gave the Bactrian kings memorable personalities and lofty ambitions; he knew who were their fathers, brothers, wives, and sons. He argued chronological points down to specific years, seasons, and even months, and he traced the movements of armies and generals across Central and South Asia as if he had captured their campaign maps. Tarn saw intimate connections between Bactria and Syria that rewrote Hellenistic history, and he even suggested that the Bactrians managed to repeat Greek history step for step in the Far East: "Euthydemus was Philip II, Bactria was Macedonia, the derelict Mauryan empire was the Persian empire, and Demetrius was a second Alexander."[17] Perhaps most important, Tarn pontificated all this with breathtaking certainty. More like a partisan lawyer than a dispassionate scholar, he pounded home his points with little patience for doubts or reservations.[18]

A good illustration may be cited in the matter of Eucratides' parentage. In 1886, the numismatist Percy Gardner had determined that Eucratides' origins were hopelessly obscure, although he conceded that the coins bearing the images and names of Heliocles and Laodice must denote his father and mother. Because Laodice's portrait often shows a diadem, she had to be of royal blood: "But we must remain in ignorance whose daughter she was."[19] In 1909, Rawlinson tentatively stepped away from that cautious appraisal. He thought it "fairly clear that Laodice is a Seleucid princess, and the most reasonable supposition is that she was the daughter of Demetrius by his marriage with the daughter of Antiochus III."[20] Rawlinson then deftly two-stepped by also stating that "the most tenable theory" is perhaps that Laodice "was *not* the *daughter* of Demetrius by his Seleucid wife, but a relation—sister, cousin, or some such connection—who had accompanied her to Bactria."[21] Macdonald in 1922 cared little for the association of Eucratides' mother with Demetrius's family but offered as "pure speculation" the possibility of some connection with Antiochus IV.[22] Tarn seized upon this latter idea. He called Macdonald's hesitant supposition "the first ray of light in the darkness" and built upon it his whole reconstruction of Eucratides' world.[23] Laodice, he argued, was "certainly a Seleucid princess," the sister of Antiochus III, making Eucratides without doubt the first cousin of Antiochus IV Epiphanes.

Whereas others had confessed ignorance or mere speculation, Tarn claimed ironclad certitude. According to the former barrister, Euthydemus and his son Demetrius realized the grandest ideals of Alexander by building a true partnership between Greeks and natives in Bactria, at least until the spoiler Eucratides intervened on behalf of Antiochus IV. In late 169 B.C.E., cousin Eucratides allegedly set out with a small army to recover the eastern edges of the old Seleucid Empire. He took the southern route through Seistan and then, in the spring of 168, marched north, assuming the title "king" and issuing coins when he reached Bactria, as his overlord Antiochus had allegedly instructed him to do. Eucratides made quick work of the Euthydemids, two of whom (Agathocles and Antimachus) tried to counter the invader's political appeal by issuing in the winter of 168–167 B.C.E. a parallel series of so-called pedigree coins professing their own (fictitious) Seleucid heritage. Eucratides answered with coins showing his mother to be a prominent Seleucid matron. In 167, Demetrius himself was defeated and killed as Eucratides swept toward India. In the following year, Eucratides proclaimed himself "Great" and issued his huge gold victory medallion.[24] Then, in 159 B.C.E., just ten years out from Syria, Eucratides fell to an assassin (not his own son, but apparently the scion of some Euthydemid rival). Heliocles the Just avenged his fallen father as Bactria began to shudder under waves of nomadic invasion.[25] This was indeed a Hellenistic history, one rich in detail, romantic in scope, and reassuring in its rigid argumentation. But, as some admirers eventually wondered, was all of it really true?[26]

Following World War II, the German scholar-spy Franz Altheim (unhindered by his earlier associations with Hermann Göring and Heinrich Himmler) tackled a number of Tarn's basic assumptions about ancient Central Asia.[27] Whereas Tarn saw Hellenism almost everywhere he looked, Altheim (1898–1976) sought out the influences of Iranian peoples. In his *Weltgeschichte Asiens im griechischen Zeitalter* and subsequent works, he focused upon the role of Parthia rather than the Seleucids in the shaping of Bactrian history.[28] Thus, Altheim dismissed the alleged kinship of Antiochus IV and Eucratides, declaring that the former never sent the latter to recover the East.[29] He returned to the old notion that the Heliocles and Laodice coin honored not Eucratides' parents but rather his son and daughter-in-law. She, in fact, was not royalty at all, in spite of her diadem. Altheim considered Heliocles the murderer of Eucratides following the death of Demetrius, whose defeated forces indeed numbered sixty thousand (as Justin states), because mere Indian troops were surely no match for three hundred "Macedonians" from Bactria! Altheim's reliance on narrative numismatics was very much like Tarn's, although the two differed about whether that story was essentially Parthian or Seleucid.

In 1951, when Tarn published a second edition of *The Greeks in Bactria and India,* he noted straightway that Altheim's rival work showed "vast learning that is not always matched by the use made of it."[30] This, ironically, was Tarn's criticism of the numismatists before him, and precisely the same might be said of Tarn's own work. The collector-scholar Richard Bertram Whitehead (1879–1967) certainly thought so. A veteran of the Indian civil service, Whitehead had in 1914 produced the first volume of his *Catalogue of Coins in the Panjab Museum, Lahore.*[31] Decades later, he recognized in Tarn's magnum opus a brilliant synthesis of information that was at the same time flawed by methodological weaknesses. He heaped praise upon *The Greeks in Bactria and India* but added, almost apologetically:[32]

> One feels it is ungenerous to criticize.... Still there are some aspects which cause misgiving, and some points on which a numismatist who has actually collected in the Punjab feels that he can offer useful comment.

Whitehead lamented the historian's overconfidence: "Where Dr. Tarn will find lack of agreement is in the attribution of certainty to various points concerned."[33] The rush to turn framework numismatics into narrative numismatics worried those whose expertise was mined but not practiced by men like Tarn.

Many of Whitehead's misgivings were passed on to a young protégé from India named Awadh Kishore Narain. In 1952, Narain arrived in London with a Holkar Fellowship to complete his doctorate.[34] Under the specially arranged tutelage of Whitehead, Narain worked through the numismatic evidence and crafted a strong rebuttal to Tarn's work. Although Whitehead fully approved his student's research, he at one point confided to a colleague his worries about Narain's criticisms of Tarn: Would the academic establishment react kindly to the young man's rival study? Narain weathered such concerns, and his dissertation was later published, as it happened, in the very year of Tarn's death.[35] The torch had passed to a new generation.

Whereas Tarn took a Hellenocentric approach and Altheim's can be called Iranocentric, A.K. Narain produced a book that is by comparison more Indocentric. Although Narain has strenuously challenged this characterization of his work, it is difficult to escape his deliberate (and equally inaccurate) counterpoint to Tarn's Greek emphasis.[36] As we have seen, Tarn overstated: "For in the history of India the episode of Greek rule has no meaning; it is really part of the history of Hellenism, and that is where its meaning resides." Clearly responding to this phraseology, Narain overstated in turn: "Their history is part of the history of India, and not of the Hellenistic states."[37] Even if Narain has here exaggerated his case for effect (he agrees elsewhere that these events have their place, too, in Hellenistic history), he did champion a renewed focus on India.[38] This is a fact, as shown by a comparison of how much space Tarn and Narain each devoted to, say, the Seleucids on the one hand or, on the other, the Indo-Greeks from Menander onward.[39] Narain intended to restore Bactria to Indian history: "I was only bringing the old truth back out to its right place."[40] This, unfortunately, created the impression of a renewed struggle for Bactrian history.[41] To what extent this tug of worlds had its roots in the modern fate of British imperialism in India has been keenly debated. One scholar proposes that "by and large, Tarn, the Englishman, represented a moribund and an already nostalgic imperialism while Narain, the Indian, personified in 1957 a freshly victorious nationalism."[42] The title of Narain's work, *The Indo-Greeks,* has been said to betray his bias since it privileges the Indians ahead of the Greeks.[43] This, however, is unfair. Narain did not invent this hyphenated term; he inherited it from his British teacher, Whitehead.[44]

In the final analysis, it was Narain's numismatic acumen rather than his politics that first set him at odds with Tarn.[45] He, like Tarn, determined that there was indeed "a clear distinction" growing between history and numismatics, but he disagreed about the relative merits of each discipline. Narain believed that the historian identifies his craft with literature, the numismatist with science. The historian tends to be less concerned with accuracy, less restrained in his judgment, and more inclined to hero worship.[46] These traits were evident to Narain in the antithetical approaches taken by Tarn and Whitehead. "Numismatics," Narain observed, "is one of those 'unwritten sources' which give scope to the historian to wander off into the land of romance."[47]

The history reconstructed by A.K. Narain certainly has a sounder grounding in the basics of framework numismatics than does the more romantic narrative of W.W. Tarn. For example, Narain challenged Tarn's clumsy argumentation about the various coinages struck in the name of Demetrius.[48] This meant that Tarn's grand notions surrounding the invasion of India by Demetrius I, son of Euthydemus, had to be reconsidered. For Narain, Euthydemus's son was no "second Alexander" at all. The real conqueror was Demetrius II, whose fame Tarn stole away based "entirely on a concatenation of slender threads of evidence."[49] Thus, Eucratides the usurper (with no kinship to the Seleucids) fought against Demetrius II, who was perhaps a son of Antimachus the God. Then Plato, at the instigation of the Parthians, allegedly assassinated Eucratides in about 155 B.C.E.[50]

Narain, of course, had the advantage not only of sound numismatic training but also of evidence not found or fully published until after Tarn's research was done. Tarn had made little use of the coin hoards known in his day and missed most of the really important finds.[51] Fortunately, Narain had some knowledge of the huge Qunduz and Mir Zakah hoards recovered in 1946 and 1947.[52] It was the Qunduz treasure that brought to light the Greek monolingual Attic-weight mintages of several kings previously known only to have produced bilingual coins struck on an Indian standard; these rulers were Lysias, Theophilus, Archebius, Philoxenus, Hermaeus, and Amyntas. Five specimens of King Amyntas were exceptional double decadrachms, the largest silver coins ever minted in the ancient world. (See plates 3 and 4.) Narain was able to incorporate these (and subsequent) numismatic, epigraphic, and archaeological discoveries into his second edition of *The Indo-Greeks* (2003).

Meanwhile, in the few years between the completion of Narain's dissertation and its first publication as a book, another major study found its place on the shelves of Bactrian scholars. In 1956, Marie-Thérèse Allouche-LePage's *L'art monétaire des royaumes bactriens* took a different tack.[53] Allouche-LePage attempted to orient the coins within the history of art and religion. She examined portraiture, titulature, dynastic cults, iconography, monograms, and other artistic and technical aspects of the coinage in a wide-ranging work that nevertheless emphasized the "Macedono-Seleucid" heritage of Bactria. The coins, she concluded, were one means by which the canons of Hellenism penetrated deep into the East.[54] Clearly, on the eve of Narain's breakthrough publication, Allouche-LePage followed the lead of Tarn as she sought an artistic rather than historical narrative but one still focused on Hellenism.

Tarn had claimed no competence in art and so vowed steadfastly from the beginning "it is no part of my purpose to write about art."[55] Yet, where coins were concerned, he could not resist. In fact, he claimed to track a whole school of numismatic artists through the mints of Bactria, and called their leader X. Confident

in his own aesthetic judgments, Tarn reached some extraordinary conclusions that even Allouche-LePage could not help but
criticize.[56] Unfortunately, Tarn and most of his contemporaries
(including at times also Narain and Allouche-LePage) operated
under assumptions that few scholars questioned at the time and
that persist even now. These bad habits stem from the undeniable
attractiveness of the Bactrian coins, particularly the alluring portraits they so often display, and the usefulness of such portraits
in fleshing out an imaginative story. Among devotees of narrative
numismatics, these images have frequently inspired speculations
that border on pure whimsy.

In 1937, the year before Tarn published his book about Bactria,
Edward T. Newell (1886–1941; fig. 14) produced a successful little
guidebook that is still held in high regard among numismatists
today: *Royal Greek Portrait Coins*.[57] This book shows that even a
coin expert might easily succumb to the charms of narrative
numismatics.[58] Wealthy and well traveled, E. T. Newell was
widely considered the greatest numismatist of his time. He
amassed a personal collection of over eighty-seven thousand
coins, wrote over thirty monographs, and served the longest term
of any president of the American Numismatic Society. A true
connoisseur, Newell wrote enthusiastically about the portrait
coins minted by Greek kings and queens. He stated: "They present us with an extraordinary series of living portraits—portraits
of a quality such as only a Greek artist could produce."[59] He
believed that these "splendid" likenesses reveal character; they
make the monarchs "real to us once more."[60] But not all of them,
for Newell limited his study by excluding any coinages that had
"lost all Greek feeling" (that is to say, were "tainted" by Roman
or Oriental qualities) and by omitting "the petty rulers of
Bithynia, Cilicia, Commagene, Trachonitis, Nabataea, etc."[61] In

Figure 14. Edward T. Newell, America's leading numismatist and a major benefactor to the American Numismatic Society.

terms of what warranted the reader's attention, and why, this volume was a product of its time, but it has also served as a continuing model for many investigators down to the present.[62] It is Newell's numismatics that we can still detect in the words of the archaeologist Edvard Rtveladze when he writes: "It is not merely the outward appearance that distinguishes portraits of those [Graeco-Bactrian] kings, but the artist's desire to express *the inner world* of the portrayed ruler."[63]

Here, then, is a basic assumption underlying narrative numismatics as it relates to Hellenistic Bactria:[64]

> And what portraits they are! They posses not only the purely objective and brutal frankness of later Roman portraiture, but to this they add that spiritual quality, that revelation of the inner soul and character of the subject which only Greek artists seemed able to secure.

Newell's two stated premises (that the coin portraits have a "spiritual quality" sufficient to reveal the king's "inner soul and character," and that only Greek artists could manage this) certainly squares with Tarn's own methodology. For instance, Tarn could allegedly detect a king's character with a simple glance at his coins. Tarn explained Euthydemus's rise to power based on "the wonderful coin-portrait of him taken in old age," as if by the participle "taken" Tarn imagines a photograph: "One has only to look at his face to see why he seized the crown: he meant to rule because he could."[65] Tarn went on to claim that "the smile of Mona Lisa" on the portrait of Euthydemus's putative son Antimachus I reveals that the latter was a self-effacing, playful man who loved irony: "One has only to look at Antimachus' face to see that there is no overweening pride there; he is rather amused at himself."[66] This man was "amused at himself" because Tarn preferred that Antimachus not have taken his cult title *Theos* ("the God") too seriously, because that would be an unwelcome sign of hubris. Thus, the portrait is turned into hard evidence for Antimachus's innermost religious feelings (fig. 15). Tarn stretched the smile even further. This "peculiar half-mocking smile" allegedly appeared only twice in all of Hellenistic art—once on the portrait coins of Antimachus, and again on a portrait of Euthydemus found on the so-called pedigree coinage of Agathocles (but not, curiously, on Antimachus's similar coin honoring Euthydemus).

Figure 15. Tetradrachm of Antimachus I, showing the portrait that some scholars believe to be a window into the king's personality.

Tarn argued that some unknown Greek artist from the "school of X" remembered, twenty years after Euthydemus's death, that the dead king had had the same smile as Antimachus, and that this "fact" proves how reliable coin portraits are for reconstructing character and kinship.[67]

Tarn the historian and Newell the numismatist were not alone in their psychoanalysis of the portraits. Indeed, this practice has become commonplace. In 1975, numismatist Claire-Yvonne Petitot-Biehler claimed undeniable proof that Apollodotus I was a Euthydemid based on his portrait, and she further identified this Apollodotus with the king of that name mentioned by Trogus because of the strong personality ("forte personnalité") detectable in his portrait.[68] Another instance occurs in the otherwise sober work of Otto Mørkholm, formerly keeper of the Royal Danish Coin Cabinet, who wrote of Euthydemus:[69]

> It is, however, with his aged portrait that the die engravers in Bactria showed their remarkable skill, an impressive rendering of the old ruler affected by many years of toil and effort that have left obvious marks on his face. The corners of the mouth are drawn down, and a

deep furrow running from the nose downwards enhances the impression of fatigue and worry. Nevertheless the glance of the eye is calm and confident, showing a man old and battered but far from beaten. It is a wonderful study in human psychology.

While there is no question that we may observe this king growing older and older on his coins, it is something else altogether to say that those years were filled with toil, trial, worry, and fatigue. That is a narrative wanted by the historian but not one warranted by the coins.

The confidence with which Tarn and others have utilized the portraits to enliven their narratives should naturally worry us.[70] In her 1940 study of Graeco-Bactrian art, the Russian orientalist Kamila Trever claimed that, contrary to Tarn, Antimachus could not have been Euthydemus's son because the former's un-Greek face meant that he was probably a Sogdian![71] This is a remarkably bold conclusion. Even the normally restrained A.K. Narain allows himself to argue that Antimachus's coins "leave *no doubt* about his powerful and very individual personality."[72] Narain's confidence seems astonishing. About two other kings he avers in *The Indo Greeks:*[73]

> Surely Euthydemus and Demetrius I, whose portraits are sufficient to show their determination and prowess, were not rash adventurers; they were wiser, though perhaps not greater, than historians have thought them.

More recently, in 1997 Stanislav Kalita of the Jagiellonian University described Antimachus as "dignified, thinking, and determined."[74] He also wrote of Euthydemus's "rather ugly, obese face with a fleshy nose, which is yet expressive and suggests intelligence and persistence."[75] Similarly, former keeper of the Department of

Coins and Medals at the British Museum Gilbert K. Jenkins found it easy in 1990 to assert that "a glance" at old Euthydemus's portrait "soon makes it clear that he was indeed one of the most formidable characters of his time" and that Antimachus's portrait, too, is "a masterpiece of characterization."[76] He added:[77]

> We have not only a vivid and accurate record of Antimachus' personal appearance but also an unequalled suggestion of a personality in which strength of character is combined with a civilized skepticism and sense of humour—such is the immediacy and impact of this superb head.

Such phrases as "vivid and accurate record" and "civilized skepticism" suggest the excesses by which framework numismatics expanded into narrative numismatics. Too often, these speculations take on the mantle of undisputed fact for want of other evidence. According to the prolific essayist and travel writer George Woodcock:[78]

> And, though their portraits give us an idea of their appearance and even of their characters—the humour that irradiates the face of Antimachus, the brutality of Heliocles—there are few [such kings] of whose actions we have any specific knowledge.

Woodcock writes evocatively of King Strato that "in his last coins, the plump, spoilt face of the boy-king is replaced by the toothless, vulpine features of an old, embittered man."[79] Framework numismatics gave us the portrait of an old, perhaps toothless monarch, but narrative numismatics has added the adjectives "spoilt," "vulpine," and "embittered."

Indeed, how can numismatists possibly test these specific (and sometimes contradictory) characterizations when, as Woodcock admits, all other evidence is lacking? What restrains anyone from channeling through these portraits anything they wish for the sake of a good story? For example, the great classicist and historian Peter Green sees some of these same kings in a very different light from other commentators.[80] In Euthydemus's portrait, he senses "decrepitude," whereas others have seen competence, confidence, and wisdom. Green finds Antimachus "coarsely jovial" although others have marked him as cultured and calculating. Menander, according to Green, was the only "serious thinker of the bunch" in spite of Kalita's rival assessment of Antimachus. In each case, one interpretation is no more likely or provable than another.[81]

Narrative numismatics responds to our desire for a Bactria animated by kings who have distinctive and interesting temperaments. Thus, we look into lumps of silver and gold to find their souls. The less we know about these rulers from other sources, the more we let ourselves remedy the deficiency based on the coins alone. We take a person like Antimachus and make him real by ascribing to him a powerful personality, sense of humor, civilized skepticism, modesty, dignified bearing, determination, intelligence, and/or coarseness. This becomes the sort of man whose life we can weave into a narrative largely of our own making, since we have no governing texts. As for Eucratides, scholars tend to see in his portraits the hard-nosed career soldier implicit in Justin's abbreviated account. Peter Green describes him as "a leathery old long-service officer," while the Harvard archaeologist and art historian George Hanfmann, eyeing Eucratides' gold medallion, recognized "all the brutal power of Renaissance *condottieri* rendered by ugly but powerful features."[82] Tarn looked closer to home; his Eucratides resembled "a British officer in a sun-helmet."[83]

As metallic Rorschach tests, Bactrian coin portraits probably reveal more about modern scholars than about ancient kings. The problem remains whether experts have discovered what the artist intended (within his level of skill) or the ruler instructed (within his level of involvement in coin manufacture), and whether either case reflects a portrait or personality that is real or contrived. The underlying assumption of narrative numismatics, of course, is that the modern scholar actually observes the ancient ruler in some direct sense: The image truly is the king, heart and soul. Such faith in the historical reliability of the portraits rests upon an enabling assumption, the second in Newell's statement quoted above: Greek artists (and only Greek artists) were capable of producing such things. What can be said about this self-serving corollary?

If the Greek aesthetic quality of the portrait (what Newell called "a quality such as only a Greek artist could produce") somehow validates the psychological profile derived from it, then how do scholars know (short of a circular argument) when they are witnessing the handiwork of a Greek artist? Identifying what is Greek (and what is not) has long been a problem in Bactrian studies. For example, Tarn considered the huge gold medallion of Eucratides to be "of finest Bactrian work."[84] H.G. Rawlinson called it magnificent and in every way unique, the coin of a king who was thoroughly Greek.[85] The numismatist Sudha Narain described the coin as[86]

> a remarkable example of superb portraiture and vigorous delineation in art. The unparalleled artistic execution of the coin qualifies this as one of the finest art object [*sic*] of the Greek world.

Yet Allouche-LePage saw it in a much less flattering light; she deemed the artistry vulgar and ordinary, echoing the sentiments of the famous French numismatist Jean Babelon (1889–1978), who

deemed the workmanship very poor.[87] In fact, Anatole Chabouillet himself had expressed dissatisfaction with the portrait on this
specimen. He went so far as to suggest that the two sides of the
coin might represent the skills of two different artists.[88] On the
obverse, Eucratides' portrait seemed to Chabouillet so unlike
the work of contemporary Greek die engravers that he attributed
this image to some poor native artist ("quelque pauvre artiste
indigène"), whereas he saw in the reverse a noble Greek style that
transferred to Central Asia the fine arts of Periclean Athens. He
likened the elegant mounts of the Dioscuri to the horses carved
into the Parthenon, the quintessential masterpiece of the classical
Greeks. One possible explanation for the artistic anomaly
between the coin's obverse and reverse, he reiterated, is that men
of different races, "l'un de race bactrienne … l'autre de race
grecque," made the dies.

Chabouillet's theory prepared the way for Newell's popular
notion of "portraits of a quality such as only a Greek artist could
produce." Besides the discomforting dichotomy of the elevated
Greek and the poor, inferior native of Bactria, we confront a
subjective methodology that can describe the same portrait as
both a superb example of the finest Greek artistry (S. Narain),
and as something banal, weak, and disappointingly non-Greek
(Allouche-LePage, Babelon, Chabouillet). Deciding between
these diverse judgments is as impossible as it is pointless. Only
someone convinced that the work of a Greek artist, and only a
Greek artist, could produce a portrait capable of capturing the
"inner soul and character of the subject" would care or dare to
guess the ethnicity of an unknown artist based on the subtleties
of style alone.[89] Thus Chabouillet's disingenuous alternative to
his theory that a non-Greek engraved the portrait on the Eucratidion is to suppose that a Greek artist created the portrait

"d'après nature."[90] In other words, the portrait is either a poor likeness done by an inferior non-Greek artist or a good likeness of the king rendered by a talented Greek!

Tarn walked a similarly twisted path when he pored over Eucratides' portrait coins. A good die engraver allegedly produced the king's early coins, "where his face is quite ugly and bears a strong resemblance to the ugly features of his son Heliocles."[91] Tarn therefore considered the later issues to be the idealized renderings of a lesser artist, and certainly not the product of his X, whose portraits always reflected "uncompromising truth and fidelity to facts."[92] Unfortunately, we would need to know these truths and facts independently in order to say that X was uncompromisingly faithful to them. This question-begging argument is tortured: X always created true likenesses of the kings, for his portrayals are the most faithful—to his own portrayals! Portraits are evidence of some things, surely, but not so authoritatively as Tarn claims.[93] The problem arises, in part, from the demands of the narrative tradition itself. As the archaeologist Olivier Guillaume has shown, "stating historical facts as a linear story, as Tarn and Narain have chosen to do, compels the historian to establish a continuity of facts."[94] In other words, these authors begin by suggesting some tentative ideas that, within a few pages, quickly become truths in order to derive from them more and more facts to keep the story moving forward.

Narrative numismatics tells tales replete with heroes and histrionics. It spins a web of wives and widows to link together royal families, whether attested in any source or not. We meet evil stepmothers, scheming widows, and spoiled brats in what-if scenarios that sound like soap operas: What if Diodotus II were the son of Diodotus's first wife, and what if a second wife were the sister of the Seleucid king, and what if this second wife grew angry at her stepson, and what if she had a daughter, and what if she wed that daughter to Euthydemus to overthrow and kill Diodotus II? This, wrote Tarn, is all a "quite certain fact."[95] Too often, then, narrative numismatics advances the narrative at the expense of the numismatics. Whether this results from a self-conscious distinction between the goals of the numismatist and the historian is not always clear, but surely Bactrian studies suffer whenever a partisan researcher champions one side over the other. One safeguard is the corrective influence of other kinds of sources, particularly archaeological and epigraphic. These finds, however, were slow to emerge from the same soils that seemed to bring forth coins in such abundance in Central and South Asia.

Plates

Plate I. The land of the Silk Road, looking across Bactria to China.

Plate 2. The Eucratidion, one the most extraordinary numismatic artifacts from the ancient world.

Plate 3. Amyntas double decadrachms (obverse), the largest silver coins struck by ancient rulers.

Plate 4. Amyntas double decadrachms (reverse).

Plate 5. A portion of the Kuliab Hoard, composed mostly of silver drachms.

Plate 6. Bactrian tetradrachm die, said to be from the pillaged site of Ai Khanoum.

Plate 7. Bactrian tetradrachm die, showing Hercules design of Demetrius I (reverse).

Plate 8. Bactrian tetradrachm die impression, showing Hercules, the reverse type of Demetrius I.

Plate 9. Eucratides tetradrachm depicting the king on the obverse and the Dioscuri on the reverse. Note the parallel arrangement of the inscription on the reverse.

Plate 10. Diodotus gold stater from Mir Zakah Hoard II, neatly halved, showing several chisel cuts into the obverse portrait of the king.

CHAPTER FIVE

Wanted—One Greek City

Archaeology

Coins suggest a world of mints and markets, a land where the kings and queens who were displayed on their money must have lived in palaces and cities, where the armies paid by this cash built and guarded fortresses, where the deities honored on these metal disks were worshipped in temples, and where the merchants who relied on this currency maintained warehouses, workshops, and homes. The exponential rise in the number of Bactrian coins recovered from Central Asia had long created the expectation of these related finds, as well as the tools, tombs, inscriptions, and other objects of an ancient society. After all, coins have purpose; they are not manufactured in a vacuum. What had happened to all these things? How could the soil of Central Asia yield so much ancient money and yet no monuments? Scholars desperately wanted to know.

Throughout the decades of the Great Game, enterprising souls had sought not just coins as they risked their lives exploring the mountains and valleys of Afghanistan. Ancient writers had described Bactria as the land of a thousand cities, filling modern minds with dreams of great discoveries.[1] What explorers found, however, did not much impress the scholarly world. In 1902, W.W. Tarn complained that "neither Bactria nor India has yet furnished a single Greek inscription."[2] He supposed that Eucratides' capital city, if ever located, would be the place "where Greek architectural remains might be expected, *if the Bactrians ever produced such architecture*."[3] This frustration came on the heels of a hundred years of digging by European explorers. Unfortunately, much of that excavating had been done by collectors seeking fame and fortune by all available means, no matter how undisciplined and destructive. Archaeology, after all, did not fully mature as a science until the twentieth century. In Afghanistan, this slow maturation was further hindered by cycles of political instability, religious intolerance, and local indifference, making it virtually impossible for scholars to establish anything like Bactriology, on the model of, say, Assyriology or Egyptology. Men like William Matthew Flinders Petrie, destined to become the Father of Egyptology, dreamed of exploring Bactria but never did.[4]

In the nineteenth century, every ancient ruin and monument in Afghanistan seemed fair game for the treasure hunter. Charles Masson, Dr. Honigberger, and the European officers serving Ranjit Singh (Court, Ventura, Allard) could not resist shoveling into the grand reliquary mounds (stupas) that dotted the landscape between Kabul and Manikyala.[5] The relics deposited inside these Buddhist monuments often included coins and other valuables. Men like Masson, "the stupa ripper," thrived on the search for these collectible artifacts.[6] His forays into the countryside around Kabul had another object besides stripping ancient monuments: Masson ached to find an entire lost city. He longed in particular to discover the site of Alexandria *sub Caucaso* (Alexandria "below the Caucasus"), a city founded by Alexander the Great somewhere at the foot of the Hindu Kush Mountains.[7] In 1833, he claimed success at Begram (Bagram), as noted above in chapter 2. Located some 37 miles (60 km) north of Kabul near the confluence of the Panjshir and Ghorband rivers, this large urban site featured walled enclosures and other signs of extensive settlement. There Masson and his local agents gathered not only coins but also pottery, engraved seals, arrowheads, rings, amulets, and other "trinkets."[8] The datable coins from this site spanned a long era of occupation, from the late fourth century B.C.E. to the early thirteenth C.E. Specimens of Eucratides and Menander proved especially common.

The early work carried out at Begram by Charles Masson was important but inevitably piecemeal and poorly documented by modern standards; academic archaeology did not arrive in Afghanistan until almost a century later.[9] During his reign (1919–29), Amanullah Khan harbored hopes of modernizing his nation while also freeing it from the old giants of the Great Game, Russia and Britain. Archaeology became one tool of this political agenda.[10] Amanullah turned to the French, whose good standing in the Islamic Middle East and record of archaeological success there made a promising match. Thus, in 1922 a formal Franco-Afghan agreement created the Délégation Archéologique Française en Afghanistan (DAFA), which gave French archaeologists nearly exclusive rights to excavate within the country.[11] First directed by Alfred Foucher (1865–1952), a specialist on Buddhist iconography and its connections to Greek art, the DAFA inaugurated a new and certainly more disciplined era in Afghan archaeology. Reflecting Foucher's interests, the origins and evolution of Gandharan (Graeco-Buddhist) art dominated the research agenda for many years.[12] Foucher believed that somewhere in the sands of Afghanistan lay the missing link of Greek colonial cities whose artists first gave the transcendent Buddha the trendy face of Apollo. The French vowed to find those cities.

One of the DAFA's earliest projects took up the chase where Masson had left off—at Begram. Initial surveys in 1924–25 led to targeted excavations between 1936 and 1946.[13] These endeavors brought forth numerous finds, topped by the discovery of the so-called Begram treasure in 1937 and 1939. This famous deposit contained Graeco-Roman glassware and statuary, Chinese lacquers, and Indian ivories.[14] These eclectic luxury items were uncovered by Joseph and Ria Hackin in two sealed storerooms that formed either part of an ancient palace or a prosperous merchant's warehouse—scholars continue to champion both views.[15] These extraordinary objects naturally fueled the ongoing debate surrounding the production and trade of ancient art in the region. The dating of the treasure remains contentious, but the settlement itself almost certainly existed during the period of Greek rule in Bactria.[16]

Another part of that lost world existed north of the Hindu Kush at Balkh, a walled ruin celebrated in Islamic tradition as the mother of all cities, oldest in the world. Called both Bactra and Zariaspa in classical sources, this site was the capital of ancient Bactria, famed for thwarting the two-year siege of Euthydemus by Antiochus the Great (208–206 B.C.E.).[17] Few modern explorers doubted that somewhere under its rubble lay perhaps the grandest of the fabled thousand cities of Bactria. As noted in chapter 2, above, Burnes, Gerard, Honigberger, and others had poked around amid the debris of Balkh; Moorcroft was buried there. Foucher himself gathered large numbers of ancient Greek coins from the locals, driving up the prices in the process.[18] The coins from Balkh included the issues of Euthydemus I and II, Eucratides, Demetrius, and Heliocles.[19] For Foucher, a city of this importance constituted an obvious priority for the DAFA, and he worried that a clause in the Franco-Afghan agreement might give the British, Germans, or Russians access to the site if the French did not immediately claim it.[20] Foucher's decision proved to be the most frustrating of his archaeological career. In 1924 and 1925, Foucher's team dug deep into Balkh with disappointing results; they found no grand Hellenistic monuments, statues, mosaics, or inscriptions.[21] In spite of all expectations, the metropolis of Balkh showed no signs of being the missing link between Greek and Gandharan art. Poor Foucher despaired that Graeco-Bactrian art had never been more than a cruel mirage in Afghanistan's desolate landscape.[22] As a later director of the DAFA would put it, "Bactra became the tomb of the hopes of Foucher."[23]

Immediately following World War II, the charismatic British archaeologist Sir Mortimer Wheeler was keen on visiting Balkh as part of a cooperative exchange between the archaeological services of India and Afghanistan.[24] Wheeler, director general of archaeology in India, confessed the irresistible tug of these ruins: "Probably no site in Asia surpasses Balkh in its appeal to the historical imagination."[25] Wheeler felt obliged to criticize the methods employed there by the French. He chastised Foucher's "superbly Gallic" predisposition to dig the one part of the site that "a less charmingly sentimental investigator would unhesitatingly have shunned."[26] Sir Mortimer clearly believed that the British had set a higher standard excavating in India than the French could yet manage in Afghanistan.[27] For years afterward, Wheeler nurtured the hope of digging the site himself, but he could never convince the Afghan government to permit a joint British, Indian, and French expedition to excavate at Balkh.[28] An archaeological version of the Great Game patently played out along nationalistic lines deep into the twentieth century.

It had been the British numismatist Sir Alexander Cunningham who founded the Archaeological Survey of India (ASI) back in 1870, more than a half-century ahead of the French in Afghanistan.[29] Important results rewarded the ASI's excavation of Taxila (now in Pakistan) by Sir John Marshall, who devoted over twenty years to this site (1913–34).[30] Trained in classics at Cambridge, Marshall approached his task "filled with enthusiasm for anything Greek," and he looked upon Taxila as "a bit of Greece itself" far afield in the Punjab.[31] He admitted that his expectations grew from Taxila's reputation in the classical sources, where the city is mentioned from the time of Alexander onward. Marshall's work showed multiple phases in the development of the site. Bhir mound represented the period of occupation from the Achaemenid Persians to the Mauryan Empire. Under Ashoka, this Taxila grew into a notable center of Buddhist culture. In the second century B.C.E., the Greeks invaded from Bactria and expanded the city on a grid plan associated with the nearby district of Sirkap.[32] Still, the scattered traces of Hellenism at Taxila disappointed the diggers, who could scarcely explain the presence of Greek-styled coins on the one hand and yet the absence of Greek inscriptions on the other.[33] As for art, Mortimer Wheeler later proposed that the Gandharan style might be more Romano-Buddhist than Graeco-Buddhist, its inspiration deriving from trade with Rome rather than from the somewhat disappointing evidence for Greek settlements in the region.[34]

The birth of the modern state of Pakistan, in 1947, eventually led to a renewed focus on the art and artifacts of early Buddhism in Gandhara and its environs. Sir Mortimer Wheeler himself excavated the large site of Charsadda (ancient Pushkalavati to the Indians, Peucelaotis to the Greeks), which seemed to have expanded from the Bala Hisar ("Upper Citadel") to nearby Shaikhan Dheri

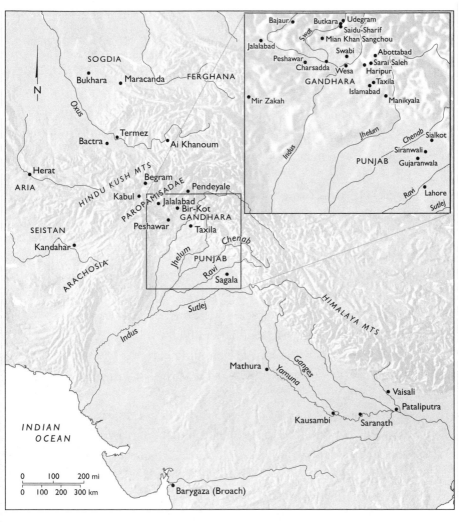

Map 2. Ancient India.

along the same lines as Taxila.[35] On this site, Wheeler could see only an incomprehensible "tumult of heaps and hollows marking the spots where the local villagers have dug up ancient brick walls" to be hauled away as phosphatic fertilizer.[36] So in 1958, on his first day of work there, Wheeler brought in the Pakistan Air Force to take aerial photographs, which "suddenly and vividly" revealed the telltale grid pattern of the Hellenistic city hidden in the Shaikhan mound.[37] Seen from the air, the trenched-out walls of the ancient city made a passable map of its houses and streets, and at least one stupa. The same farmers who had grubbed up the walls had also uncovered several important coin hoards and stray finds.[38]

An Italian archaeological mission (Instituto Italiano per il Medio ed Estremo Oriente) sponsored the large-scale excavation of Butkara I, in Swat, directed by Domenico Faccenna from 1956 to 1962. Faccenna's six volumes on this endeavor qualify Butkara I (the so-called Sacred Precinct) as "the best excavation ever made and published of a Gandharan Buddhist site."[39] The Great Stupa at Butkara underwent five building phases from the third century B.C.E. to the tenth C.E., with the chronology based largely on numismatic finds.

Meanwhile, Article II of the Franco-Afghan archaeological convention (which had so troubled Foucher) provided other nations a few opportunities to work in Afghanistan. American teams began working at selected sites, such as Balkh, in the 1950s. Italian and Japanese missions opened in 1954. A joint Soviet-Afghan archaeological survey of Turkestan commenced in 1969; a German team explored Seistan in the early 1970s, and the British Institute of Afghan Studies started excavating at Kandahar in 1974.[40] Along the Amu Darya (ancient Oxus) Valley, in northern Afghanistan, only Soviet archaeologists were generally permitted to work, in order to ease border tensions. At Dilberdjin Tepe, a fortified-town site about 25 miles (40 km) northwest of Balkh, the Soviet-Afghan mission revealed a temple of the Dioscuri, so called because it contained murals depicting the twin Greek deities Castor and Pollux. Since Eucratides featured these same gods on his silver and gold coinage, the excavators naturally suggested that this king may have built the shrine.[41]

But where and when might the archaeological breadcrumbs of Bactria lead excavators to find an actual Greek city such as the king's own Eucratidia, with its houses, government buildings, fortifications, artwork, and inscriptions? In 1960, it was lamented that "apart from the coins, all the material remains of this realm might easily be displayed in a couple of shelves of an exhibition case."[42] All that changed the next year. In 1961, while on a royal hunt along the northern borders of his nation, King Muhammad Zahir Shah of Afghanistan recognized Greek architectural remains at Ai Khanoum ("Lady Moon" in Uzbek), a site that may once have been Eucratidia itself.[43] Jules Barthoux, a French geologist, had recommended to Foucher that the DAFA excavate at Ai Khanoum in 1927, but Foucher focused instead on Balkh and thus narrowly missed the find of his dreams.[44] In November 1961, the king informed Daniel Schlumberger and the DAFA that he had seen a Corinthian capital and another carved stone at the confluence of the Amu Darya and the Kokcha River. An inspection of the site startled the experts.[45] Just inches beneath the soil, the outlines of an entire city bulged in plain sight: ramparts, gateway, streets, courtyards, theater, and other buildings of various sizes. Remarkably, the Hellenistic site had never been reoccupied, so that no Kushan or later city rested upon its ruins.

Under the skilled direction of Paul Bernard, who succeeded Schlumberger as head of the DAFA, full-scale excavations commenced in 1965 and continued until 1978. During that time, the

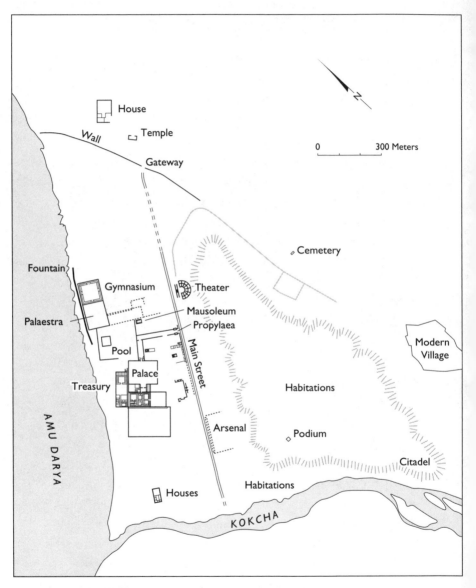

House

Temple

Wall

Gateway

0   300 Meters

Cemetery

Fountain

Gymnasium   Theater

Palaestra   Mausoleum

Propylaea

Pool

Modern
Village

Palace

Main Street

Treasury

Habitations

AMU DARYA

Arsenal

Podium

Citadel

Houses   Habitations

KOKCHA

Map 3. Ai Khanoum.

trenches at Ai Khanoum became the training ground for the next generation of DAFA archaeologists, including F. Grenet, H.-P. Francfort, C. Rapin, and O. Guillaume. In view of earlier agreements regarding this fragile Afghan-Soviet frontier, several Russian archaeologists (including G. Koshelenko, R. Munchaev, I. Kruglikova, and B. Litvinsky) labored alongside the French during the first years of excavation. In sixteen campaigns spaced over thirteen years, the main features of the ancient city came to light, dispelling Foucher's mirage to give scholars at last an intimate look inside the Graeco-Bactrian kingdom. Bernard and his team assiduously published annual reports in academic journals, and an interim assessment appeared as the first volume of *Fouilles d'Ai Khanoum* in 1973.[46] Seven subsequent volumes of *Fouilles d'Ai Khanoum* have been completed thus far, each devoted to a major feature of the site: propylaea (vol. II), temple (vol. III), stray coins (vol. IV), ramparts (vol. V), gymnasium (vol. VI), small objects (vol. VII), and treasury (vol. VIII).[47] Yet to come are volumes on the palace, theater, domestic architecture, religious and funerary monuments, arsenal, and the all-important ceramics.[48] Some materials have been separately published in scholarly journals, such as the ornate stone fountain fronting the Amu Darya (Oxus River) and the coin hoards found in and around the city.[49] Without question, Ai Khanoum is the most thoroughly excavated and published Hellenistic site in Central Asia.[50]

Given his classical training in Greek archaeology, Paul Bernard brought to this task a somewhat traditional emphasis upon art, architecture, inscriptions, and an eventful narrative of the site. Like many French archaeologists, he first worked at Thasos, in the Aegean Sea, before moving on to other assignments, in his case ever eastward until he joined the DAFA and its excavations of the Kushan temple site at Surkh Kotal.[51] As this dig neared completion, Ai Khanoum became his next—and defining—mission. Bernard's early focus at Ai Khanoum was the sprawling peristyle courtyard and associated structures in the so-called administrative quarter of the lower city.[52] After all, it had been a Corinthian capital from this edifice that first led archaeologists to explore Ai Khanoum.[53] From the outset, the excavators stressed the Greekness of what they found:[54]

> The over-all impression that these [initial] two campaigns of digging give us is that Ai Khanoum was first of all a Greek city whose colonists strove to maintain the integrity of the civilization they had brought with them. The official language was Greek, as were Greek the gods and in all probability the institutions.

Subsequent seasons did little to change that assessment as the work expanded to include other parts of the city, although Bernard did acknowledge the shadowy backdrop of a non-Greek population whose influence could be seen in some of the architecture and minor arts.[55] For example, the posh residential sector has private houses built in non-Greek style but strewn with very Greek housewares.[56] The main temple of the city appears in form and function to combine an array of Greek and non-Greek elements.[57] Stressing Hellenization, however, the archaeologist Claude Rapin insists that "no Indian or Buddhist cults were practiced at Ai Khanoum, although Indian religious symbols appear on Indo-Greek coins and on a coral pendant."[58]

To understand Ai Khanoum in its broader geographic and human context, Jean-Claude Gardin began in 1974 a series of regional archaeological surveys.[59] His team focused on the ceramics and ancient irrigation canals scattered across eastern Bactria, hoping thus to balance the evidence for urban (Greek?) and rural (native?) populations. Methodologically, this endeavor appended to the classical archaeology practiced at Ai Khanoum some of the approaches favored by the so-called New Archaeologies that arose in the 1960s.[60] Among other things, the work guided by Gardin showed that Ai Khanoum should not be categorized solely, or perhaps even principally, as a military foundation. The ancient city itself consisted of a steep natural acropolis nearly 200 feet (60 m) high that sloped down on its northern flank to a large rectangular plateau (the lower city) that stretched over a mile (1,800 m) along the banks of the Oxus, 66 feet (20 m) high. A massive rampart and ditch enclosed the northeast side of the lower city, and the Kokcha River sealed off the southwest. A wall edged the entire triangle formed by the acropolis and lower city, averaging over one mile (1,600 m) per side.

This well-chosen site clearly exploited every advantage provided by man and nature to secure itself against possible attack. These defenses, plus the strategic location of the city on the Bactrian frontier and the presence of a huge arsenal inside the walls, suggest that Ai Khanoum served, at least in part, a military function. But Gardin demonstrated that important economic factors may also have influenced the development of the city. The surrounding plain showed signs of extensive irrigation, with the potential to support a dense agrarian population. Indeed, the area had clearly been developed as a farming zone long before the arrival of the Greeks. This site also lies near sources of great mineral wealth within the Badakhshan Mountains, where mines yield copper, iron, lead, silver, rubies, and lapis lazuli. At Shortughai on the plain of Ai Khanoum, archaeologists discovered a metalworking colony of the Harrapan civilization dating back to the Bronze Age of India.[61] At Khuna Qal'a, sometimes called "Ai Khanoum II," just 1.25 miles (2 km) north of the main city, a circular fortification may have served in Achaemenid times as the original town in the plain. During the Hellenistic period, this site may have become an outpost guarding the northern approaches to the Greek city, or it may simply have become a suburb or local estate. Commanding the confluence of two rivers in a rich agricultural and mining zone, Ai Khanoum and its environs clearly possessed commercial as well as military importance.

Although several inscriptions were recovered by the DAFA at Ai Khanoum (for which see the following chapter), none provides the ancient name of the city. The site has been variously identified as Alexandria Oxiana, Diodoteia (or Diodotopolis), Dionysopolis, Ostobara, and Eucratidia.[62] The close association of the city with Eucratides arises from the fact, based on coin finds, that this king was the last Graeco-Bactrian to rule there, and at that time the city was undergoing a major renovation. This building activity is most evident in the expansion of the palace complex on a grand scale, including additions to the treasury.[63] Indeed, the enlarged treasury contained numerous items from India, which archaeologists have linked to Eucratides' plunder of Taxila and other cities.[64] The huge palace suggests that this was at times a royal residence and not merely a frontier outpost. The presence, too, of a large theater (with special loges), a gymnasium, and numerous so-called mansions gives the strong impression of a veritable capital, in which other prominent officials lived in close proximity to their king. There exists also some compelling evidence that a mint functioned at Ai Khanoum. Ten bronze flans (blanks ready for striking) were excavated in the city.[65] Reinforcing this view is the very recent discovery of an actual coin die (see plate 6; cf. plate 7) used to strike tetradrachms for King Demetrius. This invaluable artifact is reportedly among a group of objects removed clandestinely from the site. If this provenance is reliable, the die may suggest a royal precious-metal mint at Ai Khanoum;

it would accordingly place Demetrius's sovereignty there (and not just in India, as once imagined); and it may link a particular monogram (✦) to a specific mint, whether that mark represented the city or a magistrate operating in that city. (See chap. 8, below.)

The coinage recovered archaeologically from Ai Khanoum includes (besides the unstruck flans) a total of 212 identifiably Greek or Indian stray finds.[66] In addition, two large hoards were excavated.[67] One, found within the city in 1970, contained 683 coins minted in India and later looted from the palace when Ai Khanoum fell. The other, discovered in 1973 within the kitchen of a house outside the walls of Ai Khanoum, comprised 63 Greek and Bactrian tetradrachms. A third hoard, found by a farmer in the winter of 1973–74 and subsequently dispersed, contained about 141 Greek and Bactrian coins.[68] A few other hoards have been reported but not published in any detail, such as a deposit of some 1,500 Bactrian coins found at or near Ai Khanoum in 1994.[69] In every case, the latest specimens have belonged to Eucratides and not his successors, which is why the fall of Ai Khanoum has been so closely tied to this king.

What happened to Ai Khanoum remains something of a mystery. The archaeological evidence indicates a sudden abandonment of the site at or near the end of Eucratides' reign. If Bernard's interpretation of a Greek memorandum from the treasury is correct, then the latest datable administrative activity in the king's palace occurred in the twenty-fourth year of his rule (ca. 146 B.C.E.).[70] A surprising number of valuables were left in that treasury when the Greek inhabitants of Ai Khanoum hastily departed.[71] Rooms 104 and 109 warehoused semiprecious stones, artworks, and jars of coins, while magazines 120 and 126 held costly liquids. As soon as the Greeks departed, a fire swept through parts of the palace, and the treasury was quickly rifled.

For a while, locals lived and worked in the storerooms, scavenging the treasures, until they too fled—perhaps in the face of an invasion (a second one?). The city suffered a major destruction as buildings were razed, colonnades hacked down, and its stone and bricks removed. As a result of these activities, items from the treasury were scattered about the dead city, apparently lost, abandoned, or hidden by whoever came after the Greeks.

The assumption is that the Sakas, nomadic invaders pressing down from the northeast, sacked the city soon after the Greeks had fled from their approach.[72] Evidence of a battle at Ai Khanoum is conspicuously absent. In a city whose massive walls consumed an estimated ten million bricks, having been refortified three times, the inhabitants apparently suffered a crisis of confidence yet to be adequately explained.[73] Local peoples then took possession of the site as so-called squatters, salvaging what remained as they took up residence indiscriminately in the wreckage of the public and private buildings. A second nomadic incursion followed, this time led by the Yuezhi tribes whose descendants established the Kushan empire.[74]

This next phase of Afghanistan's ancient history can be witnessed in the 1978–79 excavations conducted by Victor Sarianidi and Zemaryalai Tarzi at Tillya Tepe ("Golden Hill"), near Shiberghan, west of Balkh. There, in a rain-soaked earthen mound surrounded by cotton fields, a series of impressive Kushan graves came to light.[75] Over twenty thousand pieces of gold had been interred with the five women and one man buried in the necropolis; this hoard became famous as the Bactrian treasure featured in museum shows, popular literature, and documentaries of various kinds.[76] The eclectic assemblages of grave goods included items from India, China, Parthia, and Rome, as well as from local workshops. A few items bore Greek inscriptions, and images of several Greek deities graced the jewelry. One pectoral (worn by the man) featured a cameo of a helmeted king reminiscent of Eucratides.

Unfortunately, archaeological work at Tillya Tepe—and throughout Afghanistan—suddenly ended in 1979, just ahead of the disastrous Soviet intervention and subsequent civil war. These calamities not only drove out the excavators but also invited a relentless pillage of sites and museums from Tillya Tepe and Ai Khanoum to Balkh and Kandahar. For the next twenty years, the scientific search for the lost civilization of Bactria was nearly impossible. In September 1982, the Afghan government shut down the DAFA. During the next decades, the French and others shifted their explorations to safer areas north and west of Afghanistan, ironically in regions such as Bukhara that had been so treacherous during the Great Game.[77] For many years, Russian archaeologists had been working on sites north of the Amu Darya (Oxus River) such as Khojend-Leninabad (ancient Alexandria Eschate) and Samarkand-Afrasiab (ancient Maracanda), where Vasily Bartold ("the Gibbon of Turkestan") explored before the Russian Revolution.[78] Subsequently, the interests of a distinctive, centralized Soviet archaeology diverged from those of the West, whose "bourgeois" practitioners were criticized for extolling the imperialist invasions of ancient peoples into Central Asia. Archaeologically speaking, Alexander and the Greeks were out, whereas the indigenous peoples were in. Well-financed Soviet missions shifted their priorities from "naked thingology" ("goloye veshchevedeniye") to modes of production and questions of ethnogenesis. The material culture of Bactria, especially under the Kushans, was seen as a local product rather than as an importation of Graeco-Roman civilization.

The collapse of the Soviet Union in 1991 seriously curtailed the funding of state-sponsored archaeology, yet the independence of the Central Asian republics created new opportunities for joint expeditions. At Afrasiab, for example, a Franco-Soviet mission transitioned into a Franco-Uzbek mission between the first and second seasons of excavation.[79] The French-Uzbek archaeological mission also excavated at Koktepe (19 miles [30 km] north of Samarkand), Termez (on the right bank of the Amu Darya), and the so-called Iron Gates (near Derbent); other missions, such as the International Pluridisciplinary Archaeological Expedition in Bactria, continue to explore throughout the Surkhan Darya and surrounding regions.[80] An Uzbek expedition directed by Edvard Rtveladze discovered a Hellenistic outpost at Kampyr Tepe that once guarded the Oxus crossing west of Termez.[81] Although part of the site has eroded into the river, finds included numerous Greek inscriptions (see chap. 6, below) and coins. Further excavations by Russian archaeologists uncovered evidence of body armor from the time of Eucratides, resembling that found at Ai Khanoum.[82] At Takht-i Sangin ("Throne of Stone"), Russian archaeologists of the South Tadjikistan Archaeological Expedition (1976–91) found an extraordinary cache of weaponry among other items associated with a temple dedicated to the Oxus River.[83] This ancient museum of military equipment includes bone-plated composite bows, several varieties of arrowheads, spearheads, swords, daggers, scabbards, armor plate, helmets, and shields. No greater collection of Greek armament has been found anywhere in the ancient world.

Meanwhile, the International Merv Project took up the earlier work of the South Turkmenistan Archaeological Multidisciplinary Expedition in the Merv Oasis.[84] These excavations clarified the historical development of the Achaemenid site at Erk Qal'a and its larger Hellenistic successor called Gyaur Qal'a, as well as the Parthian and Sassanian fortifications of Gobekli-tepe. The coin finds, though limited, resemble in distribution those uncovered at Ai Khanoum and Takht-i Sangin, and may indicate that Eucratides was the last Graeco-Bactrian king to control these areas.[85]

These extensive archaeological operations have considerably improved our knowledge of settlement patterns and land use in Hellenistic Sogdia and Margiana, and of the movements of nomadic peoples during and after the reign of Eucratides.[86] The resulting archaeological picture is one of a network of fortifications monitoring the northern approaches to Bactria through Sogdia, indicating the ancient perception that this was a dangerous frontier.[87] In fact, the archaeological data from Afrasiab signal that Greek military occupation of the area was interrupted for a time before the reign of Eucratides.[88] Numismatic evidence may support this conclusion.[89] Excavations at Kurgan-zol Fortress in the Surkhan Darya region of Uzbekistan show that this Greek stronghold was lost late in the third century B.C.E. and not recovered.[90]

In 2002, following the U.S.-led invasion of Afghanistan that drove the Taliban from power, the DAFA reestablished itself in the country. By then, of course, archaeology had taken the form of a rescue mission in the aftermath of a radical regime that had brazenly pulverized the magnificent Buddhas of Bamian and systematically looted many museums.[91] Over 70 percent of the material in the National Museum at Kabul had disappeared, representing a nation's cultural patrimony callously sold abroad or hammered into dust.[92] Many stolen coins were brashly auctioned away on eBay as the ePlunder of rapacious thieves. A few Afghan curators with nerves of steel managed to hide the other 30 percent, so that now these salvaged artifacts can again be studied and appreciated.[93] To some extent, the ravaging of Afghanistan shows the redeeming value of the now defunct and villainized system of archaeological *partage,* whereby finds used to be divided between the host country and foreign missions. The impressive—and safe—collections of the Musée Guimet in Paris testify to this value.

Beyond the Afghan museums, other antiquities became victims. In a lawless land plagued by want, the arduous work that had documented some 2,800 archaeological sites in Afghanistan unfortunately served the robbers as a road map to buried treasure. Known archaeological sites such as Begram, Tillya Tepe, Surkh Kotal, Ai Khanoum, and Balkh were attacked in a criminal frenzy of despoliation.[94] Some of this damage was done by impoverished locals, but in many cases well-equipped syndicates brought in bulldozers and heavy trucks. The profits from this activity rivaled the billions made from the Afghan drug trade, and some of the same unsavory characters engaged in both. Too much of this activity still continues unabated: Afghanistan today has become like the Egypt of a century ago, when the great archaeological pioneer Flinders Petrie described the Nile Valley as "a house on fire, so rapid was the destruction going on."[95]

During the Afghan civil war, clandestine diggers at Balkh located what had so long eluded Foucher, Schlumberger, and others—the remains of Hellenistic Bactra. In 1947, Schlumberger had recovered the first slim sign of an actual Greek presence at Balkh—a broken potsherd bearing the relief of a young king of Bactria.[96] The ceramic was found at the Bala Hisar ("Upper Citadel"), but the French also tentatively explored a nearby mound called Tepe Zargaran ("Jeweler's Hill"), only about half a mile (1 km) southeast of the main excavations. Schlumberger noted the promising nature of this site, but it was left for looters in the 1990s to unearth there the same sort of Greek architectural features as found at Ai Khanoum.[97] Coins and silver wine vessels have also been unearthed. Thankfully, a fresh mission is now under way to excavate what remains of the Hellenistic city at Tepe Zargaran, and another is exploring the nearby Achaemenid site at Chesm-e Shafa, where local villagers had long been looting the citadel.[98] Sadly, no such effort attends the unfortunate site of Ai Khanoum. Paul Bernard had once written:[99]

> The Greek city of Ai Khanoum is right at the surface of the soil, never having been covered by later settlements. Under the thin shroud of earth, we hoped to find the dead body intact. What we discovered was a brutally mutilated corpse.

His reference is to the damage done to the city by nomadic invaders at the end of Eucratides' reign. Unfortunately, that "corpse" was savagely desecrated again in modern times by scavengers unsated until they had picked the bones clean. The ground at Ai Khanoum has been churned so thoroughly by pillagers that the ancient city revealed by the DAFA is now hardly recognizable.[100] Wondering what had happened to the Greek columns and capitals that once graced the city, archaeologists finally found them reused to build a teahouse in nearby Khwaja Bahuaddin, the village where Commander Ahmad Shah Massoud was assassinated by the Taliban on the eve of 9/11. Thus, the trigger for the terrorist attacks far away in America was pulled among stolen ruins from Ai Khanoum.

Some sense of what Bernard's interrupted excavations had left for the looters to find can be gleaned from watching the antiquities market closely.[101] Glassware, coins, ivories, statuettes, signet rings, and beautifully decorated silver and gilt bowls hint at these spoils. Some of the looted bowls bear images of Tyche, Dionysus, satyrs, dolphins, and Eros; one has a sculpted attachment recognizable as a royal portrait bust, perhaps of Eucratides. All these objects have been openly linked to the ruin field that once was Ai Khanoum, blatantly plundered under the direction of the local commander, Mamoor Hassan. An infamous looter named Mahbuhbullah boasted to a reporter in 2001 that he had wrested three hundred pounds (136 kg) of jewelry and coins from Ai Khanoum and decorated his home with fine Greek architecture.[102] Similarly, other stunning artifacts have come from ransacked archaeological sites around Herat, Kandahar, Bajaur, and Taxila.

The current state of Central Asian archaeology remains as friable and politically charged as ever. An independent Afghan archaeological service with well-trained and securely funded local excavators is some years away and likely to be hampered in its development by lingering security issues in some vital regions. Particularly troubling is the dearth of technical skills in restoration and conservation, which leaves monuments of all periods waiting for urgent intervention before it is too late.[103] Meanwhile, international help is hard to mobilize. Many Russian archaeologists struggle to find adequate institutional support in the post-USSR world, and its fine cadre of experienced specialists is aging. The DAFA is vitally active again, but as an arm of the French foreign ministry its own political functions cannot be overlooked. A few American and British universities are sponsoring work in Afghanistan by a handful of dedicated students and faculty, but without coordinated and sustained funding. Efforts to explore the region remotely using satellite imagery show promise, but work on the ground is also necessary.[104] Given the many problems faced at the moment by the Afghan people, their security forces, and their government, costly scientific archaeology exists on the fringe and largely as a piecemeal endeavor by interested individuals. Even at that, no one can be sure how long this somewhat shattered window of opportunity may remain open.

Meanwhile, the hard-won fruits of Afghan archaeology continue to serve political agendas in and outside Afghanistan. It hardly seems a coincidence that the spectacular exhibition of Afghan archaeological artifacts entitled "Hidden Treasures from the National Museum, Kabul," has toured France, Italy, the Netherlands, the United States, Canada, Germany, and Great Britain—all of them NATO members of the International Security Assistance Force operating in Afghanistan, including the top six contributors of troops. The items selected for this goodwill tour all derive from four pre-Islamic sites and cater primarily to the Western cultural traditions of the peacekeeping forces. This trend manifests itself in countless tiny ways. Take, for instance, the "Respect Afghan Heritage" playing cards issued to troops by the well-intentioned Legacy Resource Management Program of the U.S. Department of Defense. The deck is literally stacked: it includes only three cards featuring Islamic remains, as compared with numerous cards devoted to the pre-Islamic antiquities of Ai Khanoum, Begram, Tillya Tepe, Takht-i Sangin, Rabatak, Bamian, Balkh, Tepe Zargaran, and other sites. Four of the cards actually picture sites in the United States!

The undisguised aim of many archaeologists working in Afghanistan and its environs has long been to find Greek remains, and it is only natural to celebrate their success after so many years of struggle.[105] This compelling archaeological narrative reflects a very real prime directive: Discover the kingdom that created the kings. The coins suggested not only the existence of those kings and their subjects, but also their ethnicity—hence, the presumption of Hellenic culture waiting to be unearthed. Finally identifying traces of that long-sought Greekness may, however, tend to exaggerate its importance. That is always the danger in finding what you are looking for in the archaeological record. Some features of Ai Khanoum appear quintessentially Greek, such as the theater and gymnasium; other structures bear the hallmarks of unmistakable Mesopotamian influence, such as the palace and main temple. Even so, archaeologists and historians routinely describe the site as Greek and refer to its inhabitants as Greeks. Is that a balanced assessment, or simply shorthand for "mission accomplished"? In many ways, what people build about themselves (theaters or palaces) can be less informative than what they say about themselves. Since language—and what it is used to express—plays a vital role in cultural identity, special attention must be paid to the written as well as unwritten evidence recovered from the ground.[106]

CHAPTER SIX

Letters Here and There

Epigraphy

Historians have a strong predisposition to favor the written word. The Greek letters on Bruce's tetradrachm, not its other features, first led Bayer to associate it with Bactria; his next step was inevitably to scan all of ancient literature to learn more about the king and his kingdom. Thereafter, the little inscriptions on coins constituted the only immediate hope of expanding that knowledge, one royal name at a time, during the pursuit of framework numismatics. Wanting more words, explorers naturally fantasized that someday one of them might stumble upon a long text etched in stone, perhaps a royal decree or religious dedication like the famous Rosetta Stone of Egypt or the Behistun Inscription of Persia. For those keen to sort out the cultural and ethnic landscape of Hellenistic Bactria, inscriptions were an important desideratum. Would those texts be Greek, or bilingual? Or, as it long seemed, were the inhabitants of Bactria eerily mute, as though they had nothing to say except on their currency?

Curiously, until 1946 the only nonnumismatic inscriptions associated with the Hellenistic kingdom of Bactria were found on an Aegean island rather than in Afghanistan or India.[1] Unearthed between 1885 and 1903, several Greek texts from the island of Delos record temple dedications made in the second century B.C.E. by one "Hyspasines son of Mithroaxus, a Bactrian."[2] His name approximates that of Hyspaosines, a king from Characene, near the Persian Gulf, late in the second century B.C.E.[3] Curiously, this monarch copied from afar the main coin type of Euthydemus I.[4] By its very nature, epigraphy like this poses some interesting questions: What does it mean when a man identifies himself in Greek as a Bactrian? Does he consider himself a Bactrian by virtue of ethnicity, or merely of geography? Does he (dare) think of himself as both Bactrian and Greek? Would Hyspasines be considered more Greek back home than he was at Delos? Does his name matter in terms of his ethnocultural identity? Did he, or men like him, set up similar inscriptions in Bactria—or was Greek the language of a Bactrian only when he found himself in Greece?

Answers to such questions depended upon the discovery, or nondiscovery, of epigraphic and related material from the lands of ancient Bactria itself. The first hint of nonnumismatic Greek epigraphy in Afghanistan appeared on a potsherd recovered in 1946 at Tepe Nimlik, an ancient habitation mound located 22 miles (36 km) west of Balkh (fig. 16). Daniel Schlumberger of the DAFA made this discovery while accompanying Mortimer Wheeler on the Afghan archaeological mission mentioned in the previous chapter.[5] The Greek letters ATPOC had been scratched along the rim of a pottery vessel before firing.[6] Not much could be made of this broken text, but another discovery made thirty years later may be relevant. In 1976, the South Tadjikistan Archaeological Expedition led by Soviet specialists Boris Litvinsky and Igor Pichikyan began exploring the site of Takht-i Sangin,

Figure 16. Inscribed potsherd from
Tepe Nimlik, the first nonnumismatic
Greek inscription found in Afghanistan.

just outside Afghanistan.[7] This impressive temple yielded an
inscribed altar dated by the excavators to the time of Eucratides.[8]
The stone altar supported a bronze statue of the Greek river god
Marsyas playing a double flute; the base bore the Greek inscription "Atrosokes dedicated this to the [god] Oxus."[9] The language
and form of this votive offering is Greek, but the deity is not.[10]
Furthermore, the dedicant has an Iranian name meaning something like "Possessing the Power of Divine Fire" that begins with
precisely the same letters (ATPOC) as were found on the potsherd
from Tepe Nimlik. Who this man may have been no one yet
knows. We can see, however, that indeed someone in Bactria with
an indigenous name set up a dedicatory inscription using Greek
at about the same time that his countryman Hyspasines did so at
Delos.

Other Greek potsherd inscriptions have been recovered in the
decades since 1946. In 1962, a fragment beginning with just three
Greek letters (NOY) surfaced at Udegram, in Pakistan.[11] This
old mountain fortress in the Swat Valley had previously been
visited by the renowned explorer (and scavenger of coins) Sir
Marc Aurel Stein in 1926; Stein identified the site as Ora, an
Indian stronghold captured by Alexander the Great.[12] A few
miles downstream at Bir-Kot, an imposing site teeming with

coins and identified by Stein as the ancient town of Bazira, excavations produced in 1981 a potsherd inscription with six Greek letters arrayed in two lines.[13] While the letters could represent parts of the names Euthydemus and Amyntas, the text is really too truncated to fathom its meaning.[14] An ostracon turned up at Emshi Tepe, near Tillya Tepe, in 1969 bearing the Greek letters ΔΙΟΔ, perhaps the beginning of a name such as Diodotus or Diodorus.[15] A few years later, another Greek name was found on a broken pot excavated at Afrasiab (ancient Maracanda), testifying to the existence of a certain Nicias.[16] At about the same time, a fragmentary Greek inscription of six lines was discovered at Jiga Tepe, a fortified Hellenistic site near Dilberdjin.[17] The text, perhaps a funerary epigram incised on a terra-cotta tablet, clearly mentions a Greek named Diogenes and perhaps, too, the Greek god Hades. The name Antiochus, or perhaps a place called Antiochia, may be read in Middle Persian on a potsherd from Termez.[18] The name Sokrakes has been found on a Greek pottery fragment from Tadjikistan.[19] Greek potsherd inscriptions and some papyrus fragments from Kampyr Tepe, in southern Uzbekistan, have also been excavated.[20] One shows the first letters of, perhaps, a proper name: ΚΛΕ.[21] Others record in Greek various amounts of commodities, probably the original contents of the vessels.[22] Third-century-b.c.e. ostraca found at Qala-i Sam, just outside southern Afghanistan, also record objects (including animal hides) and quantities.[23]

Sometimes Greek names and other information appear on ancient jewelry found in Afghanistan.[24] A bracelet in the form of a sea monster (*kētos*) bears the signature of its maker: ΜΗϹΤΩΡ ΕΠΟΕΙ ("Mestor made this").[25] The name Mestor is Homeric, as are other Greek names now known from ancient Afghanistan (e.g., Palamedes, Diomedes, Telephus, Thersites, Sarpedon).[26]

Another piece of jewelry, a gold bracelet in the shape of a coiled serpent, has its weight marked in Greek letters: ΛA, meaning thirty-one Attic drachms. Both these bracelets have been dated to the reign of Eucratides. A gold ornament that may have been a turban pin from first-century-B.C.E. (or C.E.) Kashmir features a female figure wearing two serpent bracelets and holding a tiny scroll, on which the Greek word "goddess" (ΘEA) has been spelled in gold droplets.[27] Among the twenty thousand gold objects excavated from six nomadic graves at Tillya Tepe, archaeologist Victor Sarianidi found a gold cista (round lidded container) with its weight recorded in Greek. He also recovered several pieces of jewelry with the name Athena engraved on them.[28] A broken seal from the region of Samarkand also has a figure of Athena, but with part of a name (ΑΙϹΙΝΟΥ) on it.[29] The inscription ΔΙΟΔώΡΟΥ ("belonging to Diodorus") appears retrograde on a second-century-B.C.E. seal stone acquired at Peshawar in 1972. The stone shows a nude Aphrodite gesturing toward the owner's name.[30]

Greek inscriptions have been found on silver plate as well.[31] A cup recovered somewhere in Afghanistan or Pakistan records the cumulative weight of it and its mate: "This pair [equals] 194 drachms."[32] A group of unpublished silver vessels from someplace in Pakistan, most probably Taxila, includes a few with bilingual (Greek and Prakrit) inscriptions. One of them reads: "The meridarch Calliphon dedicated this to the Zeus of the Chaones." The office of meridarch, normally associated with Hellenistic Syria and Judaea, represents a subdivision of a satrapy (province). The title is attested in other Prakrit inscriptions from Taxila, as noted long ago by Sir John Marshall in relation to some Buddhist dedications.[33] The name Calliphon is known from the Mollossian region of Greece, near the oracular shrine of Chaonian Zeus. This gives us a Greek name, a Greek deity, a Hellenistic administrative title, and a Greek text—alongside a non-Greek Kharoshthi version of the same. The growing list of these dedications by Taxilan meridarchs suggests a vibrant interplay of cultures.[34] Similarly, a curious bilingual stamp (Greek and Prakrit) purchased at Peshawar in 1957 attests someone with a Greek name (Philaxius) whose father (Ochus) had a Persian name.[35]

A knucklebone found at Maracanda bears some Greek letters that may be the abbreviation of a proper name.[36] Also at this site were discovered bricks variously stamped with nearly all the letters in the Greek alphabet (only iota, mu, nu, xi, and sigma are missing) plus the rare koppa and san.[37] A cave inscription at Kara Kamara attests in Greek a dedication made there by someone named Rhipus.[38] From a cave near Sangcharak, in northern Afghanistan, a Bactrian document rich in detail has lately been found inked on a leather strip. This bureaucratic text found its way into the hands of the noted coin collector R. C. Senior early in the 1990s.[39] He managed to rescue the crumpled hide from a distracted seller who habitually pulled and rubbed the artifact in a way that threatened to erase the entire text on it. Now in the Ashmolean Museum, the parchment turned out to be a Greek tax receipt from the lost world of Hellenistic Bactria. The text reads:

> During the reign of Antimachus the God, and of Eumenes and Antimachus [his sons?], year 4, month of Olous, in Asangorna, when [name] was guardian of the law: The tax collector Menodotus, in the presence of [name], who was also sent out by Demonax the former…, and [in the presence] of Simus, who was… by the agency of Diodorus the controller of revenues, acknowledges receipt from [name] the son of Dataes from the priests… the dues relating to the purchase…

This receipt acknowledges a payment made by a son of Dataes (a non-Greek name) to Menodotus the tax collector; the transaction was duly witnessed by several persons.[40] The priestly reference may indicate a purchase of sacrificial animals, but that is only one possibility. A variant reading of the smudged last line has been taken to mean that the payment amounted to twenty staters.[41] This would be a large sum, and would show the widespread use of Greek currency. As part of its dating formula, the Greek text begins with the same verb form found on King Antimachus's commemorative coins and on the Rosetta Stone, as discussed above, in chapter 2.[42] The mention of two additional royal names comes as a surprise and raises many questions about the governance of the region.[13] It seems, however, to support the statement found in Justin that Eucratides, Antimachus's contemporary, shared his throne with a son.[44] The text mentions a regnal year (4), a Macedonian month (Olous), a town (Asangorna), and several bureaucratic officials with Greek names and titles.[45]

Two additional parchment documents have lately been published. These probably derive from a different find spot, nearer to Balkh, and were discovered about a decade later than the leather tax receipt.[46] The text of the better-preserved example seems to read:

> During the reign of Antimachus[?], year 30, [month of?], in Amphipolis near[?] ... mercenaries[?] ... numbering forty Scythians, of 100 drachms of struck silver ... the quantity of silver ...

This perplexing document seems to name Antimachus as the reigning monarch, but unfortunately experts are not entirely sure of this reading.[47] Unlike the previous text, this one includes neither an epithet nor the names of associated kings. It also provides a date (year 30) more likely to be based on some unknown era rather than serving as a regnal year. More certain is the reference to a city with a well-known Greek name (Amphipolis) brought to Bactria from the Balkans. The document may record a payment of a hundred drachms to a detachment of Scythian mercenaries; the amount and ethnic are at least legible. The remaining parchment document, very poorly preserved, records a payment to someone named Archises for the transport of stone. It cannot be said whether this may have been building material or something more exotic, like the locally mined lapis lazuli.[48] Such texts, even though challenging to interpret, add much to our knowledge of administrative affairs in Bactria. While limited in number, they represent well the repertoire and palaeography of documentary material found elsewhere in the Hellenistic world.

Several interesting persons left substantial Greek inscriptions at Kandahar, the large urban site in southern Afghanistan that still bears the name of its founder, Alexander the Great.[49] One of the first to do so was Indian, not Greek, at a time when southern Afghanistan was not in the hands of Alexander's successors. Before Bactria broke free as an independent state, the Seleucids had already ceded territories south of the Hindu Kush to the Mauryan rulers of India. Bactrian kings would later regain these lands, but meanwhile the Greeks settled at Kandahar answered to the dictates of Indian rulers such as Chandragupta, Bindusura, and Ashoka. Extensive epigraphic material from their Mauryan empire has been found in South Asia, particularly from the reign of Ashoka (ca. 269–232 B.C.E.).[50] His various rock and pillar edicts have aroused keen interest not only because of this king's own historical importance but also because of the very wide geographic distribution of his monuments and the number of scripts employed on them (Brahmi, Kharoshthi, Aramaic, Greek). James Prinsep had begun reading some of this material early in the nineteenth century, when he used the bilingual coins of Agathocles and Pantaleon to help decipher them. That Ashoka had himself set up bilingual texts using Greek would later come as a complete surprise. In 1958, an Ashokan rock edict cut in both Greek and Aramaic was found on a fallen boulder at Kandahar.[51] This proclamation shows the interplay of Indian, Persian, and Greek cultures among the people for whom the bilingual text was inscribed in about 260 B.C.E. The fourteen-line Greek text reads:

> Ten years having passed, King Piodasses [Ashoka] revealed piety to men, and thereby he made them more pious and made all things to flourish throughout the whole land. And the king abstained from [eating] living creatures, and other men did likewise, and all who were the king's huntsmen or fishermen have ceased their work. And whosoever lacked self-control has, as far as possible, overcome his weakness and has become more obedient to his father, mother, and elders. And by doing all these things, they henceforth will lead better and more desirable lives.

In 1963, a German physician found at Kandahar another inscription that preserves in Greek portions of Ashoka's edicts XII and XIII.[52] The fragmented stones, perhaps originally part of a public building, enjoin his followers to respect all sects and to seek piety, confessing that

> when he had reigned eight years, King Piodasses conquered Kalinga, capturing and leading away from there 150,000 persons. He killed 100,000 more, and almost as many others died. From that time on, mercy and compassion seized him, and weighed heavily upon him.

This dramatic conversion set the remorseful raja on his famous path to social justice and royal responsibility, one of the most extraordinary events in all ancient history.

Ashoka clearly took pains to make his Buddhist creed known

to all within his realm, including the colonial remnants of the previous Macedonian and Persian empires conversant in Greek, Aramaic, or both.[53] He went further. Missionaries, presumably fluent in Greek, were dispatched to the courts of five Hellenistic kings (Antiochus II of Syria, Ptolemy II of Egypt, Magas of Cyrene, Antigonus Gonatas of Macedonia, and Alexander of Epirus), with unrecorded results.[54] Ashoka's father, Bindusura, had earlier requested from the Seleucid king Antiochus I the purchase of a Greek philosopher, along with some sweets and figs.[55] Diplomatic, commercial, and cultural contacts between East and West apparently remained active through Seleucid Bactria and Mauryan Arachosia, facilitating the survival of Hellenism until the time when Bactria, no longer Seleucid, governed Arachosia, no longer Mauryan.[56]

In December 1978, the British Institute of Afghan Studies unearthed at Kandahar an alabaster statue base with the remains of a Greek metrical inscription that mentions a "son of Aristonax."[57] The stone was damaged, having been reused for the threshold of a later Hellenistic house. The text is therefore difficult to reconstruct, but it probably commemorates a dramatic rescue from a dangerous animal:

> [This statue] of the wild beast, I,
> [name] the son of Aristonax,
> Having been rescued by
> [name] from its attacks,
> Set up in this sacred glen
> Among my fellow countrymen.

In about 2002, a stele came to light in Kandahar with a funerary epigram honoring a man named Sophytos son of Naratos.[58] Although father and son do not have Greek names, the inscription is nevertheless a clever Greek acrostic that spells out its origins down the left margin and at the head of each line. The stone reads:

Stele of Sophytos

B Beguiled by the Fates, my once prosperous clan
Y Yielded its wealth to another's hand.
S So I, Sophytos, Naratos's son,
O Outlined a plan for what should be done.
P Putting my hopes in the Muses of old,
H Honoring Apollo and gathering some gold.
Y Young though I was, I had to believe
T That if I dared to take my leave
O Of home, then maybe someday hence
S Some change of fortune would recompense
S Setting off with so much confidence.
O Out on the road, I promised myself
N Not to return without great wealth.
O Over many years, I traveled and traded
F From city to city until, elated,
N Now I find myself surrounded
A At the home my fathers founded,
R Restored to all its former glory,
A And telling friends my joyous story.
T Take heed, my sons and grandsons; you
O Ought to remember what I am due:
S Safeguard this house and my tomb too.

The poem, from roughly the time of Eucratides, sets forth a remarkable autobiography enlivened with Hellenic allusions, suggesting that its author had a good Greek education, of which he was proud.[59] This Sophytos (an Indian name?) restored the fortunes of his family by venturing abroad as a merchant, although it is not at all clear where he traveled.[60] His public display of pride in these accomplishments indicates that there were others in his native city who could appreciate them. Clearly, Greek culture remained strong at Kandahar, where at least some part of the population could read the inscriptions of Sophytos, Ashoka, and the son of Aristonax.[61] Other residents were more conversant in Aramaic or Prakrit.

Another fascinating inscription was recently discovered in the neighborhood of Kuliab, in Tadjikistan, and dated to circa 200 B.C.E.[62] This stone records in Greek verse a remarkable dedication made by a man named Heliodotus:

> For you, esteemed Hestia, Heliodotus has made
> This perfumed altar in the shade
> Of beautiful trees in Zeus's Wood
> Whereon from time to time he could
> Pour rich libations and sacrifice
> In order that he might entice
> You, dear goddess, in all things
> To guard the greatest of all kings,
> Euthydemus, his son as well,
> Demetrius, who, truth to tell,
> Is already making history
> And christened "Glorious in Victory."
> With Fortune's help, may this be done,
> Hestia, the Honored One.

This document from Kuliab, located almost 62 miles (100 km) north-northeast of Ai Khanoum, is thoroughly Greek in form and function. It invokes Hestia and Fortune (*Tychē*), and refers to a sacred grove of Zeus. The ostentatious concern expressed for Euthydemus and his son suggests that Heliodotus was perhaps a person of some standing with a strong connection to the king. The language indicates that Euthydemus was still alive and considered, by the dedicant at least, as "the greatest of all kings." There may be some hint here of Euthydemus's success against Antiochus the Great (208–206 B.C.E.): the Seleucid was *Megas* ("Great"), but the Bactrian is *Megistos* ("Greatest").[63] Apparently, young Demetrius did not yet hold the royal title, but he was already accomplished and renowned—so much so, that he is given here the epithet *Kallinikos* ("Glorious in Victory"). Whether this is in any way an official epithet remains unclear, since it is not the same one (*Anikētos*) assigned to Demetrius on Agathocles' commemorative coins. Then again, Euthydemus was styled *Theos* by Agathocles and Antimachus but *Megistos* in the inscription, and *Megas* on a unique coin said to be from Ai Khanoum.[64]

The identity of the dedicant Heliodotus is unknown, although a unique bronze coin minted by a King Heliodotus has recently come to light in Jammu, Kashmir. It is a small, square, bilingual issue, poorly struck, but it shows the king wearing a cavalry helmet and, on the reverse, Hercules crowning himself—the same type introduced by Demetrius I son of Euthydemus. It is chronologically unlikely that the Heliodotus who so admired Euthydemus and Demetrius in the Kuliab inscription later became the king who minted the new coin with Demetrius's type. Some descendant, however, is certainly a good candidate. The area around Kuliab would have fallen at about the same time as Ai Khanoum, some fifty years after the inscription was set up by Heliodotus. The family of the pious dedicant may have fled across the mountains and established a small, ephemeral Indo-Greek kingdom near Kashmir that preserved their ancestor's name and his loyalties.

In the course of their work at Ai Khanoum, archaeologists found coins, art, armaments, sundials, ceramics, mosaics, and other objects evocative of everyday life. They also found nearly seventy texts, some inscribed on stone, some inked onto pots, and some written on papyrus and parchment. This collection of written material offers a welcome archive of information from a single site, which can be contextualized in ways impossible for stray finds. The first text was found on October 22, 1966. On that day, the French uncovered fragments of a most remarkable inscription.[65] The left side of one stone reads, in verse:

> These wise words of illustrious men,
> Men of long ago,
> Stand today within the shrine
> Of holiest Pytho.
> There Clearchus copied them down,
> Accuracy's avatar,
> And inscribed them here at Cineas's tomb,
> Blazing from afar.

This Greek epigram describes the cultural mission of one Clearchus, who carefully copied at Delphi the long list of maxims revered there by the Greeks as the sayings of Apollo and the elder sages. Clearchus then carried these 147 maxims across mountains, seas, and deserts to Ai Khanoum, where they were inscribed for the edification of all Hellenes living far from their native land. The stele stood prominently within the sacred precinct of Cineas, the presumed founder of the city.[66] Although all 147 maxims are known from other sources, only the last five remain etched on this broken monument:

> As a child, be well behaved.
> As a youth, be self-controlled.
> As an adult, be just.
> As an elder, be wise.
> Die contented when you are old.

Parts of two additional maxims were recovered on a fragment excavated near the main text: "Speak well of everyone" and "Be a philosopher." The renowned epigrapher Louis Robert, who first published these texts, argued that Clearchus was the famous student of Aristotle known for his philosophical interests in the East, although a few scholars now doubt this.[67]

Within weeks of this epigraphic discovery, the excavators unearthed a dedicatory inscription honoring Hermes and Hercules, the patron deities of the Greek gymnasium.[68] Erected by two brothers, the Greek text reads:

> Triballus and Strato, sons of Strato, [dedicate this] to Hermes and Hercules.

The name Strato, of course, eventually became a royal one, as attested by coin finds from Gandhara, but any familial link must be conjectural. Closer to the mark, the name Strato is attested several times in the treasury documents of Ai Khanoum, discussed below. Louis Robert identified Triballus as a putative descendant of a Thracian soldier who served in Alexander's army. He dated the inscription early in Ai Khanoum's history, whereas scholars now place it in the last years of the city.[69] In 1971, Paul Bernard's team found the names Lysanias, Isidora, and Cosmas written on funerary urns dug from a necropolis outside the city walls; they also unearthed an urn inscribed simply "[The remains] of a little boy and a little girl."[70] One stone fragment from the cemetery mentions unnamed "kings," and another bears traces of a metrical memorial.[71]

Dozens of Greek administrative texts were recovered from the palace treasury at Ai Khanoum. Many take the form of storage jars bearing mundane notes written on them, usually identifying contents, the names of supervisory treasury officials, workers, and details of actions taken.[72] These treasury receptacles contained various commodities such as imported olive oil, incense, Greek currency, and Indian karshapana coins (plundered?) from Taxila. For example, one text states:[73]

> In the year 24…: Container A of olive oil, partly empty, holding one and a half measures decanted from two ceramic jars by Hippias, one sealed by [Molos]sus and the other by St[rato].

A series of notations on another large pitcher reads:[74]

a. From Zeno [received]: 500 drachms, counted by Oxyboakes and Oxybazus; sealed [within] by Oxyboakes.

b. From Timodemus [received]: [number] *taxaēna,* counted by Oxyboakes and Hermaeus.

c. From Philiscus [received]: 10,000 *kasapana taxaēna,*… by Aryandes and Strato.

Over a period presumably of several years, this particular jar at first held drachms and later κασαπανα ταξαηνά ("karshapana from Taksa-sila"), the Indian rectilinear punch-marked silver coins of Taxila. A hoard of such coins was discovered elsewhere in the palace, hidden in apparent haste by looters.[75] Unlike Greek coins, karshapana coins (fig. 17) were cut from metal strips and trimmed to the appropriate weight; these were stamped with several punches and then circulated. In the Ai Khanoum treasury, however, both Greek and Indian coins were clearly managed in the same fashion, by count rather than by weight.

Most members of the treasury's bureaucracy had Greek names (Zeno, Timodemus, Philiscus, Theophrastus, Callisthenes, Molossus, Hippias, Strato, Hermaeus, Niceratus, Cosmos), but a few bore native names (Oxyboakes, Oxybazus, Aryandes, Xatrannus,

Figure 17. Example of an Indian karshapana coin, stamped with various symbols.

Tarzus, Oumanes). The latter seem never to have exercised supervisory positions:

Supervisors	→	*Subordinates*
Zeno	→	Oxyboakes, Oxybazus
Timodemus	→	Oxyboakes, Hermaeus
Strato	→	Strato, Molossus, Tarzus
Philiscus	→	Strato, Aryandes, Theophrastus
Niceratus	→	Cosmos

The treasury text mentioning a date of "year 24" has been understood by Paul Bernard to mean the twenty-fourth year of Eucratides' reign.[76] Based on this supposition, some archaeologists have proposed a perhaps overly ambitious chronology that assigns each of these treasury directors a specific year in office: Zeno in 150 B.C.E., Timodemus in 149, Strato in 148, Philiscus in 147, and Niceratus in 146.[77]

Inside the palace treasury, perhaps in a chamber containing the royal library, archaeologists in September 1977 uncovered the remnants of papyrus texts.[78] The ravages of time and nature left little more than the ancient ink impressed into the soil, but enough could be read to determine that one literary text contained a Platonic or Aristotelian dialogue.[79] Nearby, fragments of parchment preserved lines of poetry, perhaps from a Greek tragedy. The palaeography of these texts matches that found on similar documents from contemporary Mediterranean sites.

Scattered around the site of Ai Khanoum were scores of Greek potsherd inscriptions quite like those found in the rest of Afghanistan. For example, one seems to identify Thersites, a name that calls to mind the Homeric epics.[80] Not all such inscriptions are Greek, however. In the main temple at Ai Khanoum, the DAFA recovered in 1970 a potsherd with what appears to be an Aramaic inscription listing some Iranian names.[81] This may represent an attempt to employ Aramaic script to write a local Iranian language, and its presence in the temple may be significant for our understanding of who worshipped there.[82] Some bronze and silver coins with the types of Euthydemus I, found north of Afghanistan, bear Aramaic legends that some scholars associate with Sogdian independence at the end of the third century B.C.E.[83]

Beyond Ai Khanoum, some ancient documents are not written in Greek per se but either mention individuals with Greek names or represent other languages that borrowed from the Greek alphabet.[84] Two Brahmi pillar inscriptions are noteworthy examples of the former type. The so-called Reh Inscription from northern India, found in 1979, seems to honor King Menander with various epithets such as "King of Kings, Great Savior, Just, Victorious, and Invincible."[85] The stone, however, is battered, and the reading disputed.[86] The famous Besnagar Inscription, on the other hand, provides a sure reference to a Greek named Heliodorus the son of Dion, from Taxila.[87] This Brahmi pillar reads:[88]

> This Garuda pillar of Vasudeva, the god of gods, was commissioned by Heliodorus son of Dion, a worshipper of Vishnu from Taxila who came as the Greek ambassador from Antialcidas, the Great King, to Bhagabhadra son of Kasi, the Savior, who was then in the fourteenth year of his prosperous reign.

Three timeless precepts, when correctly practiced, lead to heaven: Self-control, Charity, and Diligence.

This Heliodorus from Taxila, a Greek patently receptive to Indian cultural and religious influences, made this dedication at the end of the second century B.C.E. He acts in India very much as Hyspasines had done when making a Greek offering at Delos a few generations earlier. King Antialcidas the Great (heretofore known only from coins, though there with the epithet "Victory-Bearing") maintained diplomatic ties to the court of Raja Bhagabhadra the Savior. This text therefore supplies important information on several levels about the interactions of Greeks and Indians. A clay sealing from Mathura bears the name of Apollodotus in Brahmi script.[89] Similarly, an inscribed reliquary mentions a Nika, perhaps derived from *Nikē,* among a group of sisters otherwise bearing Indian names.[90]

Inscriptions using Greek letters to write native languages are also known. In the period following the fall of Hellenistic Bactria, mention continued to be made of Greek gods, dating formulas, and administrative offices.[91] During DAFA excavations of the monumental Kushan shrine at Surkh Kotal (1952–63), several important inscriptions emerged that adapted the Greek alphabet to express an Iranian dialect (called Bactrian).[92] One text actually includes the intrusive Greek phrase ΔΙΑ ΠΑΛΑΜΗΔΟΥ ("by Palamedes"). This suggests that Palamedes was the Greek-named architect, engraver, or overseer responsible in some way for this monument. At Dasht-i Nawar, in Ghazni Province, a French geologist discovered in 1967 a series of inscriptions that included texts carved in Greek, Bactrian, and Kharoshthi.[93] Several of these inscriptions refer to the Macedonian month Gorpaeus and use a Greek numerical system. At Rabatak, about 12.5 miles (20 km) northwest of Surkh Kotal, Afghan residents in March 1993 stumbled upon a grand inscription commissioned by the Kushan emperor Kanishka the Great.[94] The Bactrian text records, among other things, a remarkable ruling by the emperor that henceforth Aryan (i.e., Bactrian) should replace the Ionian (Greek) language. This measure, in year 1 of Kanishka's reign, variously dated by scholars between 78 and 128 c.e., marks a significant cultural shift away from the Hellenic legacy that still, quite obviously, lingered in the region long after the Greek kingdom was gone.

Inscriptions, then, provide a rough but important linguistic map of ancient Central and South Asia. We can see that Aramaic persisted in some local contexts in Bactria (Ai Khanoum, Bactra), Sogdia (coins), Arachosia (Kandahar), Paropamisadae (Laghman), and Gandhara (Taxila).[95] Kharoshthi (probably derived from the Aramaic script) and Brahmi were used in the latter territory, as attested also by coins. The use of Greek appears in all these regions, and its legacy endured in the writing of Bactrian. There also exist some inscriptions (at Ai Khanoum, for example) in languages that have yet to be identified or deciphered.[96] Clearly, the lost civilization of Bactria was polyglot, a fact long evident in the coins but much more complex now that epigraphy has begun to make its contribution.

The Bactria known to scholars sixty-five years ago was inhabited by a few dozen kings and queens—all brought to light through relentless effort and no little peril. This small royal population issued fascinating coins that displayed their Greek names, titles, and epithets, with some of these translated into Kharoshthi and Brahmi south of the Hindu Kush. Their religious and mythological world included a few familiar Greek deities and heroes, such as Zeus and Hercules. Epigraphy now adds a new dimension to this coin world, just as archaeology has done.

Texts show us the spread of various languages. They mention known and unknown Greek kings (Antialcidas, Demetrius, Euthydemus, Eumenes, Apollodotus) and numerous commoners (Archises, Aristonax, Calliphon, Callisthenes, Cineas, Clearchus, Cosmas, Cosmos, Demonax, Diodorus, Diogenes, Dion, Heliodorus, Heliodotus, Hermaeus, Hippias, Isidora, Lysanias, Menodotus, Mestor, Molossus, Niceratus, Nicias, Nika, Palamedes, Philaxius, Philiscus, Philoxenus, Polyxenus, Rhipus, Simus, Sokrakes, Sosipatrus, Strato, Theophrastus, Thersites, Timodemus, Triballus, Zeno). They provide non-Greek names as well (Aitanes, Aryandes, Piodasses [Ashoka], Atrosokes, Bhagabhadra, Dataes, Kasi, Naratos, Ochus, Oumanes, Oxybazus, Oxyboakes, Sophytos, Tarzus, Xatrannus).[97] Inscriptions in various languages invoke Apollo, Athena, the Buddha, Hades, Hercules, Hermes, Hestia, the Muses, the deified Oxus, Tyche, Vasudeva, Vishnu, and Zeus. Dating formulas include the Macedonian months Olous and Gorpaeus. Inscriptions give us actual place names (Amphipolis, Asangorna) and refer to a widening array of officials and occupations (kings, meridarchs, strategi, tax collectors, treasury supervisors, priests, merchants, stone haulers, Scythian mercenaries). We encounter a fascinating inventory of commodities, from honey, olive oil, incense, and cinnamon to stone, hides, and coins. Clearly, the words etched and inked on stone, pottery, papyri, and parchment provide some of our most useful sources for the lost civilization of Bactria.

One theme throughout the history of Bactrian studies seems obvious: sometimes, no evidence is not evidence at all. The total absence of Greek inscriptions from Afghanistan seemed meaningful early in the twentieth century, when this glaring fact suggested that Hellenism could not have taken root there.[98] Since World War II, however, epigraphic discoveries have exceeded everyone's expectations. It turns out that Greek and other texts have lain hidden all across the region, their previous nondiscovery being proof of nothing more than poor luck. At any given moment, scholars must inevitably work at the mercy of available evidence. To this must be added the sad corollary that sometimes the worst circumstances bring about the most discoveries. Such has been the fate of Afghanistan over recent decades, as the next chapter will demonstrate.

CHAPTER SEVEN

A Perfect Storm

Rescue and Revisionist Numismatics

Over the past thirty years (1980–2010), the ongoing political and military crisis in Afghanistan has forced many scholars to explore the unfortunate but necessary methodologies of rescue numismatics. Hand in hand with the despoliation of archaeological remains during this period (see chap. 5, above), vast troves of numismatic evidence have been dispersed or destroyed by a perfect storm of poverty and lawlessness in league with supply and demand. Some sense of this problem can be gleaned by reviewing the offerings of Bactrian and Indo-Greek coins in sales catalogues over the past thirty years, where nearly ten thousand newly found specimens have been auctioned worldwide.[1] These coins represent the tip of a much larger tragedy, since many additional examples surely have left no detectable trace in the market literature. For scholars, this brings to mind the haunting vision of ancient Bactria's lifeblood being spilled before its history can be saved.

This crisis affects every category of numismatic evidence. Consider the special tetradrachms issued by Agathocles and Antimachus to honor their royal predecessors, discussed above in chapter 2. In 1984, a comprehensive study of the known examples of these commemorative coins produced a corpus of 37 tetradrachms discovered since 1843.[2] That number has since grown to over 120 coins in this latest flood tide of largely unprovenanced evidence, taking us from an average yield of fewer than three commemorative coins per decade to over thirty examples per decade. The problem is that not one of these new specimens has come from a controlled excavation, and few have ended up in museums. Of course, we are now facing the added worry that even those artifacts formerly considered safe in an Afghan museum may be in jeopardy. Of the fifty-seven recorded hoards from Bactria and India found between 1821 and 1979, only six were recovered under controlled circumstances and transported substantially intact to a museum.[3] Of these, the first more or less complete Bactrian hoard to reach the National Museum in Kabul was the Qunduz treasure of 627 coins found at Khisht Tepe in 1946.[4] To this were added two hoards excavated at Ai Khanoum in 1970 (containing 677 Indian karshapana coins and six Indo-Greek coins) and in 1973 (containing 63 Greek coins).[5] These three hoards, half the total of intact deposits preserved from ancient Bactria and India, were not protected for long; in the turmoil since 1980, many of these coins have been pillaged from the National Museum, so that only those hoards housed outside Afghanistan have thus far escaped modern plunderers.[6] The number of Bactrian and Indo-Greek coins (as opposed to Indian punch-marked coins) derived from secure contexts amounted, therefore, to fewer than a thousand specimens, of which many have now been scattered to the winds by way of theft and the antiquities market.[7] Consequently, the past three decades have been especially damaging to scientific research on a scale that exceeds the worst days of the old Great Game in Central Asia.

Confronted by these grim realities, some experts must now devote at least a portion of their energies to rescue and recovery in order to make future research possible. Hoards in general provide essential guidance in the study of chronology, patterns of circulation, and political and military conditions—so much so, that considerable pains have been taken to record all such discoveries from throughout the homelands of ancient civilizations.[8] This is true even though most of these hoards derive from non-archaeological contexts. In fact, only about 8 percent of all reported Hellenistic coin hoards from Greece to India have been recovered scientifically.[9] To triage the other 92 percent, scholars must employ a makeshift methodology fraught with epistemological if not also personal dangers. The first hints of such a hoard usually stem from rumors in the coin trade about some spectacular find, triggered by any sudden influx of artifacts on the market. By this point, the discovery has probably been irrevocably compromised in any purely scientific sense and the scholar can only try to work backward to piece together the key data about provenance and composition: Where was the hoard discovered, and what was originally in it? The find spot cannot always be reliably ascertained; nor, in Afghanistan, can the actual finder (or finders) easily be interviewed. Everything depends on word-of-mouth reports, hampered by the suspicion that investigators may be deliberately misled by those who wish to protect a clandestine source of revenue. As for composition, hoards generally must be reconstructed based on the lamentable but necessary process of placing some trust in the timing of entry into the market. In other words, scholars must watch for the possible contents of a hoard as they show up, in dealers' shops or in auctions, following the rumors of a discovery. Here the problems multiply the more distant these potential contents appear in time and place from the original find. Hoards tend to travel quickly through bazaars and auction houses, where there is little reluctance to break them into lots for easier sale. The most collectible specimens may be culled for the connoisseurs, and extraneous merchandise may be pitched into the mix to satisfy everyone else. This may continue for months, or even years, and span several continents or even spill into cyberspace by way of electronic merchandising. Sometimes, special circumstances (such as a distinctive patina) may help in identifying the scattered coins of a given hoard, but normally the researcher must balance probabilities. Although this methodology is patently flawed and potentially very misleading, the alternative is to surrender the study of Bactria to only six intact, published hoards (three of them now pillaged).

What, then, are the realities of rescue numismatics in a place like Afghanistan? A good example may be found in the so-called Ai Khanoum Hoard III, recorded and studied under less than ideal circumstances.[10] In October 1975, curator Nancy Waggoner of the American Numismatic Society was shown by a New York dealer a large group of silver coins said to have been unearthed in Afghanistan. She quickly penned some notes about the lot, which at that time contained 135 tetradrachms and 6 drachms. In January 1976, Waggoner forwarded these notes to Claire-Yvonne Petitot-Biehler in Paris, who published a summary of them in her article about the 1973 hoard excavated at Ai Khanoum by Paul Bernard (AK Hoard II, found on 7 October).[11] According to Petitot-Biehler, Bernard had heard rumors of a clandestine hoard while in Afghanistan in 1974, which had been found near Ai Khanoum and then quickly spirited away. These were presumably the coins seen by Waggoner in New York. Thus, it appeared that some Afghan had dug up and sold a large cache of coins just a few months after the DAFA excavated a very similar hoard from an ancient house outside the walls of Ai Khanoum. (See chap. 9, below.) This led to immediate confusion. When the editors of *Coin Hoards* (vol. II, hoard 88) first tried to publish these two hoards in 1976, the finds were conflated into a single discovery reportedly made at Balkh! This error was caught and partly corrected in the next issue of *Coin Hoards*, for 1977 (vol. III, hoard 53).[12]

Meanwhile, the coins seen by Waggoner continued to travel the world, with stops in London and Switzerland. She examined them in New York again in 1976, noting that three specimens were now missing and that four others had been added, producing a slightly different record of 142 coins. The dealer agreed to supply Waggoner with black-and-white photographs of the coins, which she later consigned to this author while he was a seminar student at the ANS in 1980. (One example, a coin of Demetrius I, is shown here in fig. 18.) As it turned out, the coins in these photographs did not all tally with the two lists made by Waggoner, and one coin seems to be a forgery and another may be an intrusion, as noted in the final publication of the hoard.[13] Furthermore, there are no known weights or die axes for the 139 coins in the photographic record, a serious deficiency remedied only in cases where a given specimen later appeared in an auction catalogue furnishing such data.

In addition to the somewhat protean nature of the hoard as it moved through the market, eventually to be sold piecemeal, there appear to have been portions separated from the main lot before it reached New York. Henri-Paul Francfort published two commemorative coins of Agathocles that passed through the Kabul bazaar in the summer of 1975, one of them a heretofore unknown issue honoring Pantaleon Soter.[14] Then, in April 1976 during a visit to England, Parmeshwari Lal Gupta happened to

Figure 18. Tetradrachm of Demetrius I from Ai
Khanoum Hoard III, seen in New York City in 1976.

notice three commemorative coins of Agathocles in an
unidentified auction catalogue (which turned out to be Bank Leu
15), one of them also in honor of Pantaleon.[15] This last coin,
unfortunately broken during its travels, turned out to be the same
one reported by Francfort before it was damaged; the other three
coins were different. Although Gupta did not know that one
specimen was common to both lots, he nevertheless suggested
that all of them "might have originated from one and the same
find."[16] To these four coins can be added several more, since one
of the specimens spotted by Gupta in the Bank Leu auction had
previously been in the company of seven other Bactrian coins.[17]
Although some of these tetradrachms had not yet even been
cleaned for sale, they were all fine specimens that outshone the
lot photographed in New York.

The methodologies of rescue numismatics use this kind of
circumstantial evidence to posit the existence of a large hoard
found in Afghanistan, perhaps near Ai Khanoum, in the winter
of 1973–74. Before its contents ever left the country, dealers in
Kabul extracted the most prized specimens, including all the
highly collectible commemorative coins of Agathocles. Some of

these gleanings ended up in Switzerland while the bulk of the hoard passed from country to country, its contents subject to adulteration, until all the coins were dispersed over the course of several years. Fortunately, Nancy Waggoner at the ANS was able to examine the main lot on two separate occasions and to secure a partial photographic inventory, which led to the publication of Ai Khanoum Hoard III in 1981. This represented the first foray into the field of rescue numismatics for the period 1980–2010.

Since then, the exertions of Osmund Bopearachchi in particular have been fundamental to these endeavors. Born and educated in Sri Lanka, Bopearachchi completed his advanced studies at the Sorbonne working, in part, under the tutelage of Paul Bernard. Thereafter, he commenced publishing major public collections (Bibliothèque Nationale, Smithsonian Institution, American Numismatic Society) and private holdings (Aman ur Rahman) of Bactrian and Indo-Greek coins.[18] At the same time, he began investigating the numerous hoards from Afghanistan and Pakistan that were spilling onto the coin market. Materials that might otherwise have disappeared were instead partly documented, as conditions allowed, in a growing list of his books and articles. Most notable among these hoards was the so-called second deposit from Mir Zakah, Afghanistan (MZ II).[19] Stumbled upon by villagers in 1992, the contents of MZ II soon reached the Shinwari bazaar, at Peshawar, and thence the broader antiquities market. Throughout 1993, talk of this treasure confounded the numismatic community.[20] In March 1994, Bopearachchi personally examined a number of 110-pound (50-kg) sacks groaning with artifacts from MZ II during a visit to Pakistan; he found in them an unimaginable array of about 550,000 coins as well as jewelry, statuettes, vessels, and other artworks (fig. 19).[21] This single hoard remains the largest deposit of gold, silver, and bronze coins ever

Figure 19. Part of Mir Zakah Hoard II, the largest
cache of ancient coins ever found.

recovered from the ancient world, and its ill-fated contents have
glutted the coin trade in America, Europe, Asia, and the Middle
East.[22] Even so, tons of coins from MZ II are rumored still to be
unsold, lying in locked storage containers somewhere in Switzerland. Eventually, these will increase the number of marketed
Bactrian coins recently auctioned far beyond the ten thousand
currently known from sales catalogues.

Although the integrity of this spectacular treasure has been
irrevocably compromised, Bopearachchi managed to identify and
publish some of the important specimens it once contained.[23] He
did likewise for smaller hoards, ranging in size from a few coins
to several thousands, coming from Afghanistan, Tadjikistan,
Pakistan, and India.[24] One or more hoards containing a total
exceeding fifteen hundred coins, about half of them examined by
Bopearachchi, has been published as Ai Khanoum Hoard IV.[25]
The composition of this hoard mirrors that of the other finds
from Ai Khanoum. In 1996, a similar treasure of more than eight

hundred coins came to light at Kuliab, site of the discovery of the Heliodotus inscription. (See chap. 6, above.) Learning of this find through a private collector, Bopearachchi managed to study about a fourth of the coins directly or through photographs.[26] (See plate 5.) Many of these specimens are small denominations (drachms and obols), yet the composition of the hoard corresponds to those found at Ai Khanoum (AK II–IV), which extend from the reigns of Alexander to Eucratides.[27] A similar hoard of Bactrian tetradrachms spanning the reigns of Diodotus I to Agathocles was discovered at Tokhmach Tepe, near Bukhara, in 1983 and published by archaeologist Edvard Rtveladze.[28]

During regular investigative missions to Pakistan during the 1990s, Osmund Bopearachchi recognized an interesting phenomenon of rescue numismatics. Many Indo-Greek hoards were being reported from regions hosting large throngs of Afghan refugees. In the process of setting up camps and digging foundations, often on unrecognized archaeological sites, busy shovels were striking silver and gold.[29] Indeed, any increase in population or resource development tends to produce new coin finds through digging, dredging, or plowing. In 1992, a broken pot in the Swat River near Saidu-Sharif yielded about eight hundred coins, some of them unique. In October 1993, a hoard of the same size entered Western markets from Bajaur, where two similar deposits had been uncovered in 1942. Another eighty-three coins were unearthed in Mian Khan Sanghou (Dec. 1993), plus about 1,220 coins in the village of Wesa (Jan. 1994). At Sarai Saleh, near Haripur, a bulldozer leveling the ground for the tomb of a village leader struck a bronze vase in 1994. About two thousand Indo-Greek and Indo-Scythian coins tumbled out and were sold in the bazaars of Haripur, Islamabad, and Peshawar. Subsequent investigations revealed that a substantial ancient city once stood on the site, and archaeological excavations commenced there in 1995. Likewise, another set of finds in a farmer's fields at Siranwali produced not only a hoard of four hundred coins (mainly of Menander) but also fragments of Hellenistic pottery suggesting the presence of an ancient settlement.[30]

Rumors spread in April 2001 about an unusual discovery of gold coins minted by the first independent kings of Bactria: Diodotus I, Diodotus II, and Euthydemus I.[31] Villagers digging clay from the Ganges near Vaisali, deep in India, allegedly hauled up a clay pot containing the treasure. Some of the artifacts were precipitously melted down by local jewelers, but within a few months others went to European and American dealers; this trove is still being actively marketed. The estimated number of specimens actually found has been greatly reduced over time, from over a thousand to fewer than two hundred, but this discovery may yet help to rewrite the history of these kings.

Out of these many recent finds have emerged previously unknown rulers (such as Nashten and Heliodorus), unexpected coin types, monograms, or denominations (of Alexander, Eucratides, Menander, Amyntas, Artemidorus, etc.), and examples of new overstrikes of one coinage over another (such as Euthydemus on Diodotus, and Agathocleia on Menander). All this information is valuable, even if so much more might have been learned had these hoards been subject to careful scrutiny in a public collection. As it stands, many of the coins from these hoards will never be properly cleaned, weighed, photographed, or published. They are hostages in an ongoing war against error, a struggle for truth waged by scholars armed with the clumsy but essential weaponry of rescue numismatics.

Bactrian evidence comes at such a price that even the oldest of discoveries must from time to time be rerescued. At the British Mu-

seum, a special initiative was launched in 1993 to recover and catalogue the vast collections made by Charles Masson.[32] This explorer's sixty thousand coins sped through the arteries of
nineteenth-century British numismatics, many ending up in private hands and others at the East India Company, the British Museum, the India Office Museum, the Ashmolean Museum, the
Fitzwilliam Museum, and so forth, until a portion actually made
the return trip to India. The archival research necessary to retrieve this data is no mere parlor game or academic's pastime; the
results matter a great deal to our understanding of the sites stripped
by Masson, such as the city of Begram.[33] Similar work is also pro-
gressing on the early collections assembled and then dispersed by
the French officers serving Ranjit Singh, such as General Court.[34]

The surge of new evidence drawn from these many facets of
rescue numismatics has pushed Bactrian studies far beyond the
compass of narrative numismatics, even though a public that pre-
fers its facts in story form still accords writers like Tarn and
Narain a powerful hold over Bactrian history. Rescue numismatics has led to revisionist numismatics, an approach that more or
less abandons the crafting of elaborate narratives for the specialist's emphasis on technical analysis. The aim is to revise earlier
views by tackling specific problems in light of fresh evidence and
emerging technologies, including computer-enhanced analyses
and advanced laboratory methods (X-ray fluorescence spectrom-
etry, scanning electron microscopy, atomic absorption spectrom-
etry, etc.).[35] Electronic archives and databases are fast becoming
the essential tools of the academic trade. Meantime, the rudimentary, now outdated catalogues of the nineteenth and early
twentieth centuries have been superseded on the shelf by more
scientific, comprehensive reference works on the model of Bopearachchi's *Catalogue raisonné* of the much-expanded collection in

the Bibliothèque Nationale.[36] Centuries-old problems, such as sorting out the coinages of Diodotus I from those of Diodotus II, have now been tackled with some success.[37] Tarn's imaginative interpretation of the so-called pedigree coins has been proven false by closer analysis of these issues.[38] Epigraphic evidence has been tied to the coinages in order to rethink the chronologies of the Indo-Greeks.[39] Sequences of currency are being refined by the study of overstrikes.[40] All this progress results from a notable increase in the amount of specialized research being published on Bactrian numismatics.[41]

One welcome aspect of revisionist numismatics is its underlying emphasis upon proper methodology. In 1992, Osmund Bopearachchi announced a new approach to the study of Bactrian history, one that challenged the works of Tarn, Narain, and others.[42] Addressing one of the oldest problems in Bactrian numismatics, Bopearachchi proposed a different methodology for the study of monograms. He noted that the total number of these markings had been vastly inflated by the gradual accumulation of errant readings. Cutting that figure by more than half, he then grouped the monograms into units with their hypothetical variants, so that the control marks ᚼ and ᚺ might be *officinae* within the mint represented by ᚠ. Bopearachchi then tried to localize these units based on find spots.[43] In the cases of long-lived monogram groups, Bopearachchi then sought new data such as die links and overstrikes to posit a better chronology.[44] Drawing on a wide range of evidence, he argued that previous scholars had been completely mistaken in their reconstructions of the final period of Greek rule in India.[45]

More recently, Peter Mittag has again addressed the methodological *Kernproblem* in Bactrian studies, namely the handling of material and written sources.[46] In order to unravel the basic questions still surrounding ancient Bactria (Where, in what order, and exactly when did its forty-five known sovereigns reign?), Mittag discusses a series of access points to each problem. For example, chronologies can be established by way of a few coins possibly bearing dates (Plato, e.g.), the series of commemorative issues (*Erinnerungsmünzen*) struck by Agathocles and Antimachus, nearly three dozen recorded overstrikes, kinship (as attested in texts or surmised from coins), die links, iconographic borrowing, hoards, stylistic differences, letter forms, monograms, and the legends on coins. Mittag rightly stresses that not all these methods are of equal value, with overstrikes clearly ranking as the most deterministic, since they establish a relative order of issues. Less reliable in his view are chronological conclusions drawn from the study of iconography, hoards, style, or letter forms. Geographic areas controlled by specific rulers might be reconstructed from find spots, the languages used on the coins, monograms, coin types, style, and letter forms; however, none of these is considered particularly reliable. Mittag's hierarchy of evidence serves as his basis for a schematic reconstruction of the Bactrian and Indo-Greek reigns.[47]

Only one attempt has been made to address these matters in a comprehensive epistemological fashion. In 1987, the noted archaeologist and numismatist Olivier Guillaume embarked upon this ambitious mission in his book *L'analyse de raisonnements en archéologie: Le cas de la numismatique greco-bactrienne et indo-grecque*, a work so important that it was quickly reissued in an English edition.[48] Its author proclaimed:[49]

> The purpose of this study is to sum up the present situation of numismatics within the field of Graeco-Bactrian and Indo-Greek studies from a methodological point of view. We shall examine how numismatists describe the coins in their catalogues and how historians use the catalogues to establish their historical reconstructions.

Guillaume used the logicist analysis then in vogue among pro-
ponents of the so-called New Archaeology (see chaps. 5 and 8),
inspired by theoreticians such as Jean-Claude Gardin, who had
also worked at Ai Khanoum.[50] The approach is therefore
described as a kind of calculus that first exposes how the numismatic data have been processed in a sample of six standard catalogues: Cunningham (1884), Gardner (1886), Smith (1906), Whitehead (1914), Lahiri (1965), and Mitchiner (1978). These seemingly
straightforward compilations of hard evidence are shown, in fact,
to be laden with all sorts of ambiguous language and reasonings.
Thus, the development of Bactrian studies has depended not only
on the expansion of numismatic evidence but also on how that
material has been arranged and described: one cataloguer's Bactrian coin may be another's forgery or barbarian imitation; one
expert's Apollo may be another's Artemis or Anaitis.

In the second half of his book, Guillaume examines how these
catalogues have been used by historians to create their narrative
accounts, specifically those of Tarn (1951) and Narain (1957).[51] The
goal is to unveil the sequence of propositions (P1, P2, P3 ...) that
leads from the cataloguers' data to the historians' reconstructions, based on eleven variables such as metals, overstrikes, and
epithets.[52] For example, the use of nickel (or cupronickel) for
some coinages is a fact stated in most of the catalogues, which
then becomes another kind of fact in the works of Tarn and
Narain, who draw different conclusions from it regarding trade
and conquest, respectively.[53] The same is true of overstrikes,
which Tarn and Narain take as proof both of conquest and of a
desperate shortage of metals, depending upon the needs of their
narratives.[54] In terms of epithets, each author explains a given
title according to preconceived notions.[55] For Tarn, the epithet
ΔΙΚΑΙΟΣ ("Just") was taken by Heliocles in order to win favor

among the Euthydemids, whereas Narain saw it as Heliocles' honorific for killing Plato, the murderer of their father, Eucratides. The same epithet, ΔΙΚΑΙΟΣ, on the coins of Menander has a possible Buddhist connection in the eyes of Narain, but not for Tarn.

In the end, Guillaume concludes that the foundational works of Tarn and Narain are both flawed by weak methodologies and ideological biases.[56] He suggests that "the literary form of the narrative is singularly inadequate" for Bactrian studies.[57] In fact, it is characterized as a dead end: "as long as historical reconstructions are presented—as they are—as narratives one cannot hope for any progress."[58] Instead, Guillaume calls for closer attention to numismatic typologies and hypothesis testing as the best ways to move forward. To some extent, revisionist numismatics has answered that appeal for more scientific, problem-oriented investigations.[59]

Yet some authors still cling to the worst enticements of narrative numismatics. As one example, in his recent books about Bactria, anthropologist Homayun Sidky offers what has been called a "critical narrative" to supersede the outdated, impressionistic classic by Tarn.[60] Curiously, Sidky takes a hostile tone toward professionals, specialists, and experts—terms he usually sets apart derisively in quotation marks; the methods and interests of these unnamed and allegedly "obtuse" specialists are deemed antithetical to Sidky's self-professed emphasis upon a "narrative approach" and descriptive imagery.[61] Without conducting any original research of his own, Sidky shuffles the basic reconstructions of others, particularly Tarn and Narain, into a synthetic narrative that perpetuates the kinds of problems identified by Guillaume. Thus, for example, Sidky tells the story of Demetrius's fight against Eucratides:[62]

And so, Demetrius, who as a young man alongside his father had faced Antiochus the Great, whose conquests south of the Hindu Kush considerably increased the size of the Greek kingdom, and whose military successes had earned him the epithet *Aniketos,* "the Invincible," met his end on the field of battle. This was not at all a shameful death for a rash adventurer, with more ambition than skill, as Narain makes of Demetrius.

As Narain makes of which Demetrius? Here lies the hopeless mélange: Narain never says that Demetrius I, son of Euthydemus, met a shameful death at the hands of Eucratides because of rashness, ambition, or anything else. Narain chides that Tarn would have it thus, but that *Demetrius II* actually fought Eucratides.[63] Nor, of course, does any source report that either Demetrius died on the battlefield. That bit of descriptive imagery is a narrative builder. In fact, Sidky admits that the battle he envisions is not mentioned anywhere but asserts that one is required nonetheless to complete his story of Eucratides' conquest of India.[64]

Even in the pages of an academic numismatic journal published both in Greek and in English, the shadow of Tarn and narrative numismatics still lingers. Jens Jakobsson criticizes "the far from satisfying status of current scholarship" and advocates for a better methodology.[65] He worries that the recent trend of specialized research (i.e., revisionist numismatics) has once again driven a wedge between coin collectors or numismatists on the one hand and historians or philologists on the other.[66] One solution, he proposes, is to revisit "the somewhat abandoned field of relations between different rulers."[67] We return, therefore, to speculations regarding possible marriage connections between various kings. For example, Jakobsson interprets the commemorative coins of Antimachus as a record of actual ancestry, whereas those of Agathocles were not. This leads to the supposition that[68]

Antimachus I was a younger son of Euthydemos I, who had been married to a daughter of Diodotos I, *as could well be imagined*. Antimachus was then the *most legitimate heir* to Euthydemos II, whereas Agathokles and Pantaleon belonged to a sideline.

Similarly, Jakobsson argues that "Eukratides I had probably been married to a daughter of Apollodotos I" and that Heliocles the Just "was not necessarily a relative of Eukratides, but was perhaps married to Eukratides' sister or daughter Laodike, or if Laodike was Eukratides' queen, Heliokles was her brother or father."[69] It is difficult to see how these guesses are indeed any "better rooted in facts" than the "fanciful speculations" of W. W. Tarn.[70]

There have appeared three larger studies of Hellenistic Bactria and India since 2005, all keen to revive the study of the written evidence for whatever clues may have been missed. The premature death of Stanislaw Kalita in 2000 during the early stages of his promising academic career means that we have only an undeveloped version of his book *Grecy w Baktrii i w Indiach*, redacted by his university colleague Edward Dabrowa.[71] It was Kalita's aim to examine anew the history of the Greeks in Bactria and India "through the prism of the narrative sources" in order to compare more closely the written and numismatic evidence.[72] This work therefore deals only with those problems for which there is textual evidence, such as the chronology of Bactria's secession from the Seleucids, the war between Euthydemus I and Antiochus III, and the reign of Menander. In its unfinished state, this study glosses over the career of Eucratides.

On the other hand, a well-researched and richly documented dissertation by Omar Coloru, a student at the University of Pisa, has recently been published as *Da Alessandro a Menandro: Il regno greco di Battriana*.[73] Although written very much in the tradition of narrative numismatics, with emphases on chronology and dynastic relationships, the work is revisionist in its up-to-date incorporation of epigraphic, archaeological, and numismatic evidence.[74] Like Tarn, Coloru treats the reigns of Euthydemus and his son Demetrius as the golden age of Bactria—followed by civil war and the disastrous usurpation of Eucratides. The wars of the latter king are reconstructed in great detail (pp. 209–29) along the lines suggested by Justin's epitome of Trogus, with special attention to affairs in the West involving the Seleucids, Mithridates, and Timarchus. Although the local religions of Bactria and India made some inroads into the Greek-ruled state, Coloru considers the area as very much a satellite of the Seleucid empire.

The work of François Widemann (director of research, CNRS) offers a sweeping treatment based on technical analyses of the coinages coupled with new archaeological and epigraphic evidence and a rehabilitative faith in the surviving scraps of literary sources.[75] The author accepts the impracticality of creating an "histoire événementielle" and addresses the many "hypothèses invérifiables" of Tarn.[76] The work, however, is (by the author's own admission) uneven, speculative, and essentially narrative in its approach. Widemann tells the story of Bactria idiosyncratically, his own interests reflected in a chronicle that is at some times meticulous and at others superficial. For example, he takes no notice of recent research published on the Diodotids; yet the short reigns of the so-called Nickel Kings (Euthydemus II, Pantaleon, Agathocles) receive twice as much attention as Diodotus I, Diodotus II, Euthydemus I, and Demetrius I combined. This is largely due to the author's fascination with the cupronickel coinages of Bactria.[77] Widemann contends (following Tarn) that Bactria suffered a perpetual "penury of precious metals" in spite of the fact that it minted such huge amounts—and huge denominations—of gold and especially silver.[78] The narrative sometimes assumes a Tarnlike precision in its chronology, as in the calculation of kings' ages and reigns, and in its reconstruction of family relationships.[79] Truly a Tarn for the twenty-first century, Widemann concocts from thin air a remarkable institutional structure for Bactria. In order to bridge the gaps between various dynasties, he imagines a powerful "conseil de Bactres" while admitting that there is no evidence for it ("mais aucune source ne renseigne sur ce point").[80] He posits a formal system of epithets ("épiclèses") peculiar to Bactria, which allegedly were conferred by this Bactrian council as legal indicators of rank among co-ruling kings. To make this work, Widemann must arbitrarily switch the epithets normally assigned to Diodotus I and II, and suppose that Eucratides I did not adopt the requisite epithet *Theos* because the council refused to grant it to him.[81] There are even identifiable factions of Greeks, Indians, and Sakas that allegedly animate the politics of Taxila, and like Tarn's Euthydemids, Widemann's King Maues champions Alexander's alleged dream of a brotherhood of all mankind.[82]

It seems, therefore, that Bactrian studies remain partly mated to the old methodologies of narrative numismatics even while rescue and revisionist numismatics struggle to chart a new path for the twenty-first century. The numerous finds of fresh archaeological, epigraphic, and numismatic evidence may someday make clear the subtleties of Bactrian history, but for now a fundamental impasse remains. Bactrian studies began in the eighteenth century with compilations of king lists and other ostensible facts derived from classical literary sources, as was the norm for most aspects of ancient history. Old texts were deemed authoritative and scarcely needed validation; at most, scholars hoped to illustrate the content of those sources by means of ancillary monuments, art, and coins recovered from the earth. Gradually, the material record became important in its own right and sometimes served as a counterweight to the writings of poets, geographers, and historians. Whether the subject was Egypt, Greece, or Rome, the past revealed itself through an increasingly sophisticated system reliant upon what we might call the generation, verification, and integration (GVI) of data. Wherever source materials have been plentiful and diverse, the GVI process has worked quite well, but we have seen that Bactria is not yet such a place. Our ability to generate, verify, and integrate purported facts is severely hampered and seems incapable so far of sustaining the kinds of histories the public craves.

The literary texts, for example, claim that King Eucratides ruled a thousand cities, but neither numismatics nor archaeology can verify this. We know from Strabo that one of those cites was named for Eucratides himself, but we cannot confirm the belief of many that the archaeological site of Ai Khanoum is that place. It is no easy task to verify and integrate the results drawn from one kind of source with those from another. In the main, we have generated a large number of isolated literary, epigraphic, numismatic, and archaeological facts, but these seldom lend themselves to verification or integration on any scientific basis. Thus, the evidence about Bactria remains compartmentalized and little stronger than its unconnected pieces. As a result, almost any potential fact generated by even a respected source such as Polybius can be doubted if there is no corroborating testimony.[83]

Take the unusually multifaceted case of Demetrius I. Historians can generate seven or more facts about this man based on ancient literary sources (L1–7), two facts based on epigraphy (E1 and E2), eleven facts derived from numismatics (N1–11), and a pair of archaeological facts (A1 and A2):

L1: Demetrius was the son of Euthydemus I (Polybius).

L2: As a young man (*neaniskos*) in about 206 B.C.E., Demetrius confirmed the treaty negotiated by Teleas between Antiochus III and Euthydemus I (Polybius).

L3: Demetrius was deemed by Antiochus III worthy of kingship based upon his appearance, dignified bearing, and conversation, and Euthydemus was allowed to call himself king (Polybius).

L4: Demetrius was promised a daughter of Antiochus III as a bride (Polybius).

L5: Demetrius the son of the Bactrian king Euthydemus conquered part of India (Strabo).

L6: A Demetrius (I or II?) king of India ("rex Indorum") fought against Eucratides (Justin).[84]

L7: A city named Demetrias existed in Arachosia (Isidore of Charax).[85]

E1: Demetrius was the son of Euthydemus I (Kuliab Inscription).

E2: Demetrius was hailed as *Kallinikos,* "Glorious in Victory" (Kuliab Inscription).

N1: Demetrius was given the epithet *Anikētos* on the commemorative coins of Agathocles.

N2: Demetrius issued Attic-standard silver portrait coins showing the draped king with a diadem and wearing an elephant-scalp headdress.

N3: These coins of Demetrius used the reverse coin type of Hercules crowning himself while holding a club and lion pelt.

N4: Demetrius issued Attic-standard bronze coins of three varieties: (obverse) Hercules,(reverse) standing Artemis; (obverse) elephant head, (reverse) caduceus; (obverse) shield, (reverse) trident

N5: Demetrius's coins all bear the legend ΒΑΣΙΛΕΩΣ ΔΗΜΗΤΡΙΟΥ.

N6: Silver coins with this same inscription but different portrait and coin type (standing Athena) may belong to a later king.

N7: Demetrius did not strike gold or cupronickel coinage.

N8: Demetrius's silver coins are relatively few in hoards as compared with his father's: Ai Khanoum Hoard II (Euthydemus 27, Demetrius 3), Ai Khanoum Hoard III (Euthydemus 81, Demetrius 8), Bukhara Hoard (Euthydemus 51, Demetrius 0), Qunduz Hoard (Euthydemus 12, Demetrius 8), although the partly reported Kuliab Hoard may be an exception (Euthydemus 29, Demetrius 50)

N9: Demetrius struck his coinage on a fixed 12:00 axis.

N10: Demetrius used over a dozen monograms, but mostly ℞ and ✤.

N11: A reverse coin die of Demetrius may derive from the area of Ai Khanoum.[86]

A1: Demetrius's bronze coins are relatively few as compared with his father's in the Ai Khanoum excavations (Euthydemus 49, Demetrius 5).

A2: A bronze statuette of Hercules crowning himself, excavated at Ai Khanoum, resembles Demetrius's coin type.

This list provides us with the best-attested fact in all Bactrian studies: Demetrius I was the son of Euthydemus I, as verified independently by two literary sources and an inscription (L1, L5, and E1) and not contradicted by any known numismatic or archaeological evidence.[87] No other relationship, not even that of Diodotus I and II, can attain this level of certainty, much less the dozens of reconstructed family connections and invented persons commonly found in modern histories. This does not mean that Heliocles and Laodice were not the parents of Eucratides, or that Pantaleon and Agathocles were not brothers; but these are conjectures at best, with numerous scholars vigorously disagreeing about them. The sundry rulers identified as additional sons of Euthydemus (Euthydemus II, Antimachus, Agathocles, Pantaleon) are not corroborated anywhere; all written sources mention only young Demetrius. One source gives his epithet as "Glorious in Victory" (E2); another says "Invincible" (N1), but his own issues offer neither (N5). Dare we link the military epithets to Demetrius's alleged conquests in India (L5, L6) and Arachosia (L7)? The elephants on his coins have been logically associated with these wars (N2, N4), although not always with due consideration for the chronological crux of when these conquests took place. The coins indicate that any such campaigns were completed before Demetrius began to strike coins, since the elephant scalp is featured from the very outset. We might assume, therefore, that Demetrius either struck his father's coinage in the beginning of his reign (N8, A1) or that he achieved his military successes before his accession.[88] The latter view is supported by Polybius's remarks that Euthydemus I (but not his son, though worthy) was granted the royal title (L3), that Demetrius was *Kallinikos* when not yet king (E2), and that his father alone was identified as the ruler of Bactria at the time when Demetrius invaded India (L5). Yet there are no Indo-Greek coins attributed to Demetrius I, and the jury remains out on whether he could be the same "rex Indorum" who fought Eucratides (L6).[89]

Most of these twenty-two facts, therefore, do not verify each other, nor are they readily integrated into a reliable narrative of Demetrius's career. From Polybius to Chaucer, we may say that no Bactrian ruler enjoyed a better reputation than young Demetrius, but we cannot with any certainty explain what he did to earn that acclaim. There is no mention of him in the actual fighting against Antiochus the Great, and he was not yet twenty when his diplomatic skills impressed the Seleucid overlord. He was pledged a royal wife, but no one knows if he got one. He was thought kingly in manner, but apparently did not share that title with his father, Euthydemus. What sort of military glory did he have in the eyes of the man who commissioned the Kuliab Inscription or designed the commemorative coins? Must we seek that glory hidden somewhere in the king's elephant headdress? Did Demetrius restore Bactrian honor by invading India during his father's reign, in spite of the treaty between the Indians and the Seleucids, in order to grab elephants, which were the only symbolic spoils of war taken from Euthydemus by Antiochus? Or did Demetrius merely accompany Antiochus to India at the head of the Seleucid's elephant corps? In the end, we see that generating facts can be relatively easy, but not verifying them independently or integrating them into a sound narrative.

Even a case seemingly custom-made for GVI fails us in Bactria when *On the Circumnavigation of the Red Sea,* a literary source, appears to generate a blatantly numismatic fact: "Even now in Barygaza [modern Broach, Bharuch], old drachms stamped with inscriptions in Greek lettering come to hand, the coins of Apollodotus and Menander, who were kings after Alexander."[90] This one should be simple; but alas, there are no significant finds of these coins in the region of modern Bharuch that would substantiate the testimony of the anonymous author of this sailing manual. Only a handful of Menander coins have ever been recovered from this area, and most of the Apollodotus (II) examples derive from a single hoard dispersed from Gogha.[91] Even these specimens were unknown to the historian Tarn, who nevertheless sided with the texts and integrated this fact into his account as a reliable guide to the extent of Apollodotus's realm: "Consequently Apollodotus' rule in Barygaza cannot be in doubt."[92] The numismatist Narain, on the other hand, noted the paltry coin data and integrated this contrary fact into his narrative as evidence that Tarn's Apollodotus I never reigned there and probably never even existed at all.[93] The tremendous efforts of rescue and revisionist numismatics have yet to resolve these problems.[94] One possible solution may be sought in another approach, one that uses coins to answer a different set of questions.

CHAPTER EIGHT

A New Beginning

Cognitive Numismatics I

In 1941, three pioneers perished at the height of their professions. Edward T. Newell was at the time one of the world's greatest numismatists; Sir Arthur Evans was its most celebrated archaeologist, and Professor James Westfall Thompson was the prolific sitting president of the American Historical Association. What is most striking about their passing is the subsequent history of their respective fields over precisely the same period. Today, numismatics remains very much Newellian in its methods and interests. The ghost of Newell could feel quite at home reading a recent journal or book in his area of expertise, written likely as not by a knowledgeable collector having no formal academic training in the discipline—indeed, few still are the degrees actually granted in numismatics. The same cannot be said of Evans, whose brand of archaeology has long ceased to be practiced. In fact, the methods if not the interests of Evans would be something of a scandal in any excavation today, and the knighted hero could scarcely understand the terminologies and techniques of current archaeological research. Thompson's brand of history has fallen from favor among those less enthralled by his own regard for kings, popes, saints, artists, and intellectuals. In the AHA Presidential Address that he never lived to deliver, Thompson would have said something anathema to the "new social historians" of the next generation: "the prime movers of human affairs ... are Law and Government, Religion, Literature, and Art."[1] This capitalized hierarchy leaves little room for the lowercase histories of the lower-class peoples now in vogue. Clearly, the past seventy years have seen the rise of a New Archaeology and a New History—but not yet a New Numismatics.

This is not to say that progress has stalled in the study of coinages; previous chapters have amply demonstrated the fruits of many labors. But in spite of hard-won advances, there is still a lot more that coins can tell us about places like Bactria. The key is for numismatics to become relevant to the kinds of questions being asked today. The new archaeologies and histories have pushed aside traditional preoccupations with ruling elites, pretty objects, descriptive catalogues, and eventful narratives. Instead, the focus has shifted to the study of ordinary people, everyday objects, explanatory models, systems analysis, and scientific hypothesis testing.[2] Hence we find a proliferation of subfields ranging from women's history, ethnohistory, and cliometrics to processual, postprocessual, and logicist archaeology. Historians now investigate phenomena such as hybridity, urbanization, and colonialism as seriously as their predecessors tracked the reading habits of Thomas Jefferson; archaeologists study olive pits and pollen samples as thoroughly as their forebears did palaces and pyramids. Meanwhile, most numismatists remain fixated on the same questions that bothered Vaillant, Bayer, Pellerin, and Wolff centuries ago. For this reason, many experts in the history and archaeology of Hellenistic Bactria are finding numismatics of secondary importance in answering the dominant questions of the day.[3] What can we know about the subhistoric peoples of Bactria, who lived below the threshold of our written sources? How were identities constructed and negotiated in a world too often reduced to a stark struggle of Greek versus non-Greek? How do we correctly combine different kinds of material evidence in order to understand the dynamics of the region? Why do we stress events rather than processes?

For nearly three hundred years, Bactrian numismatics has concentrated on the names, number, and order of kings; their kinship and marriage ties with each other; their personalities and appearance; their rivalries and their conquests. Archaeological and epigraphic discoveries have done little so far to alter this numismatic obsession with those who ruled rather than those who were their subjects. History and archaeology have become bottom-up in orientation, whereas numismatics remains top-down. We look at the coins and wonder too much about the kings and not enough about their kingdoms, as if this approach simply cannot be helped. As one numismatist has recently put it:[4]

> The coins naturally put the focus on the kings who issued them rather than on broader knowledge of these societies, *but this is a limitation we have to accept.*

That is a false constraint. Perhaps it is time to try a different methodology in our search for the lost civilization of Bactria. Let us turn, therefore, to what might be called cognitive numismatics.

Taking a cue from that branch of the New Archaeology known variously as processual or cognitive, let us forget for a moment the kings of Bactria and concentrate instead on the nameless and faceless people around them.[5] Who appears on the coins matters less than who made them (this chapter) and how they were used (next chapter), for these themes give us unique access to the thoughts and actions of at least part of the subhistoric population. Coins preserve patterns of behavior across a broad spectrum of society, and we begin with the mint and the mind-set of those working there. Coins, after all, are the products of labor and the patterns of thought that guide that labor. Cognitive numismatics, like its older cousin cognitive archaeology, asks how material objects may illuminate the mental processes that shaped them. How did anonymous ancient craftsmen, both individually and as a group, plan out a complex task or respond to new challenges in the workplace? These are key questions because, as is well known, "the amount of information which survives in our [written] sources on the subject of the minting of coins is meager in the extreme."[6]

We must first of all treat coins as a process instead of simply as end products. An archaeological *chaîne opératoire* ("operational sequence") makes explicit the various steps necessary to create an artifact, from acquisition of raw materials and manufacture to its use and eventual abandonment, or loss, or reuse.[7] The Bactrians gained access to gold, silver, copper, tin, and cupronickel by means of mining, panning, war, and trade.[8] The volume of surviving coinages suggests that considerable effort was expended in these endeavors, although it is not yet possible to quantify the workforces and military expeditions marshaled specifically to acquire these metals.[9] Alluvial gold occurs in many rivers in and around Bactria, and lode deposits have been identified throughout the region. Silver and copper mines, some of them ancient, exist in the Badakhshan and Hindu Kush mountains. One of the world's largest deposits of copper, worked since the second century B.C.E., lies sixteen miles (25 km) southeast of Kabul at Ainak. Local sources for cupronickel are also known. Tin, necessary to make bronze, was mined very early in Afghanistan.[10]

Our knowledge of mining operations elsewhere in the ancient world provides a grim picture of what it may have been like for the slaves, condemned criminals, and desperately poor who were the likely diggers in Bactria.[11] In dangerous underground shafts, the rock had to be heated by fires and then cracked with splashes of water. Large chunks of ore had then to be pounded into smaller and smaller pieces by relentless labor. High-temperature cupellation separated the gold and silver from base metals. It should not, of course, be assumed that the requisite metallurgical skills were limited to the Greeks who colonized the region, since metalworking was practiced in Central Asia long before and after the Hellenistic period. Following the large-scale exodus from Ai Khanoum, those who salvaged the site took pains to recover in a systematic way the gold and silver left there. Their ingots have been excavated alongside a balance and weights, and these workers marked one lump in a non-Greek language yet to be deciphered.[12]

Once the requisite raw materials had reached the mint, skilled artisans armed with a cognitive map of the desired mintage could transform the metal into money.[13] Here is where we see through the eyes of some nonroyal Bactrians and discover their daily habits. Most ancient coins were made by hammering a piece of pre-weighed metal, called a flan or blank, between two carved dies.[14] The metal required a complicated system of assaying in order to produce a uniform alloy, which was then cast, often *en chapelet* (using molds), to the appropriate weight standard.[15] The flan would then be cleaned with an acid treatment before being hammered between the dies. One shortcut in this method was to use old coins as blanks, resulting in an overstrike. The frequent inability to obliterate altogether the designs of the host coin (the undertype) provides valuable chronological data. For example,

the mints of Heliocles II overstruck the coins of numerous contemporary or earlier rulers, including Eucratides I, Agathocleia,
Strato I, Antialcidas, Philoxenus, and Hermaeus.[16]

By numismatic convention, the lower die is called the obverse
(or heads) and the upper die is named the reverse (tails). Workers
had to engrave each of these two dies as a mirror image of the
desired coin. Thus, to produce the dies for any set of coins, the die
cutter took up his tools and carved everything backwards, including the inscription. This could be quite challenging and time-
consuming, with commensurate pressures whenever production
rates increased.[17] Especially for tiny coins with minute details, the
use of some sort of magnifier may have been necessary, such as a
plano-convex lens; otherwise, the craftsmen had to be young, myo-
pic, or both.[18] Even so, eyestrain was certainly an occupational
hazard.[19] Needless to say, this method of manufacture meant that
no two dies were exactly the same, and therefore coins minted
using the same die (or dies) were identifiable as die-linked.

Only a few coin dies actually survive from the ancient world,
but one of them happens to be from Bactria and, more precisely,
is said to have been recovered at Ai Khanoum.[20] (See plates 6–8.)
Extant dies are rare not so much because few were ever made;
the coins in the Qunduz Hoard alone represent the production
of 973 separate dies (425 obverses, 548 reverses).[21] Surviving dies
are uncommon because they had to be closely controlled while
in use, and afterward they were generally destroyed or deposited
in temples to keep them out of unscrupulous hands. If the extant
Bactrian die came from Ai Khanoum, it may have been stored in
the palace treasury or, more likely, consigned to one of the city's
temples. It was not being used at the time when the site was
abandoned because its outdated purpose was to strike the reverses
of tetradrachms issued by Demetrius I.

This die is about the size and shape of a small sewing spool (39 mm high; 37 and 35 mm diameters at the ends: 1.5 × 1.4 × 1.4 inches). It is made of heterogeneous bronze, containing 78.4–84.2 percent copper, 15.3–21.1 percent tin, and a trace of iron.[22] It seems likely that its concave shape accommodated tongs or some other clamping device that held the die firmly against the flan as the hammer did its work. The coinage of Demetrius I was struck with an adjusted die axis of 12:00, meaning that the designs on both faces were aligned upright when the finished coin was spun on its vertical axis. To achieve this, the mint workers had to orient the two dies properly for each strike. The small notch on the hammered end of the die may have served this purpose, since it happens to be aligned with the bottom of the reverse composition.[23] Because reverse dies took so much of the force, they tended to wear out more quickly than the obverses, which were anchored securely into an anvil. This surviving example does not seem particularly worn or cracked on its engraved surface, although the hammered end has been badly damaged on the side opposite the notch, and this may explain why the specimen was withdrawn from service. Another possibility is that the die was intentionally broken and retired following the demise of Demetrius. No coins have yet been identified as products of this particular die. While tens of thousands of strikes are possible with a good die, this example may have left little or no trail in the numismatic record of Hellenistic Bactria.

If we could be certain of the die's provenance, which of course we cannot, it might be possible thus to link a particular monogram to a specific place. While ✦ is not especially common on coins found at Ai Khanoum, it is noteworthy that this monogram appears on coinages struck by Demetrius I, Euthydemus II, Agathocles, Pantaleon, Antimachus I, and Eucratides I.[24] This means that ✦ disappeared at the same time that Ai Khanoum was abandoned, and it is the only major monogram to have done so.[25] Nevertheless, a Demetrius die employed elsewhere could have been sent to Ai Khanoum for decommissioning in its treasury or one of its temples. Also, a monogram used at Ai Khanoum need not end with the city's fall, since a magistrate represented by, say, ℞ could have evacuated the area and then continued to use the same monogram at a different locale. Thus, we must stop short of attributing all Bactrian coins bearing ✦ to the mint at Ai Khanoum.

We can, however, see plainly the handiwork of the die's inscriber, no matter where he happened to live and work. It must have taken some skill to fashion a serviceable die out of hardened metal. To give the standing nude figure of Hercules his lifelike pose, the artisan had to sink the hero's impression into the metal. The deeper the cuts and drills into the die, the higher the relief on the resulting coins—the face of Hercules, for example, and the dots governing the shallower strokes for the monogram and lettering. This intaglio technique was the same as that for engravers of gemstones and signet rings—commissions the die cutters may also have performed.[26] The worker responsible for Demetrius's die did a fine job of rendering Hercules in the act of crowning himself, with his club and lion pelt in hand.[27] This artwork accompanies well the inscription that frames it.

As part of his cognitive map, the worker had obviously to be mindful of etching ΒΑΣΙΛΕΩΣ ΔΗΜΗΤΡΙΟΥ backwards, since letters more than images could betray carelessness or error. Carving the Greek words retrograde could be tricky, especially for letters such as Β, Σ, Ε, and Ρ that had to be reversed. Fortunately for the engraver, twelve of the seventeen letters inscribed on this die were symmetrical on a vertical axis and therefore were engraved the same way whether forward or backward: A, I, Λ, Ω, Δ, H, M, T, O, and Υ. The propensity for error was therefore relatively low on this task, as compared with carving backward something more demanding, such as ΒΑΣΙΛΕΩΣ ΣΩΤΗΡΟΣ ΜΕΝΑΝΔΡΟΥ. The difference is analogous to writing the common names ΤΟΜ and STAN retrograde: the s and N require greater care to invert properly and are more likely to cause trouble.

Obviously, numismatists can study the engraving of thousands of dies without actually seeing each one, since the coins struck from the dies faithfully preserve their features. Even the wear and tear on dies, such as distinctive die-breaks, can be tracked. We have only to visualize the missing dies as mirror images of the extant coins, either by reversing photographs of them or by making impressions in clay. In this fashion, it is possible to recreate the cognitive maps of the Bactrian workers as they planned and executed their various tasks. For example, the *chaîne opératoire* for carving a die usually began with the image in the central field, followed afterward by any necessary text. This procedure is evident on many Bactrian coins where the lettering has been squeezed into remaining spaces after the type has been finished. Similarly, some letters have been cramped or displaced to accommodate the central image. (E.g., the lettering beneath the jugate busts in fig. 20.)[28] This is evident, too, on those issues where the legend has intentionally been interrupted by the artwork.[29]

The inscriptions on Bactrian coins reveal a lot about the men chiseling them. When tasked to engrave the inscription, one option would have been for workers to ignore the finished product as a mental template and to proceed instead by copying an already reversed text. Doing so would not require as much thought about the actual words; mere duplication would not even oblige the

Figure 20. Eucratides commemorative tetradrachm, showing his parents, Heliocles and Laodice. Note the displaced lettering beneath the jugate busts, indicating that the images were carved prior to the inscription.

engraver to understand what he was writing.[30] But the artisans indeed did know. It can be demonstrated that Bactrian die cutters were thinking in Greek as they toiled, because whenever words in the Greek coin inscriptions fall out of alignment, they generally do so at the end rather than the beginning.[31] This is the tendency of engravers who were thinking out each word in Greek, engraving the text retrograde from its beginning as though spelling it out from right to left (producing a coin to be read left to right). On tetradrachms of Eucratides with the arched legend ΒΑΣΙΛΕΩΣ ΜΕΓΑΛΟΥ, engravers sometimes used the long spears of the Dioscuri to delineate the beginning and end of these words. Often the text on the coin commences with evenly spaced lettering (ΒΑΣΙΛ...) but ends with a jumble of mashed letters at the end (...ΑΛΟΥ), because room has run out at the spear points.[32] This happens if the artisan knows (or believes he knows) the language and starts each word at its real (not reversed) beginning. Simply put, our unseen workers were spelling Greek, not just replicating a string of meaningless symbols set before them. As an example, persons unfamiliar with the Cyrillic alphabet might copy backwards a Russian text by working as readily from the end of the text as its beginning. But given a text in familiar English, French, or German, the same person is more likely to work retrograde while starting at the text's beginning.

Another proof that die cutters did not simply follow an already reversed text can be found on a coin of the Indo-Greek king Lysias.[33] Here the name of the king appears backwards on the coin, meaning that it was accidentally engraved forward as ΛΥΣΙΟΥ on the die. The workman thought and inscribed the name without remembering to invert it on the die. Some early Seleucid issues from Bactria show similar lapses.[34] It is significant, of course, not only that these errors were made in the first place but also that coins struck from faulty dies were not withheld from use. This compounds the nature of all stumbles, because botched coins in circulation represent several missteps within the mint.

Errors, in fact, can provide our best evidence for what was (or was not) on the minds of Bactria's workers. On another bronze coin struck in the name of Lysias, for example, someone did catch an error and then, rather halfheartedly, tried to fix it.[35] The die cutter absentmindedly omitted the letters IK in the middle of the epithet AN[IK]HTOY. His solution was simply to insert these missing letters incongruously at the bottom of the die, just ahead of the king's name. No supervisor apparently noticed or cared about this slipshod behavior. Such coin legends remain as material expressions of ancient states of mind. One is reminded of the Roman whose thoughts must have wandered as he engraved a child's tombstone. The distracted workman looked up his model and etched what he saw: HIC IACET CORPVS PVERI NOMINANDI ("Here lies the body of the child *name to be supplied*").[36]

Cognitive numismatics tries, literally, to connect the dots in order to understand planning as well as execution in the engraving process. We can discover on many coins the telltale signs of preparatory draftsmanship, usually in the form of small guide dots sunk into the die. These could be drilled to help form individual letters and the monograms (as on the Demetrius die), or to align the inscription as a whole, or both. The guide holes for individual letters probably served to keep the text properly sized, since rounded letters engraved without the use of dots (O, Θ, Ω) often appear too short: ΑΝΤΙΜΑΧΟΥ or ΑΓΑΘΟΚΛΕΟΥΣ.[37] While these dots are a common feature on Bactrian and other Hellenistic coins, the oversized monsters of Eucratides and Amyntas reveal them most clearly. They allow us to see that the mind of the man who created dies for the latter coins was fastidious and focused; the former was indecisive, careless, and yet also perhaps brilliant.[38]

The die cutter of the Amyntas double decadrachms had firmly in mind a finished product that exhibited a semicircular arrangement of letters for the royal title and epithet.[39] To achieve this end, he first devised a tool to use as a master template for his dies, probably in the form of a simple multipointed punch that transferred to each new reverse die a set of two concentric circles of guide dots. This arrangement of dots appears on all the reverse dies for this series, and the dots extend into the exergue (lower quadrant) where they are not needed, since the king's name was engraved there horizontally.[40] This means that there are guide dots even where none would be necessary, showing that indeed the master template was applied as step one in the engraving process (fig. 21). Next, within the inner circle of dots, the engraver neatly framed the coin type. Finally, he cut (backwards) the upper inscription ΒΑΣΙΛΕΩΣ ΝΙΚΑΤΟΡΟΣ within the arc of concentric circles, and the lower inscription ΑΜΥΝΤΟΥ

Figure 21. Reverse of a double decadrachm of Amyntas, shown as a mirror image in order to replicate the appearance of the die (dot pattern emphasized).

straight across at the bottom. The strokes forming individual letters (except, of course, for round omicrons) were guided by an independent set of deeper dots. It is obvious here as on other coins that the spacing of the text accommodates the already engraved type (at the tip of Zeus's scepter, for example) and not the other way around.

As we follow the process of the artisan who some years earlier made the dies for Eucratides' famous twenty-stater coin, we observe a very different pattern of thought and behavior.[41] This anonymous worker seems not to have begun his commission with an appropriate cognitive map, since he obviously had to erase part of his work and start again. Clear traces of this debacle can still be observed on the reverse. Unlike the engraver of Amyntas's dies a half-century later, this die cutter did not use a visible template for the overall design. Nevertheless, the centering of the type is quite expertly done. The only oversight on this part of the die is that the engraver failed to continue the shaft of the background sarissa at the horse's rump.[42] When the worker finished the Dioscuri design, he began cutting the monogram 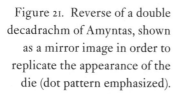. Extraneous guide dots here suggest a slight repositioning of the symbol. The upper inscription ΒΑΣΙΛΕΩΣ ΜΕΓΑΛΟΥ was at first aligned retrograde straight across the top of the die.[43] The engraver did not anticipate that this text would not fit properly. When the problem finally became apparent, he chiseled out his first attempt and substituted a less crowded semicircular alignment that followed a precise arc for the letters B through M, after which the last six letters strayed outward. The king's name was also cut slightly off center at the bottom of the die.

Obviously, this artisan did not bother to remove all traces of his fumbling, and he had no intention of starting fresh with a new die after already carving the Dioscuri on this one. His lack of foresight at one end of the *chaîne opératoire,* and his indifference at the other, give us pause. This was no innocuous local bronze issue, but rather the most ostentatious coin ever produced in antiquity. It must have been a noteworthy assignment to make this die, and it seems unlikely that sloppy work would go unnoticed—or even unpunished. What, then, was going on inside his workshop the day this man made this die? Was the engraver careless, carefree, overworked, or preoccupied? Was he an ancient free spirit given to trial and error even on the weightiest of royal commissions, or was he just in over his head?

Some scholars have theorized that this engraver was the very first to make a Eucratides die after that king ordered the title ΜΕΓΑΛΟΥ added to his coinage; therefore, the artisan did not anticipate the challenges of inserting these seven extra letters.[44] Even so, this means that the man gave no prior thought to this special task. He worked with an old cognitive map unhindered by grabbing a sketch pad or measuring tools. Now fresh numismatic evidence shows that this engraver was not the first or only worker to deal with the expanded text (see plate 9); tetradrachms with the longer inscription engraved horizontally have now come to light, albeit with different monograms (Ρ and Φ).[45] Had the engraver of the twenty-stater die not seen already the crowding of letters on these circulating varieties? Did a better idea not occur to him until after he had carved himself into a corner? The innovation of the semicircular legend was a stroke of genius, but a belated one that tells us that some workers in Eucratides' day did not plan ahead.

Another interesting example of a reworked die can be found in the Qunduz Hoard. Coins 47 and 48 with monogram ☐, minted by Demetrius II, share obverse and reverse dies. These tetradrachms show a clear anomaly on the reverse, where the ends of Athena's spear appear twice. Raoul Curiel and Gérard Fussman thought this to be the result of deliberate restriking after flipping the reverse die to correct the coins' die axis from 6:00 to 12:00.[46] Colin Kraay suggested a simpler explanation.[47] Noting the difficulties surrounding the repositioning of the dies so precisely, Kraay argued that the extra spear points must have existed on the die itself. So, either an old die was partly ground down and reengraved, or some lapse occurred while cutting a die and the worker rotated it, erased most of it, and started fresh; one way or the other, the original spear points lingered as telltale signs of the process. This episode indicates a certain degree of stress in the mint, either from an initial engraving or striking error, or from the need to recycle quickly an old die. More will be said about the die-linked obverses of these same coins below.

Cognitive numismatics therefore tasks us to consider general working conditions as well as an individual worker's competence. What was the rate of error on inscribed dies in Bactria as a whole, and what circumstances might explain those errors?[48] At times, engravers in Bactria so blundered their craft that they actually misspelled their king's name, the sort of behind-the-scenes mistake that could hardly be made more public. From the area of

Bactra, for example, we find an obol of Eucratides I with two letters missing from the king's name: EΥPATIAΥ.[49] Is this mere carelessness, or the inability to recognize and rectify carelessness? Both possibilities seem significant for a basic understanding of life in Hellenistic Bactria. Periods of carelessness on a large scale betoken poor training, lax supervision, or stressful overwork, which may be signs of larger troubles beyond the mints. The inability to identify and correct mistakes raises the question of linguistic background and facility, which may be clues about the ethnicity of the workforce.[50] After all, some coinages (of Heliocles II, e.g.) exhibit clear linguistic variations in the rendering of the king's name in Kharoshthi (*Heliyakreya, Heliyakresa, Heliyakrea*). Furthermore, these variations seem to be regional, since they are specific to particular monograms.[51] This may indicate local recruitment of die cutters. The practice noted earlier of engraving the text as though spelling out each word does not support the idea of completely Greekless die cutters who merely copied meaningless symbols, so occurrences of error in the Greek are indeed consequential. Do these deviations from expected norms mean that Hellenism occasionally weakened or broke down in Bactria?

The question of Bactria's cultural matrix used to be argued on aesthetic grounds—for example, the artwork on these coins looks less Greek than on those; this royal portrait appears Sogdian, but that one is purely Hellenic; one side of the Eucratides gold giant (the reverse with the erasure) is the work of a talented Greek, but not the other. These historical judgments remain woefully subjective and qualitative. The notion that in Bactria good art is Greek and bad art is native invites bias and bigotry. The rightness or wrongness of a seemingly Greek sculpture simply cannot be measured with the same precision as that of a

Greek text. Thus, unlike perceived lapses in art, errors in language can be quantified and lend themselves to objective analysis.

Using a controlled sample of dies that eliminates the selective bias of marketed, collectible coins or forged intrusions, reign-by-reign error rates may be ascertained for the Bactrian kingdom (table 1).[52] The data encompass all mistakes, from simple one-stroke errors (e.g., failure to add the crossbar to letter A) to multiple and more complex blunders (e.g., missing or intrusive letters).

Overall, the Greek vocabulary engraved on Bactrian coins remained quite small and repetitive during this period (just two dozen words and names all together), yet the rate of error increased meaningfully during the reign of Euthydemus I and again before and after the fall of Ai Khanoum, which seems to have occurred during or soon after the reign of Eucratides I.[53] All the errors on the dies of Euthydemus I and Antimachus, however, are of the simple variety, whereas 55 percent of the flawed dies for Eucratides I and II have complex errors.[54] For Demetrius II, the percentage of error dies with complex problems rises to 75 percent, and for Heliocles it is 62 percent. This suggests that the mints of Bactria experienced both a rise in the rate, and in the magnitude, of error shortly before and after the abandonment of Ai Khanoum. These data are statistically relevant for the deterioration of work in the mints, for the probability of an increase in error this large occurring merely by chance is much less than 1 percent.[55]

Table 2 uses as a control word in our sample the genitive-case form (ΒΑΣΙΛΕΩΣ) of the ubiquitous Greek title ΒΑΣΙΛΕΥΣ, found on nearly every coin of every king. The engraving errors can be one-stroke oversights, or (especially in the reign of Heliocles) serious spelling lapses. The increase in both the rate and the severity of mistakes can readily be appreciated in these blun-

TABLE 1

Incidence of Error on Bactrian Coin Dies, 250–130 B.C.E.

King	Inscribed dies	Error dies	Flawed (percent)
Diodotus I or II	31	0	0
Euthydemus I	160	11	7
Demetrius I	18	0	0
Euthydemus II	9	0	0
Agathocles	18	0	0
Apollodotus	1	0	0
Antimachus	20	3	15
Eucratides I	145	7	5
Eucratides II	118	4	3
Plato	10	0	0
Demetrius II	44	4	9
Heliocles	180	43	19

dered dies from the workshops of Euthydemus I, Antimachus I, Eucratides I–II, Demetrius II, and Heliocles. What was going on?

One might immediately assume that die cutters less familiar with Greek were responsible for these changes. This would be evidence of a *culture mixte* and a rapid influx of indigenous artisans employed at the mints.[56] But even so, it does not necessarily follow that good Greek could be written only by good Greeks. Sophytos at Kandahar, Atrosokes at Takht-i Sangin, Hyspasines at Delos, and Oxybazus, Oxyboakes, and others at Ai Khanoum were men with non-Greek names whose facility with the Hellenic language has been attested. (See chap. 6, above.) The latter who served in the treasury, of course, were supervised by personnel with Greek names. If we blame the rise of error on the linguistic incompetence of an increased non-Greek workforce, then there remains the problem of why their presumably Greek over-

TABLE 2

Incidence of Specific Engraving Errors in the Word
ΒΑΣΙΛΕΩΣ, 250–130 B.C.E.

Control Word Error	King	Number
ΒΛΣΙΛΕΩΣ	Euthydemus I	1
	Demetrius II	1
	Heliocles	10
bΑΣΙΛΕΩΣ	Antimachus	2
	Eucratides I	1
	Heliocles	4
ΒΑΣ:ΛΕΩΣ	Eucratides I	2
ΒΛΣΙ.ΛΕΩΣ	Demetrius II	2
bΛΣΙΛΕΩΣ	Heliocles	7
.ΛΣΙΛΕΩΣ	Heliocles	1
ΙΛΣΙΛΕΩΣ	Heliocles	5
ΒΑΣΙΛΕΣ	Heliocles	1
ΒΑΣΙΛΕΕΩ	Heliocles	1
ΒΑΣΙΛΛΕΩΣ	Heliocles	1
ΒΑΣΙΙΛΕΩΣ	Demetrius II	1
	Heliocles	1
ΒΑΙΛΛΕΩΣ	Heliocles	1

seers did not catch and correct the lapses. Also, the notion that
most ancient Greeks read everything aloud raises the question
of whether their cousins in Bactria did so even with their currency. If so, this surely would have tested the mass of coinage
through the mouthing of the inscriptions on them by Greeks all
across the kingdom. Were they, too, less skilled in the language
of their ancestral homeland?

The chief excavator of Ai Khanoum does not think so. According to Paul Bernard, the Greeks in that city assiduously preserved their language as the veritable cement of their national

identity: "They continued to speak and write Greek in an uncontaminated form right to the end, as evidenced by the inscriptions found during the excavations."[57] Setting aside the lack of evidence for spoken language, it is true that at Ai Khanoum and elsewhere in Central Asia there is growing epigraphic documentation of the high standard of written, even self-consciously erudite, Greek. Clearchus set up the Delphic maxims with a verse preamble. Heliodotus honored his favorite kings. The non-Greek Sophytos boasted of his Hellenic education and put it on public display. But this is evidence from a certain stratum of the ancient population, one that had the means and inclination to set up expensive monuments at Ai Khanoum, Kuliab, and Kandahar. What about everyone else? The linguistic landscape of Central and South Asia was shaped by numerous factors, including intermarriage and bilingualism. Although we lack the same level of documentary evidence as found elsewhere in the Hellenistic world, particularly Egypt, it is significant that the treaties between the Seleucids and India included provisions for intermarriage.[58] The children of such unions might learn a mixture of languages, as had the Branchidae of Sogdia who became bilingual ("bilingues") and gradually spoke a degenerated form of Greek ("paulatim a domestico externo sermone degeneres").[59] The significance of local languages used alongside Greek has now been demonstrated by bilingual inscriptions on everything from coins and bowls to royal edicts.

Were die cutters and their supervisors as competent in Greek as were the ruling Hellenes and wealthier native peoples of the region? The coin inscriptions provide a negative answer, even though they actually appear on official state documents. Some people somewhere in Bactria's cities, thinking in Greek, botched the Greek. Their handiwork does not exactly square with Homayun Sidky's characterization of places like Ai Khanoum as "a purely Greek city" where "there can be no doubt that the inhabitants ... were Greeks who retained their full ethnolinguistic identity" until the site was suddenly overrun and "all traces of Greek civilization [were] swept away."[60] Sir William Tarn, who did not know of Ai Khanoum or the inscriptions, nevertheless reached the same conclusion based on his aesthetic judgments about the coins. He wrote of the nomad conquest of Bactria in the time of Heliocles:[61]

> One section [of Greeks]—a very small one—is known to have been exterminated: the Greek coinage of Bactria remained fine to the end, and then the great Bactrian artists vanished from the world; no trace of their peculiar skill in portraiture ever occurs again, in India or anywhere else. The likeliest supposition is that one battle sufficed to destroy most of the Greek aristocracy.

Tarn's old theory about the artist X and his school of gifted Greek die cutters (see chap. 4, above) draws a dramatic line: the end of X marks the spot where Hellenism succumbed to a holocaust. Those adhering to the narrative tradition in Bactrian studies tend to envision a sudden, stark, violent boundary between a Greek Bactria and then a barbarian Bactria. The change, whether explained archaeologically or numismatically, allegedly came about as a single tragic event. Cognitive numismatics, however, favors a different approach that uses quantitative coin analysis and focuses on processes. This allows us to understand that the Greek coinages and the texts on them were not fine to the end. A period of increasingly corrupted engraving, either tolerated or unnoticed, was under way in Bactria's mints before the fall of Ai Khanoum and the eventual collapse of Hellenistic Bactria north of the Hindu Kush after the demise of Heliocles.

This may mean, of course, that the mints were being staffed in this period by workers whose Greek-language skills were marginal—either ethnic Hellenes who were losing their language or Central Asians not altogether fluent in Greek. But this trend must be examined in conjunction with a larger question: Why were their failings tolerated by those whose language skills allegedly remained high? The answer to this quandary may stem from production rather than personnel. A change in the ethnicity or education of the workers may be just part of a larger transformation in basic working conditions brought on by overtaxing demands. The first period of elevated incidence of error occurred during the reign of Euthydemus I, when simple one-stroke mistakes show up on the dies. This happened in the context of the disruptive Seleucid invasion of Bactria by Antiochus the Great. The capital, Bactra, in fact, endured a prolonged siege during which its dependency Sogdia seems to have gained its independence. These circumstances may have adversely impacted workers' abilities or inclination to produce pristine dies at a time when coinage had to be manufactured quickly under wartime conditions. In other words, times of anxiety and urgency may be manifested in the mental lapses of die cutters and the inattentiveness of officials to those lapses. The escape of an obvious mint error into circulation from one of Euthydemus's main mints exemplifies this problem.[62] While striking a rare gold distater with monogram ⟨symbol⟩, a flan was set on the anvil die without first removing the previous strike. The hammer then drove down the reverse die, so that the fresh coin received the design of the punch and the same design, only incuse, from the last strike. This so-called brockage of a high-value coin apparently caught no one's attention at the time.

The next, and far more serious, wave of error commenced before the abandonment of Ai Khanoum and grew worse thereafter. This runs counter to the notion that the city fell without any prior signs of trouble in Bactria.[63] Quantifiable mistakes on the coins betoken a buildup of significant strains throughout the Bactrian workforce, for the problem was widespread and not isolated to one or two mints or magistrates. The incidence and tolerance of error reflect a period of increased production demands, lax supervision, less training, and perhaps major internal distractions. Procedural as well as personnel changes in the mints may have abbreviated or eliminated a quality control step that allowed the manufacture of a less consistent product. One sign of such a change is not only the use of dies that were improperly engraved but also the continued employment of dies that had become badly worn or even cracked. The run of ten coins in the Qunduz Hoard that were among those struck from a progressively more defective obverse die suggests that quantity trumped quality.[64] Significantly, one reverse die used in this sequence had an obvious misspelling of the king's name that slipped past the minters.[65] Another pair of coins in this run shared the reengraved reverse die discussed above, which itself indicated stress in the mint.[66] A further signal of new production obligations is the rapid increase in the number of monograms being used, whether they signify more mints or more magistrates, from about fifteen for Euthydemus I to over fifty for Eucratides I.[67]

Chronologically, the coinage manufacturing system became strained under circumstances leading up to the nomadic incursions. Clearly, everything in the region was not fine right to the day (or, in Tarn's scenario, the battle) that doomed the Greek rulers and their artisans. In fact, those invasions may have been the consequence rather than the cause of Bactria's collapse. Whatever the immediate contingencies (civil war, plague, earthquake, environmental poisoning, or some other series of disas-

ters) that prompted the Greeks to evacuate the city at Ai Khanoum, conditions may have already led the workers in the mints
and their supervisors to abandon the highest standards of their
craft. The nomadic invaders may simply have moved in to take
advantage of some worsening situation, much as they had done
in Sogdia when Greek fought Greek during the siege of Bactra.
Conditions deteriorated further after the assassination of Eucratides as the stresses on the resources and peoples of Heliocles'
realm pushed the rate and severity of mint errors higher. The
nomads have become a convenient scapegoat for the entire
decline and fall of Hellenistic Bactria, but on this frontier—as
later on the Roman—internal crises and systems collapse may be
a better explanation.[68]

What seems certain now is that maintaining a pure and uncontaminated form of Hellenism was not the paramount aim of the
Bactrian population in those times of crisis. Care was still apparently taken in all other stages of the *chaîne opératoire,* ensuring that
there was an adequate—indeed increased—supply of bullion
properly assayed. Yet, flawed dies pounding out tens of thousands
of coins each were tolerated. Was there no time to check one in
five dies, or one in every few thousand coins? If not, the situation
must have been dire. Perhaps, too, many of the coins were meant
for those who had different expectations from the Greeks, such as
foreign mercenaries. The mass-produced coinages, as opposed to
a few monuments and inscriptions, prove that Bactrian society
was in a state of flux and that normative behaviors were less
guarded. That, at least, seems to be the lesson of cognitive numismatics as it examines the front end of the *chaîne opératoire.* Next,
we turn to behaviors reflected beyond those mints.

CHAPTER NINE

Coins and the Collapse of Civilization

Cognitive Numismatics II

In the autumn of 1962, a freshly plowed field in the town of Rawa Mazowiecka yielded an unexpected find.[1] Near the picturesque castle ruins, a silver drachm minted over two millennia earlier in Afghanistan emerged incongruously from the soil of central Poland.[2] No one knows how this coin of Menander I Soter got there, or when—such are the mysterious travels of money.[3] But in its movements beyond the mint, a coin like this reflects additional human behaviors besides those of its makers, from transporting, spending, losing, hoarding, defacing, reissuing, wearing, imitating, and counterfeiting to collecting and perhaps studying. There are even some nonhuman behaviors that may come into play, such as the Suffolk chicken that carried around an ancient gold coin in its crop having mistaken it for a kernel of corn.[4] These are all links in the *chaîne opératoire* that might take an artifact from mine to mint to market to museum. In these last steps, too, scholars may glimpse the ancient world that bustled below the Bactrian king list.

When a bronze or cupronickel coin left its mint, it tended to circulate nearby, since its extrinsic value depended on local conventions.[5] This was the medium for most daily business—the small change of the regional economy. Hellenistic hoards of bronze coinages are therefore very rare; household savings normally took the form of silver and sometimes gold. As official conduits to the masses, the ability of token money to reach down into the poorest levels of society was seldom fully utilized. For quite some time, fiduciary currency in Bactria kept its messages plain and simple, forgoing royal portraits, fancy titles, and commemorations. Instead, bronzes usually showed deities rather than kings, along with totem animals and objects (fig. 22). Some of these designs had specifically local significance.[6] In time, it was on this low-denomination currency that the state generally acknowledged the importance of native cultures in terms of local scripts, square shapes, and non-Greek deities.

Large-denomination silver and gold mintages, on the other hand, appeared more obviously royal and more steadfastly Greek; they held their intrinsic value over great distances and were as acceptable in Syria as in Central Asia. Bactria's mints pounded out more tetradrachms than anything else. (The Indo-Greek mints produced more drachms.) This silver's first stop was normally in the hands of soldiers, suppliers, and various state officials. Indeed, most Hellenistic economies were military in nature, and the striking of coinage in sudden surges usually betokens a war.[7] Coins would then trickle through the markets and banks, and sometimes return to the state treasury as payments for tolls and taxes. As tetradrachms slowly wore out (at about a rate of 5–18 milligrams per year), the state treasury would hold them back for remelting and restriking.[8] Along the way, some coins became immobilized in hoards, as random losses, or as something other than currency—such as jewelry. Those coins

Figure 22. Bronze coin of Diodotus II, depicting laureate Zeus (obverse) and Artemis running with a torch (reverse). A hunting dog bounds at her feet.

that eventually escaped the melting pot might be collected and studied millennia later by a Bayer or Bopearachchi.

A more concrete sense of this *chaîne opératoire* may be found at Ai Khanoum. There, a large private house stood about 165 yards (150 m) outside the walls, its back to the city and its front court-yard facing the northeast frontier beyond.[9] (See map 3.) No one knows who lived there, halfway between the main gate and the banks of the Oxus River, but its inhabitants had a front-row seat to watch everything that came or went—kings, commerce, armies, or enemies. We might imagine that the massive defensive ramparts and ditch of Ai Khanoum gave some comfort to those living nearby in this house. The fortified city with its impressive palace and arsenal was nevertheless a relatively small settlement on an exposed border of Hellenistic Bactria. Its walls stretched a total of 3.8 miles (6.12 km), whereas those of Alexandria Eschate were reportedly 6.1 miles (9.84 km) and the ramparts at Mara-canda and Antiochia Margiana longer still, at about 7.1 miles (11.48 km).[10] Crammed with monumental public buildings, Ai Khanoum reminds us more of Washington, D.C., than of Houston or Chicago. Just as monuments, memorials, and the National Mall dominate the modern U.S. capital, Ai Khanoum beneath its acropolis was a sprawl of impressive state structures leaving space for little else. In fact, the French archaeologists sought but never found a marketplace, workshops, or the remains of other everyday establishments.[11] Yet, there was ample public opulence; one archaeologist imagines the pomp and ceremony of the palace, with its elaborate displays of wealth.[12] The city was built to impress anyone who strolled its avenues in antiquity, just as its monumental remains have mesmerized modern scholars. Militarily, however, it turned out to be no more effective than the Maginot Line.

Depending upon which buildings excite them most—for instance, the theater, gymnasium, or main temple—modern investigators either insist how thoroughly Hellenized Bactria became or stress how marginally the Greeks were able to impose themselves on Central Asia. Fair enough; but how did those in the house outside Ai Khanoum perceive this world? Were they smug cultural elitists? If so, who sat beside them in the six thousand seats of the theater, since the other forty mansions in the city could not possibly supply so many patrons? Did Greek settlers come from many miles around to claim those seats; or could (some) non-Greeks attend; or was the great theater all but empty at every performance? Between that house and theater on more urgent days, were there Greek warriors enough to man those massive walls, or was the idea just to awe potential troublemakers—Greeks, natives, and nomads alike—hoping that none would call the bluff? Was the finery of the arsenal's parade shields, silvered buckles, and gilded weapons meant for much real fighting—just as the theater may not have been meant for much real entertainment?[13] We inevitably wonder, because for some reason (or reasons) the people in that house joined a great exodus from this site that no longer seemed safe enough to shelter them. There was no trusting the walls of Ai Khanoum as there had been at Bactra against the huge, sophisticated army of Antiochus the Great. There was no waiting for relief forces to arrive. Instead, the excavations reveal a crisis of nerve so complete that many people scurried away from this house, this palace, this city, this region—and never came back.

In the movement of coins beyond the mints, we glimpse the cusp of that process. Over the years, the members of the household living outside Ai Khanoum handled many kinds of coins circulating through the region; they left sixty-eight of them behind when their home was abandoned. Five of these specimens were lost on the premises in the same way that coins always slip away during the routines of everyday life.[14] The oldest examples of this lost money had been minted during the reigns of the first Seleucid monarchs and, being quite small and made of bronze, these two items probably inspired no real effort to recover them—if they were missed at all—in rooms 2 and 3 of the house. The next two were larger bronze denominations, one struck by Euthydemus II with (local?) monogram Φ and the other an as yet unidentified issue considerably corroded; these were lost in the kitchen. The only silver coin dropped and not found by its owner was a small Indian punch-marked example excavated in the courtyard of the house, one of only four such coins among the stray finds at Ai Khanoum—two of them excavated in the main temple within the city, and the other in the theater.[15] Whether these karshapana issues circulated regularly as currency in Bactria is not certain, but the temple and theater were high-traffic areas, and there were thousands stored in the Ai Khanoum treasury, from which at least 677 were subsequently pillaged.[16] (See above, chap. 6.) The assumption among archaeologists is that the latter represent the spoils of Eucratides' wars but that the specimen lost in the courtyard of the extramural house may have been obtained in some other way and used as currency or bullion.[17] An isolated coin found far beyond its mint, like the Indo-Greek drachm in Poland, had perhaps transitioned from currency to commodity. The karshapana at Ai Khanoum, however, may have been familiar enough to pass in trade.[18] It was more valuable in any case than the fiduciary bronze coins lost about the house.

One might expect more determination to retrieve a silver coin than a bronze, which is the normal behavior.[19] Yet, some unknown circumstance prevented success in this case, just as misfortune bedeviled those who never found the other three Indian punch-marked coins, plus an obol of Antimachus I, an obol of Eucratides I, an Indo-Greek drachm of Apollodotus I, and even one gold stater of Antiochus II lost about the city.[20] The mislaying of money has an archaeological pattern that reflects a nearly universal human behavior: coin losses are proportional to the value, volume, and appearance of the artifacts.[21] Thus, the everyday losses at Ai Khanoum were this handful of shiny, precious-metal coins, plus thirty-two times that number of bronze token coinages that were harder to see in the soil and not always worth searching for with diligence. What is unusual in the case of Ai Khanoum is that most of the precious-metal losses came relatively late in the city's life, and half came from India.

The owner of the house left behind a far greater treasure than a dropped karshapana. Hidden in the wall of his kitchen lay a stash of sixty-three silver tetradrachms, a collection of considerable value deliberately secreted away in a bag or box. The oldest coins in the hoard had been struck more than 150 years earlier and were from as far away as Macedonia; the most recent came from the Bactrian mints of Apollodotus I and Eucratides I.[22] This bundle of concealed wealth might be classified as either a savings or an emergency hoard.[23] The former were amassed over time, tended to be of a single denomination, often contained heavier examples of a mintage, generally were kept in a house, sometimes remained chronologically stratified in their containers, and might be known only to the owner—whose sudden death or dementia could prevent his heirs from reclaiming the treasure. On the other hand, emergency hoards were set aside quickly in the face of imminent danger, frequently buried away from dwellings, often held a miscellany of valuables alongside the coins reflecting whatever was available in circulation, and were meant to be unhoarded as soon as the peril had passed—unless the owner did not survive or could not safely return. The Ai Khanoum hoard seems to fit better the savings profile, as money perhaps set aside for a dowry or taxes, but individual occurrences are notoriously difficult to assess.[24] Using the general pay scale for a foot soldier in this period, this hoard might represent over eight months' salary (or four months' for cavalry).[25]

The key question is not why the coins were hidden but why they were never reclaimed. It is this nonrecovery of hoards that tells us about conditions at the time, for finding groups of hoards from a given period at a given place provides a useful misery index. Simply stated, valuable caches of coins do not get retrieved for many reasons, most of them bad: conscription, civil disturbances, epidemics, military invasions, famines, and natural disasters.[26] One of these things probably happened to the owner of this house, and several other hoarders nearby, during the reign of Eucratides, since no later coins are among the stray finds or hidden coins from Ai Khanoum or its environs. (See chap. 5, above.) The small but significant cluster of unreclaimed hoards from Ai Khanoum and Kuliab suggests a regional crisis of some complexity. For example, we now know that the Greeks never returned to resettle the area, but the evidence does not clearly show whether the refugees anticipated this or not. The amount of transportable wealth left behind at Ai Khanoum could indicate a sudden abandonment with every intention to return.[27] In this case, an emergency initially thought temporary later grew more dire than expected, precluding repatriation. On the other hand, the exodus may have been too desperate to allow the retrieval of hoarded coinage from the treasury or some private houses. These people would put immediate self-preservation above all other considerations. Of course, a single crisis might elicit a full range of responses, depending upon the individuals involved: Some might take the time to unhoard; others might simply take to the hills. Persons might even reverse their behaviors (as at Pompeii during the eruption of Vesuvius), first hiding their valuables and anticipating return, then deciding to take their valuables with them—leaving behind fewer hoards to be found in modern times. This practice of reverse hoarding must be taken into account for extreme emergencies. Thus, the comparatively small number of private hoards left at Ai Khanoum may represent a growing crisis of confidence.

For some, the traditional explanation of a nomadic blitzkrieg into Bactria may suffice to account for this behavior. The present state of evidence cannot rule out so simple and straightforward an interpretation. After all, the building boom at Ai Khanoum associated with Eucratides' successful wars in India would appear to support the narrative of a thriving kingdom suddenly caught unaware by advancing nomads. In the past, archaeologists and historians have generally favored such dramatic explanations for the collapse of any ancient city or civilization. They opt for a vigorous cause proportional to a devastating effect, namely an overwhelming horde sufficient to force the abandonment of a site like Ai Khanoum in which so much had been invested. A few might go so far as to make the event personal; for example, it has been proposed that the nomads despoiled Ai Khanoum specifically to punish Eucratides for his previous reconquest of Sogdia.[28] Other scholars advocate a systems approach that allows for multiple and sometimes disproportionate causation. These investigators do not search in vain for the first arrow fired, nor even for those who may have aimed it. Such actions are likely unknowable and often unimportant, since what really matters in a dynamic system are its aggregate reactions to any variety of such stimuli, large or small.[29]

Interest in the general problem of systems collapse has inspired a number of models, most of them drawing attention to the relative complexity of the city, state, or civilization involved.[30] One of the latest approaches, called self-organized criticality (SOC), has been borrowed from the realms of the physical and biological sciences and applied to all sorts of historical phenomena (e.g., riots, wars, revolutions, famines, failed states).[31] Soc models tend to be very reliant upon the mathematical analysis of more data than a Bactria can supply, and even where quantifiable data are rich (such as in modern market collapses) there is still much debate about the explanatory value of these models.[32] Yet, even the critics of SOC acknowledge the utility of these models as a means to conceptualize problems like societal collapses in a way that encourages fresh thinking.[33] It may be helpful, therefore, to examine the fall of Ai Khanoum and the subsequent collapse of Hellenistic Bactria in terms of something (or some things) other than just one or two massive nomadic invasions.[34] To do so, we must seek evidence that Bactria was becoming an increasingly complex, hypersensitive state subject to any shock, trivial or not, that might trigger a collapse (a so-called complexity cascade). This complexity entails not necessarily a more advanced society but rather one that is expanding and becoming increasingly complicated, interconnected, and interdependent while at the same time exhibiting hierarchies and inequalities. Such states self-organize until they reach a threshold of instability, prone thereafter to cascade out of control. In these cases, a system may rapidly collapse to a less complex level without any apparent or agreed-upon trigger, much like an avalanche or a stock-market crash.

The literary and archaeological evidence in a traditional exercise of the generation, verification, and integration of data (GVI) do hint at an increased rate of complexity growth for Bactria. Written sources describe, albeit briefly, the expansion of royal power into India during a period of widespread civil war among competing Bactrian dynasties. We read that the Parthians and nomads threatened the region, that at least one Bactrian ruler shared his throne (a practice now independently confirmed by documentary texts), and that this king was inexplicably assassinated and desecrated by his co-ruling son while a contemporary rival was revered in India. Signs of increasing complexity and instability also appear in the archaeological record. Frontier defenses were expanded in the north and, whether for show or not, the walls of Ai Khanoum underwent repeated rebuilding. The palace and its treasury at Ai Khanoum were being enlarged on a grand scale and packed with valuables drawn from far afield, through either commerce or war. Managing those materials in the treasury was a mixed but stratified bureaucracy of men bearing Greek and non-Greek names. The architecture of the city was also intricately mixed, yet archaeologists describe a city that restricted access to certain areas based perhaps on social and ethnic identities.[35]

The tantalizing hints offered by these kinds of sources can be enhanced by drawing upon the more continuous record supplied by numismatic data. In general, coinages reflect the societies that produce and use them. Without question, the mintages immediately preceding the collapse of Hellenistic Bactria had grown far more complex than those of a few generations earlier. The coins document a much greater societal concern about royal legitimacy, kinship, projections of power, and divinity. Coins help to prove that the pace of kingmaking quickened considerably after Euthydemus I, from three Bactrian kings in a period of fifty years (ca. 250–200 B.C.E.) to about twelve Bactrian and Indo-Greek kings over the next fifty.[36] The number of monograms employed by Euthydemus and then Eucratides more than tripled, a sure indicator of complexity growth, as shown above in chapter 8. The messages on the money also became rapidly more complicated, with a broadening audience from different cultures. Thus, the simple coins of Euthydemus I carry a portrait bust, name, and royal title in a single language, whereas those of Eucratides I mirror a far more complex society respondent to multiple languages and additional varieties of portraiture, regalia, weight standard, shape, denomination, deities, and titulature. The extraordinary commemorative coinages of Eucratides, Agathocles, and Antimachus manifest a quantum leap in the interplay of society and coinage. Even more striking, perhaps, are the remarkably multicultural mintages of a king like Agathocles, whose use of Indian deities and scripts attests to the interdependent nature of his realm. One might argue that Bactria had progressed from a colonial typology of *terra nullius* in the fourth century B.C.E. to a shared cultural milieu in the third and then a middle ground in the second.[37] In the end, this evolution made Bactria the most numismatically complex state in the world.

Hellenistic Bactria became a boiling pot as well as a melting pot. It has already been demonstrated that mints were pounding out coins at an unprecedented and error-prone rate, suggesting a system under considerable stress. Those strains must not be limited to cities alone, for in a complex society the interdependent subsystems directly impact each other. The numismatic *chaîne opératoire* carried these stresses all the way back to the mines themselves, located in the hinterland of Ai Khanoum. There the procurement of ore had to keep pace with the demand for massive outlays of coinage, and the dire environmental byproducts of ancient mining surely included watershed metal contamination and bioaccumulation of toxins, all perilously upstream from the city.[38] It is perhaps noteworthy that, once abandoned, Ai Khanoum was never rehabilitated as a city by subsequent societies—unlike other urban sites in Central Asia.

Whether we call the result a complexity cascade, a systems collapse, or a societal overshoot, in the parlance of various models, the basic premise is that Hellenistic Bactria reached a critical level of unstable complexity before some additional shock (political, military, economic, environmental, viral . . .) reverberated through the state. This explains why the similar conditions of 206 and 146 B.C.E. produced different outcomes. At both points, Bactria experienced the stresses of a civil war, nomads pressuring from the north, and a high rate of error on its coinages. In the latter period, however, a much more significant rate of minting error occurred within a state showing a far greater complexity in other ways: intensive building, military expansion, and a more pronounced but unequal interconnectivity between Greeks, Bactrians, and Indians. In an SOC scenario, we might expect the complexity cascade to act as a domino effect across Bactria, slowing only when the system self-organized into a simpler, less volatile territory. The numismatic result of such a process might be a royal coinage more like that of earlier Bactria, without the dazzling variety needed in the mintages of Eucratides, during whose reign this cascade apparently began. As it happens, Eucratides' immediate successors (Eucratides II, Plato, and Heliocles I) did fall back upon a simpler currency for Bactria.

When Justin uses the phrase "velut exsangues" ("as if bled dry," 41.6.3) to characterize Bactria's plight, there is no need to speculate about one military campaign or another, for he seems correct in the general sense that Bactria had stretched its resources of warriors and workers to a dangerous degree.[39] Ai Khanoum, perhaps something of a showpiece built around an impressive main boulevard, gave up without any evidence of a fight, perhaps before the first (Saka?) nomads crossed upriver and rode past the abandoned house and through the city gate. The chance of mounted archers capturing a manned fortified city seems otherwise remote. The city of Bactra, at least, maintained its independence for another generation, but when the Chinese traveler Zhang Qian visited the region in about 128 B.C.E., he described a disunified population of shopkeepers and merchants in towns whose armies had no stomach for war. The region had clearly reorganized itself as a temporarily less complex state. Next, we ought to expect a gradual increase again in Bactria's complexity under new circumstances. Based upon current archaeological evidence, Bactria and its surroundings rebounded with more urban development under the Yuezhi and Kushans than under the Greeks—the case of Ai Khanoum notwithstanding.[40]

The image of Greeks fleeing from unexpected waves of savage nomads should be replaced by a greater appreciation for the achievements of these so-called barbarians, who may have been more opportunistic than aggressive. Cognitive numismatics renders a similar verdict. In the first century C.E., for example, a Roman gold coin minted at Lugdunum (modern Lyon, France) by Emperor Tiberius ended up in a Kushan grave (no. III) at Tillya Tepe, Afghanistan.[41] The burial of this artifact ended its active life as both coin and commodity, but it hints at the renewed commerce connecting various peoples along the overland Silk Road and the sea routes via Egypt and India. A silver Parthian coin at least a century older than the Roman gold also ceased its rounds of circulation by coming to rest in this grave.[42] The selection of these items, one distant in place and the other in time, reflects a conscious act of ritual and respect about which we can only speculate.

Another tomb located nearby, that of a young female (no. VI), provides more clues. In her right hand she gripped a golden scepter and in her left a gold coin.[43] She also had in her mouth a worn silver Parthian coin of Phraates IV (ca. 38–2 B.C.E.).[44] The placement of these items calls to mind the Greek burial rite of Charon's fee, whereby one or more coins were situated in the mouth or hand (or both) of the deceased to pay a toll into the underworld.[45] The use of high-value coins for this purpose at Tillya Tepe, as opposed to the more customary bronzes, may be a mark of status for these nomadic royals.[46] This discovery may indicate an ongoing amalgamation of diverse cultural legacies in Central Asia or, at the very least, a general religious-magical employment of coins at the threshold of the afterlife.[47] Among the graves of (Yuezhi?) nomads excavated in the 1980s at Ksirov, in southern Tadjikistan, 20 percent included offerings of imitation obols of Eucratides.[48] A century earlier, an exploration at Ahin Push Tepe, near Jalalabad, uncovered a large Kushan site with a stupa-monastery complex.[49] Although the excavation was hardly scientific, the stupa did yield a gold amulet case set with garnets and numerous gold Kushan and Roman imperial coins.[50] This is but one of many instances of coins from local and long-distance mints being placed into Buddhist reliquary mounds, indicating that coins in Central and South Asia were not used solely as marketplace money.

The act of selecting such coins to accompany the dead may have been somewhat random, but it is interesting that both examples in Tillya Tepe grave VI had been countermarked, meaning that a small secondary image was stamped into the coin after it had left the original mint. This was done as a convenient way to retariff or revalidate a currency. Such recycling gave coins a second life as new money.[51] The gold example in tomb VI shows a small unidentified facing head, punched into the obverse of the host coin (an imitation of Gotarzes) with care not to obstruct the original portrait bust. Likewise, the silver coin has a helmeted profile carefully applied.[52] Whether the countermarking gave these coins special meaning in the context of this burial cannot be known.

The Tillya Tepe necropolis yielded no Bactrian coins as adjuncts of the dead, except as numismatic shadows. The helmeted countermark, for instance, resembles its distant model, the bust of Eucratides. In fact, this coin was then imitated with the helmeted countermark engraved into the die as if part of the Parthian host coin.[53] Specific Bactrian designs can be traced through centuries of emulation and imitation in a process that has its parallels in other parts of the ancient world, especially those where Greek settlements interacted with nomadic neighbors. The Celtic tribes of Europe perpetuated in their own evolving styles the original coin types of Philip II of Macedonia.[54] Gallic mercenaries paid with Philip's gold staters probably helped to spread this Greek cognitive map for coinage as far away as Britain. Across time and territory, the original images on the obverse and reverse (Apollo and chariot) evolved into less naturalistic abstractions as tribes singled out some features for exaggeration (the all-important horse, e.g.) while allowing others to diminish or disappear altogether (inscriptions, the charioteer). The once alien concept of coinage was thus made meaningful through the development of new cognitive maps. To call these barbarian imitations is not to suggest that the artwork degenerated as the realistic images of chariot and king became increasingly more abstract, for this implies that for centuries the Celts tried but failed to reproduce faithfully the prototype.[55] This is tantamount to disparaging the canvases of Picasso as if they were intended to be like those of Caravaggio.

In Central Asia, too, the peoples who came to dominate the region slowly transformed Bactrian coinage into something of their own choosing based upon a different aesthetic (and sometimes weight) standard.[56] Had the Yuezhi or Kushan tribes wanted to maintain an Hellenic coinage, with Greek artistic realism and pristine Greek inscriptions, they probably could have succeeded; but they cared little for these numismatic canons and steadily departed from them.[57] The first such imitations have been attributed to Sogdia in the time of Euthydemus.[58] These coins exhibit some of the same aberrations in the spelling of Greek as found on Euthydemus's own issues (see chap. 8, above), but the two groups can be separated by the much lighter weight standard adopted among the Sogdians.[59] The inscriptions on the imitations became progressively more garbled; and the artwork, more abstract. Whether Euthydemus employed Sogdian mercenaries in his war against Antiochus III is unknown, although the warning he issued to the Seleucid king may hint that this was an option.[60] By this means in Central Asia, as in Europe, the payment of such soldiers may explain the spread of a given coin type beyond its point of origin.[61]

We stand on firmer ground when addressing the next phase of imitation, beginning sixty or more years later in the time of Eucratides and Heliocles. A parchment document from the Bactrian town of Amphipolis, inked during the reign of Antimachus I, records a payment in Greek currency (100 drachms) to a detachment of forty Scythian mercenaries. (See above, chap. 6.) This text establishes the practice of recruiting and paying northern nomadic mercenaries during the crisis leading up to the abandonment of Ai Khanoum, a city that already had cataphract armor and Sakan bronze arrowheads in its arsenal alongside more ceremonial gear.[62] The probable kinsmen of those mercenaries benefited directly from the collapse of Greek power and minted their own coinages after the last Greek kings were gone. Some of this mintage borrowed from the coins that had recently come from Eucratides' and Heliocles' mints.[63] That some of the same workers are responsible for the last of the one and first of the other seems possible, since we have disposed of Tarn's old notion that the Greek die cutters were suddenly and totally exterminated in one day by the invaders. For example, the rare monogram NA exists on a Eucratidean tetradrachm with aberrant lettering and a portrait "presque caricaturaux" that Osmund Bopearachchi hedges as a lifetime issue or a posthumous imitation.[64] The same monogram also shows up on a tetradrachm with ill-formed letters from Ai Khanoum Hoard III, which suggests (but cannot prove) that these were indeed lifetime issues.[65] Later, this same monogram appears on an undisputedly posthumous issue (fig. 23).[66] The apparent continuity of this monogram shows either that some magistrates or mints did carry over from one period to the next, or that symbol systems (including some control marks) lost their original meanings but were still more or less maintained as significant to the concept of coin.

Figure 23. A so-called barbarian imitation of a coin issued by Eucratides.

As models, then, the old coins represented simply money and not a particular monarchy. The Yuezhi and later Kushans were not extending the sovereignty of a Eucratides or Heliocles, but rather perpetuating the idea of coinage as something generic and useful. The imitators did not apparently worry over what the prototypes meant in terms of nomenclature, titulature, or original propaganda, and thus it mattered little to them whether the Greek was correctly engraved and the Dioscuri or Zeus appropriately arrayed. Obviously, too, as minting errors had become increasingly more tolerated on the Eucratides and Heliocles lifetime issues, then these might be perpetuated on the imitations struck by peoples even less concerned with such lapses. Simply put, the new moneyers did not see or think in exactly the same way; their cognitive maps charted a new world.

Modifications in the coinage mirror patterns of perception. For example, the guide dots used on the Bactrian coinage became exaggerated and almost a thematic element unto itself, not just in the lettering but also in the figural art. On the imitations, things like horses' legs appeared more and more as straight lines that connected two or more prominent dots.[67] Even the faces of the riders might be rendered simply as a cluster of three contiguous dots.[68] Some depictions of horses look remarkably similar to those on Celtic coins in Europe, and the more stylized versions recall the famous Uffington White Horse chalked into a hillside of Bronze Age Britain. Imitations of Heliocles' coins showcase a similar departure from the prototypes. It is interesting that a horse sometimes replaces the standing Zeus of the originals, better capturing the nomads' own value system.[69] It has also been suggested that imitations of Heliocles' coins intend to show not the Bactrian king himself but rather avatars of his successors with Asiatic features.[70]

So, beyond the mints of Hellenistic Bactria, coinages divulge a number of fascinating behaviors ranging from hiding and losing to imitation and reuse. Through alteration, a few specimens changed function and became personal adornments or talismans.[71] Since this is a millennial practice, scholars cannot always tell when a given coin was modified for its new purpose, but ancient examples are well attested.[72] Furthermore, the manufacture of imitative coin jewelry (not fashioned from actual coins) illustrates that the ancients had a penchant for monetiform pendants. A recent discovery in Afghanistan takes the form of a gold disk imitating the Roman coin type of the she-wolf nursing Romulus and Remus. The replica's shaggy, bearlike wolf is surrounded by a nonsense inscription. An example made in northwest India during the fourth century C.E. copies on one side a Roman coin from the house of Constantine, and on the other a Kushan coin of Huvishka or Kanishka.[73] This is a so-called fantasy piece, since it does not replicate a coin that ever really existed. The maker simply paired two designs—obverse and reverse—from states thousands of miles apart and set them into an ornate gold frame with a loop for suspension. As already observed, such imitations lend themselves to new cultural norms: the Latin inscription is not correct, and the Roman emperor sports a large dangling earring.

There are earlier Bactrian and Indo-Greek coins that have loops attached or still bear signs that such appendages once existed. For example, the British Museum holds the first known Eucratides tetradrachm commemorating Heliocles and Laodice (see chap. 2), which has a residual nodule visible on both sides, just above the portraits.[74] Similar scars can be seen on other coins, such as tetradrachms of Diodotus (fig. 24) and Euthydemus I, and an Agathocles tetradrachm commemorating Euthydemus.[75] The connection between the nodules and now missing loops can be confirmed on the British Museum coin, which was found "in perfect preservation, having been worn as an ornament probably, as it has a loop attached to it."[76] The fitting was removed only after this specimen reached England. The British Museum owns as well at least two drachms of Menander I with loops still in place, while the Bibliothèque Nationale, in Paris, has a square bronze of Menander and a Eucratides II tetradrachm with intact suspension loops.[77] The placement of the loop in most of these cases does not obscure the types and tends to indicate that the owner wanted to display the coins as such and not merely use them as shiny metal squares or disks.[78]

The Diodotus and Euthydemus examples offer interesting test cases, since the coins' inverted (6:00) die axis means that, as a pendant, only one side appears upright, namely the reverses, showing Zeus and Hercules, respectively. This fact could suggest the wearers' devotion to these Greek deities or, at the least, some personal affinity for these particular designs. Yet, there is literally another way of looking at it. From the viewpoint of the wearers handling and admiring the suspended artifacts, the obverse portrait of the king appears upright. This intimates a purpose

Figure 24. Tetradrachm of Diodotus, showing royal portrait (obverse) and thundering Zeus (reverse). Note the scars on each side where a suspension loop was once attached.

beyond adornment, since an owner privileges his or her own relationship with the pendant over that of pleasing the eye of others. In either instance, the placement of the loop constitutes a thoughtful choice about the display of the coin.

A related but considerably larger sample of Bactrian and Indo-Greek coins were deliberately pierced. These holed specimens tend to be monolingual coins struck in the period from Demetrius I through Eucratides I.[79] The size and location of the holes follow a range of choices and may provide some clues about their purpose. On some bronze and cupronickel examples, a relatively large hole has been drilled or cut through the center, with no regard for sparing the images (fig. 25).[80] These may have been strung on a cord or nailed or riveted to some object as a decoration or charm.[81] It cannot be certain whether this kind of defacement rendered a coin unsuitable as currency, but it seems likely. In most instances, however, the holes have been positioned near an edge, without seriously affecting the types. On two

Figure 25. Bronze coin of Agathocles (reverse), with a square hole cut through the center..

Demetrius examples in bronze, the hole passes through the bottom on one (6:00) but through the top on the other (12:00), so that—if suspended—both obverse and reverse of the first would always appear upside down, and the other always upright.[82] These choices do not seem random, but why the first should be inverted on purpose makes little sense unless the pendant was meant to be viewed by the wearer. It may be noted that some silver coins were drilled at or near the 12:00 position, just like one of the Demetrius bronzes, so that they hung upright on both faces.[83] On at least four tetradrachms, the hole lies in front of the portrait.[84] That the intention of the owners was to display the king's portrait can be confirmed in two of these cases. On a tetradrachm of Euthydemus II, the hole was clearly positioned and punched through from the obverse side. On a Eucratides coin, the hole avoids the portrait but obliterates some of the lettering on the reverse. Three heterogeneous examples were holed behind the portrait, including one Indo-Greek bilingual drachm and one bronze square bilingual imitation.[85] Piercings at 3:00 and 9:00 would seem better suited for a bracelet than for a necklace if they functioned as jewelry. Unfortunately, none of these modified coins comes from an archaeological context that might further clarify its purpose.[86] Yet, the proven existence of pierced costume spangles, some of them imitating coins, may be relevant.[87] Also, the treasury at Ai Khanoum contained a pierced anthropomorphic bronze pendant with a suitable loop nearby.[88]

Some coins of Bactria were altered for an altogether different reason, whether to test the metal, decommission the currency, insult the ruler, or adjust the weight. Three (of forty-three) Euthydemus I tetradrachms in the Bukhara Hoard were cut in an apparent effort to determine whether they were plated or solid silver.[89] A common practice elsewhere in the ancient world, this slashing was rarely done to Bactrian silver issues.[90] Yet, Bactrian silvered *fourrées* are well attested and warranted the Bactrians' concern about plated forgeries.[91] Only a few Bactrian plated gold coins are known (e.g., from the second Mir Zakah Hoard), yet we know that very many Diodotid staters were cut.[92] Why should this be the case? If intended as an insult, it is strange that only gold coins were deemed suitable for this public denunciation; the silver portrait coins of Diodotus I and II were not generally treated in this way. Furthermore, in virtually every case the mark does not cross the king's face but falls behind the diadem and may in fact be quite small and inoffensive.[93] The precision of this cutting also argues against mass demonetization; the state would simply recall this good gold rather than bother to chisel it piece by piece to then circulate as bullion. We know, for example, that Euthydemus I did overstrike some Diodotid staters.[94] This, along with melting down the previous currency as was done in early Hellenistic Egypt, would be the normal means to demonetize a coinage.

Another explanation has been proposed that attempts to account for why only some coins were cut, and why in the same fashion but to variable degrees.[95] Was a slight lightening of cer-

tain coins the real intention? The weights of known uncut Diodotid staters range from about 8.18 to 8.56 grams, with an Attic
standard of 8.48. Mints tended to strike coinage a little below the
standard in order to turn a profit. Indeed, most uncut examples
fall within a few hundredths of 8.30 grams. The same is true of
the known population of cut staters, although we might anticipate
that a random practice of slashing coins would leave the latter
set with a lower median weight than for the unaltered group.
The result seems to be that the cut coins generally conform to
the practical standard of the uncut examples, apparently by
design. In other words, heavier gold pieces were singled out for
cutting, with variable amounts of metal removed that created,
beyond the mint, fewer circulating coins at or above the Attic
standard. This would especially apply if the state itself incremen-
tally reduced the practical standard over time. This idea, however, may be contradicted by the subsequent discovery of the
large Vaisali Hoard in India.[96] The many die-linked specimens
in the hoard exhibit a very broad range of weights for uncut
staters that were minted literally side by side, meaning that the
standard was not closely controlled or lowered in stages.

This leaves the test-cut theory for Bactria's gold as for its silver. In the Vaisali Hoard, local cutting by Indian merchants
would readily determine whether a foreign coin minted far away
was plated.[97] Yet, we must wonder why not all the staters in the
hoard were tested similarly. A consistent pattern should prevail
if the coins discovered at Vaisali mattered there only as bullion.
Even those coins that were cut betray more care in this operation
than a rudimentary examination would require.[98] Gold Diodotid
coins found in India were rarely just hacked apart or sliced
through the edges, whereas one Diodotus stater from the second
Mir Zakah Hoard in Afghanistan was cut three times and then

sliced in two.[99] (See plate 10.) Since the state would not likely test or demonetize its own currency in this way, who in the anonymous population of Bactria would cut these specimens? The test cuts are remarkably consistent in form. This seems to rule out a widespread practice by lots of different persons, who might individually choose any number of ways to carve into a specimen of gold. Furthermore, staters enjoyed a relatively brief period of production in Bactria and, since they circulated above the means of poor farmers and tradesmen, were not handled by most people. Currency of this type had limited velocity, meaning that it did not participate in the majority of day-to-day transactions. Worth ten times its weight in silver, gold served as a high-end unit of accounting in the economies of the Hellenistic world and circulated primarily for large state payments and long-distance trade.[100] Thus, it is possible that the test cuts were carried out by one or more vigilant bankers as staters randomly passed through their hands. This hypothesis explains all the variables in the observed material record and provides more insight into the monetary habits of subhistoric Bactria.

For all their beauty, then, Bactrian coins were first and foremost money in the eyes of careful bankers. The state might expend great energy designing this currency for maximum effect, loading it with sentiments and symbols that needed dissemination to target audiences, but the medium mattered more than the message to many buyers, sellers, borrowers, and hoarders. People of all eras tend to be very practical about cash. Those Americans today who disapprove of Thomas Jefferson the slave owner are not liable to forego all use of nickels as a matter of principle, nor will they favor the cents honoring Lincoln the emancipator. Most atheists do not refuse to handle money that professes IN GOD WE TRUST. Many ancient Bactrians acted simi-

Figure 26. Detail of an Afghan bank note that incorporates the reverse design of a coin of Eucratides. Note that the king's name has been misspelled.

larly.[101] They surely admired an impressive coin, but in the end it served all its normal economic functions—and some others besides—whether it was properly engraved or had later been cut. And the more unsettled the times, the less it mattered to officials and users alike if the error rate on dies reached 19 percent. In their workaday habits, we see history at a new, lower level.

Beyond the mint and the marketplace, coins also stretched the long Greek shadow across Central and South Asia. Their reuse as ornaments and models suggests that, whatever native peoples thought of the passing of Greek power, a certain prestige still clung to Hellenic culture.[102] Traces of the Greek language and its letters remained a feature of Bactrian life long after Eucratides and Heliocles were gone.[103] The Macedonian calendar stayed in vogue, as did certain units of measure. And while some moderns may perhaps be disappointed in the survival of Greek sculpture only in terms of its Buddhist forms, the widespread penchant for jewelry and adornment called upon Bactrian coins for inspiration. The money of Hellenistic Bactria is said to be the missing

link between the arts of Greece and India.[104] Thus, the Greek
things that required people to circulate among them, such as the
theater, gymnasium, or monumental architecture, mattered less
than the Greek things that circulated among the people—coins,
language, and calendars. This Hellenic culture need not be pure,
but it was itself a useful currency, and it remains so today. The
observant numismatist will notice a drawing of Eucratides'
Dioscuri coin type on the modern paper currency of Islamic
Afghanistan (fig. 26). There the twin sons of Zeus still gallop
beneath the royal titles of the Great King, whose name is nonetheless misspelled ΕΥΚΡΑΤΙΛΟΥ, to no one's apparent dismay.

Conclusion

The Lost World of the Golden King

Nearly seven hundred years ago, Bactria existed as a more or less mythical land kept alive by the imaginations of Renaissance poets. Some four hundred years later, it was still little more than a mere tally of kings who conquered, coined, and died. One of those kings, Eucratides the Great, set Bactrian studies on a new course when a coin bearing his name finally came to light. We may recap the progress made over the next centuries by using this king as a paradigm. Many great minds have pondered the problem of the Golden King and his lost world, each one anxious to tease from the evidence every available fact. Those truths have come and gone like guests at a dinner party—some fascinating and full of enlightenment, others loud but lacking substance, all welcome for whatever they might inspire in the conversation.

In 1738, Theophilus Bayer determined that Eucratides reigned from 181 to 146 B.C.E., during which time the Bactrian ruler enjoyed many military exploits across Central and South Asia. Eucratides' coin confirmed that he was indeed called Great, and its Dioscuri design seemed to credit his cavalry for his successes.

In the end, however, Eucratides' pro-Parthian policies outraged his like-named son, who cruelly assassinated his father and desecrated the body. In 1762, Joseph Pellerin thought that he had found a coin minted by the murderous son, Eucratides II. Heinrich Köhler published in 1826 a coin of Demetrius, the son of Euthydemus allegedly vanquished by Eucratides I when the Indian king was a staggering eighty-seven years old. Since Köhler still maintained the view that all Eucratides coins with a young portrait must belong to the supposed Eucratides II, he and others attributed the dynamic spear-thrower type to the wrong king and postulated from it a reform in Bactrian armaments.

Progress continued to be muddled by the rapid accumulation of new coins throughout the treacherous Great Game, making it exciting but difficult to sort properly the numismatic evidence. In 1836, James Prinsep briefly identified Eucratides I as the son of a Greek military officer and a Hindu mother named Kanlodice. When that erroneous reading of a coin was corrected by Alexander Cunningham, Laodice became to some scholars the royal Bactrian or Seleucid mother of Eucratides, to a few his wife, and to still others his sister-in-law or daughter-in-law, who was married to Heliocles. Horace H. Wilson professed the latter view in 1841, adding that Laodice's husband was the same Heliocles the Just who had been wandering up and down the Bactrian king list since the identification of his coin by Théodore Mionnet in 1799. Heliocles the Just, claimed Mionnet, Wilson, Prinsep, and Jean de Bartholomaei, was the son who killed poor Eucratides, thus absolving Eucratides II, whose very existence many denied.

According to Cunningham in 1869, Eucratides the Great was the great-grandson of Diodotus I. In about 190 B.C.E., this Eucratides led a rebellion against Demetrius with the assistance of Antimachus Nicephorus (fig. 27) because Demetrius's father,

Figure 27. Silver drachm of Antimachus Nicephorus (obverse), showing the winged goddess of victory.

Euthydemus I, had tried to wipe out the families of Diodotus, Pantaleon, and Antimachus I Theos. The success of the revolt made Eucratides the master of a thousand cities, one of which Cunningham conjured from a Greek monogram that allegedly read Apollonia, founded in honor of the god Apollo. Cunningham, like Raoul Rochette, did not believe that Heliocles killed his father, but neither did he blame a Eucratides II; instead, Cunningham fingered King Apollodotus as the eldest son and assassin of the great Eucratides. Avenging this crime, good King Heliocles took the title ΔΙΚΑΙΟΣ, "the Just." The murder of Eucratides allegedly occurred in 165 B.C.E.

Cunningham had already become embroiled in the controversy surrounding the numismatic monster acquired in July 1867 by Anatole Chabouillet of the Bibliothèque Imperiale, in Paris. The massive twenty-stater gold coin of Eucratides emerged from a murky background that involved many of the leading authorities of the nineteenth century, most notably Gaston Feuardent. For all its notoriety, however, this piece played little part in Cunningham's reconstruction of Eucratides' reign, and Feuardent mainly relied on the story of the Eucratidion's discovery and purchase to thrill readers of various newspapers. Chabouillet fumbled to explain why one side of the world's largest ancient gold coin seemed to be the work of a gifted Greek artist and the other the lesser scratchings of a poor native Bactrian. He also noticed that the supposedly Greek engraver had botched his first attempt to etch the king's titles across the reverse. Whatever its artistic merits or its historical significance, the Eucratidion henceforth made the Golden King something of a popular sensation.

In 1886, Percy Gardner published the first major museum catalogue of Bactrian coins. Gardner understood these coins in the British Museum to tell much the same story laid out by Cunningham, whose own collection was soon to join those curated by Gardner. The latter did, however, expand the list of Euthydemid kings who allegedly opposed Eucratides: Demetrius, Euthydemus II, Pantaleon, Agathocles, and Antimachus I. By associating the commemorative coins of Agathocles and Antimachus with this war against Eucratides, Gardner set the stage for the elaborate narratives soon to follow in the twentieth century. Hugh Rawlinson in 1912 cast the Golden King as a pro-Seleucid who bested his grandfather Demetrius I in battle. This victory made Eucratides the Great King of Bactria and the Maharaja of India, although his true temperament remained thoroughly Greek in Rawlinson's eyes. The Eucratidion represented the high-water mark of Hellenism in the East, after which Bactria declined. In *The Cambridge History of India* (1922), Edward Rapson wrote of Eucratides' rise to power in 175 B.C.E. and of his death in 155 at the hands of Heliocles— the last *Yavana* (i.e., Greek) king to rule in Bactria before the nomad conquest. In the same volume, George Macdonald added as pure speculation the idea that Eucratides' mother, Laodice, may have been a near relative of King Antiochus IV Epiphanes of Syria.

In 1938, William Tarn turned that speculation into the cornerstone of his breathtaking reconstruction of the lost world of

Eucratides. Still working without the safety net of archaeology and epigraphy, Tarn vaulted over the gaps in the numismatic record by describing connections between widely disparate events and believing dogmatically that what he imagined was real. Thus, when the Seleucid king celebrated at Daphne in Syria, the reason was found far away in Bactria, where his supposed cousin Eucratides had been sent with a small army to overthrow Demetrius I. Eucratides' invasion began in 168 B.C.E. with victories over Demetrius's viceroys Agathocles and Antimachus. Both sides tried to vouch that they were bona fide Seleucids—Eucratides with his "Heliocles and Laodice" coins, and the Euthydemids with their so-called pedigree tetradrachms tracing their fictitious bloodline back through Demetrius, Euthydemus, Diodotus, Antiochus II, and finally to Alexander himself. Greek loyalties in Bactria aligned with Eucratides not simply because he was the son of a Seleucid princess but because his cousin the king believed in forced Hellenization, contrary to the unpopular partnership of Greeks and non-Greeks championed by the Euthydemids.

Tarn's Eucratides defeated Demetrius in 167 B.C.E. The victor's Dioscuri coinage, replacing his earlier Apollo types, allegedly reflected the role of Antiochus and Eucratides as twin saviors of the Eastern Greeks. Antiochus celebrated at Daphne, and Eucratides at a new city named Eucratidia, where he added Great to his royal title and struck the largest of all ancient gold coins. The king then replaced the defunct Euthydemids with co-rulers from his own family, such as his sons Heliocles and Eucratides II, and his brother Plato—discovered in 1871—who supposedly received a little kingdom to play with somewhere in Bactria (fig. 28). Naturally, given the way numismatists such as Edward Newell treated coin portraiture, Tarn animated each of these players with a distinctive personality to suit his narrative, thanks to the master

Figure 28. First publication of a tetradrachm
of Plato, depicting the helmeted king (obverse)
and Helios driving a chariot (reverse).

engraver X and his school. Meanwhile, Tarn's Eucratides drove eastward into India to depose the kings Apollodotus and Menander, minting square bilingual coins along the way. In 159, having killed Apollodotus but not Menander, Eucratides returned suddenly to Bactria in order to face a Parthian invasion led by Mithridates I. In that same year, the Golden King died ignominiously at the hands not of his own son but rather of the son of some Euthydemid prince allied with the Parthians—perhaps a Demetrius II. Heliocles the Just secured control of Bactria once but not twice: after invading India, he allied with the Seleucids against Parthia and then lost Bactria once and for all to the Yuezhi.

Tarn's detailed recreation of Eucratides' world convinced many scholars but not A.K. Narain. With a stronger grounding in numismatics, and benefiting from discoveries made subsequent to Tarn's work, Narain's accounts (revised ed. 2003) offered a different Eucratides. This king was an upstart from some bypassed branch of the royal family tree in Bactria. His main enemy was Demetrius II (confused in the classical sources with Euthydemus's son), who was the real "rex Indorum" and the first king to issue bilingual coins. This Demetrius II, a scion of the Diodotids, was linked with Antimachus I Theos, Agathocles, and Pantaleon. Eucratides prevailed over them, proclaimed himself Great, and produced the ostentatious Eucratidion. He then fell victim to his son Plato in about 155 B.C.E. and was avenged by his loyal son, Heliocles the Just. All this cleared the way for Menander, brother-in-law or son-in-law of Agathocles, to emerge as the greatest of all the *Yavana* kings—a distinction, chided Narain, too often misattributed to Eucratides (fig. 29).

The rival narratives of Tarn and Narain thereafter served as fixed points in the development of Bactrian studies. Their ideas have endured, sometimes with little regard for fresh evidence or new methodologies. The personality-from-portrait approach continues to turn every king into a crowd, *ex uno plura,* as a single historical figure like Antimachus becomes variously coarse, civilized, Sogdian, Greek, pensive, playful, and so on. The recent Eucratides of Homayun Sidky (2000, 2004) has Narain's origins but fights Tarn's wars. The Golden King seized the throne in about 171 B.C.E., probably as an ambitious cavalry commander in the Bactrian army with no ties to Antiochus IV. He conquered Demetrius I, Euthydemus II, Pantaleon, Agathocles, Antimachus I, and Apollodotus I (whose existence Narain erroneously discounted for many years). Eucratides perished in about 160 B.C.E., perhaps as an act of revenge by Demetrius II during a Parthian incursion. The demise of Demetrius II in turn left Bactria in the hands of Heliocles the Just, but the exhausted Greeks abandoned the kingdom (including, of course, Ai Khanoum) as the Saka and Yuezhi tribes bore down from the north. The Indo-Greeks continued on, but Hellenistic Bactria allegedly vanished without any trace whatsoever.

In the more recent work of Jens Jakobsson (2007), Eucratides' tangled family tree may include Apollodotus as his father-in-law

Figure 29. Drachm of Menander I Soter (obverse), showing the king brandishing a spear and depicting Athena Alcidemus (reverse).

and Heliocles the Just as his brother-in-law or son-in-law. Omar Coloru's Eucratides, in 2009, was the grandson of Euthydemus I and cousin(?) of Demetrius I, the conqueror of India. Demetrius's son Euthydemus II lost control of his inheritance to the usurpers Antimachus I, Agathocles, and Pantaleon. Eucratides reconquered these territories, defeated Menander in India, and took the title Great before allying with King Timarchus of Syria against Mithridates of Parthia. Murdered by his son Heliocles, who lost Bactria to the nomads, Eucratides' realm in India reverted to his old rival Menander. Also in 2009, François Widemann reconstituted a Eucratides with a different history based in part on the research of Osmund Bopearachchi. This Golden King was a grandson of Antiochus the Great and half-brother of Euthydemus II, because Laodice had married both Demetrius I and Heliocles. Demetrius II put Eucratides in charge of Sogdia and established Antimachus II and Menander I in control of India. Emboldened by his military successes in Sogdia, Eucratides turned against his sovereign. The overthrow of Demetrius II then led to war against Menander in India, during which Eucratides' sons Heliocles and Eucratides II occupied Bactria. Widemann's so-called Bactrian Council, however, did not recognize Eucratides and refused him the epithet *Theos,* so the king became *Megas* instead. He transferred territories seized from Menander and Antimachus II to his partisan Zoilus I but was assassinated by Heliocles. The nomads, too, got their revenge by destroying Ai Khanoum as a way to punish Eucratides.

The many ongoing permutations of Eucratides' background, family ties, various alliances, wars, and demise are a sure sign that historians, archaeologists, and numismatists are no more agreed now than they were generations ago. The customary practices of GVI have yet to gain a solid footing in Bactria. Scholars therefore still have different ideas about when this king lived, where he ruled, what he achieved, and how he died—that is, the essential building blocks of any narrative account. And what is true of the Golden King is also true of the other forty-odd rulers of this elusive realm. This is not, however, a reason to give up. The spate of salvageable new evidence offers the promise of fresh insights, and we need somehow to broaden our view. Our goal should no longer be to write royal biographies but to dig deep below the king list to understand at least something about the common people as well. We seek the lost world of the Golden King rather than just the king himself. In that respect, we have advanced very far indeed beyond what was knowable to the early giants of Bactrian studies. Bayer could scarcely imagine what can now be found in the works of, say, Bopearachchi or Bernard. Now we can see into a Bactrian city, read a Bactrian tax receipt, study tens of thousands of coins, and peer over the shoulders of anonymous Bactrian workers as they faced the challenges of their time. We can ask—and begin to answer—more nuanced questions than who reigned when or where, and we can set aside the siren song of imagined narratives.

Rescue, revisionist, and cognitive numismatics will not mark the end of the search for Bactria, any more than scholarship stopped, satisfied, with checklist, framework, novelty, or narrative numismatics. Alongside methodological progress in the handling of more and more coins, archaeology and epigraphy will certainly surprise us with unexpected new evidence. Meanwhile, ancient Bactria, as moderns now know it, was a fascinating realm that sat astride a crucial geographical and historical crossroads. There cultures clashed and coalesced; religions competed and compromised; languages met and merged; people fought and fled, saved and spent, worked and worried, while leaving a trail of thousands of coins as witnesses to it all.

NOTES

INTRODUCTION

1. The modern rediscovery of Bactria had been going on for two hundred years before the German scientist Christian Gottfried Ehrenberg invented the term "bacteria," which has since caused all manner of trouble for cataloguers and search engines that confuse these words. It is probably too late for either side to change its terminology, and given the long priority of the Latinized "Bactria" for the ancient land of Baktriana (Greek Βακτριανή), this book will retain the traditional spelling as found in, e.g., *The Oxford Classical Dictionary,* 3rd edition.

2. The precise geographic boundaries of Bactria have long been disputed: B. Lyonnet, "The Problem of the Frontiers between Bactria and Sogdiana: An Old Discussion and New Data," pp. 195–208 in A. Gail and G. Mevissen, eds., *South Asian Archaeology 1991* (Stuttgart: Franz Steiner Verlag, 1993). In this book the name refers generally to the heart of the ancient kingdom in northern Afghanistan, as well as its occasional dependencies north of the Amu Darya (technically, ancient Sogdia) and south of the Hindu Kush toward Pakistan (ancient India). Some now prefer a different generic name, the Hellenistic Far East (HFE): Rachel Mairs, *The Archaeology of the Hellenistic Far East: A Survey* (Oxford: BAR, 2011), p. 8.

3. Stanley Burstein, "New Light on the Fate of Greek in Ancient Central and South Asia," *Ancient West and East* 9 (2010): 185.

4. On the classical sources, particularly for Eucratides, see chap. 1; for Chinese and Indian sources, see the notes below.

5. On Menander, see I.B. Horner, trans., *Milinda's Questions* (Bristol: Pali Text Society, 1963–64). This work takes the form of a dialogue between Milinda (Menander) and the Buddhist sage Nagasena.

6. Osmund Bopearachchi, *Monnaies gréco-bactriennes et indo-grecques: Catalogue raisonné* (Paris: Bibliothèque Nationale, 1991), pp. 76–88. On the coin type, see Agnes B. Brett, "Athena ΑΛΚΙΔΗΜΟΣ of Pella," *American Numismatic Society Museum Notes* 4 (1950): 55–72, esp. pp. 64–65.

7. Xinru Liu, "Migration and Settlement of the Yuezhi-Kushan: Interaction and Interdependence of Nomadic and Sedentary Societies," *Journal of World History* 12.2 (2001): 261–92.

8. Burton Watson, trans., *Records of the Grand Historian by Sima Qian* (New York: Research Center for Translation, 1993), pp. 231–52.

9. Yang Juping, "Alexander the Great and the Emergence of the Silk Road," *The Silk Road* 6.2 (2009): 15–22; K. M. Baipakov, "The Great Silk Way: Studies in Kazakhstan," *Archaeological Studies* 16 (1994): 89–93; and for some exciting archaeological evidence of cultural cross-currents, see Robert Jones, "Centaurs on the Silk Road: Recent Discoveries of Hellenistic Textiles in Western China," *The Silk Road* 6.2 (2009): 23–32.

10. According to the apocryphal Acts of the Apostle Thomas, the twin brother of Jesus soon reversed this journey to Bactria and India in order to convert the East to Christianity: Albertus Klijn, *The Acts of Thomas: Introduction, Text, and Commentary* (Leiden: Brill, 2003). The pagan holy man Apollonius allegedly followed a similar path eastward, as chronicled in Philostratus's *Life of Apollonius of Tyana*. See Marco Galli, "Hellenistic Court Imagery in the Early Buddhist Art of Gandhara," *Ancient Civilizations from Scythia to Siberia* 17 (2011): 288–92.

11. The quotation in the epigraph comes from Louis's article "Concerning Language and Gold," *Old and New* 7 (Apr. 1873): 410.

I. THE ADVENTURE BEGINS

1. Jacob Spon, *Voyage d'Italie, de Dalmatie, de Grèce et du Levant* (Lyon: Antoine Cellier, 1678), pp. 17–22.

2. For the career of Vaillant, see Ernest Babelon, *Traité des monnaies grecques et romaines,* vol. I: *Théorie et doctrine* (Paris: Ernest Leroux, 1901), cols. 137–43.

3. The expedient of swallowing coins in anticipation of being captured has a long, and sometimes grisly, history. When Jewish refugees from the Roman siege of Jerusalem were seen picking coins from their own fresh excrement, some two thousand prisoners were quickly slaughtered and their intestines searched for hidden gold: Josephus, *Jewish War* 5.13.4.

4. Spon, *Voyage,* p. 21.

5. Irène Aghion, "Collecting Antiquities in Eighteenth-Century France," *Journal of the History of Collections* 14.2 (2002): 193–203; Alexander McKay, "Archaeology and the Creative Imagination," pp. 227–34 in McKay, ed., *New Perspectives in Canadian Archaeology* (Ottawa: Royal Society of Canada, 1977).

6. Warwick Ball, *The Monuments of Afghanistan: History, Archaeology and Architecture* (New York: I.B. Tauris, 2008), p. 136, n. 26.

7. See, for example, Harlan Berk, *100 Greatest Ancient Coins* (Atlanta: Whitman Publishing, 2008), part of a series of such books aimed at the collector/enthusiast market. The author polled collectors, dealers, curators, and others to establish a somewhat arbitrary checklist and then illustrated each item on it. A coin of Eucratides figures as no. 80. Similarly, Prashant Srivastava, *Art-Motifs on Ancient Indian Coins* (New Delhi: Harman, 2004), produces a list of "Masterpieces of Numismatic Art" and checks off Eucratides as no. 2.

8. J.F. Vaillant, *Arsacidarum Imperium, sive Regum Parthorum Historia ad Fidem Numismaticum Accommodata* (Paris: Moette, 1725).

9. Ibid., pp. 28–44. On Eucratides II, see below, n. 29. Another king, Apollodotus, was confused with the writer Apollodorus.

10. On Bruce's career, see Grant Simpson, ed., *The Scottish Soldier Abroad, 1247–1967* (Edinburgh: John Donald Publishers, 1992), pp. 56–63.

11. Bruce's death occurred on April 19 (Old Style, which is April 30 New Style).

12. On Bayer, see Knud Lunbaek, *T.S. Bayer (1694–1738): Pioneer Sinologist* (London: Curzon Press, 1986).

13. T. Bayer, *Historia Regni Graecorum Bactriani* (St. Petersburg: Academia Scientiarum, 1738). The appearance of Bayer's history of Bactria was much anticipated as far away as London: Omar Coloru, *Da Alessandro a Menandro: Il regno greco di Battriana* (Pisa: Fabrizio Serra, 2009), p. 34.

14. Ibid., p. 100. On the denomination of this historic coin, see F. Holt, "Bayer's Coin of Eucratides: A Miscalculation Corrected," *Zeitschrift für Papyrologie und Epigraphik* 174 (2010): 289–90.

15. On these kings, see F. Holt, *Thundering Zeus: The Making of Hellenistic Bactria* (Berkeley and Los Angeles: University of California Press, 1999).

16. Bayer (*Historia Regni*, p. 95) considered Eucratides I to have been pro-Parthian and Eucratides II to have been anti-Parthian.

17. Bayer, *Historia Regni*, p. 45. There is no indication that this specimen derived from Bruce's collection.

18. J. Pellerin, *Recueil de médailles de rois* (Paris: Guerin and Delatour, 1762), p. 129; Pellerin, *Additions aux neuf volumes de Recueiles de médailles de rois* (Paris: Desaint, 1778), pp. 95–96. See also Holt, "Bayer's Coin," pp. 289–90. The rare exception was Marie-Thérèse Allouche-LePage, *L'art monétaire des royaumes bactriens* (Paris: Didier, 1956), p. 197.

19. H.H. Wilson, *Ariana Antiqua: A Descriptive Account of the Antiquities and Coins of Afghanistan* (1841; reprint, Delhi: Oriental Publishers, 1971), pp. 3 and 218.

20. See Graham Shipley, *The Greek World after Alexander, 323–30 BC* (London: Routledge, 2000).

21. Klaus Karttunen argues that Eucratides was at one time relatively well known in antiquity: "King Eucratides in Literary Sources," *Silk Road Art and Archaeology* 6 (1999–2000): 116; see also Karttunen, *India and the Hellenistic World* (Helsinki: Finnish Oriental Society, 1997).

22. Valerii Nikonorov, "Apollodorus of Artemita and the Date of His *Parthica* Revisited," *Electrum* 2 (1998): 107–22. For a very extensive, up-to-date bibliography on Parthian history, compiled by Valerii Nikonorov,

see the new Russian edition of Neilson Debevoise's 1938 classic *A Political History of Parthia* (St. Petersburg: Akademii Nauk, 2008).

23. Strabo, *Geography* 15.1.3.

24. Strabo, *Geography* 11.9.2.

25. Strabo, *Geography* 11.11.1. Euthydemus and his son Demetrius are also mentioned in Polybius, *Histories* 10.49 and 11.34. See Holt, *Thundering Zeus*, pp. 181–82.

26. Strabo, *Geography* 11.11.2. Eucratides' namesake city is also mentioned by the geographer Claudius Ptolemy (6.11.8) and by Stephanus of Byzantium in his *Ethnica*, s.v. "Eucratidia." Strabo's Turiva may be a mistake for Tapuria, a place name cited by other ancient writers: Polybius 10.49; Ptolemy 6.14.7 and 12.

27. The connection is patent in the survival of Apollodorus's stock phrase "the thousand cities of Bactria," which Trogus passed on to Justin.

28. Justin, *Epitome of Pompeius Trogus's Philippic History* 41.6.1–5.

29. In more or less quoting Justin's passage word for word, Vaillant (*Arsacidarum Imperium*, p. 44) wrote "a filio Eucratide II," as though the name actually appeared in his source. He probably just supplied the name as a supposition of his own.

30. The story is given by the historian Livy, a contemporary of Pompeius Trogus, in his *Histories* (1.46).

31. Aelian, *On the Nature of Animals* 15.8.

32. See Lionel Casson, *The Periplus Maris Erythraei: Text with Introduction, Translation, and Commentary* (Princeton: Princeton University Press, 1989), pp. 80–81 and 204–6.

33. Plutarch, *Moralia* 821D.

34. On this strange account, see Coloru, *Da Alessandro a Menandro*, pp. 104–9.

35. The Latin of this Renaissance poet does not make it entirely clear whose son, Eucratides' or Demetrius's, was the assassin. In the 1520 Paris manuscript housed in the British Museum, an anonymous person added a clarification in the margins of Boccaccio's work explaining that "Eucratides was killed by his own son, whom he had made his co-ruler."

36. See, for example, A.D.H. Bivar, "The Death of Eucratides in

Medieval Tradition," *Journal of the Royal Asiatic Society* (1950): 7–13; Omar Coloru, "Reminiscenze dei re greco-battriani nella letteratura medievale e nella science-fiction Americana," *Studi Ellenistici* 20 (2008): 519–39. Laurent and Lydgate give variant accounts of Eucratides' death, making Demetrius's son the villain.

37. "The Knight's Tale," ll. 2155–86.

38. This literary connection would not be made, however, until Alexander Cunningham, "Coins of Alexander's Successors in the East," *Numismatic Chronicle* 9 (1869): 140–53, republished in Cunningham, *Coins of Alexander's Successors in the East* (1884; reprint, Chicago: Argonaut, 1969), pp. 146–59; see also Henry Hinckley, "The Grete Emetreus the King of Inde," *Modern Language Notes* 48 (1933): 148–49. There is little to commend the suggestion that Chaucer may have been inspired by a portrait coin of Demetrius or a so-called pedigree coin of Agathocles, for which see Rachel Mairs, *The Archaeology of the Hellenistic Far East: A Survey* (Oxford: BAR, 2011), p. 12. Nothing in Chaucer's description resembles the coins, except perhaps the king's age, and that Polybius records. Surely the poet would have been likely to incorporate from the coins something of Demetrius's remarkable elephant headdress, but he imagines instead a green laurel garland.

39. Bayer, *Historia Regni*, pp. 100 and 133–34.

40. Pellerin, *Recueil*, pp. 130–31.

41. Pellerin's collection, and the beautiful cabinets designed for it, were acquired by Louis XVI: Aghion, "Collecting Antiquities," pp. 195–96. See also Thierry Sarmant, *Le Cabinet des Médailles de la Bibliothèque Nationale, 1661–1848* (Paris: École des Chartes, 1994), pp. 136–39.

42. See above, n. 29.

43. For example, see H.K.E. Köhler, *Serapis* (St. Petersburg: Imperial Academy of Sciences, 1850), p. 7.

44. Now in the Bibliothèque Nationale, this coin is Eucratides I no. 38 (p. 205) in Osmund Bopearachchi, *Monnaies gréco-bactriennes et indo-grecques: Catalogue raisonné* (Paris: Bibliothèque Nationale, 1991). See also Dominique Gerin, "Becker et les monnaies bactriennes du Cabinet de France, Part I," *Bulletin de la Société Française de Numismatique* 38.4 (1983): 305–9.

45. Pellerin, *Additions*, pp. 95–106.

46. Ibid., p. 95: "Tout concourt à la rendre une des plus précieuses & des plus intéressantes que l'on ait jamais vues." This coin is also now in the French collection: Bopearachchi, *Monnaies gréco-bactriennes gréco-bactriennes et indo-grecques: Catalogue raisonné*, Euthydemus I no. 2 (p. 154).

47. Pellerin, *Additions*, pp. 96–106.

48. Pellerin suggested that the figure of Hercules on the reverse might be taken as a characterization of Euthydemus himself, resting from his triumphant struggles and ruling henceforth in peace. Although the French scholar immediately abandoned this notion, it still survives among some numismatists today.

49. Pellerin, *Additions*, p. 102: "sûrement d'une main grecque, l'on ne doit pas être surpris de sa beauté."

50. J. Tod, "An Account of Greek, Parthian, and Hindu Medals, Found in India," *Transactions of the Royal Asiatic Society* I (1826): 313–42.

51. Ibid., p. 314.

52. Ibid., p. 315.

53. H. K. E. Köhler, "Description d'un médaillon rapporté de Boukharie par M. le Colonel Baron Georges de Meyendorff," pp. 321–28 in E. K. Meyendorff, *Voyage d'Orenbourg à Boukhara, fait en 1820* (Paris: Librairie Orientale de Dondey-Dupré, 1826).

54. For full details of these discoveries, see Holt, *Thundering Zeus*, pp. 74–77.

2. A DANGEROUS GAME

1. Rudyard Kipling's father, John Lockwood Kipling, maintained the Lahore Museum, a splendid repository of Graeco-Bactrian and Gandharan (Graeco-Buddhist) art. Kipling showcased this museum in the opening pages of *Kim*.

2. For short biographies of some of these remarkable individuals, see John Ure, *Shooting Leave: Spying Out Central Asia in the Great Game* (London: Constable, 2009). On the Great Game in general, see Peter Hopkirk, *The Great Game: The Struggle for Empire in Central Asia* (New York: Kodansha International, 1992); and Karl Meyer and Shareen

Brysac, *Tournament of Shadows: The Great Game and the Race for Empire in Central Asia* (Washington, D.C.: Counterpoint, 1999).

3. Arthur Conolly, *Journey to the North of India through Russia, Persia and Afghanistan,* 2 vols. (London: Richard Bentley, 1834).

4. On Conolly and the phrase, see Hopkirk, *The Great Game,* p. 1.

5. Meyer and Brysac, *Tournament of Shadows,* pp. 132–33.

6. Joseph Wolff, *Narrative of a Mission to Bokhara, in the Years 1843–1845, to Ascertain the Fate of Colonel Stoddart and Captain Conolly* (London: J.W. Parker, 1845), p. v.

7. Ibid. Wolff had met Conolly at Cawnpore in 1833, and so he volunteered in 1843 to search for Conolly, who had gone, in turn, to search for Captain Stoddart. Wolff himself barely survived the emir's wrath through the timely intervention of the shah of Persia.

8. Ibid., pp. 176–77. On the fruits of Conolly's numismatic interests, see the notice in *Journal of the Asiatic Society of Bengal* 3 (1834): 246–47.

9. Wolff, *Narrative of a Mission to Bokhara,* p. 224.

10. F.-P. Gosselin and C.-P. Campion, *Catalogue des médailles antiques et modernes, du Cabinet de M. D'Ennery* (Paris: de Monsieur, 1788).

11. Ibid., pp. x and 40 (coin no. 253). This coin entered the French national collection: Osmund Bopearachchi, *Monnaies gréco-bactriennes et indo-grecques: Catalogue raisonné* (Paris: Bibliothèque Nationale, 1991), Heliocles I no. 13 (p. 224).

12. See Dominique Gerin, "Becker et les monnaies bactriennes du Cabinet de France, Part II," *Bulletin de la Société Française de Numismatique* 38.5 (1983): 321–22.

13. T.E. Mionnet, *Catalogue d'une collection d'empreintes en soufre de médailles grecques et romaines* (Paris: L'Imprimerie de Crapelet, 1799), p. 66 (coin no. 1230).

14. L. Stephani, ed., *H.K.E. Köhler's gesammelte Schriften,* vol. I, *Serapis* (St. Petersburg: Imperial Academy, 1850), pp. 4–6 and 9–10.

15. F. Holt, "The Problem of Poseidon in Bactria," pp. 721–26 in E.A. Antonova et al., eds., *Central Asia: Sources, History, Culture* (Moscow: Russian Academy of Sciences, 2005).

16. Stephani, ed., *H. K. E. Köhler's gesammelte Schriften,* vol. I, *Serapis,* pp. 2 and 5–6. The nickel specimen (types: obverse, Apollo: reverse,

tripod) is described thus: "Elle a été anciennement couverte d'une lame en argent, et il en reste des vestiges sur son avers."

17. Ibid., pp. 2–3 and 6–7.

18. Ibid., pp. 3–4 and 7–8.

19. Ibid., pp. 7–8.

20. See, for example, Augustus Wilhelm von Schlegel, "Observations sur quelques médailles bactriennes et indo-scythiques nouvellement découvertes," *Journal Asiatique* 2 (1828): 321–49.

21. Ibid., p. 327.

22. Ibid., pp. 334–35.

23. On Burnes, see James Lunt, *Bokhara Burnes* (London: Faber and Faber, 1969).

24. James Prinsep, "Continuation of the Route of Lieutenant A. Burnes and Dr. Gerard, from Peshawar to Bokhara," *Journal of the Asiatic Society of Bengal* 2 (1833): 1–22, esp. 14 and 18. On Moorcroft, see Garry Alder, *Beyond Bokhara: The Life of William Moorcroft, Asian Explorer and Pioneer Veterinary Surgeon* (London: Century, 1985).

25. A. Burnes, *Travels into Bokhara,* 3 vols. (London: John Murray, 1834).

26. H.H. Wilson and J. Prinsep, "Observations on Lieut. Burnes's Collection of Bactrian and Other Coins," in Burnes, *Travels,* vol. III, pp. 369–84. Prinsep presented an earlier report, "Notes on Lieutenant Burnes' Collection of Ancient Coins," in the *Journal of the Asiatic Society of Bengal* 2 (1833): 310–18, reprinted in Edward Thomas, ed., *Essays on Indian Antiquities* (1858; reprint, Varanasi: Indological Book House, 1971), vol. I, pp. 25–29. Uncharacteristically, Prinsep errs in his reference to "the gold [*sic*] coin from the neighborhood of the Caspian Sea, described by Bayer."

27. On the casts, see J. Prinsep, "Bactrian and Indo-Scythic Coins," *Journal of the Asiatic Society of Bengal* 2 (1833): 406.

28. Mohan Lal, *Travels in the Panjab, Afghanistan, and Turkestan to Balkh, Bokhara, and Herat* (London: William Allen, 1846), esp. pp. 31–32, and a notice in the "Proceedings" of the *Journal of the Asiatic Society of Bengal* 3 (1834): 364. On this important *munshi* (secretary), see C.A. Bayly, *Empire and Information: Intelligence Gathering and Social Communication in*

India, 1780–1870 (Cambridge: Cambridge University Press, 2000), pp. 230–32.

29. "Proceedings" in the *Journal of the Asiatic Society of Bengal* 3 (1834): 247.

30. Reported by J. Prinsep, "New Types of Bactrian and Indo-Scythic Coins," *Journal of the Asiatic Society of Bengal* 5 (1836): 721.

31. On the doctor, see his memoir *Thirty-Five Years in the East* (London: H. Ballière, 1852); on the generals, see in particular Adrian de Longpérier, "Collection numismatique du Général Court," *Revue Numismatique* (1839): 81–88; Elizabeth Errington, "Rediscovering the Coin Collection of General Claude-Auguste Court: A Preliminary Report," *Topoi* 5 (1995): 409–24.

32. Eugène Jaquet, "Notice sur les découvertes archéologiques faites par M. Honigberger dans Afghanistan," *Journal Asiatique* 2 (1836): 234–304; Longpérier, "Collection," p. 83. There is some discrepancy about how many cannon were cast from old coins. In his published article, Longpérier states that there were several ("il put faire fondre plusieurs pièces de canon avec les rebuts," whereas in his elegantly handwritten manuscript still in the Bibliothèque Nationale, Longpérier wrote that there was one ("il peut faire fondre une pièce de canon avec les rebuts."

33. Gordon Whitteridge, *Charles Masson of Afghanistan* (Warminster: Aris and Phillips, 1986); Bijan Omrani, "Charles Masson of Afghanistan: Deserter, Scholar, Spy," *Asian Affairs* 39.2 (2008): 199–216.

34. On Josiah Harlan, who also befriended Reverend Joseph Wolff, see Ben Macintyre, *The Man Who Would Be King: The First American in Afghanistan* (New York: Farrar, Straus and Giroux, 2004).

35. On the intellectual milieu of British interest in Alexander, see Christopher Hagerman, "In the Footsteps of the 'Macedonian Conqueror': Alexander the Great and British India," *International Journal of the Classical Tradition* 16 (2009): 344–92; cf. Robert Rabel, "The Imitation of Alexander the Great in Afghanistan," *Helios* 34 (2007): 97–119.

36. Harlan, *The Man Who Would Be King*, p. 65; cf. Alexander Burnes, "On the Reputed Descendants of Alexander the Great, in the Valley of the Oxus," *Journal of the Asiatic Society of Bengal* 2 (1833): 305–7, and Mohan Lal, *Travels*, p. 201.

37. C. Masson, "Memoir on the Ancient Coins Found at Beghram, in the Kohistan of Kabul," *Journal of the Asiatic Society of Bengal* 3 (1834): 153–75, esp. 154–56.

38. C. Masson, "Second Memoir on the Ancient Coins Found at Beghram, in the Kohistan of Kabul," *Journal of the Asiatic Society of Bengal* 5 (1836): 1–28, esp. 10.

39. See also P.B. Lord, "Some Account of a Visit to the Plain of Koh-i-Damin, the Mining District of Ghorband, and the Pass of Hindu Kush," *Journal of the Asiatic Society of Bengal* 7 (1838): 537, who reports on Masson's finds and adds that two children hired by John Wood gathered some twenty or thirty coins in the space of a few hours at Begram.

40. C. Lassen, *Points in the History of the Greek, and Indo-Scythian Kings in Bactria, Cabul, and India, as Illustrated by Deciphering the Ancient Legends on Their Coins*, trans. H. Roeer (1840; reprint, Delhi: Indological Book House, 1972), p. 8. Lassen's translated work appeared in *Journal of the Asiatic Society of Bengal* 9 (1840): 627–76 and 733–65.

41. Witness the important Masson Project in the British Museum begun in 1993, for which see Elizabeth Errington, "Rediscovering the Collections of Charles Masson," pp. 207–37 in Michael Alram and Deborah Klimburg-Salter, eds., *Coins, Art, and Chronology: Essays on the Pre-Islamic History of the Indo-Iranian Borderlands* (Vienna: Verlag der Österreichischen Akademie der Wissenschaften, 1999). See also the valuable collection of materials in Errington and Vesta S. Curtis, *From Persepolis to the Punjab: Exploring Ancient Iran, Afghanistan and Pakistan* (London: British Museum, 2007). See below, chapter 7.

42. To the further credit of these scholars, it must be noted that they generally took a very broad view of Central and South Asian history that encompassed far more than the Hellenistic era. Thus, they were wrestling with an enormous range of historical problems. For background, see O.P. Kejariwal, *The Asiatic Society of Bengal and the Discovery of India's Past, 1784–1838* (Delhi: Oxford University Press, 1988).

43. R. Rochette, "Deuxième supplément à la Notice sur quelques médailles grecques inédites de rois de la Bactriane et de l'Inde," *Journal des Savants*, 1836: 65.

44. R. Rochette, "Supplément à la Notice sur quelques médailles

grecques inédites de rois de la Bactriane et de l'Inde," *Journal des Savants,* 1835: 513–28.

45. Rochette, "Deuxième supplément," p. 75; C. Lassen, "Points in the History of the Greek, and Indo-Scythian Kings in Bactria, Cabul, and India," *Journal of the Asiatic Society of Bengal* 9 (1840): 649 and 752. See also the discussion of the Agathocles commemorative coins, below.

46. J. Prinsep, "Further Notes and Drawings of Bactrian and Indo-Scythic Coins," *Journal of the Asiatic Society of Bengal* 4 (1835): 327–46, esp. 328. The similar portrait on a silver specimen owned by General Ventura added to the confusion: p. 337.

47. Rochette, "Deuxième supplément," p. 75.

48. For example, Masson, "Second Memoir," p. 17.

49. Charles Masson gives an interesting tally in his "Third Memoir on the Ancient Coins Discovered at the Site called Beghram in the Kohistan of Kabul," *Journal of the Asiatic Society of Bengal* 5 (1836): 547. On the chronology, see Prinsep, "Further Notes," p. 339.

50. Multiples of homonymous kings remain a matter of dispute among scholars today. See, for example, F. Holt, "Did King Euthydemus II Really Exist?" *Numismatic Chronicle* 160 (2000): 81–91.

51. See Prinsep, "New Types of Bactrian and Indo-Scythic Coins," p. 721.

52. J. Prinsep, "Additions to Bactrian Numismatics, and the Discovery of the Bactrian Alphabet," *Journal of the Asiatic Society of Bengal* 7 (1838): 637–38.

53. Ibid., p. 638.

54. Ibid., where Prinsep appends an addendum that acknowledges a letter received from Cunningham on this matter.

55. H.H. Wilson, *Ariana Antiqua: A Descriptive Account of the Antiquities and Coins of Afghanistan* (1841; reprint, Delhi: Oriental Publishers, 1971), p. 267.

56. Recounted in Alexander Burnes, *Cabool: A Personal Narrative of a Journey to, and Residence in that City in the Years 1836, 7, and 8,* 2nd ed. (London: John Murray, 1843), pp. 204–5.

57. Prinsep, "Further Notes," p. 329. Prinsep notes that he was following up a suggestion made by Masson.

58. For a useful introduction, see Richard Salomon, *Indian Epigraphy* (Oxford: Oxford University Press, 1998).

59. Her diary has been published: Patrick Macrory, ed., *Lady Sale: The First Afghan War* (Hamden, Conn.: Archon Books, 1969).

60. A. Cunningham, "Notes on Captain Hay's Bactrian Coins," *Journal of the Asiatic Society of Bengal* 9 (1840): 543–44.

61. Ibid. Cunningham offered a more comprehensive treatment in his "Second Notice of Some Forged Coins of the Bactrians and Indo-Scythians," *Journal of the Asiatic Society of Bengal* 9 (1840): 1217–80.

62. A. Cunningham, "An Attempt to Explain Some of the Monograms Found upon the Grecian Coins of Ariana and India," *Numismatic Chronicle* 8 (1845–46): 177.

63. Cunningham began this line of research in 1841 and summarized the results in "Coins of Alexander's Successors in the East," *Numismatic Chronicle* 8 (1868): 181–218, republished in Cunningham, *Coins of Alexander's Successors in the East* (1884; reprint, Chicago: Argonaut, 1969), pp. 45–77.

64. Compare his "Attempt to Explain Some of the Monograms," pp. 178–79, and *Coins of Alexander's Successors,* p. 60. In spite of these geographic options, the same monogram was still being interpreted as a date many years later: Rudolf Hoernle, "Monograms of the Baktro-Greek King Euthydemos," *The Indian Antiquary* 8 (1879): 197–98.

65. Cunningham, *Coins of Alexander's Successors,* p. 62.

66. Ibid., p. 68.

67. Ibid., p. 61–63. See also F. Holt, *Thundering Zeus: The Making of Hellenistic Bactria* (Berkeley and Los Angeles: University of California Press, 1999), pp. 51–52.

68. Edward Thomas, "Bactrian Coins," *Numismatic Chronicle* 2 (1862): n. 2, pp. 179–80.

69. Cunningham, *Coins of Alexander's Successors,* pp. 55–56 (Syrian monogram 1) and p. 70 (Bactrian monogram 62).

70. See, for example, A.N. Lahiri, *Corpus of Indo-Greek Coins* (Calcutta: Poddar Publications, 1965), pp. 52–62; Bopearachchi, *Monnaies gréco-bactriennes et indo-grecques: Catalogue raisonné,* pp. 31–34. A novel and as yet unvetted proposal for Seleucid (and perhaps some Bactrian) monograms may be found in G.G. Aperghis, "Recipients and End-

Users on Seleukid Coins," *Bulletin of the Institute of Classical Studies* 53.2 (2010): 55–84.

71. On his travels, see Nikolai de Khanikoff, *Bokhara: Its Amir and Its People* (London: James Madden, 1845).

72. Jean de Bartholomaei, "Notice sur les médailles des Diodotes, rois de la Bactriane," *Köhne's Zeitschrift für Münze-, Siegel- und Wappenkunde* 3 (1843): 66. The current disposition of this specimen is uncertain; a similar example may be seen in Osmund Bopearachchi, *Sylloge Nummorum Graecorum: The Collection of the American Numismatic Society*, part 9, *Graeco-Bactrian and Indo-Greek Coins* (New York: American Numismatic Society, 1998), no. 259.

73. Raoul Rochette, "Troisième supplement à la Notice sur quelques médailles grecques inédites de rois de la Bactriane et de l'Inde," *Journal des Savants*, 1844: 117, describing this tetradrachm as "le monument numismatique le plus curieux peut-être et le plus rare qui ait apparu, jusqu'ici, dans toute cette suite de découverts, qui constitue un des faits archéologiques les plus neufs et les plus importants de notre époque."

74. On this controversy, see the discussion below.

75. Bartholomaei, "Notice," pp. 65–77.

76. J.G. Droysen, *Geschichte des Hellenismus*, vol. II, *Geschichte der Bildung des hellenistischen Staatensystemes* (Hamburg: Friedrich Perthes, 1843), pp. 760–64. Droysen first turned his attention to numismatics in 1836: Droysen, *Briefwechsel*, ed. Rudolf Hübner (Stuttgart: Deutsche Verlagsanstalt, 1929), vol. I, pp. 90 and 108.

77. The New Testament (Acts 6:1 and 9:29), as well as 2 Maccabees 4:13, uses the much-discussed Greek word *Hellēnistēs* (Ἑλληνιστής) to describe those natives who in some sense embraced Hellenic culture.

78. J. de Bartholomaei, "Réponse à Mr. Droysen sur ses conjectures concernant les premiers rois de la Bactriane," *Köhne's Zeitschrift für Münz-, Siegel- und Wappenkunde* 6 (1846): 129–62, esp. 144. To be fair, Bartholomaei did miss the mark in his critique of where Agathocles likely ruled.

79. See, for example, E. Thomas, "Bactrian Coins," *Numismatic Chronicle* 2 (1862): 184–86; cf. E. Thomas, "Bactrian Coins," *Journal of the Royal Asiatic Society* 20 (1862–63): 123–24.

80. E. Thomas, ed., *Essays on Indian Antiquities,* vol. I, p. xvi.

81. E. Thomas, "Bactrian Coins," *Numismatic Chronicle* 2 (1862): p. 186. Thomas later argued that the obverse portraits of the "superior" kings, such as Diodotus and Euthydemus, were actually struck from dies of those kings, modified only by the addition of the name and epithet: E. Thomas, *Bactrian Coins and Indian Dates* (London: Truebner, 1876), pp. 22–23.

82. A. Cunningham, "Coins of Alexander's Successors in the East," *Numismatic Chronicle* 8 (1868): 281, republished in Cunningham, *Coins of Alexander's Successors in the East* (1884; reprint, Chicago: Argonaut, 1969), p. 103.

83. Ibid., p. 108. Cunningham (p. 115) suggests the word "Lieu-tenant" for this relationship.

84. Ibid., pp. 92–93. Cunningham (pp. 123–25) identified this "Antiochus Nikator" with the Seleucid king Antiochus III, the adversary of Euthydemus.

85. Ibid., p. 110.

86. Ibid., p. 117.

87. Alfred von Sallet, *Die Nachfolger Alexanders des Grossen in Baktrien und Indien* (Berlin: Weidmann, 1879), pp. 14–31.

88. P. Gardner, "On Some Coins of Syria and Bactria," *Numismatic Chronicle* 20 (1880): 181–91. See also Alfred von Sallet, "Alexander der Grosse als Gründer der baktrisch-indischen Reiche," *Zeitschrift für Numismatik* 8 (1881): 279–80.

89. Gardner, "On Some Coins," p. 182.

90. Ibid., p. 184.

91. New kings still occasionally turn up in the numismatic record, such as Thrason, Nasten, and Heliodotus, but the pace of such discoveries has slowed since the extraordinary days of the Great Game.

3. THE GOLD COLOSSUS

1. For the date, and the phrase "ce monstre de la numismatique," see Anatole Chabouillet, "L'Eucratidion: Dissertation sur une médaille d'or inédite d'Eucratide, roi de la Bactriane," *Revue Numismatique* (1867): 383.

2. Ibid., p. 388.

3. Ibid., p. 389.

4. *New York Times* (Mar. 9, 1879): 4; reprinted verbatim (without attribution) in *American Journal of Numismatics* 14.1 (July 1879): 18–20; and in *Gleason's Monthly Companion* 8.6 (June 1879): 278–79. Unless otherwise noted, the quotations that follow derive from this account.

5. Parts of the story appear prominently on the back cover of Osmund Bopearachchi, *Monnaies gréco-bactriennes et indo-grecques: Catalogue raisonné* (Paris: Bibliothèque Nationale, 1991); in Frank Holt, *Alexander the Great and the Mystery of the Elephant Medallions* (Berkeley and Los Angeles: University of California Press, 2003), p. 45; and in the documentary film *The Mystery of the Afghan Gold* (where a dramatization accompanies this author's narration of the story).

6. Vincenzo Cubelli, "Moneta e ideologia monarchica: Il caso di Eucratide," *Rivista Italiana di Numismatica e Scienze Affini* 95 (1993): 252 n. 2.

7. Osmund Bopearachchi and Philippe Flandrin, *Le portrait d'Alexandre le Grand: Histoire d'une découverte pour l'humanité* (Monaco: Éditions du Rocher, 2005), pp. 19–33. In 1991, Bopearachchi, *Monnaies gréco-bactriennes gréco-bactriennes et indo-grecques: Catalogue raisonné*, p. 202 n. 16, had written of "un spécialiste français dont on ignore le nom."

8. Bopearachchi and Flandrin, *Portrait d'Alexandre*, pp. 22 and 27, were not aware of the original source of the story, nor of the additional evidence cited below; they relied instead on the *American Journal of Numismatics* reprint.

9. This information derives from the editorial section of the *American Journal of Numismatics* 14.2 (Oct. 1879): 56, which states: "The article on 'A Coin of Eucratides,' in our July number, was originally printed in the 'New York Times' of March 9, 1879. It was communicated to one of the editors of that journal by Mr. Feuardent, the well known numismatist."

10. See "Obituary: Gaston L. Feuardent," *New York Times* (June 13, 1893): 4. The firm's London office was originally located at 27 Haymarket: s.v. "Rollin, Claude Camille" in Warren Dawson and Eric Uphill, *Who Was Who in Egyptology*, 2nd ed. (London: The Egypt Exploration Society, 1972), p. 252.

11. "Born of a Ball of Fire: What Might Have Been a Very Good

Story about a Huge Sword," *New York Times* (June 17, 1883): 10. Gaston Feuardent did not tolerate untruths for the sake of a very good story.

12. See Anna Marangou, *Life and Deeds: The Consul Luigi Palma di Cesnola, 1832–1904* (Nicosia: The Cultural Centre of the Popular Bank Group, 2000), esp. pp. 297–329; Michael Gross, *Rogues' Gallery: The Secret History of the Moguls and the Money That Made the Metropolitan Museum* (New York: Broadway, 2009), pp. 23–64.

13. Gaston Feuardent, "Tampering with Antiquities: A Serious Charge against the Director of the Metropolitan Museum of Art," *The Art Amateur* (Aug. 1880): 48–50.

14. Oliver Hoover, "The History of the ANS: The Third Decade," *American Numismatic Society Magazine* 1.3 (2002): 41.

15. "Thanking Mr. Feuardent, Resolutions Passed by the Numismatic and Archaeological Society," *New York Times* (Mar. 6, 1884): 8. Feuardent sued Cesnola for libel but failed.

16. *Chicago Daily* (Dec. 17, 1882): 24.

17. M.E.G. Duff, *Notes from a Diary, 1851–1872* (London: John Murray, 1897), vol. II, p. 111.

18. Feuardent, whose Jewish background became an issue in his fight with Cesnola, did not himself refer to the Bukharan as a Jew.

19. A. Cunningham, "Literary and Miscellaneous Intelligence," *Journal of the Asiatic Society of Bengal* 36 (1867): 143. Cunningham may have attended the same council meeting referred to in Sir Mountstuart's diary.

20. A later, shorter extract (the one usually referenced by scholars) appeared in London's *Athenaeum* (Mar. 21, 1868): 2108; later still in the "Varia" of the *American Journal of Numismatics* 3 (1868): 23; and again in "Newspaper Cuttings," *American Journal of Numismatics* 8 (1874): 56; followed there by the remark: "The coin mentioned in this article certainly caused one of the real numismatic sensations of this century. The coin was brought to Europe about 1837 [*sic*], and was finally bought for the collection attached to the Bibliothèque Impériale, now Nationale, at Paris, at the price of 12,000 francs [*sic*]."

21. The tribal name Zebalun (or Zebulun) was associated with Jewish communities in Bukhara and neighboring regions: Joseph Wolff,

Narrative of a Mission to Bokhara, in the Years 1843–1845, to Ascertain the Fate of Colonel Stoddart and Captain Conolly (London: J.W. Parker, 1845), p. 287.

22. Both Clarke and Feuardent joined the Royal Numismatic Society at about the same time: Gaston on November 15, 1866, and Hyde on April 18, 1867.

23. A. Cunningham, "Coins of Alexander's Successors in the East," *Numismatic Chronicle* 9 (1869): 220, republished in Cunningham, *Coins of Alexander's Successors in the East* (1884; reprint, Chicago: Argonaut, 1969), p. 164.

24. For example, *Athenaeum* (Mar. 21, 1868): 2108; *American Journal of Numismatics* 3 (1868): 23; *American Journal of Numismatics* 8 (1874): 56; and *Otago Witness* (June 13, 1868): 3.

25. A similar pattern may be seen after the discovery of the first of Alexander's elephant medallions: Holt, *Alexander the Great and the Mystery of the Elephant Medallions*, pp. 86–90.

26. I carefully examined these casts, along with several forgeries, at the British Museum in June 1984.

27. Torrey, *Gold Coins of Khokand and Bukhara* (New York: American Numismatic Society, 1950).

28. In Greek mythology, the Dioscuri (Διόσκουροι, "Sons of Zeus") were hatched by Leda. The distinctive caps (*piloi*) worn by the twins resembled the tops of the eggs from which they had emerged; the egg caps were surmounted by a star. (See here figs. 10, 23, and 26.) This ancient myth has parallels to the Vedic Asvins.

29. Lionel Fletcher, "The Avent Sale of Oriental Coins," [*Spink and Sons*] *Monthly Numismatic Circular* 6 (Jan. 1898): 2543–44. These specimens weighed 117.09 and 148.55 grams; each bore a different monogram.

30. Ibid. The da Cunha coin was sent from Bombay to London in 1889 to be sold: "Archaeological News," *American Journal of Archaeology and of the History of the Fine Arts* 5.3 (1889): 402. According to the British Museum forgery trays, however, Mrs. da Cunha possessed a gold Eucratidion in May 1906.

31. Formerly the American Numismatic and Archaeological Society. (See chap. 4, below). Coin: Schulman Mail Bid Auction (June 1953):

805A; but note that the photograph of this piece has been switched with that of item 805B. This coin weighs 26 grams and is said to be from the Aboukir find. The ANS fake (1949-11-9) weighs 80.60 grams.

32. British Museum forgery trays, which contain an electrotype copy of this specimen with a blundered inscription.

33. Raymond Hebert, *Aditi: The Monies of India* (Washington, D.C.: Smithsonian Institution, 1985), fig. 8.

34. For yet another plated example in Paris, see *Vrai ou faux? Copier, Imiter, Falsifier* (Paris: Bibliothèque Nationale, 1988), p.142 (85g).

35. Fletcher, "The Avent Sale," p. 2544.

36. For example, E. Rtveladze, *Drevnie Monety Srednej Azii* (Tashkent: Gulyama, 1987), p. 47: "Only two coins of this series are known today: according to A.A. Semyonov one was kept in the treasury of the Emir of Bukhara, the other is now in Paris."

37. The connection of these specimens to India perhaps accounts for the assumption made by some numismatists that the Eucratidion itself came, or at least passed through, the subcontinent. See, for instance, William Hazlitt, *The Coin Collector* (New York: Longmans, Green and Co., 1896), p. 40.

38. Even in a news story about postage stamps, the gold Eucratides coin was invoked for price comparisons: F.W. Crane, "Titians in Stamps," *New York Times* (Apr. 16, 1922): 94, "The highest price paid for a coin ... was $10,000, paid several [55!] years ago in Europe for a unique specimen of a large gold piece struck by Eucratides." The pride of the collector Count Michael Tyskiewicz was that his four Tarsus medallions (a purchase also negotiated by Rollin and Feuardent) eventually rested in the Bibliothèque Nationale alongside "the large medal of Eucratides." See his *Memoirs of an Old Collector* (London: Longmans, Green and Co., 1898), p. 9.

39. Hyman Montagu, "On Some Unpublished and Rare Greek Coins in My Collection," *Numismatic Chronicle* 12 (1892): 37–38.

40. On the colorful history of this specimen, see F. Holt, "The Autobiography of a Coin," *Aramco World* 48.5 (1997): 10–15.

41. The next Eucratides stater would not be found until 1968:

Georges Le Rider, "Monnaies grecques récemment acquises par le Cabinet de Paris," *Revue Numismatique* 6 (1969): 27; F. Holt, "Eukratides of Baktria," *Ancient World* 27.1 (1996): 72–76.

42. Percy Gardner, *The Coins of the Greek and Scythic Kings of Bactria and India in the British Museum* (1886; reprint, Chicago: Argonaut, 1966); particularly useful is the information assembled by Elizabeth Errington and Vesta S. Curtis, *From Persepolis to the Punjab: Exploring Ancient Iran, Afghanistan and Pakistan* (London: British Museum, 2007).

43. The first Eucratides coins to enter the American Numismatic Society in New York were accessioned in 1911 from the bequest of Isaac Greenwood (one silver, seven bronze). See Osmund Bopearachchi, *Sylloge Nummorum Graecorum: The Collection of the American Numismatic Society,* part 9, *Graeco-Bactrian and Indo-Greek Coins* (New York: American Numismatic Society, 1998). The ANS now holds one of the finest collections of Bactrian coins in the world.

4. TELLING TALES

1. Frank Adcock, "Sir William Woodthorpe Tarn," *Proceedings of the British Academy* 44 (1958): 253–62.

2. W.W. Tarn, "Patrocles and the Oxo-Caspian Trade Route," *Journal of Hellenic Studies* 21 (1901): 10–29; Tarn, "Notes on Hellenism," *Journal of Hellenic Studies* 22 (1902): 268–93.

3. Tarn patriotically interrupted his private pursuits during World War I. He was precluded from service in the army because of poor eyesight but volunteered for the Red Cross and worked at Whitehall for the Intelligence Division of the War Office. He even drafted many leaflets that were dropped over Germany: Adcock, "Sir William Woodthorpe Tarn," p. 255.

4. See, for example, Richard Todd, "W.W. Tarn and the Alexander Ideal," *The Historian* 37 (1964): 48–55; A.B. Bosworth, "The Impossible Dream: W.W. Tarn's *Alexander* in Retrospect," *Ancient Society* 13 (1983): 131–50; and W.W. Tarn, *The Greeks in Bactria and India,* 3rd ed., ed. F. Holt (Chicago: Ares Press, 1984), pp. iii–vi.

5. Tarn, "Notes on Hellenism," pp. 270–71.

6. W.W. Tarn, *The Greeks in Bactria and India* (Cambridge: Cambridge University Press, 1938), p. 220.

7. Ibid., p. viii.

8. When Tarn took up the numismatists' catalogues, he cared little about the minutiae of weights, monograms, and die axes; he found portraiture far more interesting, as discussed below.

9. The separation into independent disciplines of those interested in the past has Balkanized ancient studies, but the new millennium has brought forth efforts to bridge some parts of this great divide: Eberhard Sauer, ed., *Archaeology and Ancient History* (London: Routledge, 2004).

10. This, of course, was the institution that had steadfastly supported Gaston Feuardent against Luigi Palma di Cesnola. (See chap. 3, above.)

11. Archer Huntington, "President Huntington's Annual Address," *Proceedings of the American Numismatic and Archaeological Society* (1907): 24–27, esp. 26.

12. H.G. Rawlinson, *Bactria: The History of a Forgotten Empire* (London: Probstbain, 1912; reprint, New York: AMS Press, 1969). Rawlinson considered kings like Eucratides to be "thoroughly Greek" (p. 83) and judged the Eucratidion to be the "high-water mark of Bactrian prosperity," after which Hellenism "gradually decayed" (p. 84).

13. E.J. Rapson, ed., *The Cambridge History of India,* vol. I (Cambridge, 1922; reprint, Delhi: S. Chand, 1962), pp. 384–419 and 487–507.

14. Tarn, *Greeks in Bactria and India,* p. lvi.

15. C.A. Robinson, Jr., "The Greeks in the Far East," *Classical Journal* 44.7 (1949): 406. See also the review by G. Bobrinskoy in *Classical Philology* 35.2 (1940): 189–99.

16. Tarn likened the writing of this book to fiddling with a jigsaw puzzle: P.M. Fraser, *Cities of Alexander the Great* (Oxford: Clarendon Press, 1996), p. viii.

17. Tarn, *Greeks in Bactria and India,* p. 410.

18. Tarn admitted in the preface to the first edition (1938) that he could not write the book impersonally. In one of his published letters, Tarn reveals that he did not see himself as unduly certain about anything: "I desired above all things to avoid creating an illusion of knowl-

edge which neither I nor anyone else could possess." See Julian Romane, "W. W. Tarn on the Art of History," *Ancient World* 15 (1987): 21–24.

19. Percy Gardner, *The Coins of the Greek and Scythic Kings of Bactria and India in the British Museum* (1886; reprint, Chicago: Argonaut, 1966), p. xxiv.

20. Rawlinson, *Bactria*, p. 154.

21. Ibid., p. 156. The italics are Rawlinson's own.

22. In Rapson, ed., *Cambridge History of India*, vol. I, p. 408.

23. Tarn, *Greeks in Bactria and India*, pp. 184 and 196.

24. Tarn ignores the fact that Eucratides' pedigree coins, issued earlier to bolster his claim against Agathocles and Antimachus, had somehow already proclaimed him *Megas*.

25. Ibid., pp. 183–224.

26. As noted by Charles Edson in a review of the second edition (1951), appearing in *Classical Philology* 49 (1954): 112–18.

27. Franz Altheim, *Weltgeschichte Asiens im griechischen Zeitalter*, 2 vols. (Halle: Max Niemeyer, 1947–48). On Altheim's work for the Nazis (arranged through his partner Erika Trautmann), see Heather Pringle, *The Master Plan: Himmler's Scholars and the Holocaust* (New York: Hyperion, 2006), pp. 102–20 and 304–5.

28. For example, Franz Altheim and Ruth Stiehl, *Geschichte Mittelasiens in Altertum* (Berlin: Walter DeGruyter, 1970).

29. Ibid., pp. 560–77.

30. See the preface to his second edition (written Jan. 1950). In this work, Tarn managed under the circumstances only to add some notes to his first edition, without revising the original text.

31. Reprinted in 1969 by Argonaut Publishers, Chicago.

32. R. B. Whitehead, "Notes on the Indo-Greeks," *Numismatic Chronicle* 20 (1940): 90.

33. Ibid., p. 95.

34. A. K. Narain recounts these events in "Approaches and Perspectives," *Yavanika* 2 (1992): 5–34, an address aimed in part at my remarks in *Alexander the Great and Bactria: The Formation of a Greek Frontier in Central Asia* (Leiden: Brill, 1988).

35. A. K. Narain, *The Indo-Greeks* (Oxford: Clarendon Press, 1957).

There is now a second edition: *The Indo-Greeks, Revisited and Supplemented* (Delhi: B.R. Publishing, 2003). This work, like Tarn's second edition, entails not a rewrite but rather a reprint with the addition of later materials. For convenience, this second edition will be cited unless otherwise noted.

36. Ibid., pp. 477–84, taking issue specifically with my remarks about the ethnocentrism of *The Indo-Greeks.* Narain agrees, however, with my statement that Tarn was ethnocentric and reactionary: p. 480.

37. Ibid., p. 18.

38. Ibid., p. 479: "I cannot agree more with Holt's statement that surely Bactria belongs to the history of both the Hellenistic and Indian worlds."

39. Tarn uses about 17 percent of his book to cover Seleucid matters; A.K. Narain, only 9 percent. Conversely, Narain devotes 55 percent of *The Indo-Greeks, Revisited* to the kingdoms in India proper; Tarn, only 46 percent.

40. A.K. Narain, *The Indo-Greeks, Revisited,* p. 480.

41. Holt, *Alexander the Great and Bactria,* pp. 1–4. The place of Bactria in world history cannot so exclusively be claimed by Greece or India, and surely Iranian history has something to say on the matter. Being Hellenistic excludes none of the constituent cultures: the period of the Ptolemies is no less a part of Egyptian history whether we call it Hellenistic, Egypto-Greek, or anything else.

42. Olivier Guillaume, "Naïve Anthropology in the Reconstruction of Indo-Greek History," *The Indian Economic and Social History Review* 27.4 (1990): 475–82, esp. p. 476. Against this historiographic trend, see Rachel Mairs, "Hellenistic India," *New Voices in Classical Reception Studies* 1 (2006): 19–30. A.K. Narain acknowledges in another context that scholars are products of their own ages and groups: *The Indo-Greeks, Revisited,* p. 490.

43. Guillaume, "Naïve Anthropology," pp. 476–77. The term "Indo-Greek" reverses the usual order for such hyphenated descriptors. As with "African-American," "French-Canadian," and "Chinese-American," the first word normally indicates whence a group originated; the latter, where they settled.

44. Whitehead, *Catalogue of Coins,* p. iii.

45. A.K. Narain, *The Indo-Greeks, Revisited,* p. 481: "I had begun detecting his [Tarn's] weaknesses in dealing with the numismatic evidence. I was a student of numismatics and was being trained in the discipline by eminent teachers."

46. Ibid., pp. 486–501.

47. Ibid., p. 493.

48. Ibid., pp. 38–40.

49. Ibid., p. 51.

50. Ibid., pp. 71–90.

51. Tarn, *Greeks in Bactria and India,* p. 229, shows his methodology. He knew of the 1926 Bajaur Hoard in his first edition, but apparently not of the 1942 Bajaur Hoard in time for his second edition. These hoards are numbers 1845 and 1846 in Margaret Thompson, Otto Mørkholm, and Colin Kraay, eds., *An Inventory of Greek Coin Hoards* (New York: American Numismatic Society, 1973).

52. A.K. Narain, *The Indo-Greeks, Revisited,* pp. 140–46. See R. Curiel and D. Schlumberger, *Trésors monétaires d'Afghanistan* (Paris: Klincksieck, 1953); and R. Curiel and G. Fussman, *Le trésor monétaire de Qunduz* (Paris: Klincksieck, 1965).

53. Subtitled *Essai d'interprétation de la symbolique religieuse gréco-orientale du IIIe au Ier s. av. J.-C.* (Paris: Didier, 1956).

54. Ibid., p. 207.

55. Tarn, *Greeks in Bactria and India,* p. lviii.

56. For example, M.-T. Allouche-LePage, *L'art monétaire des royaumes bactriens: Essai d'interprétation de la symbolique religieuse gréco-orientale du IIIe au Ier s. av. J.-C.* (Paris: Didier, 1956), p. 57.

57. Originally published by Wayte Raymond, Inc.; later by the Whitman Publishing Company of Racine, Wisconsin. This influential work has endured into the twenty-first century as required reading for graduate students attending the summer seminar of the American Numismatic Society (ANS) in New York.

58. Newell's admiration for Tarn's work is attested secondhand: Alfred Bellinger, "Review of Tarn, *The Greeks in Bactria and India,*" *American Journal of Archaeology* 45.4 (1941): 648.

59. E. T. Newell, *Royal Greek Portrait Coins* (Racine, Wisc.: Whitman Publishing, 1937), p. 9.

60. Ibid.

61. Ibid., p. 10.

62. For examples, see Norman Davis and Colin Kraay, *The Hellenistic Kingdoms: Portrait Coins and History* (London: Thames and Hudson, 1973); Marit Jentoft-Nilsen, ed., *Ancient Portraiture: The Sculptor's Art in Coins and Marble* (Richmond, Va.: Virginia Museum, 1980); and the works discussed below.

63. E. Rtveladze, *Drevnie Monety Srednej Azii* (Tashkent: Gulyama, 1987), p. 47 (emphasis added).

64. Newell, *Royal Greek Portrait Coins*, p. 78, a passage quoted approvingly by the art historian Gisela Richter, *The Portraits of the Greeks* (London: Phaidon Press, 1965), vol. III, p. 278.

65. Tarn, *Greeks in Bactria and India*, p. 75.

66. Ibid., p. 92. See also Jentoft-Nilsen, *Ancient Portraiture*, p. 26 (coin 22).

67. Ibid., pp. 75–76. The smile, or at least a hint of it, remains topical: Adrian Hollis, "Greek Letters from Hellenistic Bactria," pp. 104–18 in Dirk Obbink and Richard Rutherford, eds., *Culture in Pieces: Essays on Ancient Texts in Honour of Peter Parsons* (Oxford: Oxford University Press, 2011), p. 112.

68. C.-Y. Petitot-Biehler, "Trésor de monnaies grecques et gréco-bactriennes trouvé à Ai Khanoum (Afghanistan)," *Revue Numismatique* 17 (1975): 38–39. She quotes Tarn on the personality of Euthydemus I.

69. O. Mørkholm, *Early Hellenistic Coinage from the Accession of Alexander to the Peace of Apamea (336–188 B.C.)*, ed. Philip Grierson and Ulla Westermark (Cambridge: Cambridge University Press, 1991), p. 121. Archaeologists Svetlana Gorshenina and Claude Rapin also write of "un réalisme psychologiquement nuancé" on the coins: *De Kaboul à Samarcande: Les archéologues en Asie centrale* (Paris: Gallimard, 2001), p. 78.

70. Some have been duly skeptical: Olivier Guillaume, *L'analyse de raisonnements en archéologie: Le cas de la numismatique gréco-bactrienne et indogrecque* (Paris: Éditions Recherche sur les Civilisations, 1987); and Peter Mittag, "Methodologische Überlegungen zur Geschichte Baktriens:

Könige und Münzen," *Schweizerische Numismatische Rundschau* 85 (2006): 27–46. See chap. 7, below.

71. K. Trever, *Pamiatniki greko-baktriiskogo iskusstva* (Moscow: Akademii Nauk, 1940), p. 7; note the similar claim that Euthydemus II's "gentle, un-Greek face" suggests that his mother "was a daughter of the Iranian nobility": Davis and Kraay, *The Hellenistic Kingdoms*, p. 245. This notion persists in K.A. Sheedy, *Alexander and the Hellenistic Kingdoms: The Westmoreland Collection* (Sydney: Australian Centre for Ancient Numismatic Studies, 2007), p. 157.

72. A.K. Narain, *The Indo-Greeks, Revisited*, p. 259 (emphasis added).

73. Ibid., p. 52.

74. S. Kalita, "Portraits of Rulers on Greco-Bactrian and Indo-Greek Coins: An Attempt at Classification," *Notae Numismaticae* 2 (1997): 16.

75. Ibid., p. 10.

76. G.K. Jenkins, *Ancient Greek Coins* (London: Seaby, 1990), pp. 154 and 155.

77. Ibid., p. 155.

78. G. Woodcock, "The Indian Greeks," *History Today* 12 (1962): 563.

79. Ibid., p. 566. George Woodcock later enshrined his views in a popular narrative entitled *The Greeks in India* (London: Faber and Faber, 1966).

80. P. Green, *Alexander to Actium: The Historical Evolution of the Hellenistic Age* (Berkeley and Los Angeles: University of California Press, 1990), pp. 350–51.

81. Green (ibid., p. 351) calls Demetrius I "pompous and determined, every inch the heavy Indian conqueror."

82. Ibid.; and G. Hanfmann, "Personality and Portraiture in Ancient Art," *Proceedings of the American Philosophical Society* 117.4 (1973): 266.

83. Tarn, *Greeks in Bactria and India*, p. 209.

84. Ibid., p. 438.

85. Rawlinson, *Bactria*, pp. 83–84. The adjective "magnificent" is often used: Jens Jakobsson, "The Greeks of Afghanistan Revisited," *Nomismatika Khronika* 26 (2007): 61; cf. Vincenzo Cubelli, "Moneta e ideologia monarchica: Il caso di Eucratide," *Rivista Italiana di Numismatica e*

Scienze Affini 95 (1993): 259: "uno splendido, forse un po' arrogante documento."

86. S. Narain, "The Twenty-Stater Gold Piece of Eucratides I," *Journal of the Numismatic Society of India* 18 (1956): 217.

87. Allouche-LePage, *L'art monétaire,* p. 59, citing Jean Babelon, *Le portrait dans l'antiquité d'après les monnaies* (Paris: Payot, 1942), p. 87.

88. A. Chabouillet, "L'Eucratidion: Dissertation sur une médaille d'or inédite d'Eucratide, roi de la Bactriane," *Revue Numismatique* (1867): 389–90. This view was challenged by Charles de Linas, *Les origines de l'orfèvrerie cloisonné* (Paris: Édouard Didron, 1878), vol. I, pp. 270–72.

89. See, for example, Kjetil Kvist, "Tetradrachms of Antimachos Exhibit the High Quality of Greek Art," *The Celator* 11 (Mar. 1997): 18–20. Although generally cautious, he concludes: "I will not speculate on the ethnicity of the die engraver, but, like Head, end up in the old-fashioned view that the celator *had to be Greek*" (emphasis added).

90. Chabouillet, "L'Eucratidion," p. 391.

91. Tarn, *Greeks in Bactria and India,* p. 209.

92. Ibid.

93. For which see chapter 8, below.

94. Guillaume, *L'analyse de raisonnements,* p. 78. See further discussion below, chapter 7.

95. See the discussion in F. Holt, *Thundering Zeus: The Making of Hellenistic Bactria* (Berkeley and Los Angeles: University of California Press, 1999), pp. 68–69 and 126–27.

5. WANTED—ONE GREEK CITY

1. Strabo 15.1.3 and Justin 41.4.6.

2. W.W. Tarn, "Notes on Hellenism," *Journal of Hellenic Studies* 22 (1902): 292.

3. Ibid., p. 271 (emphasis added).

4. W. Flinders Petrie, *Seventy Years in Archaeology* (Holt, 1932; reprint, New York: Greenwood Press, 1969), p. 15.

5. The lure of Alexander proved irresistible: General Ventura dug out the Great Stupa at Manikyala because he thought it was the site of

Bucephala, a city founded by Alexander in honor of his legendary war-horse, Bucephalus: J.-B. Ventura, "Account of the Excavations of Tope Manikyala," *Asiatic Researches* 17 (1832): 600–603.

6. On Masson's nickname, see Bérénice Geoffroy-Schneiter, *Gandhara: The Memory of Afghanistan* (New York: Assouline, 2001), p. 8. To his credit, Masson did strive to document and publish what he found.

7. On this Alexandria, see P.M. Fraser, *Cities of Alexander the Great* (Oxford: Clarendon Press, 1996), pp. 140–51; and Paul Bernard, "Diodore XVII, 83, 1: Alexandrie du Caucase ou Alexandrie de l'Oxus?" *Journal des Savants*, 1982: 217–42, which responds to a different interpretation by Paul Goukowsky, *Essai sur les origines du mythe d'Alexandre (336–270 av. J.-C.)*, vol. I: *Les origines politiques* (Nancy: Bialec, 1978), pp. 155–59. The stage had been set for such investigations by James Rennell in 1788, when he correctly identified modern Patna as the location of ancient Pataliputra, known from classical sources as the capital of the Mauryan empire. On this discovery, see Dilip Chakrabarti, *India: An Archaeological History* (Oxford: Oxford University Press, 1999), p. 5.

8. A splendid summary may be found in Elizabeth Errington, "Charles Masson and Begram," *Topoi* 11 (2001): 357–409.

9. For archaeological work carried out in Afghanistan down to 1981, an indispensable reference is Warwick Ball, *Archaeological Gazetteer of Afghanistan*, 2 vols. (Paris: Éditions Recherche sur les Civilizations, 1982). This work is supplemented now by Ball, *The Monuments of Afghanistan: History, Archaeology and Architecture* (New York: I.B. Tauris, 2008). See also the convenient new introduction by Rachel Mairs, *The Archaeology of the Hellenistic Far East: A Survey* (Oxford: BAR, 2011) and, for the Achaemenid period, Henri-Paul Francfort, "Asie centrale," pp. 313–52 in Pierre Briant and Rémy Boucharlat, eds., *L'archéologie de l'empire achéménide: Nouvelles recherches* (Paris: Diffusion de Boccard, 2005).

10. On the politicization of archaeology, see S. Gorshenina and C. Rapin, *De Kaboul à Samarcande: Les archéologues en Asie centrale* (Paris: Gallimard, 2001), pp. 51–67; and discussion below.

11. Paul Bernard, "L'œuvre de la Délégation Archéologique Française en Afghanistan (1922–1982)," *Comptes-Rendus de l'Académie des Inscriptions et Belles-Lettres*, 2002: 1287–1323. Françoise Olivier-Utard, *Politique et*

archéologie: Histoire de la Délégation Archéologique Française en Afghanistan (1922–1982) (Paris: Éditions Recherche sur les Civilisations, 1997), provides a detailed account of the creation of the DAFA and its subsequent personnel, budgets, and operations.

12. Geoffroy-Schneiter, *Gandhara*, p. 9. Foucher had a passing interest in numismatics: O. Bopearachchi, "Alfred Foucher et les études numismatiques en Afghanistan," *Comptes-Rendus de l'Académie des Inscriptions et Belles-Lettres,* 2007: 1875–97.

13. Joseph Hackin, *Recherches archéologiques à Bégram: Chantier no. 2 (1937),* 2 vols. (Paris: de Nobele, 1939); Hackin, *Nouvelles recherches archéologiques à Bégram (1939–1940),* 2 vols. (Paris: Presses Universitaires de France, 1954); and Roman Ghirshman, *Bégram: Recherches archéologiques et historiques sur les Kouchans* (Cairo: Institut Français d'Archéologie Orientale, 1946).

14. These finds were among those featured in the international exhibition "Afghanistan: Hidden Treasures from the National Museum, Kabul." On the objects and arguments about them, consult the catalogue of the same title edited by Fredrik Hiebert and Pierre Cambon (Washington, D.C.: National Geographic Society, 2008).

15. Sanjyot Mehendale, "The Begram Ivory and Bone Carvings: Some Observations on Provenance and Chronology," *Topoi* 11 (2001): 485–514.

16. One excavator for the DAFA used coin finds of Eucratides to date parts of the site: Ghirshman, *Bégram: Recherches archéologiques,* pp. 23–26.

17. Polybius 10.49 and 11.39; cf. 29.12.8.

18. Robert Byron, *The Road to Oxiana* (1937; reprint, New York: Oxford University Press, 1966), p. 257: "Until Foucher came here a few years ago and bought them all up, the old Greek coins of Bactria were still in circulation. Since then, people have begun to think them priceless and ask twenty or thirty times the museum value for them."

19. Joseph Hackin, "Répartition des monnaies anciennes en Afghanistan," *Journal Asiatique* 226 (1935): 287–92.

20. Olivier-Utard, *Politique et archéologie,* pp. 59–60. Article 1 of the Convention gave a monopoly to the French, but Article 11 (later invoked) gave the Afghan government the right to allow other nations to dig sites

not being explored by the DAFA. Bernard, "L'œuvre de la Délégation Archéologique Française," p. 1290, notes that Foucher supported in vain an exception to the monopoly on behalf of Sir Aurel Stein, who had wished to excavate at Balkh since 1902.

21. Olivier-Utard, *Politique et archéologie*, p. 71.

22. A. Foucher, *La vieille route de l'Inde de Bactres à Taxila*, 2 vols. (Paris: de Nobele, 1942–47), esp. vol. I, pp. 73–141.

23. Paul Bernard, "Ai Khanoum on the Oxus: A Hellenistic City in Central Asia," *Proceedings of the British Academy* 53 (1967): 72.

24. Jaquetta Hawkes, *Mortimer Wheeler: Adventurer in Archaeology* (London: Weidenfeld and Nicolson, 1982), pp. 253–54. Wheeler later had A.K. Narain among his students: Narain, *The Indo-Greeks, Revisited and Supplemented* (Delhi: B.R. Publishing, 2003), p. 484.

25. Mortimer Wheeler, "Archaeology in Afghanistan," *Antiquity* 21 (1947): 63. The well-known historian Arnold Toynbee also felt the allure of this place: "Today I have seen Balkh with my own eyes." Toynbee, *Between Oxus and Jumna* (New York: Oxford University Press, 1961), p. 92.

26. Mortimer Wheeler, *Archaeology from the Earth* (Oxford: Clarendon Press, 1954), p. 90; see also "Archaeology in Afghanistan," pp. 62–63.

27. Wheeler, "Archaeology in Afghanistan," p. 65.

28. Hawkes, *Mortimer Wheeler*, p. 325. On subsequent work at Balkh, see R.S. Young, "The South Wall of Balkh-Bactra," *American Journal of Archaeology* 59 (1955): 267–76; and D. Schlumberger, "La prospection archéologique de Bactres (printemps 1947)," *Syria* 26 (1949): 173–90.

29. Cunningham undertook some archaeological work as early as 1861: Chakrabarti, *India: An Archaeological History*, pp. 8–9.

30. John Marshall, *Taxila*, 3 vols. (Cambridge: Cambridge University Press, 1951).

31. Ibid., vol. I, p. xv.

32. For problems surrounding the site's development, see P. Callieri, "The North-West of the Indian Subcontinent in the Indo-Greek Period," pp. 293–308 in Antonio Invernizzi, ed., *In the Land of the Gryphons* (Florence: Casa Editrice Le Lettre, 1995); and Robin Coningham and Briece Edwards, "Space and Society at Sirkap, Taxila: A Re-Examination of Urban Form and Meaning," *Ancient Pakistan* 12 (1997–98): 47–75.

33. Ibid., p. 41.

34. See the early arguments and evidence laid out by Daniel Schlumberger, "Descendants non-méditerranéens de l'art grec," *Syria* 37 (1960): 131–66 and 253–318. Mortimer Wheeler's suggestion (contra Marshall, *Taxila*) still carries weight: Kurt Behrendt, *The Buddhist Architecture of Gandhara* (Leiden: Brill, 2004), p. 271.

35. Mortimer Wheeler, *Charsada: A Metropolis of the North-West Frontier* (Oxford: Oxford University Press, 1962). The site has since been reinvestigated: R. Coningham and I. Ali, *Charsadda: The British-Pakistani Excavations at the Bala Hisar* (Oxford: Archaeopress, 2007).

36. Mortimer Wheeler, *Flames over Persepolis: Turning Point in History* (New York: Reynal, 1968), pp. 96 and 101.

37. Ibid., pp. 99–101 (with photograph).

38. Ibid., p. 101, citing also the soundings of A.H. Dani in 1963 and 1964.

39. Gérard Fussman, "Southern Bactria and Northern India before Islam: A Review of Archaeological Reports," *Journal of the American Oriental Society* 116.2 (1996): 255. See especially Domenico Faccenna, *Butkara I (Swat, Pakistan) 1956–1962*, 5 vols. (Rome: IsMEO, 1980). For other explorations, see M. Ashraf Khan, "Outline of the Archaeological Field Research in Swat Valley Carried Out by Pakistani Institutions," *Journal of Asian Civilizations* 34 (2010): 81–93.

40. Anthony McNicoll and Warwick Ball, *Excavations at Kandahar 1974 and 1975* (Oxford: Archaeopress, 1996); Svend Helms, *Excavations at Old Kandahar in Afghanistan 1976–1978* (Oxford: Archaeopress, 1997).

41. Irina Kruglikova, "Les fouilles de la mission archéologique soviet-afghane sur le site gréco-kushan de Dilberdjin en Bactriane (Afghanistan)," *Comptes-Rendus de l'Académie des Inscriptions et Belles-Lettres,* 1977: 407–27, esp. p. 410, and (in Russian) *Delbarjin, Temple of the Dioscuri* (Moscow: Nauka, 1986). Note, however, the dissenting views of Ciro Lo Muzio, "The Dioscuri at Dilberjin (Northern Afghanistan): Reviewing Their Chronology and Significance," *Studia Iranica* 28 (1999): 41–71.

42. Alberto Simonetta, "Some Hypotheses on the Military and Political Structure of the Indo-Greek Kingdom," *Journal of the Numismatic Society of India* 22 (1960): 56.

43. Bernard, "Ai Khanoum on the Oxus," pp. 73–74.

44. Z. Tarzi, "Jules Barthoux, le découvreur oublié d'Ai Khanoum," *Comptes-Rendus de l'Académie des Inscriptions et Belles-Lettres*, 1996: 595–611.

45. P. Bernard, "Ai Khanoum en Afghanistan hier (1964–1978) et aujourd'hui (2001): Un site en peril," *Comptes-Rendus de l'Académie des Inscriptions et Belles-Lettres*, 2001: 971–1029.

46. See the extensive "Bibliographie de Paul Bernard" in *Bulletin of the Asia Institute* 12 (1998): 3–11. In spite of these efforts, some specialists have strongly criticized Bernard's excavation and publication practices: Fussman, "Southern Bactria and Northern India before Islam," pp. 245–54. See Bernard, "Ai Khanoum en Afghanistan hier (1964–1978) et aujourd'hui (2001)," pp. 1012–14.

47. See the works of P. Bernard, O. Guillaume, H.-P. Francfort, P. Leriche, C. Rapin, A. Rougeulle, and S. Veuve listed below in the Select Bibliography.

48. The pottery promises to be very important for numerous problems beyond chronology, including considerations of ongoing contact between Bactria and the Mediterranean world: Jean-Claude Gardin, "La céramique hellénistique en Asie centrale: Problèmes d'interpretation," *Akten des XIII. Internationalen Kongresses für klassische Archäologie, Berlin 1988* (Mainz am Rhein: Philipp von Zabern, 1990), pp. 187–93; Bertille Lyonnet, "Contributions récentes de la céramologie à l'histoire de l'Afghanistan," *Arts Asiatiques* 40 (1985): 41–52. See also note 88, below.

49. Fountain: P. Leriche and J. Thoraval, "La fontaine du rempart de l'Oxus à Ai Khanoum," *Syria* 56 (1979): 171–205; hoards: the original French publications have been conveniently collected, translated (by Osmund Bopearachchi), and republished (with additional materials) in Olivier Guillaume, ed., *Graeco-Bactrian and Indian Coins from Afghanistan* (Oxford: Oxford University Press, 1991). Separately published: F. Holt, "The Euthydemid Coinage of Bactria: Further Hoard Evidence from Ai Khanoum," *Revue Numismatique* 23 (1981): 7–44. See chapter 7, below.

50. Some highly important questions, such as the chronology of the site, remain unsettled pending final publication. See, for example, Jeffrey Lerner, "Correcting the Early History of Ay Kanom," *Archäologische*

Mitteilungen aus Iran und Turan 35–36 (2003–4): 373–410; and note 88, below.

51. Surkh Kotal was discovered in 1951 and excavated by Daniel Schlumberger from 1952 to 1963; on its inscriptions, see the following chapter.

52. Bernard, "Ai Khanoum on the Oxus," p. 78.

53. P. Bernard, "Chapiteaux corinthiens hellénistiques d'Asie centrale découverts a Ai Khanoum," *Syria* 45 (1968): 111–51.

54. Bernard, "Ai Khanoum on the Oxus," p. 91.

55. For his recent views, see Paul Bernard, "The Greek Colony at Ai Khanoum and Hellenism in Central Asia," pp. 81–105 in F. Hiebert and P. Cambon, eds., *Afghanistan: Hidden Treasures from the National Museum, Kabul* (Washington, D.C.: National Geographic Society, 2008).

56. Olivier Guillaume and Axelle Rougeulle, *Fouilles d'Ai Khanoum,* vol. VII, *Les petits objets* (Paris: Diffusion de Boccard, 1987), pp. 3–74.

57. Henri-Paul Francfort, *Fouilles d'Ai Khanoum,* vol. III, *La sanctuaire du temple à niches indentées* (Paris: Diffusion de Boccard, 1984); Frantz Grenet, "Mithra au temple principal d'Ai Khanoum?" pp. 147–53 in Paul Bernard and Frantz Grenet, eds., *Histoire et cultes de l'Asie centrale préislamique: Sources écrites et documents archéologiques* (Paris: CNRS, 1991).

58. C. Rapin, "Greeks in Afghanistan: Ai Khanoum," pp. 329–42 in Jean-Paul Descoedres, ed., *Greek Colonists and Native Populations* (Canberra: Humanities Research Centre, 1990), pp. 340–41.

59. J.-C. Gardin and P. Gentelle, "Irrigation et peuplement dans la plaine d'Ai Khanoum de l'époque achéménide à l'époque musulmane," *Bulletin de l'École Française d'Extrême-Orient* 63 (1976): 59–99; Gardin and B. Lyonnet, "La prospection archéologique de la Bactriane orientale (1974–1978): Premiers résultats," *Mesopotamia* 13–14 (1978–79): 99–154; Gardin, Gentelle, and Lyonnet, *Prospection archéologiques en Bactriane orientale, 1974–1978,* 3 vols. (Paris: Éditions Recherche sur les Civilizations, 1980–98). See also P. Bernard and H.-P. Francfort, *Études de géographie historique sur la plaine d'Ai Khanoum* (Paris: CNRS, 1978).

60. See J.-C. Gardin, *Archaeological Constructs* (Cambridge: Cambridge University Press, 1980). On these developments (which will be relevant to discussions of numismatics in subsequent chapters), see C.

Renfrew and P. Bahn, *Archaeology: Theories, Methods and Practice*, 3rd ed. (New York: Thames and Hudson, 2000).

61. H.-P. Francfort, *Fouilles de Shortughai: Recherches sur l'Asie centrale protohistorique* (Paris: Diffusion de Boccard, 1989).

62. C. Rapin, "Nomads and the Shaping of Central Asia: From the Early Iron Age to the Kushan Period," p. 41 in J. Cribb and G. Herrmann, eds., *After Alexander: Central Asia before Islam* (Oxford: Oxford University Press, 2007); Rapin, "Le nom antique d'Ai Khanoum et de son fleuve," p. 115 in O. Bopearachchi et al., eds., *De l'Indus à l'Oxus: Archéologie de l'Asie centrale* (Lattes: Imago, 2003); A.K. Narain, *The Indo-Greeks, Revisited and Supplemented*, pp. 373–84. Alternatively, Alexandria Oxiana may have been located at Termez: Bernard, "Diodore XVII, 83, 1: Alexandrie du Caucase ou Alexandrie de l'Oxus?" p. 236.

63. See, for example, P. Bernard, *Fouilles d'Ai Khanoum*, vol. IV, *Les monnaies hors trésors* (Paris: Diffusion de Boccard, 1985), p. 9.

64. The majority of finds from storeroom 109 seem to be from India, including coins: Claude Rapin, *Fouilles d'Ai Khanoum*, vol. VIII, *La trésorerie du palais hellénistique d'Ai Khanoum* (Paris: Diffusion de Boccard, 1992), p. 282. On other Indian treasures such as a throne and inlaid plaque, assumed to have been seized by Eucratides, see Rapin, *Indian Art from Afghanistan: The Legend of Sakuntala and the Indian Treasure of Eucratides at Ai Khanoum* (New Delhi: Manohar Publishers, 1996).

65. Bernard, *Fouilles d'Ai Khanoum*, vol. IV, pp. 83–84. On this mint, see Holt, *Thundering Zeus: The Making of Hellenistic Bactria* (Berkeley and Los Angeles: University of California Press, 1999), pp. 124–25.

66. On the coins in general, see Guillaume, ed., *Graeco-Bactrian and Indian Coins from Afghanistan*, pp. 25–195.

67. These hoards have become famous for their richness: Hélène Nicolet-Pierre, *Numismatique grecque* (Paris: Armand Colin, 2005), p. 37.

68. Holt, "The Euthydemid Coinage of Bactria." See chapter 7, below.

69. Osmund Bopearachchi, "Récentes découvertes de trésors de monnaies pré-sassanides trouvés en Afghanistan et au Pakistan," *Cahiers Numismatiques*, Sept. 1994: 7–14, and "Recent Hoard Evidence on Pre-Kushana Chronology," pp. 99–149 in M. Alram and D. Klimburg-

Salter, eds., *Coins, Art, and Chronology: Essays on the Pre-Islamic History of the Indo-Iranian Borderlands* (Vienna: Verlag der Österreichischen Akademie der Wissenschaften, 1999), pp. 110–11.

70. P. Bernard, "Campagne de fouilles 1978 à Ai Khanoum (Afghanistan)," *Comptes-Rendus de l'Académie des Inscriptions et Belles-Lettres,* 1980: 435–59, esp. p. 442.

71. The archaeologists all stress the Greek abandonment of Ai Khanoum, whereas the local population apparently remained and pillaged the site. On these events, see Rapin, *Indian Art from Afghanistan,* pp. 10–11.

72. Rapin, *Indian Art from Afghanistan,* pp. 105–21, provides an ambitious narrative.

73. Pierre Leriche, "Bactria, Land of a Thousand Cities," pp. 121–53 in J. Cribb and G. Herrmann, eds., *After Alexander: Central Asia before Islam* (Oxford: Oxford University Press, 2007), p. 142 n. 47. Either the population had declined to dangerous levels or a Bactrian army had suffered a huge defeat somewhere in the field. This problem will be raised below, in chapters 8 and 9.

74. Bernard, "The Greek Colony at Ai Khanoum and Hellenism in Central Asia," p. 104.

75. V. Sarianidi, *The Temple and Tombs at Tillya Tepe* (Moscow: Nauka, 1989), in Russian with a good analysis of the pottery. For a lavishly illustrated account of the discovery, see Sarianidi, *The Golden Hoard of Bactria* (New York: Abrams, 1985).

76. For example, the 1985 History Channel film *The Mystery of the Afghan Gold* (director: David Keane) insinuates that this treasure (like King Tut's) actually carried an ancient curse.

77. Eugene Schuyler, *Turkistan: Notes of a Journey in Russian Turkistan, Khokand, Bukhara, and Kuldja* (New York: Scribner, Armstrong, and Company, 1876), p. 236 n. 1, reports on the kinds of unsystematic excavations undertaken at Afrasiab back in 1875.

78. On the background of Soviet work in the region, see B.A. Litvinsky, "Archaeology in Tadzikistan under Soviet Rule," *East and West* 18 (1968): 125–46.

79. Paul Bernard et al., "Fouilles de la mission franco-soviétique à l'ancienne Samarcand (Afrasiab): Première campagne," *Comptes-Rendus*

de l'Académie des Inscriptions et Belles-Lettres, 1990: 356–80; Paul Bernard et al., "Fouilles de la mission franco-ouzbèque à l'ancienne Samarcand (Afrasiab): Deuxième et troisième campagnes," *Comptes-Rendus de l'Académie des Inscriptions et Belles-Lettres,* 1992: 275–311.

80. See, e.g., P. Leriche and C. Pidaev, *Termez sur Oxus: Cité-capitale d'Asie centrale* (Paris: Maisonneuve and Larose, 2008); J. Gurt et al., *Preliminary Report of the First Season Work of the International Pluridisciplinary Archaeological Expedition in Bactria* (Barcelona: ERAUB, 2008); and N.A. Beregovaia, U. Islamov, and A.N. Kalandadze, *Contributions to the Archaeology of the Soviet Union, with Special Emphasis on Central Asia, the Caucasus and Armenia* (Cambridge, Mass.: Peabody Museum, 1966).

81. E. Rtveladze, *Kampyr Tepe,* 4 vols. (Tashkent: San'at, 2000–2006), and *Makedoniyalik Aleksandr i Baqtria va So'g'diyonada* (Tashkent: Academy of Fine Arts of the Republic of Uzbekistan, 2002). This site, like Ai Khanoum, has been identified as Alexandria Oxiana, and also as Pandokheion: P. Leriche, "Bactria, Land of a Thousand Cities," p. 133. (The reference not given by Leriche is V. Minorsky, "A Greek Crossing on the Oxus," *Bulletin of the School of Oriental and African Studies* 30.1 [1967]: 45–53.)

82. V. Nikonorov and S. Savchuk, "New Data on Ancient Bactrian Body-Armour (in the Light of Finds from Kampyr Tepe)," *Iran* 30 (1992): 49–54.

83. B. Litvinsky and I. Pichikyan, *Ellinisticheskiy khram Oksa v Baktrii (Iuzhnyi Tadzikistan),* 3 vols. (Moscow: Vostoknaya Literatura, 2000–2010), vol. II. For additional work, see Angelina Drujinina, "Die Ausgrabungen in Taxt-i Sangin im Oxos-Tempelbereich," *Archäologische Mitteilungen aus Iran und Turan* 33 (2001): 257–92; and Drujinina and N. Boroffka, "First Preliminary Report on the Excavations in Takht-i Sangin 2004," *Bulletin of the Miho Museum* 6 (2006): 57–69. On the important inscription found at this site, see below, chapter 6.

84. Summarized by G.A. Koshelenko, "The Fortifications at Gobekly-depe," and by V.A. Zavylov, "The Fortifications of the City of Gyaur Kala, Merv," pp. 269–83 and 313–29, respectively, in J. Cribb and G. Herrmann, eds., *After Alexander: Central Asia before Islam* (Oxford: Oxford University Press, 2007).

85. Natalia Smirnova, "On Finds of Hellenistic Coins in Turkmenistan," *Ancient Civilizations from Scythia to Siberia* 3 (1996): 260–85.

86. Sebastian Stride, "Regions and Territories in Southern Central Asia: What the Surkhan Darya Province Tells Us about Bactria," pp. 99–117 in J. Cribb and G. Herrmann, eds., *After Alexander: Central Asia before Islam* (Oxford: Oxford University Press, 2007).

87. P. Leriche, "Bactria, Land of a Thousand Cities," pp. 132–33 and 136–37.

88. Bertille Lyonnet, "Les Grecs, les nomades et l'indépendance de la Sogdiane, d'après l'occupation comparée d'Ai Khanoum et de Marakanda au cours des derniers siècles avant notre ère," *Bulletin of the Asia Institute* 12 (1998): 141–59. Lyonnet's chronology has recently been challenged, with potential repercussions for Ai Khanoum, Kurganzol Fortress, and other sites: Jeffrey Lerner, "Revising the Chronologies of the Hellenistic Colonies of Samarkand-Marakanda (Afrasiab II–III) and Ai Khanoum (Northeastern Afghanistan)," *Anabasis* 1 (2010): 58–79. Another article by Lerner, "A Reappraisal of the Economic Inscriptions and Coin Finds from Ai Khanoum," *Anabasis* 2 (2011): 103–47, has just appeared, too late for anything more than an acknowledgment of it here. It proposes a very controversial argument on the coin-based chronology of the site that must be analyzed elsewhere.

89. Osmund Bopearachchi, "The Euthydemus Imitations and the Date of Sogdian Independence," *Silk Road Art and Archaeology* 2 (1991–92): 1–21.

90. Leonid Sverchkov, "The Kurganzol Fortress (On the History of Central Asia in the Hellenistic Era)," *Ancient Civilizations from Scythia to Siberia* 14 (2008): 123–91.

91. F. Holt, *Into the Land of Bones* (Berkeley and Los Angeles: University of California Press, 2005), pp. 145–48. The Buddhas were bombed on March 11, 2001.

92. O. Massoudi, "The National Museum of Afghanistan," and C. Grissmann and F. Hiebert, "Saving Afghanistan's Heritage," pp. 35–41 and 45–53, respectively, in F. Hiebert and P. Cambon, eds., *Afghanistan: Hidden Treasures from the National Museum, Kabul* (Washington, D.C.: National Geographic Society, 2008). See also Frank Holt, "The Trag-

edies and Treasures of Afghanistan," *American Scientist* 97.3 (2009): 248–49.

93. On the recovery of the museum, see Carla Grissmann, "The Inventory of the Kabul Museum: Attempts at Restoring Order," *Museum International* 55.3–4 (2003): 71–76; Francine Tissot, *Catalogue of the National Museum of Afghanistan 1931–1985* (Paris: UNESCO, 2006). A group of ivories from the Begram treasure has recently been returned to the museum: St. John Simpson, "Ancient Afghanistan Revealed," *World Archaeology Magazine* 46.4 (2011): 16–24.

94. P. Bernard, J.-F. Jarrige, and R. Besenval, "Carnet de route en images d'un voyage sur les sites archéologiques de la Bactriane afghan," *Comptes-Rendus de l'Académie des Inscriptions et Belles-Lettres*, 2002: 1385–1428.

95. Petrie, *Seventy Years in Archaeology*, p. 20

96. Schlumberger, "La prospection," pp. 186–87. The portrait cannot be attributed, but it resembles closely the coinages of the early second century B.C.E. and, based on the diadem and cloak, could be anyone from Demetrius I to Heliocles I.

97. Ibid., pp. 189–90.

98. For the latest results, see R. Besenval and P. Marquis, "Les travaux de la Délégation Archéologique Française en Afghanistan (DAFA)," *Comptes-Rendus de l'Académie des Inscriptions et Belles-Lettres*, 2008: 973–95. On Chesm-e Shafa, see Andrew Lawler, "Edge of an Empire," *Archaeology* 64.5 (2011): 42–47.

99. Bernard, "Ai Khanoum on the Oxus," p. 75.

100. Bernard, "Ai Khanoum en Afghanistan hier (1964–1978) et aujourd'hui (2001)," pp. 991–1029.

101. Most of this material remains unpublished and in private hands. I thank Osmund Bopearachchi and others for bringing it to my attention. (See chap. 7, below.)

102. Anna Badkhen, "War Gives Cover to Antiquities Looter," *San Francisco Chronicle* (Nov. 3, 2001): p. A1.

103. Abdul Wasay Najimi, "Built Heritage in Afghanistan: Threats, Challenges and Conservation," *International Journal of Environmental*

Studies 68 (2011): 343–61. Since 2002, the Aga Khan Trust for Culture has been supporting some conservation projects and training in Afghanistan. For an indispensable assessment of the ongoing cultural heritage crisis, see Juliette van Krieken–Pieters, ed., *Art and Archaeology of Afghanistan: Its Fall and Survival* (Leiden: Brill, 2006).

104. See, for example, David Thomas et al., "The Archaeological Sites of Afghanistan in Google Earth," *Aerial Archaeology Research Group Newsletter* 37 (2008): 22–30.

105. For example, Director Daniel Schlumberger declared in 1946 that, in spite of its many commitments to Afghan history and archaeology in general, it was "pour trouver des sites grecs que la Délégation Archéologique a été constituée." See Schlumberger, "Rapport sur une mission en Afghanistan," *Comptes-Rendus de l'Académie des Inscriptions et Belles-Lettres,* 1946: 174.

106. Bernard's phrase "the Greek language as the cement for national identity" is a striking example: see p. 95 in F. Hiebert and P. Cambon, eds., *Afghanistan: Hidden Treasures from the National Museum, Kabul* (Washington, D.C.: National Geographic Society, 2008).

6. LETTERS HERE AND THERE

1. A Babylonian cuneiform text mentions an anonymous satrap from Seleucid Bactria who sent elephants to Antiochus I in about 275 B.C.E., for which see Sidney Smith, ed., *Babylonian Historical Texts* (London: Methuen, 1924), pp. 150–59.

2. Félix Durrbach, ed., *Inscriptions de Délos* (Paris: Librairie Ancienne Honoré Champion, 1929), nos. 442 B, l. 109, and 443 Bb, l. 33; F. Durrbach and P. Roussel, eds., *Inscriptions de Délos* (Paris: Librairie Ancienne Honoré Champion, 1935), no. 1432 Aa II, ll. 26–27. These dedications were made between 178 and about 166 B.C.E.

3. Monika Schuol, *Die Charakene: Ein mesopotamisches Königreich in hellenistisch-parthischer Zeit* (Stuttgart: Franz Steiner Verlag, 2000). On the name, see Rüdiger Schmitt, "Der Name Hyspasines (samt Varianten)," *Bulletin of the Asia Institute* 4 (1990): 245–49.

4. Alfred Bellinger, "Hyspaosines of Charax," *Yale Classical Studies* 8 (1942): 52–67. Bellinger guessed that this Hyspaosines was a grandson of King Euthydemus, a view disputed by Paul Bernard, *Fouilles d'Ai Khanoum*, vol. IV, *Les monnaies hors trésors* (Paris: Diffusion de Boccard, 1985), pp. 135–36.

5. Reported by Daniel Schlumberger in Edmond Faral, "Séance du 14 Mars," *Comptes-Rendus de l'Académie des Inscriptions et Belles-Lettres*, 1947: 241–42; see also Mortimer Wheeler, "Archaeology in Afghanistan," *Antiquity* 21 (1947): 63.

6. The most useful reference works on Greek inscriptions from Central Asia are now Filippo Canali de Rossi, ed., *Iscrizioni dello estremo oriente greco* (Bonn: Rudolf Habelt, 2004); and Reinhold Merkelbach and Josef Stauber, eds., *Jenseits des Euphrat: Griechische Inschriften* (Munich: K.G. Saur, 2005). For the Tepe Nimlik fragment, see Canali de Rossi, ed., *Iscrizioni*, p. 195 (no. 303).

7. B. Litvinsky and I. Pichikyan, *Ellinisticheskiy khram Oksa v Baktrii (Iuzhnyi Tadzikistan)*, 3 vols. (Moscow: Vostoknaya Literatura, 2000–2010).

8. Ibid., vol. I, pp. 305–7; B. Litvinsky, I. Pichikyan, and Y.G. Vinogradov, "The Votive Offering of Atrosokes, from the Temple of the Oxus in Northern Bactria" (in Russian with English summary), *Vestnik Drevnej Istorii* (1985): 84–110. See also Canali de Rossi, ed., *Iscrizioni*, p. 198 (no. 311); Merkelbach and Stauber, eds., *Jenseits des Euphrat: Griechische Inschriften*, p. 16 (no. 104).

9. An inscribed vessel from Takht-i Sangin records in Greek another votive offering to the Oxus: Canali de Rossi, ed., *Iscrizioni*, p. 199 (no. 312); Angelina Drujinina, "Die Ausgrabungen in Taxt-i Sangin im Oxos-Tempelbereich," *Archäologische Mitteilungen aus Iran und Turan* 33 (2001): 257–92.

10. Shaul Shaked, *Le satrape de Bactriane et son gouverneur: Documents araméens du IVe s. avant notre ère* (Paris: Diffusion de Boccard, 2004), pp. 24 and 47–48, identifies several Bactrians with theophoric names indicating veneration of Vakshu (Greek Oxus). This form of devotion preceded the arrival of the Greeks and continued unabated.

11. G. Pugliesi-Carratelli, "Greek Inscriptions of the Middle East,"

East and West 16 (1966): 35–36, who takes this to be a Greek name (*Nous*); Canali de Rossi, ed., *Iscrizioni*, p. 193 (no. 297).

12. Aurel Stein, *On Alexander's Track to the Indus: Personal Narrative of Explorations on the North-West Frontier of India* (1929; reprint, Edison, N.J.: Castle Books, 2004), pp. 53–61. Stein began his scholarly career writing about coins: Jeannette Mirsky, *Sir Aurel Stein: Archaeological Explorer* (Chicago: University of Chicago Press, 1977), p. 31.

13. Stein, *On Alexander's Track to the Indus*, pp. 30–48; Pierfranceso Callieri, "A Potsherd with a Greek Inscription from Bir-Kot (Swat)," *Journal of Central Asia* 7.1 (1984): 49–53.

14. Canali de Rossi, ed., *Iscrizioni*, p. 192 (no. 295); cf. no. 296.

15. Irina Kruglikova and Shahibye Mustamandi, "Résultats prelimi-naries des travaux de l'expédition archéologique afghano-soviétique en 1969," *Afghanistan* 23 (1970): 84–97; Canali de Rossi, ed., *Iscrizioni*, p. 195 (no. 302).

16. Canali de Rossi, ed., *Iscrizioni*, p. 228 (no. 388).

17. Irina Kruglikova, "Les fouilles de la mission archéologique soviet-afghane sur le site gréco-kushan de Dilberdjin en Bactriane (Afghanistan)," *Comptes-Rendus de l'Académie des Inscriptions et Belles-Lettres*, 1977: 425–26; Canali de Rossi, ed., *Iscrizioni*, p. 196 (no. 304).

18. P. Leriche and C. Pidaev, *Termez sur Oxus: Cité-capitale d'Asie cen-trale* (Paris: Maisonneuve and Larose, 2008), p. 32.

19. B.A. Litvinsky, "Archaeological Work in Tajikistan in 1962–1970" *Archeologiceskie Raboty v Tadzikistane* 10 (1973): 5–41 (in Russian), esp. 17; see also E. Zeymal, ed., *Ancient Tadjikistan* (Dushanbe: Akademii Nauk, 1985), pp. 136–37 (in Russian); Canali de Rossi, ed., *Iscrizioni*, p. 199 (no. 313). This name has been erroneously reported as Socrates by P. Leriche, "Bactria, Land of a Thousand Cities," pp. 121–53 in J. Cribb and G. Her-rmann, eds., *After Alexander: Central Asia before Islam* (Oxford: Oxford University Press, 2007), p. 132 n. 29.

20. Edvard Rtveladze, "Découvertes en numismatique et épigraphie gréco-bactriennes à Kampyr-Tepe (Bactriane du nord)," *Revue Numis-matique* 6 (1995): 20–24, and "Kampyr Tepe–Pandokheïon: Les Grecs ont traversé l'Oxus," *Dossiers d'Archéologie* 247 (1999): 56–57.

21. Canali de Rossi, ed., *Iscrizioni*, p. 197 (no. 309).

22. Ibid., nos. 307 and 308.

23. Pugliesi-Carratelli, "Greek Inscriptions of the Middle East," pp. 34–35; Canali de Rossi, ed., *Iscrizioni*, p. 183–84 (nos. 285–89).

24. Of course, jewelry from the region often bears inscriptions in Kharoshthi or Brahmi: Rai Chandra, *Indo-Greek Jewellery* (New Delhi: Abhinav, 1979).

25. P. Bernard and O. Bopearachchi, "Deux bracelets grecs avec inscriptions grecques trouvés dans l'Asie centrale hellénisée," *Journal des Savants*, 2002: 237–78; Canali de Rossi, ed., *Iscrizioni*, pp. 259–60 (nos. 446–48).

26. The Trojan Horse appears in at least two Gandharan artworks, signaling the popularity of the Greek saga in the East: Nazir Khan, "A New Relief from Gandhara Depicting the Trojan Horse," *East and West* 40 (1990): 315–19.

27. E. Errington and J. Cribb, eds., *The Crossroads of Asia: Transformation in Image and Symbol in the Art of Ancient Afghanistan and Pakistan* (Cambridge: The Ancient India and Iran Trust, 1992), pp. 138–40.

28. V. Sarianidi, *The Golden Hoard of Bactria* (Leningrad: Aurora, 1985); Fredrik Hiebert and Pierre Cambon, eds., *Afghanistan: Hidden Treasures from the National Museum, Kabul* (Washington, D.C.: National Geographic Society, 2008), items 55, 88, and 105.

29. Canali de Rossi, ed., *Iscrizioni*, p. 229–30 (no. 390).

30. O. Bopearachchi et al., eds., *De l'Indus à l'Oxus: Archéologie de l'Asie centrale* (Lattes: Imago, 2003), item 137, now in the Bibliothèque Nationale.

31. In general, see Michael Pfrommer, *Metalwork from the Hellenized East: Catalogue of the Collections* (Malibu: Getty Museum, 1993).

32. Canali de Rossi, ed., *Iscrizioni*, p. 259 (no. 445).

33. J. Marshall, *Taxila*, 3 vols. (Cambridge: Cambridge University Press, 1951), vol. I, pp. 40–41 ("Theodorus the Meridarch").

34. See, for example, Himanshu Ray, "The Yavana Presence in Ancient India," *Journal of the Economic and Social History of the Orient* 31 (1988): 311–25.

35. Helmut Humbach, "Eine griechische Inschrift aus Pakistan,"

Gutenberg Jahrbuch (1976): 15–17; Canali de Rossi, ed., *Iscrizioni*, p. 193 (no. 298).

36. Canali de Rossi, ed., *Iscrizioni*, p. 228 (no. 387), but misleadingly listed as κτΗϹ. The eta should be a theta: κτΘϹ.

37. Ibid., pp. 228–29 (no. 389).

38. Ibid., p. 198 (no. 310).

39. Ashmolean accession number EA 1994.79. See J.R. Rea, R.C. Senior, and A.S. Hollis, "A Tax Receipt from Hellenistic Bactria," *Zeitschrift für Papyrologie und Epigraphik* 104 (1994): 261–80; P. Bernard and C. Rapin, "Un parchemin gréco-bactrien d'une collection privée," *Comptes-Rendus de l'Académie des Inscriptions et Belles-Lettres*, 1994: 261–94.

40. G.G. Aperghis, *The Seleukid Royal Economy: The Finances and Financial Administration of the Seleukid Empire* (Cambridge: Cambridge University press, 2004), pp. 282–83.

41. Bernard and Rapin, "Un parchemin," p. 270.

42. The word also appears in the Ashoka edict found in 1963 at Kandahar, for which see below.

43. Claude Rapin, "Nouvelles observations sur le parchemin gréco-bactrien d'Asangôrna," *Topoi* 6 (1996): 458–69.

44. This document answers once and for all the doubts expressed by Alberto Simonetta about subkings or joint kings in Bactria and India: "A New Essay on the Indo-Greeks, the Sakas and the Pahlavas," *East and West* 9 (1958): 157.

45. Frantz Grenet, "ΑϹΑΓΓΩΡΝΟΙϹ, ΑϹΚΙϹΑΓΓΟΡΑΓΟ, SANGCHARAK," *Topoi* 6 (1996): 470–73.

46. W. Clarysse and D.J. Thompson, "Two Greek Texts on Skin from Hellenistic Bactria," *Zeitschrift für Papyrologie und Epigraphik* 159 (2007): 273–79.

47. Ibid., p. 276: "We are still not entirely happy with the name Antimachos."

48. Ibid., p. 278.

49. P.M. Fraser, *Cities of Alexander the Great* (Oxford: Clarendon Press, 1996), pp. 132–40. Kandahar lay within the old Persian satrapy of Arachosia.

50. Richard Salomon, *Indian Epigraphy* (Oxford: Oxford University Press, 1998), provides an essential reference.

51. Canali de Rossi, ed., *Iscrizioni*, pp. 185–87 (no. 290); Merkelbach and Stauber, *Jenseits des Euphrat: Griechische Inschriften*, pp. 35–36 (no. 202). The publication of this inscription by the Italians created some tensions between Giuseppe Tucci and Daniel Schlumberger of the DAFA, which had long monopolized Afghan archaeology: S. Gorshenina and C. Rapin, *De Kaboul à Samarcande: Les archéologues en Asie centrale* (Paris: Gallimard, 2001), pp. 60–61.

52. Canali de Rossi, ed., *Iscrizioni*, pp. 187–91 (nos. 291 and 292); Merkelbach and Stauber, *Jenseits des Euphrat: Griechische Inschriften*, pp. 25–35 (no. 201). A third Ashokan inscription from Kandahar is fragmentary, but it has both Aramaic and Prakrit lettering: E. Beneviste and A. Dupont-Sommer, "Une inscription indo-araméene d'Asoka provenant de Kandahar (Afghanistan)," *Journal Asiatique* 254 (1966): 437–65.

53. It was apparently a challenge for the scribes to translate some words and concepts into Greek: K.R. Norman, "Notes on the Greek Version of Ashoka's Twelfth and Thirteenth Rock Edicts," *Journal of the Royal Asiatic Society of Great Britain and Ireland* 2 (1972): 111–18; Émile Beneviste, "Édits d'Asoka en traduction grecque," *Journal Asiatique* (1964): 137–57.

54. Consult F.R. Allchin and K.R. Norman, "Guide to the Ashokan Inscriptions," *South Asian Studies* 1 (1985): 43–50 (Major Rock Edict XIII). The suggestion has been made that Antiochus I (not II) is referred to in this inscription: Jarl Charpentier, "Antiochus, King of the Yavanas," *Bulletin of the School of Oriental Studies* 6.2 (1931): 303–21.

55. Athenaeus, *Deipnosophistae* 14.652f–653a. Antiochus replied that figs and sweets could be obtained, but sophists were not for sale.

56. For philosophical and ethical crosscurrents, see Valeri Yailenko, "Les maximes delphiques d'Ai Khanoum et la formation de la doctrine du *Dhamma* d'Asoka," *Dialogues d'Histoire Ancienne* 16 (1990): 239–56; and David Sick, "When Socrates Met the Buddha: Greek and Indian Dialectic in Hellenistic Bactria and India," *Journal of the Royal Asiatic Society* 17.3 (2007): 253–78. For linguistic interplay, see also Alain Christol, "Les édits grecs d'Asoka: Étude linguistique," *Journal Asiatique* 271 (1983):

25–42; and Carlo Gallavotti, "The Greek Version of the Kandahar Bilingual Inscription of Ashoka," *East and West* 10 (1959): 185–92.

57. The inscription is dated 300–250 B.C.E. by P.M. Fraser, "The Son of Aristonax at Kandahar," *Afghan Studies* 2 (1979): 9–21; Canali de Rossi, ed., *Iscrizioni,* pp. 191–92 (no. 293); Merkelbach and Stauber, *Jenseits des Euphrat: Griechische Inschriften,* p. 19 (no. 106). The translation of this text, as for all other Greek metrical inscriptions discussed below, has been rhymed in order to convey its intended poetic form.

58. P. Bernard, G.-J. Pinault, and G. Rougemont, "Deux nouvelles inscriptions grecques de l'Asie central," *Journal des Savants,* 2004: 227–356; Merkelbach and Stauber, *Jenseits des Euphrat: Griechische Inschriften,* pp. 17–19 (no. 105).

59. An interesting brief commentary is now provided by Adrian Hollis, "Greek Letters from Hellenistic Bactria," pp. 104–18 in Dirk Obbink and Richard Rutherford, eds., *Culture in Pieces: Essays on Ancient Texts in Honour of Peter Parsons* (Oxford: Oxford University Press, 2011), pp. 112–16.

60. It was believed at one point that the inscription mentions China as the place where Sophytos made his fortune: P. Bernard and G. Rougemont, "Les secrets de la stèle de Kandahar," *L'Histoire* 280 (2003): 27–28.

61. For various potsherd inscriptions, see Svend Helms, *Excavations at Old Kandahar in Afghanistan 1976–1978* (Oxford: Archaeopress, 1997), pp. 101–2.

62. Bernard et al., "Deux nouvelles inscriptions," pp. 333–56; Merkelbach and Stauber, *Jenseits des Euphrat: Griechische Inschriften,* p. 4 (no. 101).

63. See also Hollis, "Greek Letters," pp. 110–12.

64. On the coin, see Osmund Bopearachchi, "Trésors monétaires découvertes et pillage," p. 104 in *Afghanistan, patrimoine en péril: Actes d'une journée d'étude* (Paris: CEREDAF, 2001).

65. Louis Robert, "De Delphes à l'Oxus," *Comptes-Rendus de l'Académie des Inscriptions et Belles-Lettres,* 1968: 416–57; Canali de Rossi, ed., *Iscrizioni,* pp. 224–27 (nos. 382–84); Merkelbach and Stauber, *Jenseits des Euphrat: Griechische Inschriften,* pp. 8–15 (no. 103 A and B).

66. Wolfgang Leschhorn, *Gründer der Stadt: Studien zu einen politisch-*

religiösen Phänomen der griechischen Geschichte (Stuttgart: Franz Steiner Verlag, 1984), pp. 314–17. Whether Cineas founded (or refounded) the settlement under the aegis of Alexander or Seleucus is not certain, and A. K. Narain argues for a much later date, under Diodotus I or II: *The Indo-Greeks, Revisited and Supplemented* (Delhi: B. R. Publishing, 2003), p. 406.

67. Merkelbach and Stauber, *Jenseits des Euphrat: Griechische Inschriften*, pp. 13–15, accept Robert's thesis; Jeffrey Lerner, "Correcting the Early History of Ay Kanom," *Archäologische Mitteilungen aus Iran und Turan* 35–36 (2003–4): 391–95, does not.

68. Canali de Rossi, ed., *Iscrizioni*, p. 223 (no. 381); Merkelbach and Stauber, *Jenseits des Euphrat: Griechische Inschriften*, pp. 7–8 (no. 102).

69. See, e.g., Lerner, "Correcting the Early History of Ay Kanom," 390–91, with bibliography.

70. P. Bernard, "Campagne de fouilles à Ai Khanoum (Afghanistan)," *Comptes-Rendus de l'Académie des Inscriptions et Belles-Lettres*, 1972: 605–32; Canali de Rossi, ed., *Iscrizioni*, pp. 218–19 (nos. 360–62).

71. Canali de Rossi, ed., *Iscrizioni*, p. 227 (nos. 385–86).

72. Claude Rapin, "Les inscriptions économiques de la trésorerie hellénistique d'Ai Khanoum (Afghanistan)," *Bulletin de Correspondance Hellénique* 107 (1983): 315–81.

73. Ibid., pp. 319–20; C. Rapin, *Indian Art from Afghanistan: The Legend of Sakuntala and the Indian Treasure of Eucratides at Ai Khanoum* (New Delhi: Manohar Publishers, 1996), pp. 15–16; Canali de Rossi, ed., *Iscrizioni*, p. 210 (no. 329). The text is written on a broken pot that served as the lid of the container of oil, which adds the workers' names.

74. Canali de Rossi, ed., *Iscrizioni*, pp. 207–9 and 211 (nos. 324, 325, and 330); Rapin, "Les inscriptions économiques de la trésorerie," pp. 326–29. The jar was pillaged from the treasury and its fragments found in the main temple.

75. Rémy Audouin and Paul Bernard, "Trésor de monnaies indiennes et indo-grecques d'Ai Khanoum (Afghanistan)," *Revue Numismatique* 15 (1973): 238–89 and 16 (1974): 6–41.

76. P. Bernard, "Campagne de fouilles 1978 à Ai Khanoum (Afghanistan)," *Comptes-Rendus de l'Académie des Inscriptions et Belles-Lettres*, 1980: 435–59, esp. p. 442; Canali de Rossi, ed., *Iscrizioni*, pp. 210–11 (no. 329).

For a different view, see A.K. Narain, "Notes on Some Inscriptions from Ai Khanoum (Afghanistan)," *Zeitschrift für Papyrologie und Epigraphik* 69 (1987): 272–82.

77. Claude Rapin, "La trésorerie hellénistique d'Ai Khanoum," *Revue Archéologique* (1987): 56.

78. Claude Rapin, "Les texts littéraires grecs de la trésorerie d'Ai Khanoum," *Bulletin de Correspondance Hellénique* III (1987): 225–66; Canali de Rossi, ed., *Iscrizioni,* pp. 269–72 (nos. 457 and 458).

79. Jeffrey Lerner, "The Ai Khanoum Philosophical Papyrus," *Zeitschrift für Papyrologie und Epigraphik* 142 (2003): 45–51.

80. Canali de Rossi, ed., *Iscrizioni,* p. 221 (no. 372).

81. P. Bernard, "Campagne de fouilles à Ai Khanoum (Afghanistan)," *Comptes-Rendus de l'Académie des Inscriptions et Belles-Lettres,* 1972: 631–32. For the use of Aramaic in pre-Hellenistic Bactria, see Shaked, *Le satrape de Bactriane.*

82. Rachel Mairs, "The 'Temple with Indented Niches' at Ai Khanoum: Ethnic and Civic Identity in Hellenistic Bactria," in Richard Alston and Onno van Nijf, eds., *Cults, Creeds and Contests in the Post-Classical City* (Louvain: Peeters, forthcoming).

83. François Widemann, "Un monnayage inconnu de type gréco-bactrien à legende araméenne," *Studia Iranica* 18 (1989): 193–97; O. Bopearachchi, "The Euthydemus Imitations and the Date of Sogdian Independence," *Silk Road Art and Archaeology* 2 (1991–92): 1–21.

84. Some inscriptions mentioning Greeks have been declared false. On the Bajaur casket inscription, see H. Falk, "The Introduction of Stupa-Worship in Bajaur," pp. 347–58 in O. Bopearachchi and M.-F. Boussac, eds., *Afghanistan: Ancien carrefour entre l'est et l'ouest* (Turnhout, 2005). Also condemned are the texts claimed by the Sri Lankan expert Senarat Paranavitana in *The Greeks and the Mauryas* (Colombo: Lake House Investments, 1971).

85. G.R. Sharma, *Reh Inscription of Menander and the Indo-Greek Invasion of the Ganga Valley* (Allahabad: Abinash, 1980).

86. See, for example, Gyula Wojtilla, "Did the Indo-Greeks Occupy Pataliputra?" *Acta Archaeologica Academiae Scientiarum Hungaricae* 40 (2000): 497–98.

87. D.C. Sircar, ed., *Select Inscriptions Bearing on Indian History and Civilization*, 2nd ed. (Calcutta: University of Calcutta, 1965), vol. I, no. 2; see also Salomon, *Indian Epigraphy*, pp. 265–66.

88. Adapted from S. Burstein, ed., *The Hellenistic Age from the Battle of Ipsos to the Death of Kleopatra* (Cambridge: Cambridge University Press, 1985), p. 72.

89. S. Godbole, "Mathura Clay Sealing of Appolodotus [*sic*]," vol. I, pp. 311–12 in Tony Hackens and Ghilaine Moucharte, eds., *Actes du XIe Congrès International de Numismatique, Bruxelles 1991* (Louvain: Association Marcel Hoc, 1993).

90. G. Fussman, "Nouvelles inscriptions Saka: Ère d'Eucratide, Ère d'Azes, Ère Vikrama, Ère de Kanishka," *Bulletin de l'École Française d'Extrême-Orient* 67 (1980): 15.

91. See Walter Posch, *Baktrien zwischen Griechen und Kuschan* (Wiesbaden: Harrassowitz, 1995), pp. 129–33.

92. D. Schlumberger, M. LeBerre, and G. Fussman, *Surkh Kotal en Bactriane*, vol. I, *Les temples* (Paris: Diffusion de Boccard, 1983); Fussman and O. Guillaume, *Surkh Kotal en Bactriane*, vol. II, *Les monnaies et petits objets* (Paris: Diffusion de Boccard, 1990); and R. Curiel, "Inscriptions de Surkh Kotal," *Journal Asiatique* 242 (1954): 189–97.

93. G. Fussman, "Documents épigraphiques kouchans," *Bulletin de l'École Française d'Extrême-Orient* 61 (1974): 1–77.

94. N. Sims-Williams and J. Cribb, "A New Bactrian Inscription of Kanishka the Great," *Silk Road Art and Archaeology* 4 (1995–96): 75–142; G. Fussman, "L'inscription de Rabatak, la Bactriane et les Kouchans," pp. 251–91 in Pierre Leriche et al., eds., *La Bactriane au carrefour des routes et des civilizations de l'Asie centrale* (Paris: Maisonneuve and Larose, 2001). The site has since been bulldozed by looters.

95. David Graf, "Aramaic on the Periphery of the Achaemenid Realm," *Archäologische Mitteilungen aus Iran und Turan* 32 (2000): 75–92, esp. 80–82.

96. C. Rapin, *Fouilles d'Aï Khanoum*, vol. VIII, *La trésorerie du palais hellénistique d'Aï Khanoum* (Paris: Diffusion de Boccard, 1992), pp. 139–42, on the silver ingot with a runic inscription.

97. Frantz Grenet, "L'onomastique iranienne à Ai Khanoum," *Bulletin de Correspondance Hellénique* 107 (1983): 373–81.

98. W.W. Tarn, "Notes on Hellenism," *Journal of Hellenic Studies* 22 (1902): 292, and Alfred Foucher, *La vieille route de l'Inde de Bactres à Taxila* (Paris: de Nobele, 1942–47), vol. I, p. 385, were both struck at the time by the total lack of epigraphic evidence found in Afghanistan.

7. A PERFECT STORM

1. The author's own tally has lately been confirmed independently by the research of Olivier Bordeaux, "Restitution des trésors monétaires d'Afghanistan et du Pakistan de 1990 à 2008," Mémoire de Master 1 (Sorbonne, 2011). This study covers the Graeco-Bactrian coins sold by 154 different vendors but does not include internet auctions; his second Mémoire covers the Indo-Greek coins.

2. F. Holt, "The So-Called 'Pedigree Coins' of the Bactrian Greeks," pp. 69–91 in W. Heckel and R. Sullivan, eds., *Ancient Coins of the Graeco-Roman World: The Nickle Numismatic Papers* (Waterloo, Ont.: Wilfrid Laurier University Press, 1984).

3. Statistics have been compiled from these standard inventories of coin hoards, taking care not to duplicate data from hoards listed more than once: Margaret Thompson, Otto Mørkholm, and Colin Kraay, eds., *Inventory of Greek Coin Hoards* (New York: American Numismatic Society, 1973), and the ten volumes of *Coin Hoards* published so far as addenda (1975–2010). Some finds listed in *IGCH* are not true hoards, such as no. 1827.

4. Raoul Curiel and Gérard Fussman, *Le trésor monétaire de Qunduz* (Paris: Klincksieck, 1965). One drachm of the original 628 coins was lost en route to the museum.

5. Olivier Guillaume, ed., *Graeco-Bactrian and Indian Coins from Afghanistan* (Oxford: Oxford University Press, 1991).

6. A small percentage of the thirty thousand coins stored in the National Museum were secretly transferred to a secure vault elsewhere in Kabul prior to the bombing and looting of the museum in 1993.

7. See F. Holt, *Into the Land of Bones: Alexander the Great in Afghanistan* (Berkeley and Los Angeles: University of California Press, 2005), p. 146. To date, more than seventy-five coins from the Qunduz Hoard have appeared for sale in auction catalogues or on eBay.

8. See, for example, Peter Berghaus, "Coin Hoards: Methodology and Evidence," pp. 16–19 in P.L. Gupta and A.K. Jha, eds., *Numismatics and Archaeology* (Anjaneri: Indian Institute of Research in Numismatic Studies, 1987). For the principal inventories of Greek hoards, see n. 3, above.

9. F. Holt, "Alexander the Great and the Spoils of War," *Ancient Macedonia* 6.1 (1999): 499–506.

10. For what follows, see F. Holt, "The Euthydemid Coinage of Bactria: Further Hoard Evidence from Ai Khanoum," *Revue Numismatique* 23 (1981): 7–44.

11. C.-Y. Petitot-Biehler, "Trésor de monnaies grecques et gréco-bactriennes trouvé à Ai Khanoum (Afghanistan)," *Revue Numismatique* 17 (1975): 23–57, esp. 54–55.

12. The problems arose from misinformation supplied to Martin Price of the British Museum, one of the editors for *Coin Hoards* (personal communication).

13. Holt, "The Euthydemid Coinage of Bactria," pp. 10–11. Intrusions are coins added to a hoard in order to sell extraneous material or introduced by mistake as groups of coins pass through various hands.

14. H.-P. Francfort, "Deux nouveaux tétradrachmes commémoratifs d'Agathocle," *Revue Numismatique* 17 (1975): 19–22. Ironically, the very next article in this journal was Petitot-Biehler's (see n. 11, above) that first announced the third Ai Khanoum hoard without any connection yet being made with these important Agathocles specimens.

15. P.L. Gupta, "Three Commemorative Tetradrachms of Agathocles," *Journal of the Numismatic Society of India* 38.2 (1976): 92–94. The unidentified auction was Bank Leu 15 (May 1976), items 357–59. All three specimens in the Bank Leu auction were purchased by William Wahler of California (personal communication) and were later auctioned off again after his death. One of them was acquired by the British Museum in 1993.

16. Ibid., p. 94.

17. *Coin Hoards* II (1976), p. 27 (fig. 10). The Leu coin is number 4.

18. O. Bopearachchi, *Monnaies gréco-bactriennes et indo-grecques: Catalogue raisonné* (Paris: Bibliothèque Nationale, 1991); *Catalogue of Indo-Greek, Indo-Scythian and Indo-Parthian Coins of the Smithsonian Institution* (Washington, D.C.: Smithsonian, 1993); *Sylloge Nummorum Graecorum: The Collection of the American Numismatic Society*, part 9, *Graeco-Bactrian and Indo-Greek Coins* (New York: American Numismatic Society, 1998); and with A. ur Rahman, *Pre-Kushana Coins in Pakistan* (Karachi: Iftikhar Rasul, 1995).

19. The first deposit (MZ 1) was found and partially recovered in 1947–48: Raoul Curiel and Daniel Schlumberger, *Trésors monétaires d'Afghanistan* (Paris: Klincksieck, 1953), pp. 65–100. The approximately thirteen thousand coins in this deposit were dispersed into various collections; those that ended up in the Kabul Museum have subsequently been looted.

20. My own notes of conversations (April–July 1993) with academics, curators, and dealers in New York, California, Italy, Pakistan, and Switzerland bear this out. Some informants believed there was a single great hoard, whereas others suspected that two or three separate finds had been mingled on the market.

21. For his personal account, see O. Bopearachchi, "A Joy and a Curse," pp. 33–73 in F. Holt and O. Bopearachchi, eds., *The Alexander Medallion: Exploring the Origins of a Unique Artefact* (Lacapelle-Mirival: Imago Lattara, 2011).

22. Osmund Bopearachchi was cleverly able to track some of these coins, as well as others from MZ I, by virtue of the distinctive patina caused by conditions inside the ancient well at Mir Zakah.

23. For example, O. Bopearachchi, "Two More Unique Coins from the Second Mir Zakah Deposit," *Oriental Numismatic Society Newsletter* 169 (2001): 21–22.

24. For examples, "Grands trésors de monnaies pré-sassanides trouvés en Afghanistan et au Pakistan," *International Numismatic Newsletter* 24 (1994): 2–3; "Récentes découvertes de trésors de monnaies pré-sassanides trouvés en Afghanistan et au Pakistan," *Cahiers Numismatiques*,

Sept. 1994: 7–14; "Recent Discoveries: Hoards and Finds of Ancient Coins from Afghanistan and Pakistan," *Yavanika* 4 (1994): 3–30; "Découvertes récentes de trésors indo-grecs: Nouvelles données historiques," *Comptes-Rendus de l'Académie des Inscriptions et Belles-Lettres,* 1995: 609–27; and "Nouvelles trouvailles archéologiques en Afghanistan et au Pakistan et la destruction du patrimoine," *La Timuride* 24 (2002): 10–20.

25. O. Bopearachchi, "Recent Coin Hoard Evidence on Pre-Kushana Chronology," pp. 99–149 in Michael Alram and Deborah Klimburg-Salter, eds., *Coins, Art, and Chronology: Essays on the Pre-Islamic History of the Indo-Iranian Borderlands* (Vienna: Verlag der Österreichischen Akademie der Wissenschaften, 1999), pp. 110–11.

26. O. Bopearachchi, "La circulation et la production monétaires en Asie centrale et dans l'Inde du nord-ouest (avant et après la conquête d'Alexandre)," *Indologica Taurinensia* 35 (1999–2000): 15–121.

27. Ibid., p. 60.

28. Edvard Rtveladze, "La circulation monétaire au nord de l'Oxus à l'époque gréco-bactrienne," *Revue Numismatique* 26 (1984): 61–76, report augmented by G. Kurbanov and M. Niyazova, *Katalog greko-baktriskikh monet iz fondov Bukharskogo muzeia* (Bukhara: Bukhara Museum, 1989).

29. Rtveladze, "La circulation monétaire," p. 64. Naturally, this material entered the antiquities market and occasionally attracted professional looters to these areas.

30. On these discoveries, see the works cited above in nn. 24–26.

31. O. Bopearachchi and Klaus Grigo, "Thundering Zeus Revisited," *Oriental Numismatic Society Newsletter* 169 (autumn 2001): 22–24.

32. See, for example, Elizabeth Errington, "Rediscovering the Collections of Charles Masson," pp. 207–37 in Michael Alram and Deborah Klimburg-Salter, eds., *Coins, Art, and Chronology: Essays on the Pre-Islamic History of the Indo-Iranian Borderlands* (Vienna: Verlag der Österreichischen Akademie der Wissenschaften, 1999).

33. Elizabeth Errington, "Charles Masson and Begram," *Topoi* 11 (2001): 357–409.

34. Elizabeth Errington, "Rediscovering the Coin Collection of General Claude-Auguste Court: A Preliminary Report," *Topoi* 5 (1995): 409–24.

35. Updated summaries of this progress may be found in the volumes of *A Survey of Numismatic Research,* published periodically by the International Numismatic Commission. See also Duncan Hook, "The Application of Science to Coins and Coin Hoards at the British Museum," in Barrie Cook, ed., *The British Museum and the Future of UK Numismatics* (London: British Museum Press, 2011), pp. 28–33.

36. See n. 18, above. The older catalogues include: A.N. Lahiri, *Corpus of Indo-Greek Coins* (Calcutta: Poddar Publications, 1965); and Michael Mitchiner, *Indo-Greek and Indo-Scythian Coinage,* 9 vols. (London: Hawkins, 1975).

37. F. Holt, *Thundering Zeus: The Making of Hellenistic Bactria* (Berkeley and Los Angeles: University of California Press, 1999); Brian Kritt, *Dynastic Transitions in the Coinage of Bactria: Antiochus–Diodotus–Euthydemus* (Lancaster, Pa.: Classical Numismatic Group, 2001); and Jens Jakobsson, "Antiochus Nicator," *Numismatic Chronicle* 170 (2010): 17–33.

38. As demonstrated in Holt, "The So-Called 'Pedigree Coins.'" Yet, the shadow of Tarn cannot always be banished by new light: M.C.J. Miller, "Antimachus (II) Nikephoros: A New Alexander?" *Ancient World* 39.1 (2008): 55–62, esp. 55.

39. For example, Jens Jakobsson, "Who Founded the Indo-Greek Era of 186/5 B.C.E.?" *Classical Quarterly* 59.2 (2009): 505–10.

40. See, for example, Robert Senior, "Menander versus Zoilos, Another Overstrike," *Oriental Numismatic Society Newsletter* 150 (1996): 12.

41. This latest surge has been noted by Peter Mittag, "Bactria and Parthia," pp. 111–16 in Michel Amandry and Donal Bateson, eds., *A Survey of Numismatic Research* 2002–2007 (Glasgow: International Numismatic Commission, 2009), p. 111. See also the earlier surveys in F. Holt, "Discovering the Lost History of Ancient Afghanistan: Hellenistic Bactria in Light of Recent Archaeological and Historical Research," *Ancient World* 9 (1984): 3–28, and "Hellenistic Bactria: Beyond the Mirage," *Ancient World* 14 (1986): 3–15.

42. O. Bopearachchi, "A New Approach to the History of the Greeks in India," *Yavanika* 1 (1992): 6–20.

43. Similarly, while rejecting the ambitious system devised earlier by Alexander Cunningham (see chap. 2, above), A.D.H. Bivar sought to

establish the geographical significance of the monograms: "Monogram Counts from the Kabul Collection," pp. 225–33 in Paul Bernard and Frantz Grenet, eds., *Histoire et cultes de l'Asie centrale préislamique: Sources écrites et documents archéologiques* (Paris: CNRS, 1991).

44. See also O. Bopearachchi, "Monnaies indo-grecques surfrappées," *Revue Numismatique* 31 (1989): 49–79, and "L'apport des surfrappes à la reconstruction de l'histoire des Indo-Grecs," *Revue Numismatique* (2008): 245–68.

45. On the range of techniques employed, see O. Bopearachchi, "Les royaumes grecs d'Asie centrale: L'apport de la numismatique à leur histoire," *Les Nouvelles de l'Archéologie* 39 (1990): 21–26.

46. P. Mittag, "Methodologische Überlegungen zur Geschichte Baktriens: Könige und Münzen," *Schweizerische Numismatische Rundschau* 85 (2006): 27–46.

47. Ibid., p. 44.

48. O. Guillaume, *Analysis of Reasonings in Archaeology: The Case of Graeco-Bactrian and Indo-Greek Numismatics*, trans. Osmund Bopearachchi (Oxford: Oxford University Press, 1990).

49. Ibid., p. 1. The great failing of Olivier Guillaume's work is that he, like those he criticizes, does not make explicit his own intermediate propositions, in his case linking the catalogues to the histories allegedly derived from them. How do catalogues published *after* the selected works of Tarn and A.K. Narain possibly influence them?

50. Ibid., p. 9. Jean-Claude Gardin wrote the foreword for the book.

51. As shown in chapter 4, above, it may be debated whether A.K. Narain should be classified as an historian or a numismatist. In fact, Narain produced a coin catalogue of his own that has been published several times, most recently as part of *The Indo-Greeks, Revisited and Supplemented* (Delhi: B.R. Publishing, 2003), pp. 299–349. See also n. 56, below.

52. The other variables are number of coins (correlated to importance or length of reign), royal and nonroyal portraiture (including the problems of personality and kinship), languages, monograms, paleography, provenance, and style.

53. Guillaume, *Analysis of Reasonings in Archaeology*, pp. 70–71.

54. Ibid., pp. 72–73.

55. Ibid., pp. 96–98.

56. Ibid., pp. 111–18. To this, A.K. Narain has thrown down a challenge in *The Indo-Greeks, Revisited and Supplemented*, pp. 484–501 (from an updated version of his 1991 presidential address for the Indian Society of Greek and Roman Studies). Narain insists that he is no nationalist and that he is a scientific numismatist (and archaeologist) rather than a subjective historian like Tarn.

57. Guillaume, *Analysis of Reasonings in Archaeology*, p. 115.

58. Ibid., p. 114.

59. Olivier Guillaume praises Bopearachchi's *Monnaies gréco-bactriennes et indo-grecques: Catalogue raisonné* as both a catalogue and an historical reconstruction: *Studies in History* 9.2 (1993): 292–94. In this review, Guillaume presses for more use of computerized databases and expanded analysis of monograms and die links. See also Guillaume, "How Can the Computer Help the Numismatist and the Historian of the Indo-Greek Period?" *Journal of the Numismatic Society of India* 47 (1985): 152–60.

60. Homayun Sidky, *The Greek Kingdom of Bactria: From Alexander to Eucratides the Great* (Lanham, Md.: University Press of America, 2000), p. ix. This is in some ways an admirable endeavor, but one fatally flawed by sloppy preparation, terrible printing, and total absence of basic proofreading. Even the table of contents is wrong. These careless errors continue right through the text, notes, bibliography, and index. The republication of excerpts from this book under another title offers little improvement: *The Rise and Fall of the Graeco-Bactrian Kingdom* (Jaipur: ABD Publishers, 2004).

61. Sidky, *The Greek Kingdom of Bactria*, pp. xiv–xv and 229 n. 23.

62. Ibid., pp. 214–15.

63. A.K. Narain, *The Indo-Greeks, Revisited and Supplemented*, p. 52.

64. Sidky, *The Greek Kingdom of Bactria*, p. 214.

65. Jens Jakobsson, "The Greeks of Afghanistan Revisited," *Nomismatika Khronika* 26 (2007): 51–88.

66. Ibid., p. 52. This is essentially Tarn's complaint some seventy years earlier, although Jakobsson stresses for some reason philologists

as well: "This criticism is directed against the general chasm between philologists and numismatists." Jakobsson himself is not a philologist.

67. Ibid., p. 53. The author rightly expresses these ideas with utmost caution.

68. Ibid., p. 59. Emphasis added.

69. Ibid., pp. 67 and 69.

70. Ibid., pp. 69 and 51. Many of the author's so-called facts may certainly be contested. For example, the author declares (p. 56) that young rulers were rare in Bactria but then describes many of them as, in fact, being young (e.g., Demetrius I, Euthydemus II, Menander, Demetrius II, Antimachus II). He calls the dated potsherd from Ai Khanoum a stele (p. 63) and reprises the old notion (p. 59) that Poseidon on the coins of Antimachus suggests a kingdom near the coast or along the Indus (but *not* in India).

71. Stanislaw Kalita, *Grecy w Baktrii i w Indiach: Wybrane problem ich historii* (Kraków: Historia Iagellonica, 2005).

72. Ibid., p. 248.

73. In the series Studi Ellenistici, volume 21 (Pisa: Fabrizio Serra Editore, 2009). Omar Coloru also studied in France with Osmund Bopearachchi and the noted specialist on Persia Pierre Briant.

74. For example, Omar Coloru, *Da Alessandro a Menandro* (Pisa: Fabrizio Serra Editore, 2009), pp. 198–206, uses the parchment documents (discussed above, chap. 6) to work out a speculative chronology for Antimachus's reign that is tied to coins and dynastic politics. He presumes that Euthydemus II was a son of Demetrius by his (promised) Seleucid wife, and that the Eumenes and Antimachus (II) in the tax document were the brother and nephew of Antimachus I.

75. François Widemann, *Les successeurs d'Alexandre en Asie centrale et leur héritage culturel* (Paris: Riveneuve, 2009). A preliminary (but often word-for-word) version was published as "Phases et contradictions de la colonization grecque en Asie centrale et en Inde du nord-ouest," *Indologica Taurinensia* 27 (2001): 215–62.

76. The phrase is Widemann's: *Les successeurs d'Alexandre*, p. 9.

77. Widemann seems to have missed only M.A.R. Khan, "The Probably Meteoritic Origin of Certain Specimens of Nickel Coins

Struck in Bactria before 200 B.C.," *Meteoritics and Planetary Science* 1 (1953): 60, a view challenged in the same issue by John Buddhue, "A Possible Explanation of the Nickel in Ancient Asiatic Coins," pp. 60–61.

78. See also F. Widemann, "Scarcity of Precious Metals and Relative Chronology of Indo-Greek and Related Coinages (1st Century B.C.–1st Century A.D.)," *East and West* 50 (2000): 227–58; cf. W.W. Tarn, *The Greeks in Bactria and India,* 3rd ed. (Chicago: Ares Press, 1984), pp. 103–4.

79. For examples: Widemann, *Les successeurs d'Alexandre,* p. 71 (on Demetrius I and Euthydemus II) and p. 161 (on Eucratides as grandson of Antiochus III of Syria).

80. Ibid., p. 74.

81. Ibid., pp. 49–50, 180, and 446–47.

82. Ibid., pp. 447–48.

83. For example, the almost universally accepted siege of Bactra by Antiochus the Great: Stanislav Kalita, "Oblezenie, którego nie bylo? Uwagi na marginesie historii wojny Antiocha III z Eutydemosem królem Baktrii," pp. 47–55 in Marciej Salamon and Zdzislaw Kapera, eds., *Studia Classica et Byzantina Alexandro Krawczuk Oblata* (Kraków: Jagiellonian University Press, 1996).

84. Reprised in Boccaccio and other Renaissance authors, along with Chaucer's "Emetreus King of India," for which see above, chapter 1.

85. On the various supposed references to Demetrius I in Indian sources, see A.K. Narain, *The Indo-Greeks, Revisited and Supplemented,* pp. 47–50, *contra* Tarn.

86. This list of numismatic facts could easily be extended by considering imitations of Demetrius's coins, etc.

87. A filial connection might be surmised on the basis of the shared Hercules motif on the coins.

88. The possibility that Demetrius II is really young Demetrius I (cf. N6 in the list above), or that Euthydemus II is actually Demetrius I, has been suggested as well. See the discussion in F. Holt, "Did King Euthydemus II Really Exist?" *Numismatic Chronicle* 160 (2000): 81–91.

89. As shown above, Tarn and A.K. Narain took opposite positions.

See also Michael Kordosis, "Οι έλληνες βασιλείς της Βακτρίας και Ινδίας ως το θάνατο του Μενάνδρου," *Δωδώνη* 20.1 (1991): 217–24; L.M. Wilson, "King Demetrios of India and Eukratides of Bactria," *Oriental Numismatic Society Newsletter* 174 (2003): 17–23.

90. *On the Circumnavigation of the Red Sea*, 47. See chapter 1, above.

91. John Deyell, "Indo-Greek and Ksaharata Coins from the Gujarat Seacoast," *Numismatic Chronicle* 144 (1984): 115–27.

92. Tarn, *Greeks in Bactria and India*, p. 149. Tarn would rather believe (p. 527) that if no Apollodotus coins were known from Bharuch, then this was not the same place as Barygaza than that the ancient writer could be wrong.

93. A.K. Narain, *The Indo-Greeks, Revisited and Supplemented*, pp. 86–87, recanted pp. 268–69. See also D.W. MacDowall and N.G. Wilson, "Apollodoti Reges Indorum," *Numismatic Chronicle* (1960): 221–28.

94. A similar assessment was reached in Erik Seldeschlachts's judicious survey of Greek and Indian evidence: "The End of the Road for the Indo-Greeks?" *Iranica Antiqua* 39 (2004): 249–96.

8. A NEW BEGINNING

1. Published posthumously in *American Historical Review* 47.2 (1942): 225–44. It should be noted that Thompson nevertheless anticipated some of the New History in his studies of literacy, espionage, and animal husbandry.

2. On these developments, consult Matthew Johnson, *Archaeological Theory: An Introduction* (Malden, Mass.: Blackwell, 1999).

3. Examples include Rachel Mairs, "Greek Identity and the Settler Community in Hellenistic Bactria and Arachosia," *Migrations and Identities* 1.1 (2008): 19–43; Mairs, "Ethnicity and Funarary [*sic*] Practice in Hellenistic Bactria," pp. 111–24 in Hannes Schroeder, P. Gardner, and Peter Bray, eds., *Crossing Frontiers* (Oxford: Oxford University Press, 2007); Grant Parker, "Hellenism in an Afghan Context," pp. 170–91 in Himanshu Ray and Daniel Potts, eds., *Memory as History: The Legacy of Alexander in Asia* (New Delhi: Aryan Books, 2007). It should be noted that the situation is considerably brighter in Roman numismatics; see,

for example, Hans-Markus von Kaenal and Fleur Kemmers, eds., *Coins in Context*, vol. I, *New Perspectives for the Interpretation of Coin Finds* (Mainz am Rhein: Philipp von Zabern, 2009).

4. Jens Jakobsson, "The Greeks of Afghanistan Revisited," *Numismatika Khronika* 26 (2007): 51 (emphasis added).

5. A debt is owed to works such as the following: Colin Renfrew and Ezra Zubrow, eds., *The Ancient Mind: Elements of Cognitive Archaeology* (Cambridge: Cambridge University Press, 1994); Michael O'Brien, Lee Lyman, and Michael Schiffer, *Archaeology as a Process: Processualism and Its Progeny* (Salt Lake City: University of Utah Press, 2005). Not seen before the writing of this book, but sharing some of the approaches advocated here and in a lecture introducing cognitive numismatics at the Metropolitan Museum of Art in New York (9/10/2009), is Fleur Kemmers and Nanouschka Myrberg, "Rethinking Numismatics: The Archaeology of Coins," *Archaeological Dialogues* 18 (2011): 87–108.

6. J.R. Melville Jones, *Testimonia Numaria: Greek and Latin Texts Concerning Ancient Greek Coinage*, vol. I (London: Spink, 1993), p. 349.

7. Sometimes called cultural formation process, with stages labeled as C-transforms. Phenomena such as corrosion are called natural formation processes (N-transforms).These are useful ways of understanding how the archaeological (and numismatic) record has been shaped.

8. It is not easy to determine which coins derive from which sources on the basis of present evidence and analysis. For instance, the treasury at Ai Khanoum contained jars of karshapana coins that may represent trade or war with India and may or may not have been intended for reuse as bullion to strike Bactrian issues.

9. The treatment of this topic is highly speculative in F. Widemann, *Les successeurs d'Alexandre en Asie centrale et leur héritage culturel* (Paris: Riveneuve, 2009). He believes that Bactria suffered chronic shortages of precious metals, and that control of Sogdia in particular was essential for access to gold.

10. On the metals and metalworking of Afghanistan and Pakistan, see Elizabeth Errington and Joe Cribb, eds., *The Crossroads of Asia: Transformation in Image and Symbol in the Art of Ancient Afghanistan and Pakistan* (Cambridge: The Ancient India and Iran Trust, 1992), pp. 241–

59. Open-pit mining at Ainak threatens a sprawling ancient Buddhist monastery site.

11. Diodorus Siculus 3.12–14 describes the gold mines of Egypt.

12. Claude Rapin, *Fouilles d'Ai Khanoum*, vol. VIII, *La trésorerie du palais hellénistique d'Ai Khanoum* (Paris: Diffusion de Boccard, 1992), pp. 70–71, 146–47, 288–94, and 318.

13. A cognitive map is an interpretive scheme for understanding the world, often existing as a communal mind-set on how a certain task should be done. A good look into an ancient mint may be found in John Camp II and John Kroll, "The Agora Mint and Athenian Bronze Coinage," *Hesperia* 70 (2001): 127–62.

14. An introduction to this process may be found in Philip Grierson, *Numismatics* (Oxford: Oxford University Press, 1975), pp. 100–111.

15. As noted above, in chapter 5, ten unstruck bronze flans were excavated at Ai Khanoum. These cast flans show the form of the mold tree. The resulting sprue will sometimes be evident on the finished coin: for example, Osmund Bopearachchi, *Monnaies gréco-bactriennes et indo-grecques: Catalogue raisonné* (Paris: Bibliothèque Nationale, 1991), plate 3, coin 22 (Euthydemus I).

16. Osmund Bopearachchi, "L'apport des surfrappes à la reconstruction de l'histoire des Indo-Grecs," *Revue Numismatique* (2008): 259–60. This proves the existence of a second King Heliocles distinct from Eucratides' immediate successor.

17. For the working conditions in a well-attested medieval mint, see Peter Spufford, "Mint Organisation in the Burgundian Netherlands in the Fifteenth Century," pp. 239–61 in C.N.L. Brooke et al., eds., *Studies in Numismatic Method* (Cambridge: Cambridge University Press, 1983).

18. Leonard Gorelick and John Gwinnett, "Close Work without Magnifying Lenses?" *Expedition* (winter 1981): 27–34; Dimitris Plantzos, "Crystals and Lenses in the Graeco-Roman World," *American Journal of Archaeology* 101 (1997): 451–64; Jay Enoch, "Early Lens Use: Lenses Found in Context with Their Original Objects," *Optical History* 73.11 (1996): 707–13.

19. Pliny, *Historia Naturalis* 37.16, mentions the problems faced by gem cutters.

20. I thank Osmund Bopearachchi for kindly sharing this information.

21. Raoul Curiel and Gérard Fussman, *Le trésor monétaire de Qunduz* (Paris: Klincksieck, 1965), pp. 49–54.

22. Analysis done by Maryse Blet-Lemarquand using scanning electron microscopy energy-dispersive X-ray analysis.

23. Whenever the dies shifted slightly between blows, a double-struck image could appear on the coin: e.g., Curiel and Fussman, *Le trésor monétaire de Qunduz,* no. 346 (obverse).

24. Bopearachchi, *Monnaies gréco-bactriennes et indo-grecques: Catalogue raisonné,* p. 397. Note that the issues listed in the name of Diodotus were minted by a later king.

25. P. Bernard, *Fouilles d'Ai Khanoum,* vol. IV, *Les monnaies hors trésors* (Paris: Diffusion de Boccard, 1985), p. 16.

26. Notice the similar guide dots and letter forms on, e.g., the Athena signet ring from Tillya Tepe: V. Sarianidi, *The Golden Hoard of Bactria* (New York: Harry Abrams, 1985), p. 168. Note also the curious steatite engraving of Eucratides' coin type listed in Baldwin's auction 2008, lot 570.

27. An unpublished signet ring found recently in Shaikhan Dheri is set with a brilliant gemstone carving of young Hercules with his lion pelt.

28. Classical Numismatic Group auction 72 (June 2006), no. 1034; see also Gorny and Mosch auction 155 (Mar. 2007), no. 171.

29. Some silver coins of Euthydemus II do this, for example, with the hand and crown of Hercules: Bopearachchi, *Monnaies gréco-bactriennes et indo-grecques: Catalogue raisonné,* p. 55.

30. There is no indication that die cutters used a method known to stone cutters whereby the text was first chalked or inked and then cut, perhaps by a different and even illiterate subordinate.

31. Bactrian die cutters desired that parallel inscriptions begin (and if possible, end) in alignment, as is evident on many dies, including those of Apollodotus I. The rare tetradrachms with his name carved with letters of the same size cannot achieve this balance, because ΑΠΟΛΛΟΔΟΤΟΥ is so much longer than ΒΑΣΙΛΕΩΣ. Yet, by shrinking the omicrons and tucking them among the other letters, this

alignment became possible. Compare Bopearachchi, *Monnaies gréco-bactriennes et indo-grecques: Catalogue raisonné,* plate II A, to Triton auction 8 (Jan. 2005), no. 642.

32. See, for example, Classical Numismatic Group auction 39 (Sept. 1996), no. 859.

33. Osmund Bopearachchi, "Some Interesting Coins from the Pandayale Hoard," *Oriental Numismatic Society Newsletter* 169 (2001): 19–21.

34. E. T. Newell, *The Coinage of the Eastern Seleucid Mints from Seleucus I to Antiochus III* (1938; reprint, New York: American Numismatic Society, 1978), nos. 669 and 670 (Bactra); P. Bernard and O. Guillaume, "Monnaies inédites de la Bactriane grecque à Ai Khanoum (Afghanistan)," *Revue Numismatique* 22 (1980): 21–23. For further discussion of blundered legends, see below.

35. Osmund Bopearachchi and Klaus Grigo, "To Err Is Human," *Oriental Numismatic Society Newsletter* 172 (2002): 14–15.

36. J. C. McKeown, *A Cabinet of Roman Curiosities* (Oxford: Oxford University Press, 2010), p. 6. Emphasis added.

37. Bopearachchi, *Monnaies gréco-bactriennes et indo-grecques: Catalogue raisonné,* plates 8 and 9.

38. It is interesting that both supercoins are multiples of twenty (drachms and staters), which may indicate that they served a similar economic function.

39. Curiel and Fussman, *Le trésor monétaire de Qunduz,* nos. 619–23.

40. This interpretation differs from the one offered in Bopearachchi, *Monnaies gréco-bactriennes et indo-grecques: Catalogue raisonné,* p. 102, because on closer inspection of photographs from the Kabul Museum the dots do appear in the exergue of coin 619.

41. Discussed at length above, in chapter 3.

42. On many early issues of Eucratides (without the epithet), the back portions of the spears do not appear at all.

43. Coin types that were essentially horizontal, like the Dioscuri, dictated parallel horizontal legends, whereas the vertical types common before Eucratides required parallel vertical legends.

44. For example, Bopearachchi, *Monnaies gréco-bactriennes et indo-grecques: Catalogue raisonné,* p. 69; see also O. Bopearachchi, "Recent Coin

Hoard Evidence on Pre-Kushana Chronology," pp. 99–149 in Michael Alram and Deborah Klimburg-Salter, eds., *Coins, Art, and Chronology: Essays on the Pre-Islamic History of the Indo-Iranian Borderlands* (Vienna: Verlag der Österreichischen Akademie der Wissenschaften, 1999), p. 119.

45. O. Bopearachchi, "Découvertes récentes de trésors indo-grecs: Nouvelles données historiques," *Comptes-Rendus de l'Académie des Inscriptions et Belles-Lettres*, 1995: 619–20.

46. Curiel and Fussman, *Le trésor monétaire de Qunduz*, p. 18.

47. C. Kraay, "Demetrius in Bactria and India," *Numismatic Digest* 9 (1985): 17–18.

48. F. Holt, "Mimesis in Metal: The Fate of Greek Culture on Bactrian Coins," pp. 93–104 in F. Titchener and R. Moorton, eds., *The Eye Expanded: Life and the Arts in Greco-Roman Antiquity* (Berkeley and Los Angeles: University of California Press, 1999).

49. O. Bopearachchi and A. ur Rahman, *Pre-Kushana Coins in Pakistan* (Karachi: Iftikhar Rasul, 1995), pp. 218–19 (no. 1068); and cf. no. 1071.

50. For a discussion of linguistic clues to the ethnicity of scribes in Achaemenid Bactria, see Shaul Shaked, *Le satrape de Bactriane et son gouverneur: Documents araméens du IVe s. avant notre ère* (Paris: Diffusion de Boccard, 2004), pp. 23–27.

51. For example, Bopearachchi, *Monnaies gréco-bactriennes et indo-grecques: Catalogue raisonné*, pp. 281–82.

52. Holt, "Mimesis in Metal," pp. 94–98. The sample includes only coins (and therefore the dies that made them) from secure contexts, not market specimens or known imitations of the interesting type found in Mariusz Mielczarek, "Two Imitations of Eucratides' Obols from the Museum Collection in Lodz," *Wiadomosci Numizmatyczne* 31 (1987): 48–51.

53. One coin attributable to Eucratides II appears in the compromised Hoard III from Ai Khanoum: F. Holt, "The Euthydemid Coinage of Bactria: Further Hoard Evidence from Ai Khanoum," *Revue Numismatique* 23 (1981): no. 129; the one bronze coin (no. 166) from Ai Khanoum identified by Paul Bernard as an issue of Demetrius II should probably be attributed to Demetrius I: Bopearachchi, *Monnaies gréco-bactriennes et indo-grecques: Catalogue raisonné*, p. 167 (series 5 C).

54. There are Antimachus coins outside this controlled sample that

have more complex errors. These occur on his square issues: see, e.g., Bopearachchi and ur Rahman, *Pre-Kushana Coins*, pp. 100–101 (nos. 189 and 190).

55. I take this opportunity to thank Professor Charles Peters of the University of Houston Mathematics Department for kindly reviewing these data.

56. As proposed by Bernard and Guillaume, "Monnaies inédites," p. 22, to explain some coinage errors at Ai Khanoum; cf. Holt, "Mimesis in Metal," pp. 99–100.

57. P. Bernard, "The Greek Colony at Ai Khanoum and Hellenism in Central Asia," pp. 81–105 in F. Hiebert and P. Cambon, eds., *Afghanistan: Hidden Treasures from the National Museum, Kabul* (Washington, D.C.: National Geographic Society, 2008), p. 95.

58. Strabo 15.2.9 cites the agreement made by Seleucus I, reportedly renewed by Antiochus III according to Polybius 11.39.11–12. See F. Holt, *Alexander the Great and Bactria: The Formation of a Greek Frontier in Central Asia* (Leiden: Brill, 1988), p. 101.

59. Quintus Curtius 7.5.29.

60. H. Sidky, *The Greek Kingdom of Bactria: From Alexander to Eucratides the Great* (Lanham, Md.: University Press of America, 2000), pp. 131 and xvi. Similarly, D.W. MacDowall and M. Taddei, "The Early Historic Period: Achaemenids and Greeks," pp. 187–232 in F.R. Allchin and N. Hammond, eds., *The Archaeology of Afghanistan from Earliest Times to the Timurid Period* (London: Academic Press, 1978), p. 198: "the pure Greek character of the city in its language, culture and system of education in Bactria."

61. W.W. Tarn, *The Greeks in Bactria and India*, 2nd ed. (Cambridge: Cambridge University Press, 1951), p. 301. Tarn then goes on, contrary to Sidky, to discuss some survivals of the Hellenic population and their culture.

62. Bopearachchi and ur Rahman, *Pre-Kushana Coins*, pp. 56–58 and 88–89 (no. 120), accepted as genuine.

63. Rapin, *Fouilles d'Ai Khanoum*, vol. VIII, *La trésorerie*, p. 292: "La ville grecque d'Ai Khanoum fut abandonée soudainement et sans avoir connu une période de décadence préalable."

64. Curiel and Fussman, *Le trésor monétaire de Qunduz*, nos. 39–48, show the development of an obvious crack at 11:00 on the obverse die.

65. Ibid., no. 39, which—given the size of the crack in the obverse—was probably not the first in this series.

66. Ibid., nos. 47 and 48.

67. Based on the monograms for lifetime issues as enumerated in Bopearachchi, *Monnaies gréco-bactriennes et indo-grecques: Catalogue raisonné*, pp. 199–214.

68. See below, chapter 9, for further discussion.

9. COINS AND THE COLLAPSE OF CIVILIZATION

1. Mariusz Mielczarek, *Ancient Greek Coins Found in Central, Eastern and Northern Europe* (Warsaw: Polish Academy of Sciences, 1989), p. 146 (no. 25). The artifact is now in the Archaeological and Ethnographical Museum, Lodz.

2. The coin bears the monogram ⊠, which Mielczarek (above, n. 1, citing A.D.H. Bivar) identified with the Pushkalavati mint but has since been attributed to Begram by Osmund Bopearachchi, *Monnaies gréco-bactriennes et indo-grecques: Catalogue raisonné* (Paris: Bibliothèque Nationale, 1991), pp. 84–85.

3. Mielczarek, *Ancient Greek Coins*, pp. 93–100, offers some speculations.

4. *The Daily Telegraph*, April 3, 1969, reported this incident at Sudbury, Suffolk.

5. On the nature of bronze coinages, see F. Holt, *Thundering Zeus: The Making of Hellenistic Bactria* (Berkeley and Los Angeles: University of California Press, 1999), pp. 107–25.

6. Ibid., p. 121: the assimilation of Artemis and Anahita.

7. M.M. Austin, "Hellenistic Kings, War, and the Economy," *Classical Quarterly* 36.3 (1986): 450–66.

8. Using the data derived by Alain Davesne and Georges Le Rider, *Gülnar*, vol. II, *Le trésor de Meydancikkale* (Paris: Recherche sur les Civilisations, 1989), pp. 256–58.

9. Excavated in 1973: Paul Bernard, "Fouilles d'Ai Khanoum

(Afghanistan), Campagnes de 1972 et 1973," *Comptes-Rendus de l'Académie des Inscriptions et Belles-Lettres,* 1974: 280–308.

10. Alexandria Eschate: Curtius 7.6.25. Marakanda: Curtius 7.6.10. Antiochia Margiana: Pliny, *Historia Naturalis* 6.18 (47). The latter two sites reportedly served as regional capitals; Arrian 3.30.6 calls Maracanda a royal residence.

11. P. Bernard, "Ai Khanoum en Afghanistan hier (1964–1978) et aujourd'hui (2001): Un site en péril," *Comptes-Rendus de l'Académie des Inscriptions et Belles-Lettres,* 2001: 1016–17.

12. Claude Rapin, *Indian Art from Afghanistan: The Legend of Sakuntala and the Indian Treasure of Eucratides at Ai Khanoum* (New Delhi: Manohar Publishers, 1996), pp. 104–5.

13. Frantz Grenet, Jean-Claude Liger, and Régis de Valence, "L'arsenal," *Bulletin de l'École Française d'Extrême-Orient* 68 (1980): 51–63.

14. Paul Bernard, *Fouilles d'Ai Khanoum,* vol. IV, *Les monnaies hors trésors* (Paris: Diffusion de Boccard, 1985), nos. 11, 58, 159, 184, and 210.

15. Ibid., nos. 191, 193, and 212.

16. Olivier Guillaume, ed., *Graeco-Bactrian and Indian Coins from Afghanistan* (Oxford: Oxford University Press, 1991), pp. 25–116. The treasury inscriptions listing such coins are discussed above, in chapter 6.

17. Bernard, *Fouilles d'Ai Khanoum,* vol. IV, p. 76. The distinctions between trade, tribute, and plunder in the archaeological record are not easy to make, as the equivocations of some scholars show: Rapin, *Indian Art from Afghanistan,* pp. 107, 111, and 118.

18. Only a few Bactrian coins reached Central and Eastern Europe, all of them silver: Mielczarek, *Ancient Greek Coins,* nos. 25 (Menander), 153 (Eucratides II), and 125 (Euthydemus imitation).

19. For example, the parable of the lost coin (Luke 15:8): "Either what woman having ten pieces [drachms] of silver, if she lose one piece, doth not light a candle, and sweep the house, and seek diligently till she find it?" (KJV).

20. Bernard, *Fouilles d'Ai Khanoum,* vol. IV, p. 5.

21. P.J. Casey, *Understanding Ancient Coins* (Norman: University of Oklahoma Press, 1986), pp. 69–74. Casey also includes political and economic factors.

22. C.-Y. Petitot-Biehler, "Trésor de monnaies grecques et gréco-bactriennes trouvé à Ai Khanoum (Afghanistan)," *Revue Numismatique* 17 (1975): 23–57; and P. Bernard, "Trésor de monnaies grecques et gréco-bactriennes trouvé à Ai Khanoum (Afghanistan): Note sur la signification historique de la trouvaille," *Revue Numismatique* 17 (1975): 58–69 (both reprinted and translated in Guillaume, ed., *Graeco-Bactrian and Indian Coins*, pp. 117–64).

23. There is a vast literature on hoard studies, but a good place to start is Casey, *Understanding Ancient Coins*, pp. 51–67. The classification of hoards began in antiquity: Justinian, *Digest* 41.1.

24. The latest coin in the hoard (Eucratides) seems to have rested near the top of the pile, based on photographs of the concreted mass before cleaning: Bernard, "Trésor de monnaies grecques et gréco-bactriennes," fig. 4.

25. G.G. Aperghis, *The Seleukid Royal Economy: The Finances and Financial Administration of the Seleukid Empire* (Cambridge: Cambridge University Press, 2004), pp. 202–5, with appropriate cautions.

26. See Holt, *Thundering Zeus*, pp. 34–35. Other kinds of hoards may have been deliberately abandoned as useless currency, grave offerings, etc.

27. On such problems in the archaeological record, see Catherine Cameron and Steve Tomka, eds., *Abandonment of Settlements and Regions: Ethnoarchaeological and Archaeological Approaches* (Cambridge: Cambridge University Press, 1993).

28. See François Widemann, *Les successeurs d'Alexandre en Asie centrale et leur héritage culturel* (Paris: Riveneuve, 2009), p. 186.

29. Systems theory in archaeology began as part of the New Archaeology: see Kent Flannery, "Archaeological Systems Theory and Early Mesopotamia," pp. 67–87 in Betty J. Meggers, ed., *Anthropological Archaeology in the Americas* (Washington, D.C.: Anthropological Society of Washington, 1968).

30. Joseph Tainter, *The Collapse of Complex Societies* (Cambridge: Cambridge University Press, 1988); Jared Diamond, *Collapse: How Societies Choose to Fail or Succeed* (New York: Penguin, 2005).

31. Most notably by Gregory Brunk, "Understanding Self-Orga-

nized Criticality as a Statistical Process," *Complexity* 5.3 (2000): 26–33, and "Why Do Societies Collapse? A Theory Based on Self-Organized Criticality," *Journal of Theoretical Politics* 14.2 (2002): 195–230.

32. Roman Frigg, "Self-Organized Criticality—What It Is and What It Isn't," *Studies in History and Philosophy of Science* 34 (2003): 613–32.

33. Ibid., pp. 625–30.

34. As Tainter, *Collapse of Complex Societies*, points out (p. 64): "But the fundamental problem with intruder theories is that they do not clarify much. The overthrow of a dominant state by a weaker, tribally-organized people is an event greatly in need of explanation. It is, standing alone, an acceptable explanation of nothing."

35. Paul Bernard et al., "Campagne de fouille 1978 à Ai Khanoum (Afghanistan)," *Bulletin de l'École Française d'Extrême-Orient* 68 (1980): 7.

36. The latter group includes Demetrius I, Euthydemus II, Antimachus I (and his co-rulers Antimachus and Eumenes), Agathocles, Pantaleon, Apollodotus I, Demetrius II, Eucratides I and a co-ruler, and Menander. Claude Rapin notes that the Bactrian and Indo-Greek king list doubles that of the Seleucids over a similar time span: *Fouilles d'Ai Khanoum*, vol. VIII, *La trésorerie du palais hellénistique d'Ai Khanoum* (Paris: Diffusion de Boccard, 1992), p. 281.

37. For these useful typologies, see Chris Gosden, *Archaeology and Colonialism: Cultural Contact from 5000 BC to the Present* (Cambridge: Cambridge University Press, 2004).

38. The chief global polluter in this period was Roman Spain, but the local impact of Bactrian mining operations should be considered. See Kevin J.R. Rosman et al., "Lead from Carthaginian and Roman Spanish Mines Isotopically Identified in Greenland Ice Dated from 600 B.C. to 300 A.D." *Environmental Science and Technology* 31.12 (1997): 3413–16; F.B. Pyatt and J.P. Grattan, "Some Consequences of Ancient Mining Activities on the Health of Ancient and Modern Human Populations," *Journal of Public Health Medicine* 23.3 (2001): 235–36.

39. Pierre Leriche, "Bactria, Land of a Thousand Cities," pp. 121–53 in J. Cribb and G. Herrmann, eds., *After Alexander: Central Asia before Islam* (Oxford: Oxford University Press, 2007), p. 143.

40. Ibid., p. 138.

41. V. Sarianidi, *The Golden Hoard of Bactria* (New York: Abrams, 1985), p. 34. See also Karen Rubinson, "Tillya Tepe: Aspects of Gender and Cultural Identity," pp. 51–64 in K.M. Linduff and K.S. Rubinson, eds., *Are All Warriors Male? Gender Roles on the Ancient Eurasian Steppe* (Plymouth: AltaMira Press, 2008).

42. This specimen was minted by Mithridates II.

43. Sarianidi, *The Golden Hoard of Bactria*, p. 47; R.C. Senior, *Indo-Scythian Coins and History* (London: Classical Numismatic Group, 2001), vol. I, pp. 105–6, and vol. II, pp. 145–46.

44. Sarianidi, *The Golden Hoard of Bactria*, p. 52.

45. Susan Stevens, "Charon's Obol and Other Coins in Ancient Funerary Practice," *Phoenix* 45.3 (1991): 215–29.

46. Ibid., p. 226.

47. Ibid., p. 227.

48. Bertille Lyonnet, "Les nomades et la chute du royaume gréco-bactrien: Quelques nouveaux indices en provenance de l'Asie centrale—Vers l'identification des Tokhares–Yueh-Chi?" pp. 153–64 in Paul Bernard and Frantz Grenet, eds., *Histoire et cultes de l'Asie centrale préislamique: Sources écrites et documents archéologiques* (Paris: CNRS, 1991).

49. William Simpson, "Buddhist Remains in the Jalalabad Valley," *Indian Antiquary* 8 (1879): 227–30.

50. F.R. Hoernle, "Gold Coins from Jalalabad," *Proceedings of the Asiatic Society of Bengal* 48 (1879): 122–38.

51. This behavior also pertains to Hellenistic Bactria: Holt, *Thundering Zeus*, p. 115. See also the "Phar" countermark on some issues of Demetrius I: Michael Mitchiner, *Indo-Greek and Indo-Scythian Coinage* (London: Hawkins, 1975), vol. I, p. 64 (type 122).

52. Senior, *Indo-Scythian Coins and History*, vol. I, p. 106, and vol. II, p. 146 (no. 199.1D).

53. Ibid., no. 199.2D.

54. See, for instance, John Creighton, *Coins and Power in Late Iron Age Britain* (Cambridge: Cambridge University Press, 2000), p. 27.

55. These mintages are variously identified as barbarian imitations, barbarous imitations, Scythian imitations, posthumous issues, or simply unofficial issues.

290 / Notes to Pages 199–200

56. Senior, *Indo-Scythian Coins and History*, vol. II, pp. 217–19. An important pioneer in these studies was E. V. Zeymal, whose works include *Drevniye moneti Tadzhikistana* (Dushanbe: Akademii Nauk, 1983) and "Problèmes de circulation monétaire dans la Bactriane hellénistique," pp. 273–79 in Jean-Claude Gardin, ed., *L'archéologie de la Bactriane ancienne: Actes du colloque franco-soviétique* (Paris: CNRS, 1985).

57. This issue is treated well by David Smith, "Will the Real Eukratides Please Stand Up?" *Numismatics International Bulletin* 40.4 (2005): 74–83, although he deems any coin with a corrupted legend to be ipso facto an imitation.

58. Osmund Bopearachchi, "The Euthydemus Imitations and the Date of Sogdian Independence," *Silk Road Art and Archaeology* 2 (1991–92): 1–21.

59. Ibid., p. 9.

60. Polybius, *Histories* 11.34, where the Bactrian king points out the dangerous presence of nomads to the north.

61. For what it is worth, one of these Euthydemus imitations was found in Ukraine: Mielczarek, *Ancient Greek Coins*, p. 178 (no. 125). See also Mielczarek, "Two Bronze Imitations of Heliocles's Coins in the Numismatic Collection of the Archaeological and Ethnographical Museum in Lodz," *Prace i Materialy Muzeum Archeologicznego i Etnograficznego w Lodzi* 7 (1987): 5–9 (in Polish with English summary); Mielczarek, "Two Imitations of Eucratides' Obols from the Museum Collection in Lodz," *Wiadomosci Numizmatyczne* 31 (1987): 48–51 (in English with Polish summary).

62. Grenet et al., "L'arsenal"; cf. Valerii Nikonorov and Serge Savchuk, "New Data on Ancient Bactrian Body-Armour (in Light of Finds from Kampyr Tepe)," *Iran* 30 (1992): 49–54.

63. Some imitations of Demetrius I also appear in the archaeological record, but at places like Kampyr Tepe issues and imitations in the name of Heliocles predominate: Edvard Rtveladze, "Découvertes en numismatique et épigraphie gréco-bactriennes à Kampyr-Tepe (Bactriane du nord)," *Revue Numismatique* 6 (1995): 23–24.

64. Bopearachchi, *Monnaies gréco-bactriennes et indo-grecques: Catalogue*

raisonné, p. 204 (no. 33); cf. D. Smith, "Will the Real Eukratides Please Stand Up?" no. 15, and Triton auction II (Jan. 2008), no. 364.

65. F. Holt, "The Euthydemid Coinage of Bactria: Further Hoard Evidence from Ai Khanoum," *Revue Numismatique* 23 (1981): no. 133.

66. Numismatic Fine Arts auction (Dec. 1989), no. 767.

67. For example, Classical Numismatic Group mail bid sale 75 (May 2007), no. 666. Note that this same practice appears on a lifetime issue of Plato, where the horses' legs seem unattached to the animals: Classical Numismatic Group mail bid sale 75 (May 2007), no. 651.

68. Heritage World auction 458 (Jan. 2008), no. 50045 (inscribed ΙΑΙΛΕΩΣ ΜΕΓΛΛΥ ΕΥΚΙΛΤΛΟΥ).

69. Osmund Bopearachchi, *Sylloge Nummorum Graecorum: The Collection of the American Numismatic Society,* part 9, *Graeco-Bactrian and Indo-Greek Coins* (New York: American Numismatic Society, 1998), nos. 666–81.

70. Widemann, *Les successeurs d'Alexandre,* p. 196.

71. For an altogether different purpose, some coins have been mutilated, probably in modern times, to obliterate the human form. An otherwise fine tetradrachm of Euthydemus II in the trays of the Hermitage Museum has the standing figure of Hercules on the reverse deliberately slashed numerous times from head to waist.

72. Joe Cribb, ed., *Money from Cowrie Shells to Credit Cards* (London: British Museum, 1986), p. 152; Cornelius Vermeule, "Numismatics in Antiquity," *Schweizerische Numismatische Rundschau* 54 (1975): 5–32. See also Jutta-Annette Bruhn, *Coins and Costume in Late Antiquity* (Washington, D.C.: Dumbarton Oaks, 1993), for examples of coins set into jewelry without damaging the coins.

73. E. Errington and J. Cribb, eds., *The Crossroads of Asia: Transformation in Image and Symbol in the Art of Ancient Afghanistan and Pakistan* (Cambridge: The Ancient India and Iran Trust, 1992), p. 146.

74. Percy Gardner, *The Coins of the Greek and Scythic Kings of Bactria and India in the British Museum* (1886; reprint, Chicago: Argonaut, 1966), p. 19 (no. 1); Robert Bracey, "Alexander's Lost Kingdom: From Diodotus to Strato III," p. 145 (ill. 11.3) in Himanshu Ray and Daniel Potts, eds.,

Memory as History: The Legacy of Alexander in Asia (New Delhi: Aryan Books, 2007).

75. Diodotus: Holt, *Thundering Zeus*, p. 152 (series B, group 2, no. 4); Euthydemus I: Fitzwilliam Museum; Agathocles: private collection of Lloyd Taylor, with part of the iron pin still in place. The removal of the metal attachments usually causes further damage, as is obvious on these coins; see also F. Holt, "The Autobiography of a Coin," *Aramco World* 48.5 (Sept.–Oct. 1997): 10–15, which takes up the case of a damaged gold stater of Eucratides now in the American Numismatic Society collection. It was once worn as a ring.

76. H.H. Wilson, *Ariana Antiqua: A Descriptive Account of the Antiquities and Coins of Afghanistan* (1841; reprint, Delhi: Oriental Publishers, 1971), p. 267 and plate XXI, no. 7.

77. Bracey, "Alexander's Lost Kingdom," p. 143 (ill. 11.1); Mitchiner, *Indo-Greek and Indo-Scythian Coinage*, vol. II, p. 123; Bopearachchi, *Monnaies gréco-bactriennes et indo-grecques: Catalogue raisonné*, p. 244 (no. 185) and p. 218 (no. 10). Vermeule, "Numismatics in Antiquity," lists as no. 5 an Agathocles tetradrachm commemorating Alexander that has two loops attached; this coin, however, is suspect: F. Holt, "The So-Called 'Pedigree Coins' of the Bactrian Greeks," pp. 69–91 in W. Heckel and R. Sullivan, eds., *Ancient Coins of the Graeco-Roman World: The Nickle Numismatic Papers* (Waterloo, Ont.: Wilfrid Laurier University Press, 1984), p. 74.

78. A curious, and perhaps spurious, example of a coin fixed in a suspension setting may be found illustrated in A.N. Oikonomides, "The Gold Coinage of the Indo-Greek King Eucratides I (171–155 B.C.)," *North American Journal of Numismatics* 7.6 (1968): 181.

79. Also an imitation Eucratides obol from Baluchistan, whence have come a high percentage of holed coins, was pierced at the 5:00 position: Edward J. Rapson, "Ancient Silver Coins from Baluchistan," *Numismatic Chronicle* 4 (1904): 321.

80. Demetrius I bronzes: Bopearachchi, *Monnaies gréco-bactriennes et indo-grecques: Catalogue raisonné*, p. 167 (no. 14); Bopearachchi, *Sylloge Nummorum Graecorum*, no. 211. Euthydemus II cupronickels: O. Bopearachchi and A. ur Rahman, *Pre-Kushana Coins in Pakistan* (Karachi: Iftikhar

Rasul, 1995), pp. 92–93 (no. 145); Bopearachchi, *Monnaies gréco-bactriennes et indo-grecques: Catalogue raisonné,* p. 170 (no. 10). Agathocles cupronickel: private collection (square hole cut cleanly). Heliocles I imitation(?) tetradrachm, considerably trimmed: Mitchiner, *Indo-Greek and Indo-Scythian Coinage,* vol. II, p. 160 (type 108).

81. Robert Graves describes such a coin in his poem "The Clipped Stater." He imagines Alexander the Great, living in obscurity as a frontier guard in China, accepting his pay, with some surprise, in the form of one of his own gold staters: "The coin is bored, to string with the country's bronze on a cord."

82. Mitchiner, *Indo-Greek and Indo-Scythian Coinage,* vol. I, p. 60 (type 108).

83. For example, Demetrius I obol: Mitchiner, *Indo-Greek and Indo-Scythian Coinage,* vol. I, p. 58 (type 105); Eucratides obol: ibid., p. 94 (type 181); and a tetradrachm: Bopearachchi and ur Rahman, *Pre-Kushana Coins,* pp. 106–7 (no. 240).

84. Euthydemus II: Bopearachchi, *Monnaies gréco-bactriennes et indo-grecques: Catalogue raisonné,* p. 178 (no. 6); Eucratides I: Timothy Gantz and Frances Van Keuren, *The Richard E. Paulson Collection of Ancient Coins* (Athens, Ga.: Georgia Museum of Art, 1981), p. 7; Agathocles: Mitchiner, *Indo-Greek and Indo-Scythian Coinage,* vol. I, p. 77 (type 137); Antialcidas: ibid., vol. II, p. 147 (type 269, with two holes).

85. Eucratides I bilingual square imitation: Bopearachchi, *Sylloge Nummorum Graecorum,* no. 573; Eucratides I obol: Mitchiner, *Indo-Greek and Indo-Scythian Coinage,* vol. 1, p. 94 (type 180); Apollodotus II drachm: Bopearachchi, *Sylloge Nummorum Graecorum,* no. 1559.

86. The only holed coin excavated at Ai Khanoum, for example, was an Islamic piece dated 1918–19: Bernard, *Fouilles d'Ai Khanoum,* vol. IV, p. 80 (no. 224).

87. See, for example, Errington and Cribb, eds., *The Crossroads of Asia,* p. 147.

88. Rapin, *Indian Art from Afghanistan,* p. 124 (item O3).

89. Edvard Rtveladze, "La circulation monétaire au nord de l'Oxus a l'époque gréco-bactrienne," *Revue Numismatique* 26 (1984): 61–76, esp. 66.

90. For example, an unusual Bactrian tetradrachm: Bopearachchi,

Sylloge Nummorum Graecorum, no. 180 (Euthydemus I, listed as a Sogdian imitation); a Demetrius I tetradrachm: Bopearachchi, *Sylloge Nummorum Graecorum*, no. 192 (on which the cut was made into the edge); and a Eucratides tetradrachm at Samarkand: Natalia Smirnova, "Coins of Eucratides in Museum Collections," *East and West* 42.1 (1992): 10 (coin 66).

91. See, for example, some tetradrachms of Demetrius I: Bopearachchi and ur Rahman, *Pre-Kushana Coins*, pp. 90–91 (no. 124) and 208–9 (no. 1013).

92. See O. Bopearachchi, "A Joy and a Curse," pp. 33–73 in F. Holt and O. Bopearachchi, eds., *The Alexander Medallion: Exploring the Origins of a Unique Artefact* (Lacapelle-Mirival: Imago Lattara, 2011), pp. 42–47.

93. Two die-linked staters, if they are genuine, provide exceptions that have deep wedge-shaped cuts across the face of the king: Ponterio mail bid auction 140 (Nov. 2006), no. 7, and Triton 8 auction (Jan. 2005) no. 615b.

94. Osmund Bopearachchi, "L'apport des surfrappes à la reconstruction de l'histoire des Indo-Grecs," *Revue Numismatique* (2008): 246 and 255.

95. Holt, *Thundering Zeus*, pp. 156 and 160. The gaps in the cut coins show that the gold there was not all simply mashed aside, but some metal had to be removed.

96. O. Bopearachchi and Klaus Grigo, "Thundering Zeus Revisited," *Oriental Numismatic Society Newsletter* 169 (autumn 2001): 22–24.

97. On the problems (and profits) of plated coins, see F. Reiff et al., "Investigation of Contemporary Gilded Forgeries of Ancient Coins," *Fresenius' Journal of Analytical Chemistry* 171.8 (2001): 1146–53.

98. The process of cutting a coin in this rather precise way required sharp (and perhaps heated) tools and some muscle. The pressure that needed to be applied to the obverse can be gauged by the frequent mashing of the reverse type. See, e.g., Classical Numismatic Group auction 66 (May 2004), no. 939.

99. Bopearachchi, "A Joy and a Curse," pp. 44–47.

100. Aperghis, *The Seleukid Royal Economy*, pp. 218–19.

101. For one possible exception, see Holt, *Thundering Zeus*, pp. 121–23.

102. Xinru Liu, "Hellenistic Residue in Central Asia under Islamic Regimes," *Journal of Interdisciplinary Studies in History and Archaeology* 1.2 (2004): 79–86.

103. Stanley Burstein, "New Light on the Fate of Greek in Ancient Central and South Asia," *Ancient West and East* 9 (2010): 181–92.

104. Michael Cosmopoulos, "The Greek Tradition in India and the Formation of Gandharan Sculpture: Coinage and Classical Iconography," *Ancient World* 36 (2005): 44–53.

SELECT BIBLIOGRAPHY

Ancillary materials such as book reviews, obituary notices, numismatic auction catalogs, and so forth have been omitted below, but full citations appear in the notes.

"A Coin of Eucratides." *American Journal of Numismatics* 14.1 (1879): 18–20.

Aghion, Irène. "Collecting Antiquities in Eighteenth-Century France." *Journal of the History of Collections* 14.2 (2002): 193–203.

Alder, Garry. *Beyond Bokhara: The Life of William Moorcroft, Asian Explorer and Pioneer Veterinary Surgeon.* London: Century, 1985.

Allchin, F.R., and K.R. Norman. "Guide to the Ashokan Inscriptions." *South Asian Studies* 1 (1985): 43–50.

Allouche-LePage, Marie-Thérèse. *L'art monétaire des royaumes bactriens: Essai d'interprétation de la symbolique religieuse gréco-orientale du IIIe au Ier s. av. J.-C.* Paris: Didier, 1956.

Altheim, Franz. *Weltgeschichte Asiens im griechischen Zeitalter.* 2 vols. Halle: Max Niemeyer, 1947–48.

Altheim, Franz, and Ruth Stiehl. *Geschichte Mittelasiens im Altertum.* Berlin: Walter DeGruyter, 1970.

Aperghis, G.G. "Recipients and End-Users on Seleukid Coins." *Bulletin of the Institute of Classical Studies* 53.2 (2010): 55–84.

———. *The Seleukid Royal Economy: The Finances and Financial Administration of the Seleukid Empire.* Cambridge: Cambridge University Press, 2004.

Ashraf Khan, Muhammad. "Outline of the Archaeological Field Research in Swat Valley Carried Out by Pakistani Institutions." *Journal of Asian Civilizations* 34 (2011): 81–93.

Audouin, Rémy, and Paul Bernard. "Trésor de monnaies indiennes et indogrecques d'Ai Khanoum (Afghanistan)." *Revue Numismatique* 15 (1973): 238–89; and 16 (1974): 6–41.

Austin, M.M. "Hellenistic Kings, War, and the Economy." *Classical Quarterly* 36.3 (1986): 450–66.

Babelon, Ernest. *Traité des monnaies grecques et romaines.* Vol. I, *Théorie et doctrine.* Paris: Ernest Leroux, 1901.

Babelon, Jean. *Le portrait dans l'antiquité d'après les monnaies.* Paris: Payot, 1942.

Baipakov, K.M. "The Great Silk Way: Studies in Kazakhstan." *Archaeological Studies* 16 (1994): 89–93.

Ball, Warwick. *Archaeological Gazetteer of Afghanistan.* 2 vols. Paris: Éditions Recherche sur les Civilizations, 1982.

———. *The Monuments of Afghanistan: History, Archaeology and Architecture.* New York: I.B. Tauris, 2008.

de Bartholomaei, Jean. "Notice sur les médailles des Diodotes, rois de la Bactriane." *Köhne's Zeitschrift für Münze-, Siegel- und Wappenkunde* 3 (1843): 65–77.

———. "Réponse à Mr. Droysen sur ses conjectures concernant les premiers rois de la Bactriane." *Köhne's Zeitschrift für Münz-, Siegel- und Wappenkunde* 6 (1846): 129–62.

Bayer, Theophilus. *Historia Regni Graecorum Bactriani.* St. Petersburg: Academia Scientiarum, 1738.

Bayly, C.A. *Empire and Information: Intelligence Gathering and Social Communication in India, 1780–1870.* Cambridge: Cambridge University Press, 2000.

Behrendt, Kurt. *The Buddhist Architecture of Gandhara.* Leiden: Brill, 2004.

Bellinger, Alfred. "Hyspaosines of Charax." *Yale Classical Studies* 8 (1942): 52–67.

Beneviste, Émile. "Édits d'Asoka en traduction grecque." *Journal Asiatique* (1964): 137–57.

Beneviste, Émile, and A. Dupont-Sommer. "Une inscription indo-araméene d'Asoka provenant de Kandahar (Afghanistan)." *Journal Asiatique* 254 (1966): 437–65.

Beregovaia, N.A., U. Islamov, and A.N. Kalandadze. *Contributions to the Archaeology of the Soviet Union, with Special Emphasis on Central Asia, the Caucasus and Armenia.* Cambridge, Mass.: Peabody Museum, 1966.

Berghaus, Peter. "Coin Hoards: Methodology and Evidence." In P.L. Gupta and A.K. Jha, eds., *Numismatics and Archaeology*, pp. 16–19. Anjaneri: Indian Institute of Research in Numismatic Studies, 1987.

Berk, Harlan. *100 Greatest Ancient Coins.* Atlanta: Whitman Publishing, 2008.

Bernard, Paul. "Ai Khanoum en Afghanistan hier (1964–1978) et aujourd'hui (2001): Un site en péril." *Comptes-Rendus de l'Académie des Inscriptions et Belles-Lettres*, 2001: 971–1029.

———. "Ai Khanoum on the Oxus: A Hellenistic City in Central Asia." *Proceedings of the British Academy* 53 (1967): 71–95.

———. "Campagne de fouilles à Ai Khanoum (Afghanistan)." *Comptes-Rendus de l'Académie des Inscriptions et Belles-Lettres*, 1972: 605–32.

———. "Campagne de fouilles 1978 à Ai Khanoum (Afghanistan)." *Comptes-Rendus de l'Académie des Inscriptions et Belles-Lettres*, 1980: 435–59.

———. "Chapiteaux corinthiens hellénistiques d'Asie centrale découverts à Ai Khanoum." *Syria* 45 (1968): 111–51.

———. "Diodore XVII, 83, 1: Alexandrie du Caucase ou Alexandrie de l'Oxus?" *Journal des Savants*, 1982: 217–42.

———. *Fouilles d'Ai Khanoum.* Vol. IV, *Les monnaies hors trésors.* Paris: Diffusion de Boccard, 1985.

———. "Fouilles d'Ai Khanoum (Afghanistan), campagnes de 1972 et 1973." *Comptes-Rendus de l'Académie des Inscriptions et Belles-Lettres*, 1974: 280–308.

———. "The Greek Colony at Ai Khanoum and Hellenism in Central Asia." In F. Hiebert and P. Cambon, eds., *Afghanistan: Hidden Treasures from the National Museum, Kabul*, pp. 81–105. Washington, D.C.: National Geographic Society, 2008.

———. "L'œuvre de la Délégation Archéologique Française en Afghanistan (1922–1982)." *Comptes-Rendus de l'Académie des Inscriptions et Belles-Lettres*, 2002: 1287–1323.

———. "Trésor de monnaies grecques et gréco-bactriennes trouvé à Ai Khanoum (Afghanistan): Note sur la signification historique de la trouvaille." *Revue Numismatique* 17 (1975): 58–69.

Bernard, Paul, and Osmund Bopearachchi. "Deux bracelets grecs avec inscriptions grecques trouvés dans l'Asie centrale hellénisée." *Journal des Savants,* 2002: 237–78.

Bernard, Paul, and Henri-Paul Francfort. *Études de géographie historique sur la plaine d'Ai Khanoum.* Paris: CNRS, 1978.

Bernard, Paul, and Olivier Guillaume. "Monnaies inédites de la Bactriane grecque à Ai Khanoum (Afghanistan)." *Revue Numismatique* 22 (1980): 9–32.

Bernard, Paul, Jean-François Jarrige, and Roland Besenval. "Carnet de route en images d'un voyage sur les sites archéologiques de la Bactriane afghan." *Comptes-Rendus de l'Académie des Inscriptions et Belles-Lettres,* 2002: 1385–1428.

Bernard, Paul, Georges-Jean Pinault, and Georges Rougemont. "Deux nouvelles inscriptions grecques de l'Asie centrale." *Journal des Savants,* 2004: 227–356.

Bernard, Paul, and Claude Rapin. "Un parchemin gréco-bactrien d'une collection privée." *Comptes-Rendus de l'Académie des Inscriptions et Belles-Lettres,* 1994: 261–94.

Bernard, Paul, and Georges Rougemont. "Les secrets de la stèle de Kandahar." *L'Histoire* 280 (2003): 27–28.

Bernard, Paul, et al. "Campagne de fouille 1978 à Ai Khanoum (Afghanistan)." *Bulletin de l'École Française d'Extrême-Orient* 68 (1980): 1–104.

———. *Fouilles d'Ai Khanoum.* Vol. I, *Campagnes 1965, 1966, 1967, 1968.* Paris: Klincksieck, 1973.

———. "Fouilles de la mission franco-ouzbèque à l'ancienne Samarcand (Afrasiab): Deuxième et troisième campagnes." *Comptes-Rendus de l'Académie des Inscriptions et Belles-Lettres,* 1992: 275–311.

———. "Fouilles de la mission franco-soviétique à l'ancienne Samarcand (Afrasiab): Première campagne." *Comptes-Rendus de l'Académie des Inscriptions et Belles-Lettres,* 1990: 356–80.

Besenval, Roland, and P. Marquis. "Les travaux de la Délégation Archéologique Française en Afghanistan (DAFA)." *Comptes-Rendus de l'Académie des Inscriptions et Belles-Lettres,* 2008: 973–95.

"Bibliographie de Paul Bernard." *Bulletin of the Asia Institute* 12 (1998): 3–11.

Bivar, A.D.H. "The Death of Eucratides in Medieval Tradition." *Journal of the Royal Asiatic Society* (1950): 7–13.

———. "Monogram Counts from the Kabul Collection." In Paul Bernard and Frantz Grenet, eds., *Histoire et cultes de l'Asie centrale préislamique: Sources écrites et documents archéologiques*, pp. 225–33. Paris: CNRS, 1991.

Bopearachchi, Osmund. "Alfred Foucher et les études numismatiques en Afghanistan." *Comptes-Rendus de l'Académie des Inscriptions et Belles-Lettres*, 2007: 1875–97.

———. "L'apport des surfrappes à la reconstruction de l'histoire des Indo-Grecs." *Revue Numismatique*, 2008: 245–68.

———. *Catalogue of Indo-Greek, Indo-Scythian and Indo-Parthian Coins of the Smithsonian Institution*. Washington, D.C.: Smithsonian, 1993.

———. "La circulation et la production monétaires en Asie centrale et dans l'Inde du nord-ouest (avant et après la conquête d'Alexandre)." *Indologica Taurinensia* 35 (1999–2000): 15–121.

———. "Découvertes récentes de trésors indo-grecs: Nouvelles données historiques." *Comptes-Rendus de l'Académie des Inscriptions et Belles-Lettres*, 1995: 609–27.

———. "The Euthydemus Imitations and the Date of Sogdian Independence." *Silk Road Art and Archaeology* 2 (1991–92): 1–21.

———. "Grands trésors de monnaies pré-sassanides trouvés en Afghanistan et au Pakistan." *International Numismatic Newsletter* 24 (1994): 2–3.

———. *Monnaies gréco-bactriennes et indo-grecques: Catalogue raisonné*. Paris: Bibliothèque Nationale, 1991.

———. "Monnaies indo-grecques surfrappées." *Revue Numismatique* 31 (1989): 49–79.

———. "A New Approach to the History of the Greeks in India." *Yavanika* 1 (1992): 6–20.

———. "Nouvelles trouvailles archéologiques en Afghanistan et au Pakistan et la destruction du patrimoine." *La Timuride* 24 (2002): 10–20.

———. "Recent Discoveries: Hoards and Finds of Ancient Coins from Afghanistan and Pakistan." *Yavanika* 4 (1994): 3–30.

———. "Recent Hoard Evidence on Pre-Kushana Chronology." In Michael Alram and Deborah Klimburg-Salter, eds., *Coins, Art, and Chronology: Essays on the Pre-Islamic History of the Indo-Iranian Borderlands*, pp. 99–149. Vienna: Verlag der Österreichischen Akademie der Wissenschaften, 1999.

———. "Récentes découvertes de trésors de monnaies pré-sassanides trouvés en Afghanistan et au Pakistan." *Cahiers Numismatiques*, Sept. 1994: 7–14.

———. "Les royaumes grecs d'Asie centrale: L'apport de la numismatique à leur histoire." *Les Nouvelles de l'Archéologie* 39 (1990): 21–26.

———. "Some Interesting Coins from the Pandayale Hoard." *Oriental Numismatic Society Newsletter* 169 (2001): 19–21.

———. *Sylloge Nummorum Graecorum: The Collection of the American Numismatic Society.* Part 9, *Graeco-Bactrian and Indo-Greek Coins.* New York: American Numismatic Society, 1998.

———. "Trésors monétaires découvertes et pillage." In *Afghanistan, patrimoine en péril: Actes d'une journée d'étude,* pp. 97–106. Paris: CEREDAF, 2001.

———. "Two More Unique Coins from the Second Mir Zakah Deposit." *Oriental Numismatic Society Newsletter* 169 (2001): 21–22.

Bopearachchi, Osmund, and Marie-Françoise Boussac, eds. *Afghanistan: Ancien carrefour entre l'est et l'ouest.* Turnhout: Brepols, 2005.

Bopearachchi, Osmund, and Philippe Flandrin. *Le portrait d'Alexandre le Grand: Histoire d'une découverte pour l'humanité.* Monaco: Éditions du Rocher, 2005.

Bopearachchi, Osmund, and Klaus Grigo. "Thundering Zeus Revisited." *Oriental Numismatic Society Newsletter* 169 (autumn 2001): 22–24.

———. "To Err Is Human." *Oriental Numismatic Society Newsletter* 172 (2002): 14–15.

Bopearachchi, Osmund, and Aman ur Rahman. *Pre-Kushana Coins in Pakistan.* Karachi: Iftikhar Rasul, 1995.

Bopearachchi, Osmund, et al., eds. *De l'Indus à l'Oxus: Archéologie de l'Asie centrale.* Lattes: Imago, 2003.

Bordeaux, Olivier. "Restitution des trésors monétaires d'Afghanistan et du Pakistan de 1990 à 2008." Mémoire de Master 1, Sorbonne, 2011.

Bosworth, A.B. "The Impossible Dream: W.W. Tarn's *Alexander* in Retrospect." *Ancient Society* 13 (1983): 131–50.

Bracey, Robert. "Alexander's Lost Kingdom: From Diodotus to Strato III." In Himanshu Ray and Daniel Potts, eds. *Memory as History: The Legacy of Alexander in Asia,* pp. 142–56. New Delhi: Aryan Books, 2007.

Brett, Agnes B. "Athena ΑΛΚΙΔΗΜΟΣ of Pella." *American Numismatic Society Museum Notes* 4 (1950): 55–72.

Bruhn, Jutta-Annette. *Coins and Costume in Late Antiquity.* Washington, D.C.: Dumbarton Oaks, 1993.

Brunk, Gregory. "Understanding Self-Organized Criticality as a Statistical Process." *Complexity* 5.3 (2000): 26–33.

———. "Why Do Societies Collapse? A Theory Based on Self-Organized Criticality." *Journal of Theoretical Politics* 14.2 (2002): 195–230.

Buddhue, John. "A Possible Explanation of the Nickel in Ancient Asiatic Coins." *Meteoritics and Planetary Science* 1 (1953): 60–61.

Burnes, Alexander. *Cabool: A Personal Narrative of a Journey to, and Residence in That City in the Years 1836, 7, and 8.* 2nd ed. London: John Murray, 1843.

———. "On the Reputed Descendants of Alexander the Great, in the Valley of the Oxus." *Journal of the Asiatic Society of Bengal* 2 (1833): 305–7.

———. *Travels into Bokhara.* 3 vols. London: John Murray, 1834.

Burstein, Stanley. "New Light on the Fate of Greek in Ancient Central and South Asia." *Ancient West and East* 9 (2010): 181–92.

———, ed. *The Hellenistic Age from the Battle of Ipsos to the Death of Kleopatra.* Cambridge: Cambridge University Press, 1985.

Byron, Robert. *The Road to Oxiana.* [1937.] Reprint. New York: Oxford University Press, 1966.

Callieri, Pierfrancesco. "The North-West of the Indian Subcontinent in the Indo-Greek Period." In Antonio Invernizzi, ed., *In the Land of the Gryphons,* pp. 293–308. Florence: Casa Editrice Le Lettre, 1995.

———. "A Potsherd with a Greek Inscription from Bir-Kot (Swat)." *Journal of Central Asia* 7.1 (1984): 49–53.

Cameron, Catherine, and Steve Tomka, eds. *Abandonment of Settlements and Regions: Ethnoarchaeological and Archaeological Approaches.* Cambridge: Cambridge University Press, 1993.

Camp, John, and John Kroll. "The Agora Mint and Athenian Bronze Coinage." *Hesperia* 70 (2001): 127–62.

Canali de Rossi, Filippo, ed. *Iscrizioni dello estremo oriente greco.* Bonn: Rudolf Habelt, 2004.

Casey, P.J. *Understanding Ancient Coins.* Norman: University of Oklahoma Press, 1986.

Chabouillet, Anatole. "L'Eucratidion: Dissertation sur une médaille d'or inédite d'Eucratide, roi de la Bactriane." *Revue Numismatique,* 1867: 382–415.

Chakrabarti, Dilip. *India: An Archaeological History.* Oxford: Oxford University Press, 1999.

Chandra, Rai. *Indo-Greek Jewellery.* New Delhi: Abhinav, 1979.

Charpentier, Jarl. "Antiochus, King of the Yavanas." *Bulletin of the School of Oriental Studies* 6.2 (1931): 303–21.

Christol, Alain. "Les édits grecs d'Ashoka: Étude linguistique." *Journal Asiatique* 271 (1983): 25–42.

Clarysse, Willy, and Dorothy J. Thompson. "Two Greek Texts on Skin from Hellenistic Bactria." *Zeitschrift für Papyrologie und Epigraphik* 159 (2007): 273–79.

Coloru, Omar. *Da Alessandro a Menandro: Il regno greco di Battriana.* Pisa: Fabrizio Serra, 2009.

———. "Reminiscenze dei re greco-battriani della letteratura medievale e nella science fiction Americana." *Studi Ellenistici* 20 (2008): 519–39.

Coningham, Robin, and I. Ali. *Charsadda: The British-Pakistani Excavations at the Bala Hisar.* Oxford: Archaeopress, 2007.

Coningham, Robin, and Briece Edwards. "Space and Society at Sirkap, Taxila: A Re-Examination of Urban Form and Meaning." *Ancient Pakistan* 12 (1997–98): 47–75.

Conolly, Arthur. *Journey to the North of India through Russia, Persia and Afghanistan.* 2 vols. London: Richard Bentley, 1834.

Cosmopoulos, Michael. "The Greek Tradition in India and the Formation of Gandharan Sculpture: Coinage and Classical Iconography." *Ancient World* 36 (2005): 44–53.

Creighton, John. *Coins and Power in Late Iron Age Britain.* Cambridge: Cambridge University Press, 2000.

Cribb, Joe, ed. *Money from Cowrie Shells to Credit Cards.* London: British Museum, 1986.

Cubelli, Vincenzo. "Moneta e ideologia monarchica: Il caso di Eucratide." *Rivista Italiana di Numismatica e Scienze Affini* 95 (1993): 251–59.

Cunningham, Alexander. "An Attempt to Explain Some of the Monograms Found upon the Grecian Coins of Ariana and India." *Numismatic Chronicle* 8 (1845–46): 175–97.

———. "Coins of Alexander's Successors in the East." *Numismatic Chronicle* 8 (1868): 93–136, 181–218, 257–83.

———. "Coins of Alexander's Successors in the East." *Numismatic Chronicle* 9 (1869): 28–46, 121–53, 217–46, 293–318.

———. "Coins of Alexander's Successors in the East." *Numismatic Chronicle* 10 (1870): 65–90, 205–36.

———. "Coins of Alexander's Successors in the East." *Numismatic Chronicle* 12 (1872): 157–85.

———. "Coins of Alexander's Successors in the East." *Numismatic Chronicle* 13 (1873): 187–219.

———. *Coins of Alexander's Successors in the East.* [1884.] Reprint. Chicago: Argonaut, 1969.

———. "Notes on Captain Hay's Bactrian Coins." *Journal of the Asiatic Society of Bengal* 9 (1840): 531–44.

———. "Second Notice of Some Forged Coins of the Bactrians and Indo-Scythians." *Journal of the Asiatic Society of Bengal* 9 (1840): 1217–80.

Curiel, Raoul. "Inscriptions de Surkh Kotal." *Journal Asiatique* 242 (1954): 189–97.

Curiel, Raoul, and Gérard Fussman. *Le trésor monétaire de Qunduz.* Paris: Klincksieck, 1965.

Curiel, Raoul, and Daniel Schlumberger. *Trésors monétaires d'Afghanistan.* Paris: Klincksieck, 1953.

Davesne, Alain, and Georges Le Rider. *Gülnar.* Vol. II, *Le trésor de Meydancik-kale.* Paris: Éditions Recherche sur les Civilisations, 1989.

Davis, Norman, and Colin Kraay. *The Hellenistic Kingdoms: Portrait Coins and History.* London: Thames and Hudson, 1973.

Dawson, Warren, and Eric Uphill. *Who Was Who in Egyptology.* 2nd ed. London: The Egypt Exploration Society, 1972.

Debevoise, Neilson. *A Political History of Parthia.* Chicago, 1938. [Russian ed., with bibliographical supplement by Valerii Nikonorov (St. Petersburg: Akademii Nauk, 2008).]

Deyell, John. "Indo-Greek and Ksaharata Coins from the Gujarat Seacoast." *Numismatic Chronicle* 144 (1984): 115–27.

Diamond, Jared. *Collapse: How Societies Choose to Fail or Succeed.* New York: Penguin, 2005.

Droysen, Johann Gustav. *Briefwechsel.* 2 vols. Ed. Rudolf Hübner. Stuttgart: Deutsche Verlagsanstalt, 1929.

———. *Geschichte des Hellenismus.* Vol. II, *Geschichte der Bildung des hellenistischen Staatensystemes.* Hamburg: Friedrich Perthes, 1843.

Drujinina, Angelina. "Die Ausgrabungen in Taxt-i Sangin im Oxos-Tempel-bereich." *Archäologische Mitteilungen aus Iran und Turan* 33 (2001): 257–92.

Drujinina, Angelina, and N. Boroffka. "First Preliminary Report on the Excavations in Takht-i Sangin 2004." *Bulletin of the Miho Museum* 6 (2006): 57–69.

Duff, M.E.G. *Notes from a Diary, 1851–1872.* 2 vols. London: John Murray, 1897.

Durrbach, Félix, ed. *Inscriptions de Délos.* Paris: Librairie Ancienne Honoré Champion, 1929.

Durrbach, Félix, and P. Roussel, eds. *Inscriptions de Délos.* Paris: Librairie Ancienne Honoré Champion, 1935.

Enoch, Jay. "Early Lens Use: Lenses Found in Context with Their Original Objects." *Optical History* 73.11 (1996): 707–13.

Errington, Elizabeth. "Charles Masson and Begram." *Topoi* 11 (2001): 357–409.

———. "Rediscovering the Coin Collection of General Claude-Auguste Court: A Preliminary Report." *Topoi* 5 (1995): 409–24.

———. "Rediscovering the Collections of Charles Masson." In Michael Alram and Deborah Klimburg-Salter, eds., *Coins, Art, and Chronology: Essays on the Pre-Islamic History of the Indo-Iranian Borderlands,* pp. 207–37. Vienna: Verlag der Österreichischen Akademie der Wissenschaften, 1999.

Errington, Elizabeth, and Joe Cribb, eds. *The Crossroads of Asia: Transformation in Image and Symbol in the Art of Ancient Afghanistan and Pakistan.* Cambridge: The Ancient India and Iran Trust, 1992.

Errington, Elizabeth, and Vesta S. Curtis. *From Persepolis to the Punjab: Exploring Ancient Iran, Afghanistan and Pakistan.* London: British Museum, 2007.

Faccenna, Domenico. *Butkara I (Swat, Pakistan), 1956–1962.* 5 vols. Rome: IsMEO, 1980.

Falk, Harry. "The Introduction of Stupa-Worship in Bajaur." In Osmund Bopearachchi and Marie-Françoise Boussac, eds., *Afghanistan: Ancien carrefour entre l'est et l'ouest,* pp. 347–58. Turnhout: Brepols, 2005.

Faral, Edmond. "Séance du 14 Mars." *Comptes-Rendus de l'Académie des Inscriptions et Belles-Lettres,* 1947: 241–42.

Feuardent, Gaston. "Tampering with Antiquities: A Serious Charge against the Director of the Metropolitan Museum of Art." *The Art Amateur,* Aug. 1880: 48–50.

Flannery, Kent. "Archaeological Systems Theory and Early Mesopotamia." In Betty J. Meggers, ed., *Anthropological Archaeology in the Americas,* pp. 67–87. Washington, D.C.: Anthropological Society of Washington, 1968.

Fletcher, Lionel. "The Avent Sale of Oriental Coins." [*Spink and Sons*] *Monthly Numismatic Circular* 6 (Jan. 1898): 2543–44.

Foucher, Alfred. *La vieille route de l'Inde de Bactres à Taxila.* 2 vols. Paris: de Nobele,1942–47.

Francfort, Henri-Paul. "Asie centrale." In Pierre Briant and Rémy Boucharlat, eds. *L'archéologie de l'empire achéménide: Nouvelles recherches,* pp. 313–52. Paris: Diffusion de Boccard, 2005.

———. "Deux nouveaux tétradrachmes commémoratifs d'Agathocle." *Revue Numismatique* 17 (1975): 19–22.

———. *Fouilles d'Ai Khanoum.* Vol. III, *La sanctuaire du temple à niches indentées.* Paris: Diffusion de Boccard, 1984.

———. *Fouilles de Shortughai: Recherché sur l'Asie centrale protohistorique.* Paris: Diffusion de Boccard, 1989.

Fraser, P.M. *Cities of Alexander the Great.* Oxford: Clarendon Press, 1996.

———. "The Son of Aristonax at Kandahar." *Afghan Studies* 2 (1979): 9–21.

Frigg, Roman. "Self-Organized Criticality—What It Is and What It Isn't." *Studies in History and Philosophy of Science* 34 (2003): 613–32.

Fussman, Gérard. "Documents épigraphiques kouchans." *Bulletin de l'École Française d'Extrême-Orient* 61 (1974): 1–77.

———. "L'inscription de Rabatak, la Bactriane et les Kouchans." In Pierre Leriche et al., eds., *La Bactriane au carrefour des routes et des civilizations de l'Asie centrale,* pp. 251–91. Paris: Maisonneuve and Larose, 2001.

———. "Nouvelles inscriptions Saka: Ère d'Eucratide, Ère d'Azes, Ère Vikrama, Ère de Kanishka." *Bulletin de l'École Française d'Extrême-Orient* 67 (1980): 1–43.

———. "Southern Bactria and Northern India before Islam: A Review of Archaeological Reports." *Journal of the American Oriental Society* 116.2 (1996): 243–59.

Fussman, Gérard, and Olivier Guillaume. *Surkh Kotal en Bactriane.* Vol. II, *Les monnaies et petits objets.* Paris: Diffusion de Boccard, 1990.

Gallavotti, Carlo. "The Greek Version of the Kandahar Bilingual Inscription of Ashoka." *East and West* 10 (1959): 185–92.

Galli, Marco. "Hellenistic Court Imagery in the Early Buddhist Art of Gandhara." *Ancient Civilizations from Scythia to Siberia* 17 (2011): 279–329.

Gantz, Timothy, and Frances Van Keuren. *The Richard E. Paulson Collection of Ancient Coins.* Athens, Ga.: Georgia Museum of Art, 1981.

Gardin, Jean-Claude. *Archaeological Constructs.* Cambridge: Cambridge University Press, 1980.

———. "La céramique hellénistique en Asie centrale: Problèmes d'interpretation." In *Akten des XIII. Internationalen Kongresses für klassische Archäologie, Berlin, 1988,* pp. 187–93. Mainz am Rhein: Philipp von Zabern, 1990.

Gardin, Jean-Claude , and P. Gentelle. "Irrigation et peuplement dans la plaine d'Ai Khanoum de l'époque achéménide à l'époque musulmane." *Bulletin de l'École Française d'Extrême-Orient* 63 (1976): 59–99.

Gardin, Jean-Claude, P. Gentelle, and B. Lyonnet. *Prospection archéologique en Bactriane orientale, 1974–1978.* 3 vols. Paris: Éditions Recherche sur les Civilizations, 1980–98.

Gardin, Jean-Claude, and B. Lyonnet. "La prospection archéologique de la Bactriane orientale (1974–1978): Premiers résultats." *Mesopotamia* 13–14 (1978–79): 99–154.

Gardner, Percy. *The Coins of the Greek and Scythic Kings of Bactria and India in the British Museum.* [1886.] Reprint. Chicago: Argonaut, 1966.

———. "On Some Coins of Syria and Bactria." *Numismatic Chronicle* 20 (1880): 181–91.

Geoffroy-Schneiter, Bérénice. *Gandhara: The Memory of Afghanistan.* New York: Assouline, 2001.

Gerin, Dominique. "Becker et les monnaies bactriennes du Cabinet de France, Part I." *Bulletin de la Société Française de Numismatique* 38.4 (1983): 305–9.

———. "Becker et les monnaies bactriennes du Cabinet de France, Part II." *Bulletin de la Société Française de Numismatique* 38.5 (1983): 321–22.

Ghirshman, Roman. *Bégram: Recherches archéologiques et historiques sur les Kouchans.* Cairo: Institut Français d'Archéologie Orientale, 1946.

Godbole, S.D. "Mathura Clay Sealing of Appolodutus [*sic*]." In Tony Hackens and Ghilaine Moucharte, eds., *Actes du XIe Congrès International de Numismatique, Bruxelles, 1991,* vol. I, pp. 311–12. Louvain: Association Marcel Hoc, 1993.

Gorelick, Leonard, and John Gwinnett. "Close Work without Magnifying Lenses?" *Expedition,* winter 1981: 27–34.

Gorshenina, Svetlana, and Claude Rapin. *De Kaboul à Samarcande: Les archéologues en Asie centrale.* Paris: Gallimard, 2001.

Gosden, Chris. *Archaeology and Colonialism: Cultural Contact from 5000 BC to the Present.* Cambridge: Cambridge University Press, 2004.

Gosselin, François-Paschal, and Charles-Philippe Campion. *Catalogue des médailles antiques et modernes, du Cabinet de M. D'Ennery.* Paris: de Monsieur, 1788.

Goukowsky, Paul. *Essai sur les origines du mythe d'Alexandre (336–270 av. J.-C.).* Vol. I, *Les origines politiques.* Nancy: Bialec, 1978.

Graf, David. "Aramaic on the Periphery of the Achaemenid Realm." *Archäologische Mitteilungen aus Iran und Turan* 32 (2000): 75–92.

Green, Peter. *Alexander to Actium: The Historical Evolution of the Hellenistic Age.* Berkeley and Los Angeles: University of California Press, 1990.

Grenet, Frantz. "ΑΓΑΓΓΩΡΝΟΙΣ, ΑΣΚΙΣΑΓΓΟΡΑΓΟ, SANGCHARAK." *Topoi* 6 (1996): 470–73.

————. "Mithra au temple principal d'Ai Khanoum?" In Paul Bernard and Frantz Grenet, eds., *Histoire et cultes de l'Asie centrale préislamique: Sources écrites et documents archéologiques,* pp. 147–53. Paris: CNRS, 1991.

————. "L'onomastique iranienne à Ai Khanoum." *Bulletin de Correspondance Hellénique* 107 (1983): 373–81.

Grenet, Frantz, Jean-Claude Liger, and Régis de Valence. "L'arsenal." *Bulletin de l'École Française d'Extrême-Orient* 68 (1980): 51–63.

Grierson, Philip. *Numismatics.* Oxford: Oxford University Press, 1975.

Grissmann, Carla. "The Inventory of the Kabul Museum: Attempts at Restoring Order." *Museum International* 55.3–4 (2003): 71–76.

Grissmann, Carla, and Fredrik Hiebert. "Saving Afghanistan's Heritage." In Fredrik Hiebert and Pierre Cambon, eds., *Afghanistan: Hidden Treasures from the National Museum, Kabul,* pp. 45–53. Washington, D.C.: National Geographic Society, 2008.

Gross, Michael. *Rogues' Gallery: The Secret History of the Moguls and the Money That Made the Metropolitan Museum.* New York: Broadway, 2009.

Guillaume, Olivier. *L'analyse de raisonnements en archéologie: Le cas de la numismatique gréco-bactrienne et indo-grecque.* Paris: Éditions Recherche sur les Civilisations, 1987.

————. *Analysis of Reasonings in Archaeology: The Case of Graeco-Bactrian and Indo-Greek Numismatics.* Trans. Osmund Bopearachchi. Oxford: Oxford University Press, 1990.

————. *Fouilles d'Ai Khanoum.* Vol. II, *Les propylées de la rue principale.* Paris: Diffusion de Boccard, 1983.

————. "How Can the Computer Help the Numismatist and the Historian of the Indo-Greek Period?" *Journal of the Numismatic Society of India* 47 (1985): 152–60.

————. "Naïve Anthropology in the Reconstruction of Indo-Greek History." *The Indian Economic and Social History Review* 27.4 (1990): 475–82.

————, ed. *Graeco-Bactrian and Indian Coins from Afghanistan.* Trans. Osmund Bopearachchi. Oxford: Oxford University Press, 1991.

Guillaume, Olivier, and Axelle Rougeulle. *Fouilles d'Ai Khanoum.* Vol. VII, *Les petits objets.* Paris: Diffusion de Boccard, 1987.

Gupta, Parmeshwari Lal. "Three Commemorative Tetradrachms of Agathocles." *Journal of the Numismatic Society of India* 38.2 (1976): 92–94.

Gurt, Josep, et al. *Preliminary Report of the First Season Work of the International Pluridisciplinary Archaeological Expedition in Bactria.* Barcelona: ERAUB, 2008.

Hackin, Joseph. *Nouvelles recherches archéologiques à Bégram (1939–1940).* 2 vols. Paris: Presses Universitaires de France, 1954.

————. *Recherches archéologiques à Bégram: Chantier no. 2 (1937).* 2 vols. Paris: de Nobele, 1939.

————. "Répartition des monnaies anciennes en Afghanistan." *Journal Asiatique* 226 (1935): 287–92.

Hagerman, Christopher. "In the Footsteps of the 'Macedonian Conqueror': Alexander the Great and British India." *International Journal of the Classical Tradition* 16 (2009): 344–92.

Hanfmann, George. "Personality and Portraiture in Ancient Art." *Proceedings of the American Philosophical Society* 117.4 (1973): 259–85.

Hawkes, Jaquetta. *Mortimer Wheeler: Adventurer in Archaeology.* London: Weidenfeld and Nicolson, 1982.

Hazlitt, William. *The Coin Collector.* New York: Longmans, Green and Co., 1896.

Hebert, Raymond. *Aditi: The Monies of India.* Washington, D.C.: Smithsonian Institution, 1985.

Helms, Svend. *Excavations at Old Kandahar in Afghanistan, 1976–1978*. Oxford: Archaeopress, 1997.

Hiebert, Fredrik, and Pierre Cambon, eds. *Afghanistan: Hidden Treasures from the National Museum, Kabul*. Washington, D.C.: National Geographic Society, 2008.

Hinckley, Henry. "The Grete Emetreus the King of Inde." *Modern Language Notes* 48 (1933): 148–49.

Hoernle, Rudolf. "Gold Coins from Jalalabad." *Proceedings of the Asiatic Society of Bengal* 48 (1879): 122–38.

———. "Monograms of the Baktro-Greek King Euthydemos." *The Indian Antiquary* 8 (1879): 196–98.

Hollis, Adrian. "Greek Letters from Hellenistic Bactria." In Dirk Obbink and Richard Rutherford, eds., *Culture in Pieces: Essays on Ancient Texts in Honour of Peter Parsons*, pp. 104–18. Oxford: Oxford University Press, 2011.

Holt, Frank. *Alexander the Great and Bactria: The Formation of a Greek Frontier in Central Asia*. Leiden: Brill, 1988.

———. *Alexander the Great and the Mystery of the Elephant Medallions*. Berkeley and Los Angeles: University of California Press, 2003.

———. "Alexander the Great and the Spoils of War." *Ancient Macedonia* 6.1 (1999): 499–506.

———. "The Autobiography of a Coin." *Aramco World* 48.5 (1997): 10–15.

———. "Bayer's Coin of Eucratides: A Miscalculation Corrected." *Zeitschrift für Papyrologie und Epigraphik* 174 (2010): 289–90.

———. "Did King Euthydemus II Really Exist?" *Numismatic Chronicle* 160 (2000): 81–91.

———. "Discovering the Lost History of Ancient Afghanistan: Hellenistic Bactria in Light of Recent Archaeological and Historical Research." *Ancient World* 9 (1984): 3–28.

———. "Eukratides of Baktria." *Ancient World* 27.1 (1996): 72–76.

———. "The Euthydemid Coinage of Bactria: Further Hoard Evidence from Ai Khanoum." *Revue Numismatique* 23 (1981): 7–44.

———. "Hellenistic Bactria: Beyond the Mirage." *Ancient World* 14 (1986): 3–15.

———. *Into the Land of Bones: Alexander the Great in Afghanistan*. Berkeley and Los Angeles: University of California Press, 2005.

———. "Mimesis in Metal: The Fate of Greek Culture on Bactrian Coins."

In Frances Titchener and Richard Moorton, eds. *The Eye Expanded: Life and the Arts in Greco-Roman Antiquity*, pp. 93–104. Berkeley and Los Angeles: University of California Press, 1999.

———. "The Problem of Poseidon in Bactria." In E.A. Antonova et al., eds., *Central Asia: Sources, History, Culture*, pp. 721–26. Moscow: Russian Academy of Sciences, 2005.

———. "The So-Called 'Pedigree Coins' of the Bactrian Greeks." In Waldemar Heckel and Richard Sullivan, eds., *Ancient Coins of the Graeco-Roman World: The Nickle Numismatic Papers*, pp. 69–91. Waterloo, Ont.: Wilfrid Laurier University Press, 1984.

———. *Thundering Zeus: The Making of Hellenistic Bactria*. Berkeley and Los Angeles: University of California Press, 1999.

———. "The Tragedies and Treasures of Afghanistan." *American Scientist* 97.3 (2009): 248–49.

———, ed. *The Greeks in Bactria and India*, by W.W. Tarn. 3rd ed. Chicago: Ares Press, 1984.

Holt, Frank, and Osmund Bopearachchi, eds. *The Alexander Medallion: Exploring the Origins of a Unique Artefact*. Lacapelle-Mirival: Imago Lattara, 2011.

Honigberger, Martin. *Thirty-Five Years in the East*. London: H. Ballière, 1852.

Hook, Duncan. "The Application of Science to Coins and Coin Hoards at the British Museum." In Barrie Cook, ed., *The British Museum and the Future of UK Numismatics*, pp. 28–33. London: British Museum Press, 2011.

Hoover, Oliver. "The History of the ANS: The Third Decade." *American Numismatic Society Magazine* 1.3(2002): 40–43

Hopkirk, Peter. *The Great Game: The Struggle for Empire in Central Asia*. New York: Kodansha, 1992.

Horner, I.B., trans. *Milinda's Questions*. Bristol: Pali Text Society, 1963–64.

Humbach, Helmut. "Eine griechische Inschrift aus Pakistan." *Gutenberg Jahrbuch*, 1976: 15–17.

Huntington, Archer. "President Huntington's Annual Address." *Proceedings of the American Numismatic and Archaeological Society*, 1907: 24–27.

Jakobsson, Jens. "Antiochus Nicator." *Numismatic Chronicle* 170 (2010): 17–33.

———. "The Greeks of Afghanistan Revisited." *Nomismatika Khronika* 26 (2007): 51–70.

————. "Who Founded the Indo-Greek Era of 186/5 B.C.E.?" *Classical Quarterly* 59.2 (2009): 505–10.

Jaquet, Eugène. "Notice sur les découvertes archéologiques faites par M. Honigberger dans Afghanistan." *Journal Asiatique* 2 (1836): 234–304.

Jenkins, Gilbert K. *Ancient Greek Coins.* London: Seaby, 1990.

Jentoft-Nilsen, Marit, ed. *Ancient Portraiture: The Sculptor's Art in Coins and Marble.* Richmond, Va.: Virginia Museum, 1980.

Johnson, Matthew. *Archaeological Theory: An Introduction.* Malden, Mass.: Blackwell, 1999.

Jones, Robert. "Centaurs on the Silk Road: Recent Discoveries of Hellenistic Textiles in Western China." *The Silk Road* 6.2 (2009): 23–32.

Kalita, Stanislav. *Grecy w Baktrii i w Indiach: Wybrane problem ich historii.* Kraków: Historia Iagellonica, 2005.

————. "Oblezenie, którego nie bylo? Uwagi na marginesie historii wojny Antiocha III z Eutydemosem królem Baktrii." In Marciej Salamon and Zdzisław Kapera, eds., *Studia Classica et Byzantina Alexandro Krawczuk Oblata,* pp. 47–55. Kraków: Jagiellonian University Press, 1996.

————. "Portraits of Rulers on Greco-Bactrian and Indo-Greek Coins: An Attempt at Classification." *Notae Numismaticae* 2 (1997): 7–26.

Karttunen, Klaus. *India and the Hellenistic World.* Helsinki: Finnish Oriental Society, 1997.

————. "King Eucratides in Literary Sources." *Silk Road Art and Archaeology* 6 (1999–2000): 115–18.

Kejariwal, O.P. *The Asiatic Society of Bengal and the Discovery of India's Past, 1784–1838.* Delhi: Oxford University Press, 1988.

Kemmers, Fleur, and Nanouschka Myrberg. "Rethinking Numismatics: The Archaeology of Coins." *Archaeological Dialogues* 18 (2011): 87–108.

Khan, M.A.R. "The Probably Meteoritic Origin of Certain Specimens of Nickel Coins Struck in Bactria before 200 B.C." *Meteoritics and Planetary Science* 1 (1953): 60.

Khan, Nazir. "A New Relief from Gandhara Depicting the Trojan Horse." *East and West* 40 (1990): 315–19.

de Khanikoff, Nikolai. *Bokhara: Its Amir and Its People.* London: James Madden, 1845.

Klijn, Albertus F.J. *The Acts of Thomas: Introduction, Text, and Commentary.* Leiden: Brill, 2003.

Köhler, H.K.E. "Description d'un médaillon rapporté de Boukharie par M. le Colonel Baron Georges de Meyendorff." In E.K. Meyendorff, *Voyage d'Orenbourg à Boukhara, fait en 1820,* pp. 321–28. Paris: Librairie Orientale de Dondey-Dupré, 1826.

———. *Serapis.* St. Petersburg: Imperial Academy of Sciences, 1850.

Kordosis, Michael. "Οι έλληνες βασιλείς της Βακτρίας και Ινδίας ως το θάνατο του Μενάνδρου." *Δωδώνη* 20.1 (1991): 217–24.

Koshelenko, G.A. "The Fortifications at Gobekly-depe." In J. Cribb and G. Herrmann, eds., *After Alexander: Central Asia before Islam,* pp. 269–83. Oxford: Oxford University Press, 2007.

———. *Grecheskij polis na ellinisticheskon Vostoke.* Moscow: Nauka, 1979.

Kraay, Colin. "Demetrius in Bactria and India." *Numismatic Digest* 9 (1985): 12–30.

Kritt, Brian. *Dynastic Transitions in the Coinage of Bactria: Antiochus–Diodotus–Euthydemus.* Lancaster, Pa.: Classical Numismatic Group, 2001.

Kruglikova, Irina. *Delbarjin, Temple of the Dioscuri.* Moscow: Nauka, 1986. [In Russian.]

———. "Les fouilles de la mission archéologique soviet-afghane sur le site gréco-kushan de Dilberdjin en Bactriane (Afghanistan)." *Comptes-Rendus de l'Académie des Inscriptions et Belles-Lettres,* 1977: 407–27.

Kruglikova, Irina, and Shahibye Mustamandi. "Résultats préliminaries des travaux de l'expédition archéologique afghano-soviétique en 1969." *Afghanistan* 23 (1970): 84–97.

Kurbanov, G., and M. Niyazova. *Katalog greko-baktriskikh monet iz fondov Bukharskogo muzeia.* Bukhara: Bukhara Museum, 1989.

Kvist, Kjetil. "Tetradrachms of Antimachos Exhibit the High Quality of Greek Art." *The Celator* 11 (Mar. 1997): 18–20.

Lahiri, A.N. *Corpus of Indo-Greek Coins.* Calcutta: Poddar Publications, 1965.

Lal, Mohan. *Travels in the Panjab, Afghanistan, and Turkestan to Balkh, Bokhara, and Herat.* London: William Allen, 1846.

Lassen, Christian. *Points in the History of the Greek and Indo-Scythian Kings in Bactria, Cabul, and India, as Illustrated by Deciphering the Ancient Legends on Their Coins.* Trans. H. Roeer. [1840.] Reprint. Delhi: Indological Book House, 1972.

Lawler, Andrew. "Edge of an Empire." *Archaeology* 64.5 (2011): 42–47.

Leriche, Pierre. "Bactria, Land of a Thousand Cities." In Joe Cribb and Georgina Herrmann, eds., *After Alexander: Central Asia before Islam*, pp. 121–53. Oxford: Oxford University Press, 2007.

———. *Fouilles d'Ai Khanoum*. Vol. V, *Les remparts et les monuments associés*. Paris: Diffusion de Boccard, 1986.

Leriche, Pierre, and Chakirjan Pidaev. *Termez sur Oxus: Cité-capitale d'Asie centrale*. Paris: Maisonneuve and Larose, 2008.

Leriche, Pierre, and Joël Thoraval. "La fontaine du rempart de l'Oxus à Ai Khanoum." *Syria* 56 (1979): 171–205.

Le Rider, Georges. "Monnaies grecques récemment acquises par le Cabinet de Paris." *Revue Numismatique* 6 (1969): 7–27.

Lerner, Jeffrey. "The Ai Khanoum Philosophical Papyrus." *Zeitschrift für Papyrologie und Epigraphik* 142 (2003): 45–51.

———. "Correcting the Early History of Ay Kanom." *Archäologische Mitteilungen aus Iran und Turan* 35–36 (2003–4): 373–410.

———. "A Reappraisal of the Economic Inscriptions and Coin Finds from Ai Khanoum," *Anabasis* 2 (2011): 103–47.

———. "Revising the Chronologies of the Hellenistic Colonies of Samarkand-Marakanda (Afrasiab II–III) and Ai Khanoum (Northeastern Afghanistan)." *Anabasis* 1 (2010): 58–79.

Leschhorn, Wolfgang. *Gründer der Stadt: Studien zu einen politisch-religiösen Phänomen der griechischen Geschichte*. Stuttgart: Franz Steiner Verlag, 1984.

de Linas, Charles. *Les origines de l'orfèvrerie cloisonné*. Paris: Édouard Didron, 1878.

"Literary and Miscellaneous Intelligence." *Journal of the Asiatic Society of Bengal* 36 (1867): 143.

Litvinsky, Boris. "Archaeological Work in Tajikistan in 1962–1970." *Archeologiceskie Raboty v Tadzikistane* 10 (1973): 5–41. [In Russian.]

———. "Archaeology in Tadzikistan under Soviet Rule." *East and West* 18 (1968): 125–46.

Litvinsky, Boris, and Igor Pichikyan. *Ellinisticheskiy khram Oksa v Baktrii (Iuzhnyi Tadzikistan)*. 3 vols. Moscow: Vostoknaya Literatura, 2000–2010.

Litvinsky, Boris, Igor Pichikyan, and Y.G. Vinogradov. "The Votive Offering of Atrosokes, from the Temple of the Oxus in Northern Bactria." *Vestnik Drevnej Istorii* (1985): 84–110. [In Russian with English summary.]

Liu, Xinru. "Hellenistic Residue in Central Asia under Islamic Regimes." *Journal of Interdisciplinary Studies in History and Archaeology* 1.2 (2004): 79–86.

———. "Migration and Settlement of the Yuezhi-Kushan: Interaction and Interdependence of Nomadic and Sedentary Societies." *Journal of World History* 12.2 (2001): 261–92.

Lo Muzio, Ciro. "The Dioscuri at Dilberjin (Northern Afghanistan): Reviewing Their Chronology and Significance." *Studia Iranica* 28 (1999): 41–71.

de Longpérier, Adrian. "Collection numismatique du Général Court." *Revue Numismatique,* 1839: 81–88.

Lord, P.B. "Some Account of a Visit to the Plain of Koh-i-Damin, the Mining District of Ghorband, and the Pass of Hindu Kush." *Journal of the Asiatic Society of Bengal* 7.1 (1838): 521–37.

Louis, A.H. "Concerning Language and Gold." *Old and New* 7 (Apr. 1873): 407–15.

Lunbaek, Knud. *T.S. Bayer (1694–1738): Pioneer Sinologist.* London: Curzon Press, 1986.

Lunt, James. *Bokhara Burnes.* London: Faber and Faber, 1969.

Lyonnet, Bertille. "Contributions récentes de la céramologie à l'histoire de l'Afghanistan." *Arts Asiatiques* 40 (1985): 41–52.

———. "Les Grecs, les nomades et l'indépendance de la Sogdiane, d'après l'occupation comparée d'Ai Khanoum et de Marakanda au cours des derniers siècles avant notre ère." *Bulletin of the Asia Institute* 12 (1998): 141–59.

———. "Les nomades et la chute du royaume gréco-bactrien: Quelques nouveaux indices en provenance de l'Asie centrale—Vers l'identification des Tokhares–Yueh-Chi?" In Paul Bernard and Frantz Grenet, eds., *Histoire et cultes de l'Asie centrale préislamique: Sources écrites et documents archéologiques,* pp. 153–64. Paris: CNRS, 1991.

———. "The Problem of the Frontiers between Bactria and Sogdiana: An Old Discussion and New Data." In A. Gail and G. Mevissen, eds., *South Asian Archaeology 1991,* pp. 195–208. Stuttgart: Franz Steiner Verlag, 1993.

MacDowall, D.W., and M. Taddei. "The Early Historic Period: Achaemenids and Greeks." In F. Raymond Allchin and Norman Hammond, eds., *The*

Archaeology of Afghanistan from Earliest Times to the Timurid Period, pp. 187–232. London: Academic Press, 1978.

MacDowall, D.W., and N.G. Wilson. "Apollodoti Reges Indorum." *Numismatic Chronicle* (1960): 221–28.

Macintyre, Ben. *The Man Who Would Be King: The First American in Afghanistan*. New York: Farrar, Straus and Giroux, 2004.

Macrory, Patrick, ed. *Lady Sale: The First Afghan War*. Hamden, Conn.: Archon Books, 1969.

Mairs, Rachel. *The Archaeology of the Hellenistic Far East: A Survey*. Oxford: BAR, 2011.

———. "Ethnicity and Funarary [*sic*] Practice in Hellenistic Bactria." In Hannes Schroeder, P. Gardner, and Peter Bray, eds., *Crossing Frontiers*, pp. 111–24. Oxford: Oxford University Press, 2007.

———. "Greek Identity and the Settler Community in Hellenistic Bactria and Arachosia." *Migrations and Identities* 1.1 (2008): 19–43.

———. "Hellenistic India." *New Voices in Classical Reception Studies* 1 (2006): 19–30.

———. "The 'Temple with Indented Niches' at Ai Khanoum: Ethnic and Civic Identity in Hellenistic Bactria." In Richard Alston and Onno van Nijf, eds., *Cults, Creeds and Contests in the Post-Classical City*. Louvain: Peeters, forthcoming.

Marangou, Anna. *Life and Deeds: The Consul Luigi Palma di Cesnola, 1832–1904*. Nicosia: The Cultural Centre of the Popular Bank Group, 2000.

Marshall, John. *Taxila*. 3 vols. Cambridge: Cambridge University Press, 1951.

Masson, Charles. "Memoir on the Ancient Coins Found at Beghram, in the Kohistan of Kabul." *Journal of the Asiatic Society of Bengal* 3 (1834): 153–75.

———. "Second Memoir on the Ancient Coins Found at Beghram, in the Kohistan of Kabul." *Journal of the Asiatic Society of Bengal* 5 (1836): 1–28.

———. "Third Memoir on the Ancient Coins Discovered at the Site Called Beghram, in the Kohistan of Kabul." *Journal of the Asiatic Society of Bengal* 5 (1836): 537–47.

Massoudi, Omara. "The National Museum of Afghanistan." In Fredrik Hiebert and Pierre Cambon, eds., *Afghanistan: Hidden Treasures from the National Museum, Kabul*, pp. 35–41. Washington, D.C.: National Geographic Society, 2008.

McKay, Alexander. "Archaeology and the Creative Imagination." In A. McKay, ed., *New Perspectives in Canadian Archaeology*, pp. 227–34. Ottawa: Royal Society of Canada, 1977.

McKeown, J.C. *A Cabinet of Roman Curiosities.* Oxford: Oxford University Press, 2010.

McNicoll, Anthony, and Warwick Ball. *Excavations at Kandahar, 1974 and 1975.* Oxford: Archaeopress, 1996.

Mehendale, Sanjyot. "The Begram Ivory and Bone Carvings: Some Observations on Provenance and Chronology." *Topoi* 11 (2001): 485–514.

Melville Jones, J.R. *Testimonia Numaria: Greek and Latin Texts Concerning Ancient Greek Coinage.* Vol. I, *Texts and Translations.* London: Spink, 1993.

Merkelbach, Reinhold, and Josef Stauber, eds. *Jenseits des Euphrat: Griechische Inschriften.* Munich: K.G. Saur, 2005.

Meyer, Karl, and Shareen Brysac. *Tournament of Shadows: The Great Game and the Race for Empire in Central Asia.* Washington, D.C.: Counterpoint, 1999.

Mielczarek, Mariusz. *Ancient Greek Coins Found in Central, Eastern and Northern Europe.* Warsaw: Polish Academy of Sciences, 1989.

———. "Two Bronze Imitations of Heliocles' Coins in the Numismatic Collection of the Archaeological and Ethnographical Museum in Lodz." *Prace i Materialy Muzeum Archeologicznego i Etnograficznego w Lodzi* 7 (1987): 5–9. [In Polish with English summary.]

———. "Two Imitations of Eucratides' Obols from the Museum Collection in Lodz." *Wiadomosci Numizmatyczne* 31 (1987): 48–51. [In English with Polish summary.]

Miller, M.C.J. "Antimachus (II) Nikephoros: A New Alexander?" *Ancient World* 39.1 (2008): 55–62.

Minorsky, Vladimir. "A Greek Crossing on the Oxus." *Bulletin of the School of Oriental and African Studies* 30.1 (1967): 45–53.

Mionnet, Théodore Edme. *Catalogue d'une collection d'empreintes en soufre de médailles grecques et romaines.* Paris: L'Imprimerie de Crapelet, 1799.

Mirsky, Jeannette. *Sir Aurel Stein: Archaeological Explorer.* Chicago: University of Chicago Press, 1977.

Mitchiner, Michael. *Indo-Greek and Indo-Scythian Coinage.* 9 vols. London: Hawkins, 1975.

Mittag, Peter. "Bactria and Parthia." In Michel Amandry and Donal Bateson, eds., *A Survey of Numismatic Research, 2002–2007,* pp. 111–16. Glasgow: International Numismatic Commission, 2009.

―――. "Methodologische Überlegungen zur Geschichte Baktriens: Könige und Münzen." *Schweizerische Numismatische Rundschau* 85 (2006): 27–46.

Montagu, Hyman. "On Some Unpublished and Rare Greek Coins in My Collection." *Numismatic Chronicle* 12 (1892): 22–39.

Mørkholm, Otto. *Early Hellenistic Coinage from the Accession of Alexander to the Peace of Apamea (336–188 b.c.).* Ed. Philip Grierson and Ulla Westermark. Cambridge: Cambridge University Press, 1991.

Najimi, Abdul Wasay. "Built Heritage in Afghanistan: Threats, Challenges and Conservation." *International Journal of Environmental Studies* 68(2011): 343–61.

Narain, A.K. "Approaches and Perspectives." *Yavanika* 2 (1992): 5–34.

―――. *The Indo-Greeks, Revisited and Supplemented.* Delhi: B.R. Publishing, 2003.

―――. "Notes on Some Inscriptions from Ai Khanoum (Afghanistan)." *Zeitschrift für Papyrologie und Epigraphik* 69 (1987): 272–82.

Narain, Sudha. "The Twenty-Stater Gold Piece of Eucratides I." *Journal of the Numismatic Society of India* 18 (1956): 217–18.

Newell, Edward T. *The Coinage of the Eastern Seleucid Mints from Seleucus I to Antiochus III.* [1938.] Reprint. New York: American Numismatic Society, 1978.

―――. *Royal Greek Portrait Coins.* Racine, Wisc.: Whitman Publishing, 1937.

Nicolet-Pierre, Hélène. *Numismatique grecque.* Paris: Armand Colin, 2005.

Nikonorov, Valerii. "Apollodorus of Artemita and the Date of His *Parthica* Revisited." *Electrum* 2 (1998): 107–22.

Nikonorov, Valerii, and Serge Savchuk. "New Data on Ancient Bactrian Body-Armour (in the Light of Finds from Kampyr Tepe)." *Iran* 30 (1992): 49–54.

Norman, K.R. "Notes on the Greek Version of Ashoka's Twelfth and Thirteenth Rock Edicts." *Journal of the Royal Asiatic Society of Great Britain and Ireland* 2 (1972): 111–18

O'Brien, Michael, Lee Lyman, and Michael Schiffer. *Archaeology as a Process: Processualism and Its Progeny.* Salt Lake City: University of Utah Press, 2005.

Oikonomides, Alcibiades N. "The Gold Coinage of the Indo-Greek King

Eucratides I (171–155 B.C.)." *North American Journal of Numismatics* 7.6 (1968): 180–83.

Olivier-Utard, Françoise. *Politique et archéologie: Histoire de la Délégation Archéologique Française en Afghanistan (1922–1982).* Paris: Éditions Recherche sur les Civilisations, 1997.

Omrani, Bijan. "Charles Masson of Afghanistan: Deserter, Scholar, Spy." *Asian Affairs* 39.2 (2008): 199–216.

Paranavitana, Senarat. *The Greeks and the Mauryas.* Colombo: Lake House Investments, 1971.

Parker, Grant. "Hellenism in an Afghan Context." In Himanshu Ray and Daniel Potts, eds., *Memory as History: The Legacy of Alexander in Asia,* pp. 170–91. New Delhi: Aryan Books, 2007.

Pellerin, Joseph. *Additions aux neuf volumes de Recueiles de médailles de rois.* Paris: Desaint, 1778.

———. *Recueil de médailles de rois.* Paris: Guerin and Delatour, 1762.

Petitot-Biehler, Claire-Yvonne. "Trésor de monnaies grecques et gréco-bactriennes trouvé à Ai Khanoum (Afghanistan)." *Revue Numismatique* 17 (1975): 23–57.

Petrie, William Matthew Flinders. *Seventy Years in Archaeology.* [1932.] Reprint. New York: Greenwood Press, 1969.

Pfrommer, Michael. *Metalwork from the Hellenized East: Catalogue of the Collections.* Malibu: Getty Museum, 1993.

Plantzos, Dimitris. "Crystals and Lenses in the Graeco-Roman World." *American Journal of Archaeology* 101 (1997): 451–64.

Posch, Walter. *Baktrien zwischen Griechen und Kuschan.* Wiesbaden: Harrassowitz, 1995.

Pringle, Heather. *The Master Plan: Himmler's Scholars and the Holocaust.* New York: Hyperion, 2006.

Prinsep, James. "Additions to Bactrian Numismatics, and the Discovery of the Bactrian Alphabet." *Journal of the Asiatic Society of Bengal* 7 (1838): 636–58.

———. "Bactrian and Indo-Scythic Coins." *Journal of the Asiatic Society of Bengal* 2 (1833): 406.

———. "Continuation of the Route of Lieutenant A. Burnes and Dr. Gerard, from Peshawar to Bokhara." *Journal of the Asiatic Society of Bengal* 2 (1833): 1–22.

————. "Further Notes and Drawings of Bactrian and Indo-Scythic Coins." *Journal of the Asiatic Society of Bengal* 4 (1835): 327–48.

————. "New Types of Bactrian and Indo-Scythic Coins." *Journal of the Asiatic Society of Bengal* 5 (1836): 720–24.

————. "Notes on Lieutenant Burnes' Collection of Ancient Coins." *Journal of the Asiatic Society of Bengal* 2 (1833): 310–18.

Pugliesi-Carratelli, Giovanni. "Greek Inscriptions of the Middle East." *East and West* 16 (1966): 31–36.

Pyatt, F.B., and J.P. Grattan. "Some Consequences of Ancient Mining Activities on the Health of Ancient and Modern Human Populations." *Journal of Public Health Medicine* 23.3 (2001): 235–36.

Rabel, Robert. "The Imitation of Alexander the Great in Afghanistan." *Helios* 34 (2007): 97–119.

Rapin, Claude. *Fouilles d'Ai Khanoum*. Vol. VIII, *La trésorerie du palais hellénistique d'Ai Khanoum*. Paris: Diffusion de Boccard, 1992.

————. "Greeks in Afghanistan: Ai Khanoum." In Jean-Paul Descoedres, ed., *Greek Colonists and Native Populations*, pp. 329–42. Canberra: Humanities Research Centre, 1990.

————. *Indian Art from Afghanistan: The Legend of Sakuntala and the Indian Treasure of Eucratides at Ai Khanoum*. New Delhi: Manohar Publishers, 1996.

————. "Les inscriptions économiques de la trésorerie hellénistique d'Ai Khanoum (Afghanistan)." *Bulletin de Correspondance Hellénique* 107 (1983): 315–81.

————. "Le nom antique d'Ai Khanoum et de son fleuve." In Osmund Bopearachchi et al., eds., *De l'Indus à l'Oxus: Archéologie de l'Asie centrale*, p. 115. Lattes: Imago, 2003.

————. "Nomads and the Shaping of Central Asia: From the Early Iron Age to the Kushan Period." In Joe Cribb and Georgina Herrmann, eds., *After Alexander: Central Asia before Islam*, pp. 29–72. Oxford: Oxford University Press, 2007.

————. "Nouvelles observations sur le parchemin gréco-bactrien d'Asangôrna." *Topoi* 6 (1996): 458–69.

————. "Les texts littéraires grecs de la trésorerie d'Ai Khanoum." *Bulletin de Correspondance Hellénique* 111 (1987): 225–66.

————. "La trésorerie hellénistique d'Ai Khanoum." *Revue Archéologique* (1987): 41–70.

Rapson, Edward James. "Ancient Silver Coins from Baluchistan." *Numismatic Chronicle* 4 (1904): 311–25.

———, ed. *The Cambridge History of India.* Vol. I. [1922.] Reprint. Delhi: S. Chand, 1962.

Rawlinson, Hugh George. *Bactria: The History of a Forgotten Empire.* [1912.] Reprint. New York: AMS Press, 1969.

Ray, Himanshu. "The Yavana Presence in Ancient India." *Journal of the Economic and Social History of the Orient* 31 (1988): 311–25.

Rea, John, Robert C. Senior, and Adrian S. Hollis. "A Tax Receipt from Hellenistic Bactria." *Zeitschrift für Papyrologie und Epigraphik* 104 (1994): 261–80.

Reiff, F., et al. "Investigation of Contemporary Gilded Forgeries of Ancient Coins." *Fresenius' Journal of Analytical Chemistry* 171.8 (2001): 1146–53.

Renfrew, Colin, and Paul Bahn. *Archaeology: Theories, Methods and Practice.* 3rd ed. New York: Thames and Hudson, 2000.

Renfrew, Colin, and Ezra Zubrow, eds. *The Ancient Mind: Elements of Cognitive Archaeology.* Cambridge: Cambridge University Press, 1994.

Richter, Gisela. *The Portraits of the Greeks.* 3 vols. London: Phaidon Press, 1965.

Robert, Louis. "De Delphes à l'Oxus." *Comptes-Rendus de l'Académie des Inscriptions et Belles-Lettres,* 1968: 416–57.

Robinson, Charles Alexander, Jr. "The Greeks in the Far East." *Classical Journal* 44.7 (1949): 405–12.

Rochette, Raoul. "Deuxième supplément à la Notice sur quelques médailles grecques inédites de rois de la Bactriane et de l'Inde." *Journal des Savants,* 1836: 65.

———. *Notice sur quelques médailles grecques inédites, appartenant à des rois inconnus de la Bactriane et de l'Inde.* Paris: L'Imprimerie Royale, 1834.

———. "Supplément à la Notice sur quelques médailles grecques inédites de rois de la Bactriane et de l'Inde." *Journal des Savants,* 1835: 513–28.

———. "Troisième supplement à la Notice sur quelques médailles grecques inédites de rois de la Bactriane et de l'Inde." *Journal des Savants,* 1844: 108–19

Romane, Julian. "W. W. Tarn on the Art of History." *Ancient World* 15 (1987): 21–24.

Rosman, Kevin, et al. "Lead from Carthaginian and Roman Spanish Mines

Isotopically Identified in Greenland Ice Dated from 600 B.C. to 300 A.D."
Environmental Science and Technology 31.12 (1997): 3413–16.

Rtveladze, Edvard. "La circulation monétaire au nord de l'Oxus à l'époque gréco-bactrienne." *Revue Numismatique* 26 (1984): 61–76.

———. "Découvertes en numismatique et épigraphie gréco-bactriennes à Kampyr-Tepe (Bactriane du nord)." *Revue Numismatique* 6 (1995): 20–24.

———. *Drevnie Monety Srednej Azii.* Tashkent: Gulyama, 1987.

———. *Kampyr Tepe.* 4 vols. Tashkent: San'at, 2000–2006.

———. "Kampyr Tepe–Pandokheïon: Les Grecs ont traversé l'Oxus." *Dossiers d'Archéologie* 247 (1999): 56–57.

———. *Makedoniyalik Aleksandr i Baqtria va So'g'diyonada.* Tashkent: Academy of Fine Arts of the Republic of Uzbekistan, 2002.

Rubinson, Karen. "Tillya Tepe: Aspects of Gender and Cultural Identity." In K.M. Linduff and K.S. Rubinson, eds., *Are All Warriors Male? Gender Roles on the Ancient Eurasian Steppe,* pp. 51–64. Plymouth: AltaMira Press, 2008.

Salomon, Richard. *Indian Epigraphy.* Oxford: Oxford University Press, 1998.

Sarianidi, Victor. *The Golden Hoard of Bactria.* New York: Abrams, 1985.

———. *The Temple and Tombs at Tillya Tepe.* Moscow: Nauka, 1989. [In Russian.]

Sarmant, Thierry. *Le Cabinet des Médailles de la Bibliothèque Nationale, 1661–1848.* Paris: École des Chartes, 1994.

Sauer, Eberhard, ed. *Archaeology and Ancient History.* London: Routledge, 2004.

Schlumberger, Daniel. "Descendants non-méditerranéens de l'art grec." *Syria* 37 (1960): 131–66, 253–318.

———. "La prospection archéologique de Bactres (printemps 1947)." *Syria* 26 (1949): 173–90.

———. "Rapport sur une mission en Afghanistan." *Comptes-Rendus de l'Académie des Inscriptions et Belles-Lettres,* 1946: 169–77.

Schlumberger, Daniel, Marc LeBerre, and Gérard Fussman. *Surkh Kotal en Bactriane.* Vol. I, *Les temples.* Paris: Diffusion de Boccard, 1983.

Schmitt, Rüdiger. "Der Name Hyspasines (samt Varianten)." *Bulletin of the Asia Institute* 4 (1990): 245–49.

Schuol, Monika. *Die Charakene: Ein mesopotamisches Königreich in hellenistisch-parthischer Zeit.* Stuttgart: Franz Steiner Verlag, 2000.

Schuyler, Eugene. *Turkistan: Notes of a Journey in Russian Turkistan, Khokand, Bukhara, and Kuldja.* New York: Scribner, Armstrong, and Company, 1876.

Seldeschlachts, Erik. "The End of the Road for the Indo-Greeks?" *Iranica Antiqua* 39 (2004): 249–96.

Senior, Robert C. *Indo-Scythian Coins and History.* 3 vols. London: Classical Numismatic Group, 2001.

———. "Menander versus Zoilos: Another Overstrike." *Oriental Numismatic Society Newsletter* 150 (1996): 12.

Shaked, Shaul. *Le satrape de Bactriane et son gouverneur: Documents araméens du IVe siècle avant notre ère.* Paris: Diffusion de Boccard, 2004.

Sharma, G.R. *Reh Inscription of Menander and the Indo-Greek Invasion of the Ganga Valley.* Allahabad: Abinash, 1980.

Shipley, Graham. *The Greek World after Alexander, 323–30 BC.* London: Routledge, 2000.

Sick, David. "When Socrates Met the Buddha: Greek and Indian Dialectic in Hellenistic Bactria and India." *Journal of the Royal Asiatic Society* 17.3 (2007): 253–78.

Sidky, Homayun. *The Greek Kingdom of Bactria: From Alexander to Eucratides the Great.* Lanham, Md.: University Press of America, 2000.

———. *The Rise and Fall of the Graeco-Bactrian Kingdom.* Jaipur: ABD Publishers, 2004.

Simonetta, Alberto. "A New Essay on the Indo-Greeks, the Sakas and the Pahlavas." *East and West* 9 (1958): 154–83.

———. "Some Hypotheses on the Military and Political Structure of the Indo-Greek Kingdom." *Journal of the Numismatic Society of India* 22 (1960): 56–62.

Simpson, Grant, ed. *The Scottish Soldier Abroad, 1247–1967.* Edinburgh: John Donald Publishers, 1992.

Simpson, St. John. "Ancient Afghanistan Revealed." *World Archaeology Magazine* 46.4 (2011): 16–24.

Simpson, William. "Buddhist Remains in the Jalalabad Valley." *Indian Antiquary* 8 (1879): 227–30.

Sims-Williams, Nicholas, and Joe Cribb. "A New Bactrian Inscription of Kanishka the Great." *Silk Road Art and Archaeology* 4 (1995–96): 75–142.

Sircar, D.C., ed. *Select Inscriptions Bearing on Indian History and Civilization.* 2nd ed. Calcutta: University of Calcutta Press, 1965.

Smirnova, Natalia. "Coins of Eucratides in Museum Collections." *East and West* 42.1 (1992): 85–102.

———. "On Finds of Hellenistic Coins in Turkmenistan." *Ancient Civilizations from Scythia to Siberia* 3 (1996): 260–85.

Smith, David. "Will the Real Eukratides Please Stand Up?" *Numismatics International Bulletin* 40.4 (2005): 74–83.

Smith, Sidney, ed. *Babylonian Historical Texts.* London: Methuen, 1924.

Smith, Vincent A. *Coins of Ancient India: Catalogue of the Coins in the Indian Museum, Calcutta.* Vol. I. [1906.] Reprint. Delhi: Indological Book House, 1972.

Spon, Jacob. *Voyage d'Italie, de Dalmatie, de Grèce et du Levant.* Lyon: Antoine Cellier, 1678.

Spufford, Peter. "Mint Organisation in the Burgundian Netherlands in the Fifteenth Century." In C.N.L. Brooke et al., eds., *Studies in Numismatic Method,* pp. 239–61. Cambridge: Cambridge University Press, 1983.

Srivastava, Prashant. *Art-Motifs on Ancient Indian Coins.* New Delhi: Harman, 2004.

Stein, Aurel. *On Alexander's Track to the Indus: Personal Narrative of Explorations on the North-West Frontier of India.* [1929.] Reprint. Edison, N.J.: Castle Books, 2004.

Stephani, Ludolf, ed. *H.K.E. Köhler's gesammelte Schriften.* Vol. I, *Serapis.* St. Petersburg: Imperial Academy, 1850.

Stevens, Susan. "Charon's Obol and Other Coins in Ancient Funerary Practice." *Phoenix* 45.3 (1991): 215–29.

Stride, Sebastian. "Regions and Territories in Southern Central Asia: What the Surkhan Darya Province Tells Us about Bactria." In Joe Cribb and Georgina Herrmann, eds., *After Alexander: Central Asia before Islam,* pp. 99–117. Oxford: Oxford University Press, 2007.

Sverchkov, Leonid. "The Kurganzol Fortress (On the History of Central Asia in the Hellenistic Era)." *Ancient Civilizations from Scythia to Siberia* 14 (2008): 123–91.

Tainter, Joseph. *The Collapse of Complex Societies.* Cambridge: Cambridge University Press, 1988.

Tarn, William W. *The Greeks in Bactria and India*. [1938.] 2nd ed. Cambridge: Cambridge University Press, 1951.

———. *The Greeks in Bactria and India*. 3rd ed. Ed. F. Holt. Chicago: Ares Press, 1984.

———. "Notes on Hellenism." *Journal of Hellenic Studies* 22 (1902): 268–93.

———. "Patrocles and the Oxo-Caspian Trade Route." *Journal of Hellenic Studies* 21 (1901): 10–29.

Tarzi, Zemaryalai. "Jules Barthoux, le découvreur oublié d'Ai Khanoum." *Comptes-Rendus de l'Académie des Inscriptions et Belles-Lettres,* 1996: 595–611.

Thomas, David, et al. "The Archaeological Sites of Afghanistan in Google Earth." *Aerial Archaeology Research Group Newsletter* 37 (2008): 22–30.

Thomas, Edward. "Bactrian Coins." *Numismatic Chronicle* 2 (1862): 178–88.

———. "Bactrian Coins." *Journal of the Royal Asiatic Society* 20 (1862–63): 123–24.

———. *Bactrian Coins and Indian Dates*. London: Truebner, 1876.

———, ed. *Essays on Indian Antiquities*. 2 vols. [1858.] Reprint. Varanasi: Indological Book House, 1971.

Thompson, James Westfall. "Presidential Address." *American Historical Review* 47.2 (1942): 225–44.

Thompson, Margaret, Otto Mørkholm, and Colin Kraay, eds. *An Inventory of Greek Coin Hoards*. New York: American Numismatic Society, 1973.

Tissot, Francine. *Catalogue of the National Museum of Afghanistan, 1931–1985*. Paris: UNESCO, 2006.

Tod, James. "An Account of Greek, Parthian, and Hindu Medals, Found in India." *Transactions of the Royal Asiatic Society* 1 (1826): 313–42.

Todd, Richard. "W.W. Tarn and the Alexander Ideal." *The Historian* 37 (1964): 48–55.

Torrey, Charles Cutler. *Gold Coins of Khokand and Bukhara*. New York: American Numismatic Society, 1950.

Toynbee, Arnold. *Between Oxus and Jumna*. New York: Oxford University Press, 1961.

Trever, Kamila. *Pamiatniki greko-baktriiskogo iskusstva*. Moscow: Akademii Nauk, 1940.

Tyskiewicz, Michael. *Memoirs of an Old Collector*. London: Longmans, Green and Co., 1898.

Ure, John. *Shooting Leave: Spying Out Central Asia in the Great Game.* London: Constable, 2009.

Vaillant, Jean Foy. *Arsacidarum Imperium, sive Regum Parthorum Historia ad Fidem Numismaticum Accommodata.* Paris: Moette, 1725.

van Krieken–Pieters, Juliette, ed. *Art and Archaeology of Afghanistan: Its Fall and Survival.* Leiden: Brill, 2006.

Ventura, Jean-Baptiste. "Account of the Excavations of Tope Manikyala." *Asiatic Researches* 17 (1832): 600–603.

Vermeule, Cornelius. "Numismatics in Antiquity." *Schweizerische Numismatische Rundschau* 54 (1975): 5–32.

Veuve, Serge. *Fouilles d'Ai Khanoum.* Vol. VI, *Le gymnase.* Paris: Diffusion de Boccard, 1987.

von Kaenal, Hans-Markus, and Fleur Kemmers, eds. *Coins in Context.* Vol. I, *New Perspectives for the Interpretation of Coin Finds.* Mainz am Rhein: Philipp von Zabern, 2009.

von Sallet, Alfred. "Alexander der Grosse als Gründer der baktrisch-indischen Reiche." *Zeitschrift für Numismatik* 8 (1881): 279–80.

———. *Die Nachfolger Alexanders des Grossen in Baktrien und Indien.* Berlin: Weidmann, 1879.

von Schlegel, Augustus Wilhelm. "Observations sur quelques médailles bactriennes et indo-scythiques nouvellement découvertes." *Journal Asiatique* 2 (1828): 321–49.

Watson, Burton, trans. *Records of the Grand Historian by Sima Qian.* New York: Research Center for Translation, 1993.

Wheeler, Mortimer. *Archaeology from the Earth.* Oxford: Clarendon Press, 1954.

———. "Archaeology in Afghanistan." *Antiquity* 21 (1947): 57–65.

———. *Charsada: A Metropolis of the North-West Frontier.* Oxford: Oxford University Press, 1962.

———. *Flames over Persepolis: Turning Point in History.* New York: Reynal, 1968.

Whitehead, Richard Bertram. *Catalogue of Coins in the Panjab Museum, Lahore.* Vol. I, *Indo-Greek Coins.* [1914.] Reprint. Chicago: Argonaut Publishers, 1969.

———. "Notes on the Indo-Greeks." *Numismatic Chronicle* 20 (1940): 89–122.

Whitteridge, Gordon. *Charles Masson of Afghanistan.* Warminster: Aris and Phillips, 1986.

Widemann, François. "Un monnayage inconnu de type gréco-bactrien à legende araméenne." *Studia Iranica* 18 (1989): 193–97.

―――. "Phases et contradictions de la colonization grecque en Asie centrale et en Inde du nord-ouest." *Indologica Taurinensia* 27 (2001): 215–62.

―――. "Scarcity of Precious Metals and Relative Chronology of Indo-
Greek and Related Coinages (1st Century B.C.–1st Century A.D.)." *East and
West* 50 (2000): 227–58.

―――. *Les successeurs d'Alexandre en Asie centrale et leur héritage culturel.* Paris:
Riveneuve, 2009.

Wilson, Horace H. *Ariana Antiqua: A Descriptive Account of the Antiquities and
Coins of Afghanistan.* [1841.] Reprint. Delhi: Oriental Publishers, 1971.

Wilson, L.M. "King Demetrios of India and Eukratides of Bactria." *Oriental
Numismatic Society Newsletter* 174 (2003): 17–23.

Wojtilla, Gyula. "Did the Indo-Greeks Occupy Pataliputra?" *Acta Archaeologica Academiae Scientiarum Hungaricae* 40 (2000): 495–504.

Wolff, Joseph. *Narrative of a Mission to Bokhara, in the Years 1843–1845, to Ascertain
the Fate of Colonel Stoddart and Captain Conolly.* London: J.W. Parker, 1845.

Woodcock, George. *The Greeks in India.* London: Faber and Faber, 1966.

―――. "The Indian Greeks." *History Today* 12 (1962): 558–67.

Yailenko, Valeri. "Les maximes delphiques d'Ai Khanoum et la formation de
la doctrine du *Dhamma* d'Asoka." *Dialogues d'Histoire Ancienne* 16 (1990):
239–56.

Yang, Juping. "Alexander the Great and the Emergence of the Silk Road." *The
Silk Road* 6.2 (2009): 15–22.

Young, Rodney S. "The South Wall of Balkh-Bactra." *American Journal of
Archaeology* 59 (1955): 267–76.

Zavylov, V.A. "The Fortifications of the City of Gyaur Kala, Merv." In J.
Cribb and G. Herrmann, eds., *After Alexander: Central Asia before Islam,* pp. 313–
29. Oxford: Oxford University Press, 2007.

Zeymal, E.V. *Drevniye moneti Tadzhikistana.* Dushanbe: Akademii Nauk, 1983.

―――. "Problèmes de circulation monétaire dans la Bactriane hellénistique." In Jean-Claude Gardin, ed., *L'archéologie de la Bactriane ancienne:
Actes du colloque franco-soviétique,* pp. 273–79. Paris: CNRS, 1985.

―――, ed. *Drevnosti Tadzhikistana.* Dushanbe: Akademii Nauk, 1985.

ILLUSTRATION CREDITS

FIGURES

Figures 1, 6, 7, 11, 13, 14, 28: Laura Holt.

Figures 2, 3: Bayer, *Historia Regni* (1738).

Figure 4: Pellerin, *Recueil* (1762).

Figure 5: Pellerin, *Additions* (1778).

Figures 8, 9: Cunningham, *Numismatic Chronicle* (1869, 1868).

Figure 10: Chabouillet, *Revue Numismatique* (1867).

Figures 12, 15–18, 22, 24–27, 29: author.

Figures 19, 21: Osmund Bopearachchi.

Figures 20, 23: www.cngcoins.com.

PLATES

Plate 1: NASA.

Plate 2: Duruy, *History of Rome* (1891).

Plates 3–10: Osmund Bopearachchi.

INDEX

Aegean, 99, 114
Aelian, 19
Afghanistan, 1, 3–4, 27, 42, 89, 107–
    8, 111, 114, 134–38, 140–42, 163, 184,
    202, 207, 210; archaeology and,
    90–91, 93–94, 96–97, 104–5, 108,
    110–11, 197; epigraphy and, 114–18,
    120, 130, 133
Agathocleia, 39, 144, 165
Agathocles, 38–39, 44, 46–49, 72,
    80, 125, 135, 139–40, 143, 147, 150–
    52, 155, 157, 165–66, 177, 194, 203,
    214–15, 217–18
Agra, 36
Ahin Push Tepe, 197
Ai Khanoum, 97, 99–112, 124–30,
    132–33, 136, 138–43, 148, 154, 156,
    164–67, 176- 81, 183, 185–93, 195–
    96, 200, 206, 217, 219
Ainak, 163
Aitanes, 133
Alexander of Epirus, 122
Alexander the Great, 1–2, 12, 16–
    17, 20, 30, 36–37, 42, 45–46, 48–

49, 58, 67, 71–72, 76, 90–91, 94,
    105, 115, 120, 127, 143–44, 153, 158,
    215
Alexandria Eschate, 105, 186
Alexandria Oxiana, 102, 256n81
Alexandria *sub Caucaso*, 37, 90
Algerian pirates, 7
Ali, Sheikh Keramat, 35–36, 39
Allard, Jean-François, 36, 90
Allouche-LePage, Marie-Thérèse,
    77–78, 85–86
Altheim, Franz, 73, 75
Amanullah Khan, 91
America. *See* United States of
    America
American Historical Association
    (AHA), 160–61
American Numismatic (and
    Archaeological) Society (ANS),
    57, 63, 69, 78, 138, 141
Amphipolis, 119, 133, 200
Amu Darya (ancient Oxus River),
    1, 17, 32, 34, 67, 96–97, 99, 101, 105–
    6, 115, 133, 186, 221

Amyntas, 39, 42, 77, 116, 144; double decadrachms of, 77, 171–72
Anaitis, 148
Aniketos ("Invincible"), 125, 130, 150, 155, 157
Antialcidas, 39, 130–31, 133, 165
Antigonus Gonatus, 122
Antimachus I, 32, 34, 39, 47–48, 72, 76, 80, 82–84, 119, 125, 135, 147, 150–51, 157, 166, 176–78, 189, 194, 200, 213–15, 217–18; parchment texts and, 118–19, 276n74
Antimachus II, 118, 212, 218–19
Antiochia (in Bactria?), 116
Antiochia Margiana, 186
Antiochus: name on commemorative coins, 47–48; name on tablet, 116
Antiochus I, 122
Antiochus II, 122, 189, 215
Antiochus III, 12–13, 24, 71–72, 92, 125, 150–51, 155, 158, 181, 188, 199, 218
Antiochus IV, 72–73, 214–15, 217
Apameia, 43
Aphrodite, 117
Apollo, 32, 43, 92, 123, 126, 133, 148, 198, 213, 215
Apollodorus of Artemita, 16–18
Apollodotus I, 13, 20, 24–26, 33, 39–40, 81, 131, 133, 151, 158–59, 177, 189–90, 213, 216–17
Apollodotus II, 159
Apolloneia, 43
Apollonia, 43, 213
Arachosia, 18, 122, 132, 155, 157
Aramaic, 41, 120–22, 124, 130, 132
Archaeological Survey of India, 94
archaeology, 3–4, 8, 41, 57, 69, 77, 79, 84, 87–88, 90–112, 114, 117, 125, 129, 132, 135, 137, 143–44, 147–48,

152–54, 157, 160–63, 180, 187, 189, 191, 193, 196, 206, 215, 219–20
Archebius, 39, 77
Archises, 120, 133
Ariana, 16–18
Aristonax, 122
Aristotle, 127, 129
armor, 106, 200
Arsaces, 18
Arsacids, 8–9, 26
arrows/arrowheads, 91, 106, 192, 200
arsenal, 99, 101, 186–87, 200
Artemidorus, 144
Artemis, 148, 156
Aryan. *See* Bactrian language
Aryandes, 128–29, 133
Asangorna, 118–19, 133
Ashmolean Museum, 118, 145
Ashoka, 94, 120–22, 124, 133
Aspionus, 17
Astrakhan, 12
Athena, 2, 117, 133, 156, 174
Athens, 15, 86
Atrosokes, 115, 133, 177
Avent, Joseph, 63–64
Azes, 39
Azilises, 39

Babelon, Jean, 85–86
Bactra, 17, 92–93, 108, 132, 175, 196; siege of, 92, 181, 183, 188. *See also* Balkh
Bactria, 1–5, 10–29, 31–36, 38, 40, 42–44, 46, 48–49, 65–68, 70–75, 77–82, 84–86, 88–90, 92–94, 97, 99–108, 113–15, 118, 120, 122, 125, 131–33, 135–36, 138, 140–49, 151–55, 157–58, 161–71, 174–88, 190–96, 198–204, 206–9, 211–12, 214–20, 221n1
Bactrian language, 131–32
Badakshan Mountains, 101, 163

Baghdad, 61–62
Bagram. *See* Begram
Bajaur, 110, 143, 244n51, 267n84
Balkh, 27, 34, 42, 97, 104, 114, 119,
  139; archaeology and, 92–93, 96–
  97, 105, 108, 111. *See also* Bactra
Bamian, 36, 107, 111
banking, 185, 208
Bank Leu, 140
Bartholomaei, Jean de, 44–46, 49
Barthoux, Jules, 97
Bartold, Vasily, 105
Barygaza, 19, 158–59
Bayer, Theophilus, 3, 10–15, 20, 22–
  25, 49, 65, 113, 161, 186, 211, 219
Bazira, 116
Begram, 37, 91–92, 108, 111, 145
Behistun Inscription, 113
Berlin, 48
Bernard, Paul, 97, 99–100, 103, 109,
  127, 129, 138, 141, 178, 219
Besnagar Inscription, 130
Bhagabhadra, 130–31, 133
Bharuch. *See* Barygaza
Bhir mound. *See* Taxila
Bibliothèque Nationale (formerly
  Impériale) de France, 50, 54–55,
  59–60, 62, 141, 146, 203, 213
Bilgrame, Syed Ali, 63
bilingual texts, 40, 77, 113, 117–18,
  120–21, 125, 179, 205, 216
Bindusura, 120, 122
Bir-Kot, 115
Boccaccio, Giovanni, 20
Bokhari, Aga Zebalun, 60, 62
Bopearachchi, Osmund, 141–43,
  145–46, 186, 200, 218–19
Brahmi script, 41, 120, 130–32
Branchidae, 179
British Institute of Afghan Studies,
  96, 122
British Museum, 48, 52, 55, 59,

61–64, 66, 83, 144–45, 203,
  214
Broach. *See* Barygaza
bronze, 115, 143, 156, 163, 166, 200,
  206; coins of, 13, 32, 36, 38, 42, 61,
  63, 66, 102, 125, 130, 141, 156, 170,
  173, 184–85, 188–89, 197, 203–5
Bronze Age, 5, 101, 202
Bruce, Jacob Daniel, 10–12, 22–23,
  32, 113
Buddha, 92, 107, 133
Buddhism, 2–3, 20, 37–38, 90–91,
  94, 96, 100, 117, 121, 149, 198, 209
Bukhara, 25, 27, 29–30, 34–35, 43–
  44, 52–54, 58–63,105, 143, 156;
  hoard from, 143, 156, 206
Burnes, Alexander, 34–35, 39, 42, 92
Butkara, 96

caduceus, 156
Calcutta, 34
calendar, Macedonian, 119, 131, 133,
  209
Calliphon, 117, 133
Callisthenes, 128, 133
Campion, Charles Philippe, 31
Canada, 111
Caspian Sea, 32
Castor and Pollux. *See* Dioscuri
cavalry, 12, 23, 32–34, 60, 64, 125, 190,
  211, 217
Celts, 198–99, 202
ceramics. *See* pottery
Cesnola, Luigi Palma di, 56–57
Chabouillet, Pierre-Marie Anatole,
  50, 52, 86, 213
chaîne opératoire, 163, 168, 173, 183–84,
  186, 195
Champollion, Jean-François, 41
Chandragupta, 120
Characene, 114
chariot, 18–19, 198–99

Charon's fee, 197
Charsadda, 94
Chaucer, Geoffrey, 20, 158, 226n38
Chesm-e Shafa, 109
Chicago, 57, 187
China, 2–3, 70, 92, 104, 196, 265n60, 293n81
Christianity, 29, 45–46
chronology, 9, 12, 18–19, 43, 46, 58, 71, 96, 125, 129, 132, 137, 146–47, 151, 153, 157, 164, 182, 190, 196, 211–17
Cineas, 126, 133
cinnamon, 133
Clarke, Hyde, 61–62, 64
Clearchus, 126–27, 133, 179
coin catalogues, 31, 66, 74, 135, 139–40, 142, 145, 147–48, 161, 214
Colbert, Jean-Baptiste, 7
Coloru, Omar, 151–52, 218
complexity cascade. *See* self-organized criticality
Conolly, Arthur, 27, 29–30, 34, 36, 42–43
control marks. *See* monograms
copper, 101, 163, 166
Corinthian architecture, 97, 100
Cosmas, 127, 133
Cosmos, 128–29, 133
Court, Claude-Auguste, 36–37, 66, 90, 145
Cunha, Guerson da, 63–64
Cunningham, Alexander, 40–43, 47–48, 60–62, 66, 94, 148, 212–14
cupronickel coinages, 32, 148, 152, 156, 163, 184, 204, 208
Curiel, Raoul, 174

Dabrowa, Edward, 151
Daphne, celebration at, 215
Darapsa, 17
Dasht-i Nawar, 131
Dataes, 118, 133

Délégation Archélogique Française en Afghanistan (DAFA), 91–93, 97, 99, 102, 105, 107, 109–10, 114, 130–31, 138
Delos, 114–15, 131, 177
Delphi, 126, 179
Demetrius I, 10, 13, 17–21, 24–26, 34, 39, 48, 71–73, 76, 82, 92, 102–3, 124–25, 133, 139, 149–50, 152, 154–58, 165–67, 171, 177, 204–5, 212, 214–15, 218
Demetrius II, 34, 76, 150, 155, 174, 176–78, 216–18
Demonax, 118, 133
demonetization, 206, 208
Derbent, 106
diadem, 12, 39, 71, 73, 155, 206
die axis, 139, 156, 166, 174, 203
die breaks, 168, 182
die links, 146–47, 165, 174, 207
dies and die cutters, 81, 86–87, 102, 156, 164–77, 179–83, 198, 200, 203, 209, 214, 216, 219
Dikaios ("Just"), 31, 34, 40, 44, 73, 151, 212–13, 216–18, 130, 148–49
Dilberdjin Tepe, 96, 116
Diodorus, 116–18, 133
Diodotus I and II, 10, 12–13, 16–17, 22, 24, 26, 33, 44, 46–48, 87–88, 102, 116, 143–44, 146, 151–53, 157, 177, 203, 206–7, 212–13, 215–16
Diodoteia, 43, 102
Diodotopolis, 102
Diogenes, 116, 133
Diomedes, 39, 116
Dion, 130, 133
Dionysopolis, 43, 102
Dionysus, 12, 109
Dioscuri, 12, 23, 50, 58, 63–65, 86, 97, 169, 172–73, 201, 210–11, 215, 238n28
dolphins, 110
Drangians, 18

Droysen, Johann Gustav, 45–47, 49
Duff, Mountstuart Elphinstone
    Grant, 59, 61–62
Duruy, Victor, 52

East India Company, 34, 145
Egypt, 3, 8, 15, 19, 46, 90, 108, 113, 122,
    154, 179, 197, 206
elephant, 25, 155–58, 259n1
Emetreus, 21
Emshi Tepe, 116
epigraphy, 3, 77, 88–90, 93, 97, 99,
    102, 104, 106, 113–34, 143, 146, 152–
    55, 157–58, 162, 179–80, 183, 215,
    220; on coins, 19, 33, 39–40, 44,
    47–48, 60, 113, 156, 158, 165, 167–
    69, 171–73, 178–79, 199, 202–3
Epiphanes ("God Manifest"), 72, 214
epithets, 41, 44, 119, 125, 130–32, 148–
    50, 153, 155, 157, 170–71, 219. *See also*
    Aniketos; Dikaios; Epiphanes;
    Kallinikos; Megas; Megistos;
    Nicephorus; Nikator; Soter;
    Theos
Erk Qal'a, 106
Eros, 110
ethnicity, 86, 105, 111, 113–14, 161, 175,
    180–81, 193, 247n89, 283n50
Eucratides I, 2–4, 10, 13, 15, 26, 34,
    39–40, 43, 48, 71–73, 76, 84, 90,
    105–6, 110, 115, 117, 123, 149–53, 157–
    58, 183, 196, 198, 200–201, 204, 209,
    211–19; Ai Khanoum and, 102–
    3, 107, 109, 129, 143, 176, 189–92;
    coins of, 12, 14, 22, 24, 26, 32–33,
    37, 39–40, 43, 46, 48, 63, 65–66,
    72, 87, 91–92, 97, 103, 107, 143–44,
    165–66, 169, 175–78, 182, 189–90,
    194, 196–97, 200, 203, 205, 211–13;
    Eucratidion of, 49–65, 73, 85–
    86, 171–75, 213–14, 217; literary
    sources for, 16–21, 119, 154–55

modern Afghan currency and,
    210
Eucratides II, 10, 13, 23–24, 26, 33–
    34, 177, 196, 203, 212–13, 215, 219
Eucratidia, 17, 97, 102, 154, 215
Eumenes, 118, 133
Euthydemus I, 10, 12–13, 17–18,
    24–26, 32–33, 35, 39, 42, 47–48,
    71–72, 76, 80–84, 88, 92, 114, 116,
    124–25, 130, 133, 144, 150–52, 155–
    58, 176–78, 181–82, 194, 199, 203,
    206, 212–13, 215–16, 218
Euthydemus II, 32, 36, 39, 92, 151–52,
    157, 166, 177, 188, 205, 214, 217–18
Evans, Arthur, 160

Faccenna, Domenico, 96
Feuardent, Gaston, 55–62, 64, 213
Feuardent, Félix, 54–55
First Afghan War, 34, 38
Fitzwilliam Museum, 145
flans, 102–3, 164, 166, 181, 280n15
forgeries, 42, 52, 56, 63–64, 139, 148,
    176, 184, 206
Foucher, Alfred, 91–93, 96–97, 99,
    108
fourrées, 206
Fox, Charles Richard, 52, 54–55,
    58, 60
France, 7–9, 20, 22, 31, 36, 38, 44,
    52–55, 57–60, 66, 85, 91–94, 97,
    99, 105–6, 108, 110–11, 126, 131, 145,
    170, 187, 197
Francfort, Henri-Paul, 99, 139–40
Fussman, Gérard, 174

Galitzin, Michael, 32–33
Gandhara, 91, 93–94, 96, 127, 132
Ganges River, 144
Gardin, Jean-Claude, 100–101, 148
Gardner, Percy, 48, 71, 148, 214
Garuda pillar, 130

Gauls, 17, 198
Gerard, Dr. James G., 34–36, 92
Germany, 44–45, 48, 73, 93, 96, 111, 121, 170
Ghazni province, 131
Ghorband River, 91
Gibbs, James, 47
Gobekli-tepe, 107
Gogha, 159
gold, 21, 104, 117, 123, 163–64, 197, 202, coins of, 1, 4, 7–8, 24, 32, 42, 49–50, 52–53, 55, 58–65, 73, 84–85, 97, 141, 143–44, 153, 156, 175, 181, 184–85, 189, 197–98, 206–8, 213–15
Gorpaeus (Macedonian month), 131, 133
Gosselin, François-Paschal, 31
Gotarzes, 198
Great Britain, 25, 27, 31, 34, 36, 38, 65–67, 70, 75, 84, 91, 93–94, 110–11, 139, 145, 198, 202–3
Great Game, 3, 26–27, 29, 31, 34, 38, 49, 89, 91, 93, 105, 136, 212
Greek language, 2, 9, 13, 16–17, 19, 22, 25, 40–41, 44, 77, 90, 94, 100, 103–4, 106, 113–15, 116–24, 126–27, 130–34, 150, 158, 167, 169, 175–77, 179, 181, 199, 201, 209, 213
Greeks, 7, 12, 21–24, 32, 50, 60, 71, 78, 80, 85–87, 91, 94, 97, 99–100, 103, 105–6, 109–11, 114–16, 119, 121, 123–24, 126–29, 131–32, 136, 175, 177–78, 180, 185, 197, 199–200, 203, 210, 214, 217; the East and, 1–4, 12–13, 16–17, 24, 29, 39–40, 46, 70, 72, 75, 81, 92–94, 101–5, 107–8, 112, 116, 120–21, 130–33, 146, 150–53, 162, 164, 178, 180, 182–83, 187, 191, 193, 195–96, 198, 200, 209, 212, 214–15, 217
Green, Peter, 84
Grenet, Frantz, 99

Grote, Arthur, 60
guide dots (on coin dies), 171–72, 201
Guillaume, Olivier, 87, 99, 147–49
Guimet, Musée, 108
Gupta, Parmeshwari Lal, 139–40
Guthrie, Charles Seton, 60
GVI (Generation, Verification, Integration), 154, 158, 193, 219
Gyaur Qal'a, 106

Hackin, Joseph and Ria, 92
Hades, 116, 133
Hanfmann, George, 84
Harlan, Josiah, 36
Harappan civilization, 101
Haripur, 143
Hassan, Mamoor, 110
Hay, Major, 42, 46
Heliocles (on Eucratides coins), 39–40, 46, 48, 71, 73, 157, 203, 212, 215
Heliocles I, 31–34, 39–40, 68, 73, 83, 87, 92, 148–49, 151, 176–78, 180, 183, 196, 200-202, 209, 212–19
Heliocles II, 165, 175
Heliodorus (ambassador), 130–31, 133
Heliodorus (king), 144
Heliodotus (commoner), 124–25, 133, 143, 179
Heliodotus (king), 125
helmet, 12, 32, 39, 60, 84, 105–6, 125, 198
Herat, 110
Hercules, 13, 125, 127, 132–33, 155–56, 167, 203
Hermaeus (commoner), 128–29, 133
Hermaeus (king), 39, 77, 165
Hermes, 127, 133
Hestia, 124, 133
Hindu, 40, 212

Hindu Kush Mountains, 1, 34, 91–
92, 120, 132, 150, 163, 180
Hippias, 128, 133
hoards, 7–8, 76–77, 96, 99, 103–4,
128, 136–44, 147, 156, 159, 165, 174,
182, 184–85, 189–91, 200, 206–8
Homeric epics, 116, 130, 262n26
honey, 133
Honigberger, Dr. Martin, 36–38,
90, 92
horse, 12, 22, 32, 34, 86, 172, 199,
201–2
Huntington, Archer, 69
Huvishka, 202
Hypanis River, 17
Hyspaosines, 114
Hyspasines, 114–15, 131, 177

incense, 128, 133
India, 1–3, 12–13, 15–16, 18–21, 25–27,
31, 33, 35, 38, 40–41, 49, 58, 60, 64,
66–67, 70, 72–77, 92–94, 100–104,
114–15, 120–21, 123, 128, 130–31, 136–
37, 142, 144–46, 150–53, 155, 157–
58, 179–80, 188–89, 191, 193–95,
197, 202, 207, 210, 212, 214, 216, 218,
221
India Office Museum, 145
Indo-Greek, 75, 100, 125, 135–36, 141,
143, 146–47, 158, 170, 185, 189, 194,
203–5, 217
Instituto Italiano per il Medio
Estremo Oriente, 96
International Merv Project, 106
International Pluridisciplinary
Archaeological Expedition, 106
International Security Assistance
Force, 111
Iranian, 73, 75, 115, 130–31
iron, 101, 166
Iron Gates, 106
irrigation, 100–101

Isidora, 127, 133
Isidore of Charax, 155
Islamabad, 143
Islamic, 5, 91–92, 111, 210
Islington, 53
Israel, Lost Tribes of, 29
Italy, 8, 36, 96, 111

Jakobsson, Jens, 150–51, 217
Jalalabad, 197
Jammu, 125
Japan, 96
Jenkins, Gilbert K., 83
Jesus, 46, 222n10
jewelry, 105, 110, 116–17, 141, 185, 202–
6, 209
Jiga Tepe, 116
Judaea, 117
Justin (M. Junianus Justinus),
17–19, 73, 84, 119, 152, 155, 196

Kabul, 34, 37, 42, 90–91, 107, 111, 136,
139–40, 163
Kadlubeck, Vincenzo, 20
Kalinga, 121
Kalita, Stanislav, 82, 84, 151
Kallinikos ("Glorious in Victory"),
125, 155, 157
Kampyr Tepe, 106, 116, 290n63
Kandahar, 96, 105, 110, 120–22, 124,
132, 177, 179
Kanishka, 132, 202
Kapisa, 43
Kara Kamara, 118
karshapana coins, 128, 136, 188–89,
279n8
Kasan, 12
Kashmir, 35, 117, 125
Kasi, 130, 133
Kensington, 52–53
Khan Ali. *See* Conolly, Arthur
Khanikoff, Nikolai de, 43–44

Kharoshthi script, 25, 41, 118, 120,
131–32, 175
Khisht Tepe, 136
Khojend-Leninabad, 105
Khuna Qal'a, 101
Khwaja Bahuaddin, 109
Khyber Pass, 27
Kipling, Rudyard, 27, 29, 37
Köhler, Heinrich, 25, 32–33, 212
Kokcha River, 97, 101
Koktepe, 106
Koshelenko, Gennady A., 99
Kraay, Colin, 174
Kruglikova, Irina, 99
Ksirov, 197
Kuliab, 124–25, 143, 155–56, 158, 179,
191
Kurganzol Fortress, 107
Kushan, 97, 99, 104–5, 131–32, 196–
97, 199, 201–2

Laghman, 132
Lahiri, Amarendra N., 148
Lal, Mohan, 35, 42
"land of a thousand cities," 1, 16–17,
89, 92, 154, 213, 225n27
Laodice, 40, 46, 48, 71–73, 151, 157,
203, 212, 214–15, 218; 'Kanlodice'
and, 39, 212
lapis lazuli, 101, 120
Lassen, Christian, 37–38, 47
Latin language, 2, 9, 11, 17, 203,
221n1, 225n35
Laurent de Premierfait, 20
lead, 101
Legacy Resource Management
Program, 111
lenses, magnification, 165
Lewis, James. *See* Masson, Charles
lightning bolt, 32, 44
lion pelt, 155, 167, 281n27

Litvinsky, Boris, 99, 114
London, 52, 54–55, 58–59, 61, 67,
74, 139
Lord, Dr. P., 40
Louis XIV, 7, 9
Ludhiana, 38
Lugdunum (Lyon), 197
Lydgate, John, 20
Lysanias, 127, 133
Lysias, 39, 77, 170

Macdonald, George, 70–72, 214
Macedonia, 2, 12, 16, 71, 73, 77, 122,
190, 198. *See also* calendar
Magas of Cyrene, 122
Mahbubullah, 110
Manikyala, 90
Maracanda. *See*
Samarkand-Afrasiab
Margiana, 107, 186
Marseilles, 8
Marshall, John, 94, 117
Marsyas, 115
Massaga, 43
Masson, Charles, 36–39, 66, 90–
92, 145
Massoud, Ahmad Shah, 109
Mathura, 131
Maues, 39, 153
Mauryan Empire, 71, 94, 120, 122
Megas ("Great"), 10, 12, 15, 22, 24,
26, 32–34, 37, 39–40, 73, 92, 125,
130–32, 150, 158, 181, 188, 210–15,
217–19
Megistos ("Greatest"), 125
Menander, 2–3, 13–14, 33, 39, 75, 84,
151, 216–19; coins of, 2, 20, 24–26,
40, 91, 144, 149, 158–59, 184, 203;
literary sources for, 2, 10, 17,
19–20, 130, 158
Menodotus, 118, 133

mercenaries, 10, 119–20, 133, 183, 198–200
meridarch, 117–18, 133
Merv, 52, 106
Mesopotamia, 112
Mestor, 116, 133
Metz, 31
Meyendorff, Georges de, 25–26, 34
Mian Khan Sanghou, 143
Michelet d'Ennery, 31
mines, 101–2, 120, 163–64, 184, 195
mints, 4, 42–43, 77, 89, 102–3, 146, 163–67, 170, 174–77, 180–85, 188–90, 195, 198, 200, 202, 207, 209
Mionnet, Théodore Edme, 31, 212
Mir Zakah, 77, 141–42, 206–7
Mitchiner, Michael, 148
Mithridates, 15, 18, 20, 152, 216, 218
Mittag, Peter, 146–47
Mollossi, 117
Molossus, 128–29, 133
monograms on coins, 22–23, 33, 42–43, 64–65, 77–78, 103, 144, 146–47, 156, 166–67, 171–75, 181–82, 188, 194, 200, 213
Moorcroft, William, 34, 92
Morgan, John Pierpont, 63
Mørkholm, Otto, 81
Moscow, 10, 32–33
Munchaev, Rauf, 99
Muses, 123, 133

Napoleon I, 9, 36
Napoleon III, Louis, 50, 54, 58
Narain, Awadh Kishore, 74–78, 82, 87, 145–46, 148–50, 159, 216–17
Narain, Sudha, 85–86
Naratos, 122–23, 133
Nashten, 144
Nasrullah, Emir of Bukhara, 30

National Museum, Kabul, 107, 111, 136
NATO, 111
Nautaka, 42
Netherlands, 111
Newell, Edward T., 78–81, 85–86, 160, 215
New York, 55, 57, 138–40
New York Times, 52, 55, 57–58
Nicephorus ("Victory-Bearing"), 131, 212
Niceratus, 128–29, 133
Nicias, 116, 133
nickel. *See* cupronickel
Nika, 131, 133
Nikator ("Conqueror"), 16, 47
Nike ("Victory"), 131
Nimlik, Tepe, 114–15
nomads, 2, 73, 104, 107, 109, 117, 180, 182–83, 187, 191–93, 195–98, 200, 202, 214, 218–19

Ochus, 118, 133
olive oil, 128, 133
Olous (Macedonian month), 118–19, 133
Ora, 115
Ostobara, 102
Oumanes, 129, 133
Ouseley, Gore, 33–34
overstrikes, 144, 146–48, 164–65, 206
Oxus River. *See* Amu Darya
Oxybazus, 128–29, 133, 177
Oxyboakes, 128–29, 133, 177

Pakistan, 94, 96, 115, 117, 141–43
palace: at Ai Khanoum, 99, 102–3, 112, 127–29, 165, 186–88, 193; at Begram, 92
Palamedes, 116, 131, 133

Panjshir, 91
Pantaleon, 39, 47–48, 121, 139–40, 151–52, 157, 166, 213–14, 217–18
papyrus, 4, 14–15, 116, 126, 129, 133
parchment, 4, 118–20, 126, 129, 133, 200
Paris, 22, 50, 54–55, 58–59, 61, 64, 108, 138, 203, 213
Paropamisadae, 132
Parthenon, 86
Parthia, 8–10, 15–20, 27, 43, 73, 76, 104, 107, 193, 197–98, 212, 216–18
Patalene, 17
Pella, 2
Pellerin, Joseph, 22–24, 33, 161, 212
Perimula, 19
Persia, 8, 33, 52, 64, 71, 94, 113, 116, 118, 121–22; Achaemenid dynasty of, 94, 101, 106, 109
Persian Gulf, 114
Peshawar, 42, 117–18, 141, 143
Peter the Great, 10
Petitot-Biehler, Claire-Yvonne, 81, 138
Petrie, William Matthew Flinders, 90, 108
Peucelaotis. *See* Charsadda
Philaxius, 118, 133
Philip II, 48, 71, 198
Philiscus, 128–29, 133
Philoxenus (commoner), 133
Philoxenus (king), 39, 77, 165
Phraates IV, 197
Phryni, 17
Pichikyan, Igor, 114
Piodasses. *See* Ashoka
Plato (king), 76, 146, 149, 177, 196, 215, 217
Plato (philosopher), 129
Plutarch, 20, 25
Poland, 184, 189
Polybius, 24, 154–55, 157–58

Polyxenus, 133
Pompeii, 191
portraiture on coins, 9, 14, 23–24, 31–33, 39, 44, 48, 65, 71, 77–87, 155–56, 175, 180, 185, 194, 198, 200, 203, 205–6, 212, 215, 217
Poseidon, 32
pottery, 4, 91, 99–100, 108, 114–16, 125–26, 128, 130, 133, 143–44, 252n48
Prakrit, 40–41, 117–18, 124
Prinsep, James, 34–35, 39–42, 66, 120, 212
Ptolemies, 8, 15, 122
Punjab, 74, 94
Pushkalavati. *See* Charsadda
Pytho, 126

Qala-i Sam, 116
Qin Shihuangdi, 2
Qunduz Hoard, 77, 136, 156, 165, 174, 182

Rabatak, 111, 131
Rahman, Aman ur, 141
Rapin, Claude, 99–100
Rapson, Edward James, 70–71, 214
Rawa Mazowiecka, 184
Rawlinson, Henry, 41
Rawlinson, Hugh George, 70–71, 85, 214
Reh Inscription, 130
Renaissance, 1, 84, 211
Rhipus, 118, 133
Robert, Louis, 127
Robinson, Jr., Charles Alexander, 70
Rochette, Raoul, 38, 47, 213
Rome, 3, 7–8, 15–17, 19, 52, 78, 80, 92, 94, 104–5, 154, 170, 183, 197–98, 202–3

Romulus and Remus, 202
Rosetta Stone, 40, 46, 113, 119
Royal Asiatic Society, 24, 59–60
Royal Numismatic Society, 52, 55
Rtveladze, Edvard, 79, 106, 143
rubies, 21, 101
Russia, 10, 25, 27, 32, 43–44, 46, 66, 82, 91, 93, 96–97, 99, 105–6, 110, 114, 170
Russian Imperial Academy, 25
Russian Imperial Museum, 10

Saidu-Sharif, 143
Saint Petersburg, 10, 25, 32
Sakas, 104, 153, 196, 200, 217
Sale, Florentia Wynch and Robert, 42
Sallet, Alfred von, 48
Samarkand-Afrasiab, 105–7, 116–17
Sangcharak, 118
Sanskrit, 37, 39, 70
Sarai Saleh, 143
Saraostus, 17
Sarianidi, Victor, 104, 117
sarissa, 12, 172
Sarpedon, 116
satellite imagery, 110
satrapy, 17, 117
satyrs, 110
scepter, 32, 172, 197
Schlumberger, Daniel, 97, 108, 114
Scythians, 16, 119–20, 133, 143, 200
sea monster (*ketos*), 116
Seistan, 72, 96
Seleucids, 8, 13, 16, 24, 31, 40, 72–73, 75–77, 87, 120, 122, 125, 151–52, 158, 170, 179, 181, 188, 199, 212, 214–16
Seleucus I, 16
self-organized criticality (SOC), 192–93, 195–96
Senior, Robert C., 118
Seres, 17

Servius Tullius, 19
Shah, Muhmmad Zahir, 97
Shaikhan Dheri, 94, 96
Shiberghan, 104
shields, 106, 156, 187
Shortughai, 101
Shinwari bazaar, 141
Sicily, 8
Sidky, Homayun, 149–50, 180, 217
Sigerdis, 17
silk, 21
Silk Road, 3, 197
silver, 101, 109, 117, 163–64, 187, 208; coins of, 1–2, 7, 12, 19, 22–23, 31–32, 61–66, 77, 84, 97, 119, 128, 130, 138, 141, 143, 153, 155–56, 184–85, 188–89, 197–98, 205–7
Simus, 118, 133
Singh, Ranjit, 36–37, 90, 145
Siranwali, 144
Sirkap. *See* Taxila
Smith, Vincent, 148
Smithsonian Institution, 64, 141
Sogdia, 18, 42, 82, 107, 130, 132, 175, 179, 181, 183, 192, 199, 217–18
Sokrakes, 116, 133
Sophocles, 15
Sophytos, 122–24, 133, 177, 179
Soras, 19
Sosipatrus, 133
Soter ("Savior"), 12, 33, 44, 47, 130–31, 139, 184
South Tadjikistan Archaeological Expedition, 106, 114
South Turkmenistan Archaeological Multidisciplinary Expedition, 106
spear, 33, 106, 169, 174, 212. *See also* sarissa
Sri Lanka, 141
Stein, Marc Aurel, 115–16
Stoddart, Colonel, 29–30, 34, 43

Strabo, 16–17, 19, 25, 154–55
Strato (commoner), 127–29, 133
Strato (king), 83, 127, 165
Strutt, Charles, 65
stupa, 20, 37, 90, 96, 197
subhistoric peoples, 162–63, 208
Surkhan Darya, 106–7
Surkh Kotal, 99, 108, 131–32
Svoboda, M., 61–62
Swat, 96, 115, 143
Switzerland, 139, 141–42
sword, 56, 106
Syria, 16, 31, 43, 71, 73, 117, 122, 185,
    214–15, 218
systems collapse model, 183, 192,
    195

Tadjikistan, 116, 124, 142, 197
Takht-i Sangin, 106–7, 111, 114, 177
Taliban, 107, 109
Talikana, 42
Tarn, William Woodthorpe, 67–
    78, 80–82, 84–85, 87–88, 90, 145–
    46, 148–53, 159, 180, 182, 200,
    214–17
Tarzi, Zemaryalai, 104
Tarzus, 129, 133
Tashkurgan, 39
Taukiana, 42
taxaena, 128
Taxila, 94, 96, 102, 110, 117–18, 128,
    130–32, 153
Teleas, 155
Telephus, 116
temples, 89, 97, 99, 106, 114–15, 165;
    at Ai Khanoum, 99–100, 112, 130,
    167, 187–88
Termez, 106, 116
Thasos, 99
Theodotus. *See* Diodotus
Theophilus, 77
Theophrastus, 128–29, 133

Theos ("God"), 32, 34, 39, 47, 76,
    80, 118, 125, 153, 213, 217, 219
Thersites, 116, 130, 133
Thomas, Edward, 47
Thompson, James Westfall, 160–61
Thornton, Mrs., 64
Thracian, 127
Tiberius, 197
Tillya Tepe, 104–5, 108, 111, 116–
    17, 197–98
Timarchus, 152, 218
Timodemus, 128–29, 133
Timur, 30
tin, 163
Tod, James, 24–25
Tokhmach Tepe, 143
Torrey, Charles Cutler, 63–64
Trever, Kamila, 82
Triballus, 127, 133
trident, 156
Trogus, Pompeius, 17–18, 81, 152
Tullia, 19
Turiva, 17, 225n26
Turkestan, 21, 52, 96, 105
Tyche, 109, 124, 133

Udegram, 115
Uffington White Horse, 202
United States of America, 36, 57,
    59, 63, 65–66, 96, 109–10, 142,
    144, 208
Uzbekistan, 97, 106–7, 116

Vaillant, Jean Foy, 7–10, 12–13, 15,
    20, 22–24, 26, 49, 161
Ventura, Jean-Baptiste, 36–37, 90
Vaisali, 144, 207
Vasudeva, 130, 133
Vishnu, 130, 133

Wade, Claude, 38
Waggoner, Nancy, 138–39, 141

Wesa, 143
Wheeler, Mortimer, 9, 93–94, 96, 114
Whitehead, Richard Bertram, 74–76, 148
Widemann, François, 152–53, 218
Wilson, Horace Hayman, 34, 42, 212
wolf, 202
Wolff, Joseph, 29–30, 43, 49, 161
Woodcock, George, 83
Wudi, 2

Xatrannus, 128, 133

Yavana, 214, 217. *See also* Greeks
Yuezhi, 104, 196–97, 199, 201, 216–17

Zargaran, Tepe, 108–9, 111
Zariaspa. *See* Bactra
Zeno, 128–29, 133
Zeus, 12, 32, 44, 117, 124, 132–33, 172, 201–3, 210
Zhang Qian, 3, 196
Zoilus I, 219